AF552676

A SENSE OF SHIFTING

Queer Artists Reshaping Dance

Text by Coco Romack
Photography by Yael Malka

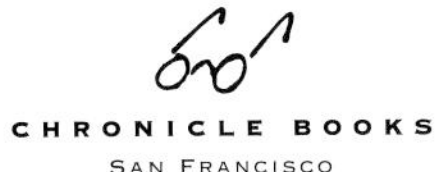

CHRONICLE BOOKS
SAN FRANCISCO

Text copyright © 2024 by Coco Romack.
Photographs copyright © 2024 by Yael Malka.
All rights reserved. No part of this book may be reproduced in any form without written permission from the publisher.

Library of Congress Cataloging-in-Publication Data available.

ISBN 978-1-7972-1977-6

Manufactured in China.

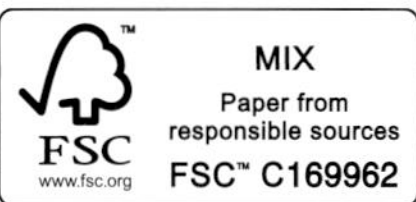

Design by Henna Crowner.
Typeset in Resolve Sans.

10 9 8 7 6 5 4 3 2 1

Chronicle Books LLC
680 Second Street
San Francisco, California 94107
www.chroniclebooks.com

Introduction 7

The Sundance Stompede 10

Ballez 34

Raja Feather Kelly and the feath3r theory 56

Kinetic Light 76

Vangeline Theater/New York Butoh Institute's *Queer Butoh* 98

Tosh Basco 116

Compañia Manuel Liñán 138

STREB Extreme Action 160

FlucT 182

Masterz at Work Dance Family 204

NIC Kay 226

Alejandro's Night 248

Acknowledgments 270

Bibliography 271

INTRODUCTION

Two dancers hurl themselves from a trampoline; the sound of their bodies crashing into a mat below creates, in the absence of music, an erratic rhythm. A man swings hip-to-hip with his partner, while a red handkerchief peeks out from the back right pocket of his jeans indicating, to those who know the code, his secret desires. The silver sequins decorating an artist's dress refract an onslaught of light pounding down from a strobe as her arms thrash and her fingers flutter during a vulnerable release. How they shimmer and shine, glamorous despite the exhausting weight of the gown pulling against the performer's frame.

These are some of the scenes documented over the course of a year by the photographer Yael Malka, my dear friend and collaborator. She has dedicated much of her career and life to celebrating LGBTQ+ people—often dancers—in tender, loving images. Like many other time-honored art forms, dance is defined in part by formalist ideas about how it must be done and what it should look like, which exclude those who don't fit a rigid mold established long ago. Yet as Yael's photographs showcase, there are many artists, dancers, and choreographers working today to push against these outdated notions—and creating startling, exciting pieces in the process.

Yael and I first met over Tecates at a bar in Brooklyn, New York, where we both live, through our mutual friend Fran Tirado, a brilliant writer and cohost of the podcast *Like a Virgin*. As conversations in our city typically begin, we started by acknowledging that we knew and admired each other's work. Much like Yael, I've spent much of my career as a writer and editor highlighting artists on the margins in my own way—through words and stories.

In March 2022, Yael and I set out to expand on our previous work by highlighting, in images and interviews, the dancers, movement-based artists, companies, and collectives who are using queerness to destabilize the traditions handed down to them. These dancers vary in training and dance style, ranging from vogue to flamenco, ballet to country western. Some have had a lifetime of rigorous training, while others are self-taught, having mastered their movements under the low lights of underground nightclubs or on the gritty streets of New York City. Yet all of their work might fit under the umbrella of what the scholar Clare Croft describes in the introduction to her 2017 anthology, *Queer Dance: Meanings & Makings*. Croft writes, "Dance has potential to have a particular power within queer work because dance emphasizes how public, physical action can be a force of social change."

Through the way they move and the communities they construct, these dancers embody expansive and liberatory means of existing. For them, beauty is not defined by achieving normative ideals or expertly deploying traditional techniques. Rather, the dancers envision beauty themselves, then showcase it for others to see. The sight of two women holding each other tightly and proudly at a hoedown in San Francisco disrupts heteronormative ideas of partnership, as well as the often-conservative nature of country-western culture. Flamenco dancers performing in drag in southern Spain invite viewers into their jubilant fantasies of long, ruffled skirts and flower-adorned hairdos. These are classic symbols associated with the genre that, to this day, are still reserved exclusively for women.

For this book, Yael and I traveled through the United States and Europe to meet groundbreaking artists and communities. The individuals we spoke with and photographed represent just a small sampling of the LGBTQ+ people creating dance on every continent and in every genre.

In this book, we give a broad look at queerness and dance, both wide and slippery concepts. While the project centers on LGBTQ+ people and the unique experiences and struggles we encounter, many queer dancers also use their work to address compounding factors of race, disability, and more. We look at queerness in much the same way as the butoh dancer Xue described it to me: a "sense of shifting and being able to transform infinitely." While many of the artists in this book are working within the traditional bounds of a genre in order to illuminate something about its history or alter it from the inside, some showcase entirely novel approaches to dance as a medium. A few don't consider themselves dancers at all. In these artists' practices, dance is not only performed onstage but also distilled in clips on the social media app TikTok. In one case, it is even painted with oils on canvas.

Of the many photographs Yael captured while we were making this book, one image still sticks out to me. Taken during a day we spent with the ballet company Ballez at a residency in upstate New York, it depicts the dancers cove barton and Arzu Salman locked in an embrace. Salman bends toward the floor and extends his arms behind him, his face cast in shadow. Barton holds him at the shoulders, mirroring his partner's posture as his back is softly kissed by sunlight. The black lines of a tattoo flow like a stream from under barton's sleeveless top and down his arm. Yael's images convey the visceral emotion contained in the body's movements. They allow me to consider and reconsider the dance through small, transient moments filled with care.

Prior to each shoot, Yael would create lengthy mood boards packed with historical references to help guide how she would consider framing and lighting each composition. Images by the artists Claude Cahun, Charles Ray, and Bruce Nauman flashed in her mind, as well as the life-size dolls fashioned by the sculptor Greer Lankton. Still, no matter how much planning she has done, photographing movement will always be, to some degree, a game of chance. And so Yael embedded herself within the rehearsal, capturing hundreds of snapshots. In one moment, she climbed high up into a lofted perch to grab an overhead angle. The next, she was crouched close to the dancers, or lying on the ground with her back arched toward them, zeroing in on the angle of one dancer's foot. On that day, it often seemed to me that Yael's process of documentation, demanding constant motion and an acute awareness of her surroundings, became its own kind of dance.

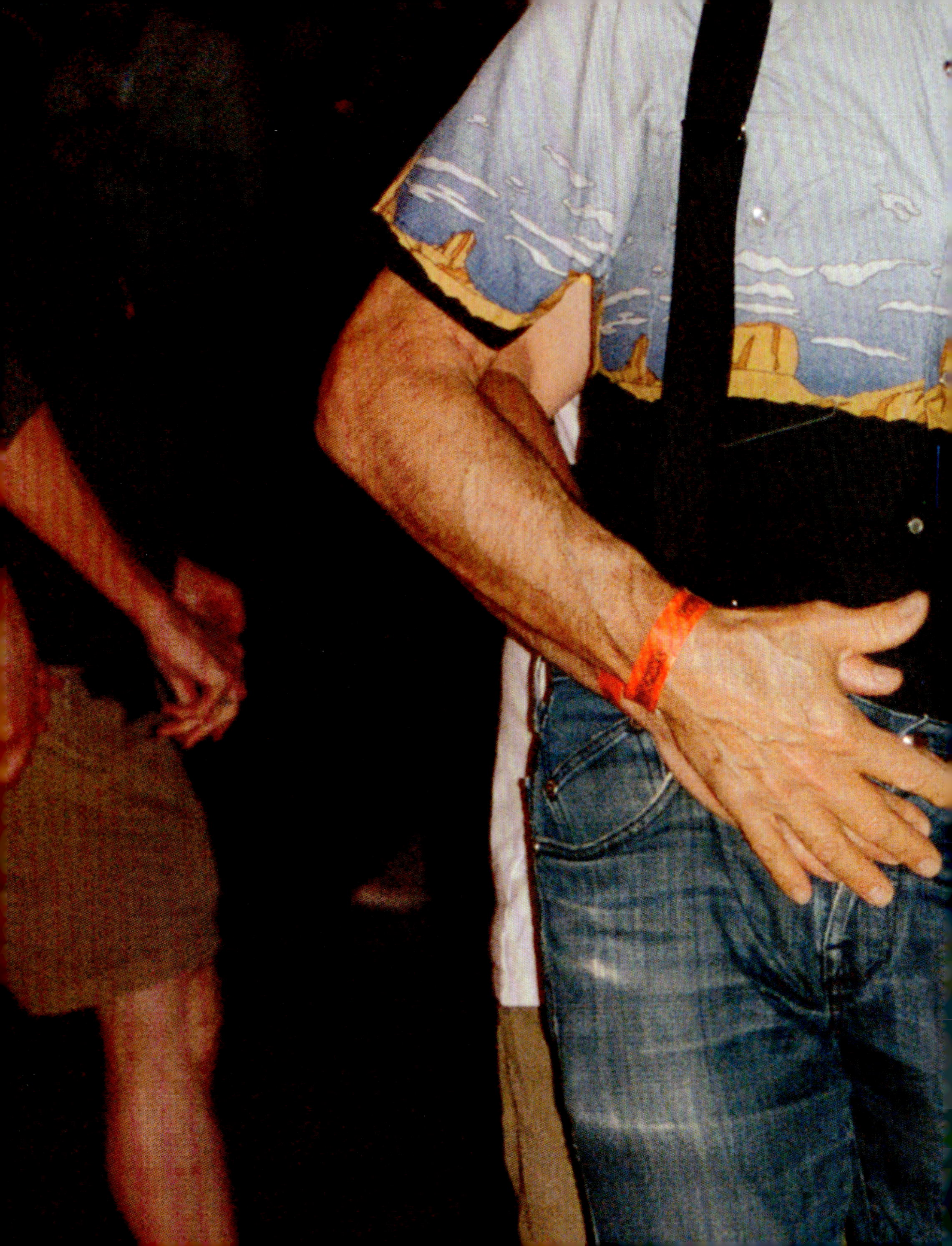

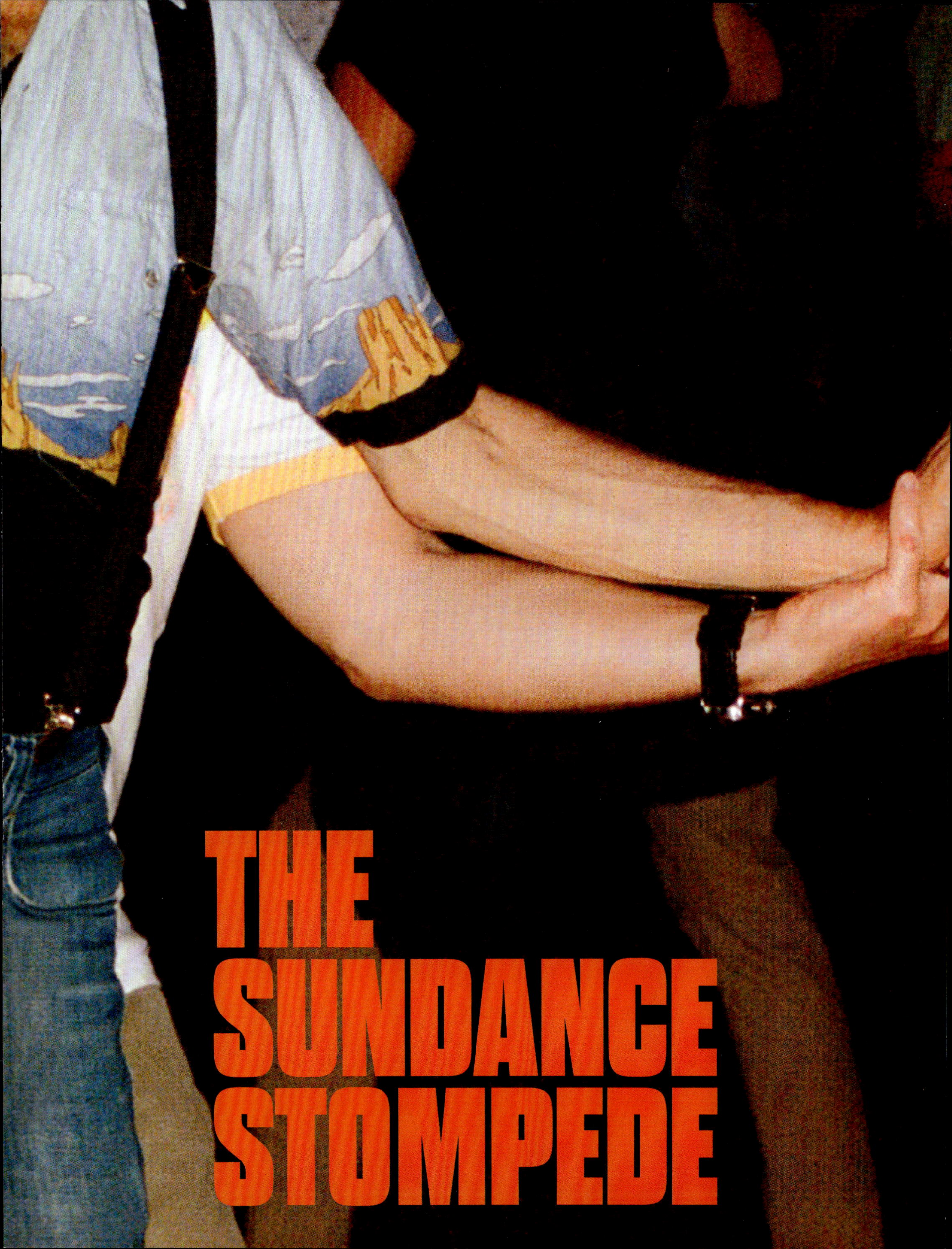
THE
SUNDANCE
STOMPEDE

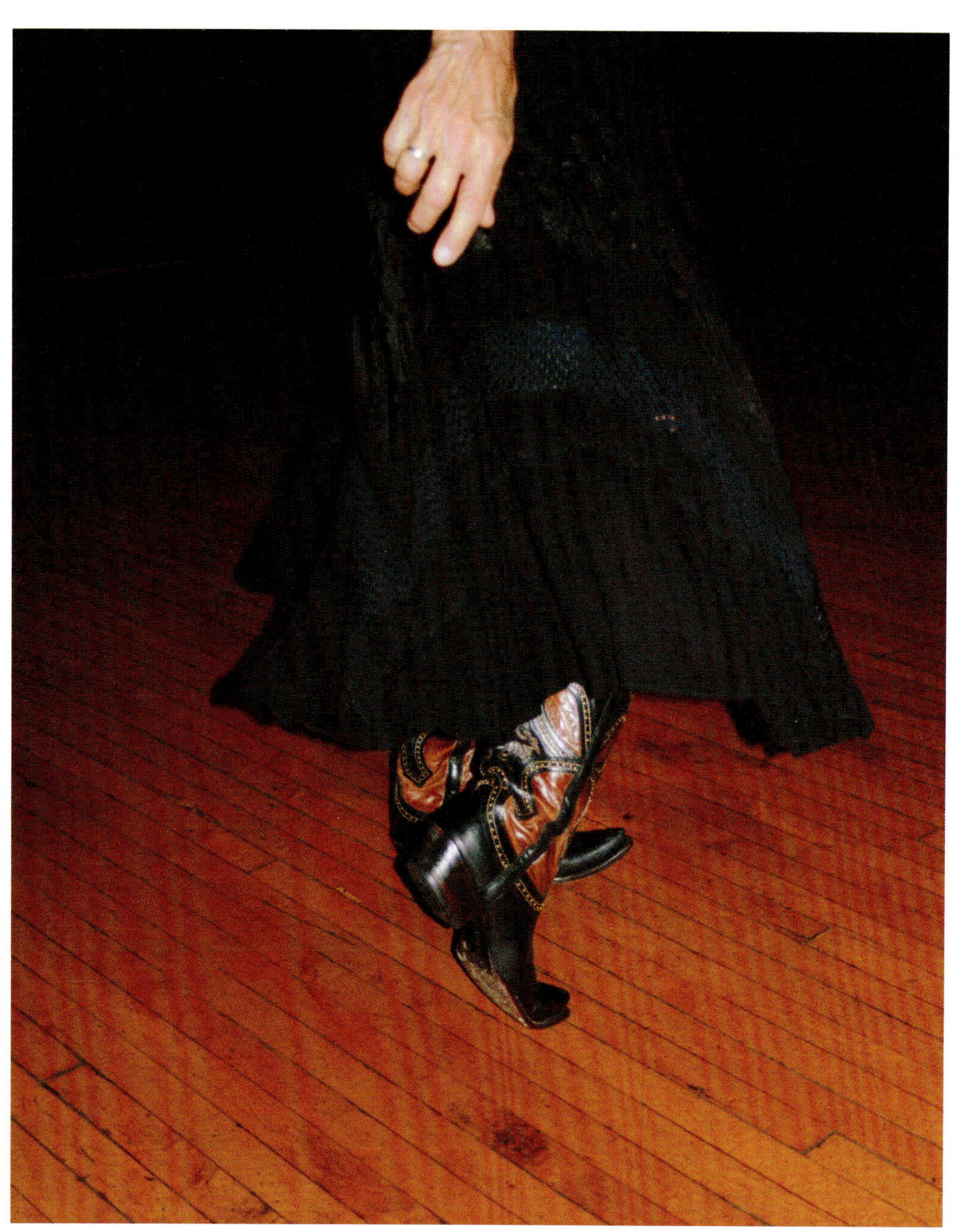

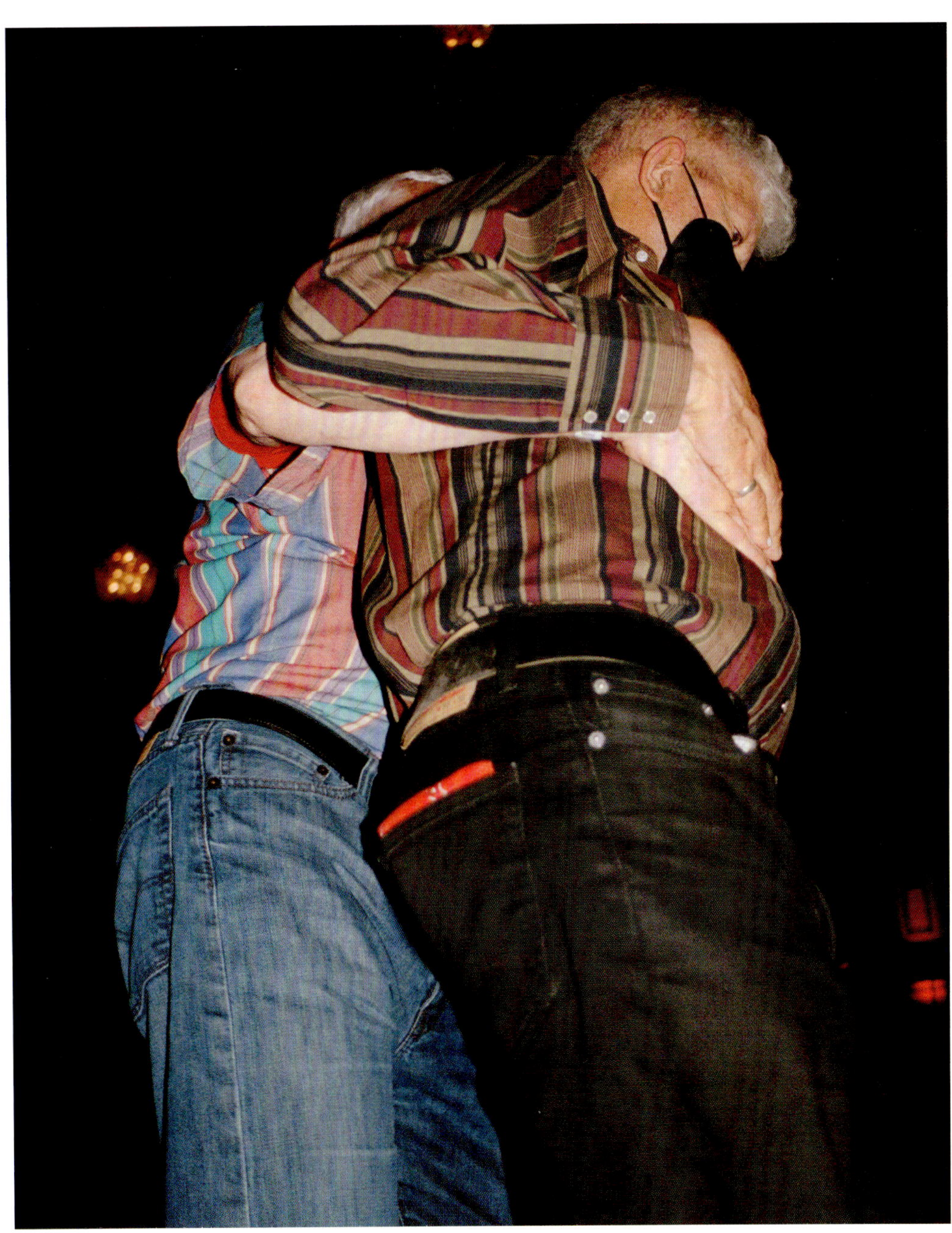

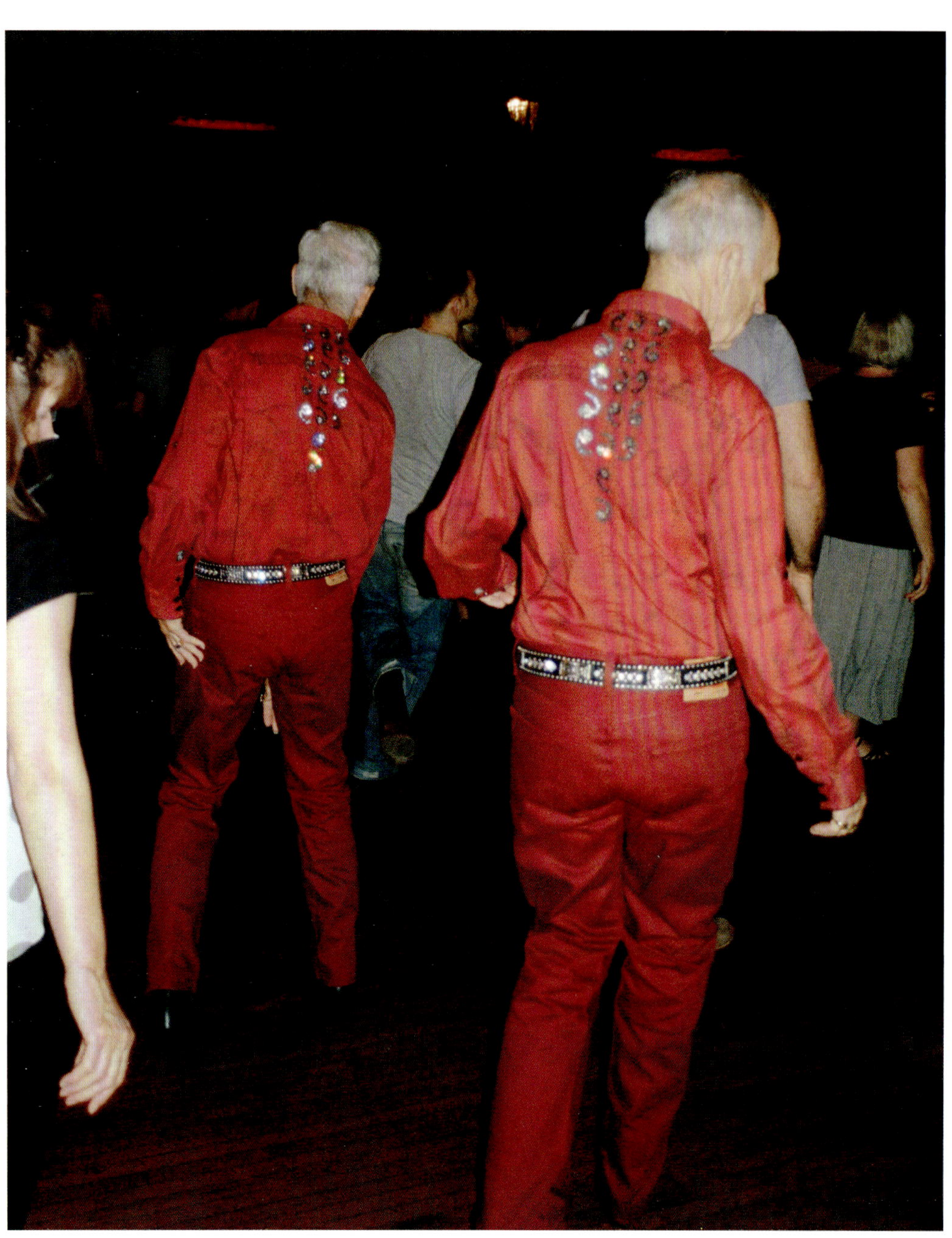

TWO WOMEN CLUTCH EACH OTHER TIGHTLY AT THE EDGE OF the Regency Ballroom's sprawling main dance floor They're positioned front to back, leisurely swaying in unison with their knees bent. The leader stands behind with her hand resting on her companion's waist, directing their movements while they turn and weave through the crowd that has gathered here. This is an intimate variation on two-step known as shadow dancing, named for the parallel arrangement of the dancers' bodies.

The follower here is Dawn Larson, a retired executive administrative assistant. A fan of country music since childhood, she began dancing to it publicly after becoming sober in 1995. The gay bar Oil Can Harry's, which had fostered a thriving country-western scene in Studio City for over fifty years, became a haven for Dawn to do what she loved without temptation, as drinks were barred from the dance floor. It was at Oil Can Harry's that, in 2013, she met the woman who would become her wife as well as her lifelong dance partner: Los Angeles Fire Department Assistant Chief Kris Larson.

"I had started coming back, looking to reclaim my own passion," Dawn recalls. "I was sitting on the stage at Oil Can's, and when I yawned, she came up and stuck her finger in my face: 'There's no yawning on the dance floor.'"

Oil Can Harry's was sold and shuttered in January 2021, one of many LGBTQ+ watering holes forfeited to the financial strains caused by the coronavirus pandemic. The Larsons felt the loss as if it were a death in the family. The community they had built around a mutual affinity for Americana aesthetics, old-timey tunes, and the flashy movements they inspire had splintered—but it had not broken. They trusted that some 380 miles north, at a converted Masonic lodge in San Francisco, they would see their friends again. In May 2022, they made the trip to the Sundance Stompede together for the first time.

For aficionados of country-western dancing, the Sundance Stompede is an experience to be savored. An annual four-day festival dedicated to creating an inclusive culture around this dance style, it is the largest LGBTQ+ country-western dance gathering. It draws hundreds of people from around the world to participate in welcoming workshops, raucous exhibitions, and, for some, even steamy late-night underwear parties. There are entry-level lessons for beginners and lighthearted competitions for seasoned performers. Many dancers come with partners, but swapping is encouraged. Stand on the sidelines for a couple minutes and you'll soon be invited into the dance by a wandering cowpoke with a friendly face.

Since 2001, the Stompede has brought the collective joys of two-stepping, line dancing, and swing dancing to San Francisco, and it has been volunteer-run for just as long. Behind it is the Sundance Association, a nonprofit that facilitates biweekly dance classes and stages performances at Pride events, at local street fairs, and aboard gay cruises. The association formed in 1999 as a grassroots effort to preserve San Francisco's LGBTQ+ country-western dancing community when they no longer felt welcome at the bar that primarily housed them. At the time, no one involved wanted to kick-start an organization. They simply wanted a safe, comfortable place to be together.

"The Sundance Association came out of the actions of the bar owner . . . alienating its customers," says Stompede Event Director Dave Hayes. "He would kick people out for spinning too much on the dance floor, for not ordering enough drinks, stuff like that. [Stompede Assistant Director Ingu Yun] and some friends said, 'You know what? I think we've had enough of this.' So they met with an event

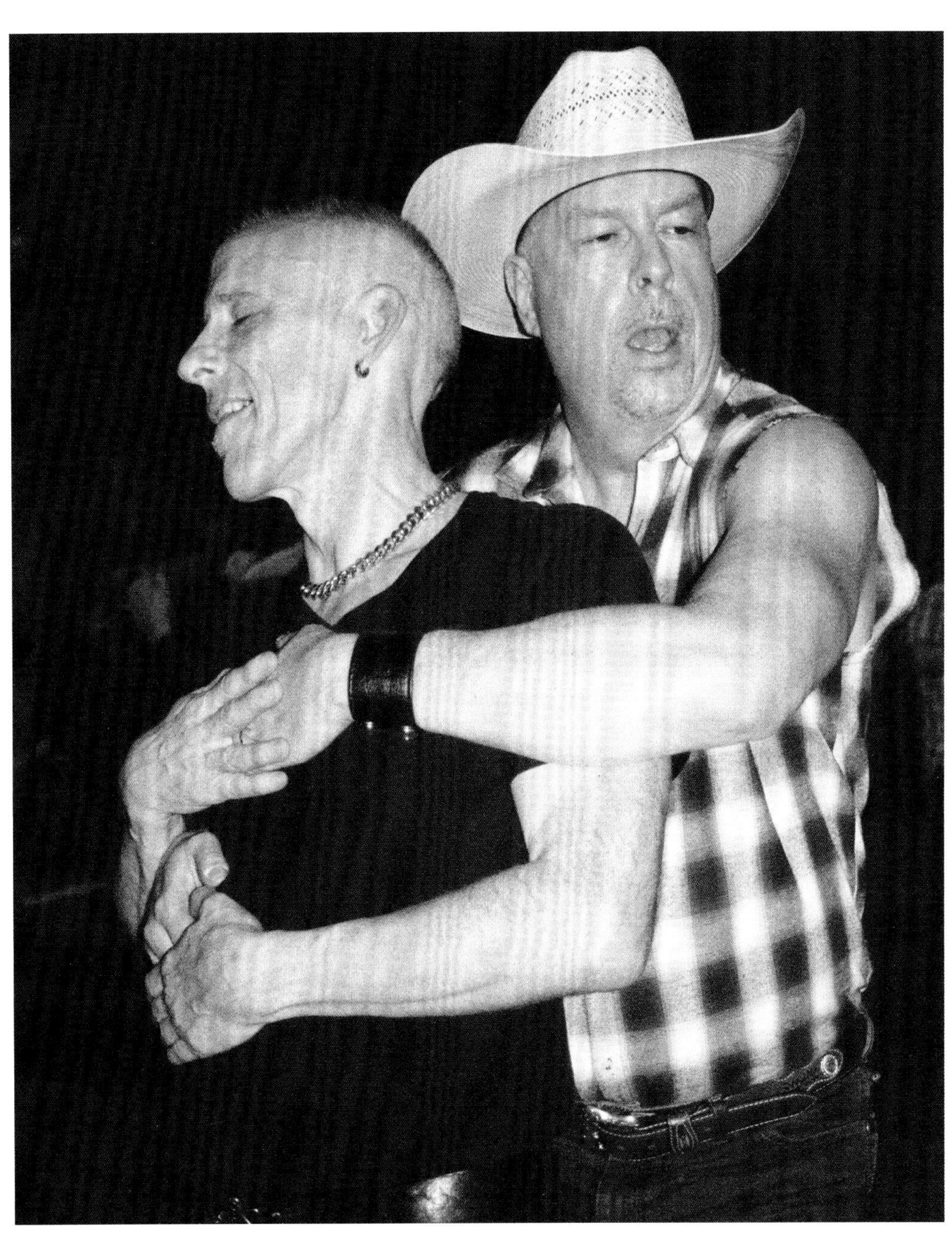

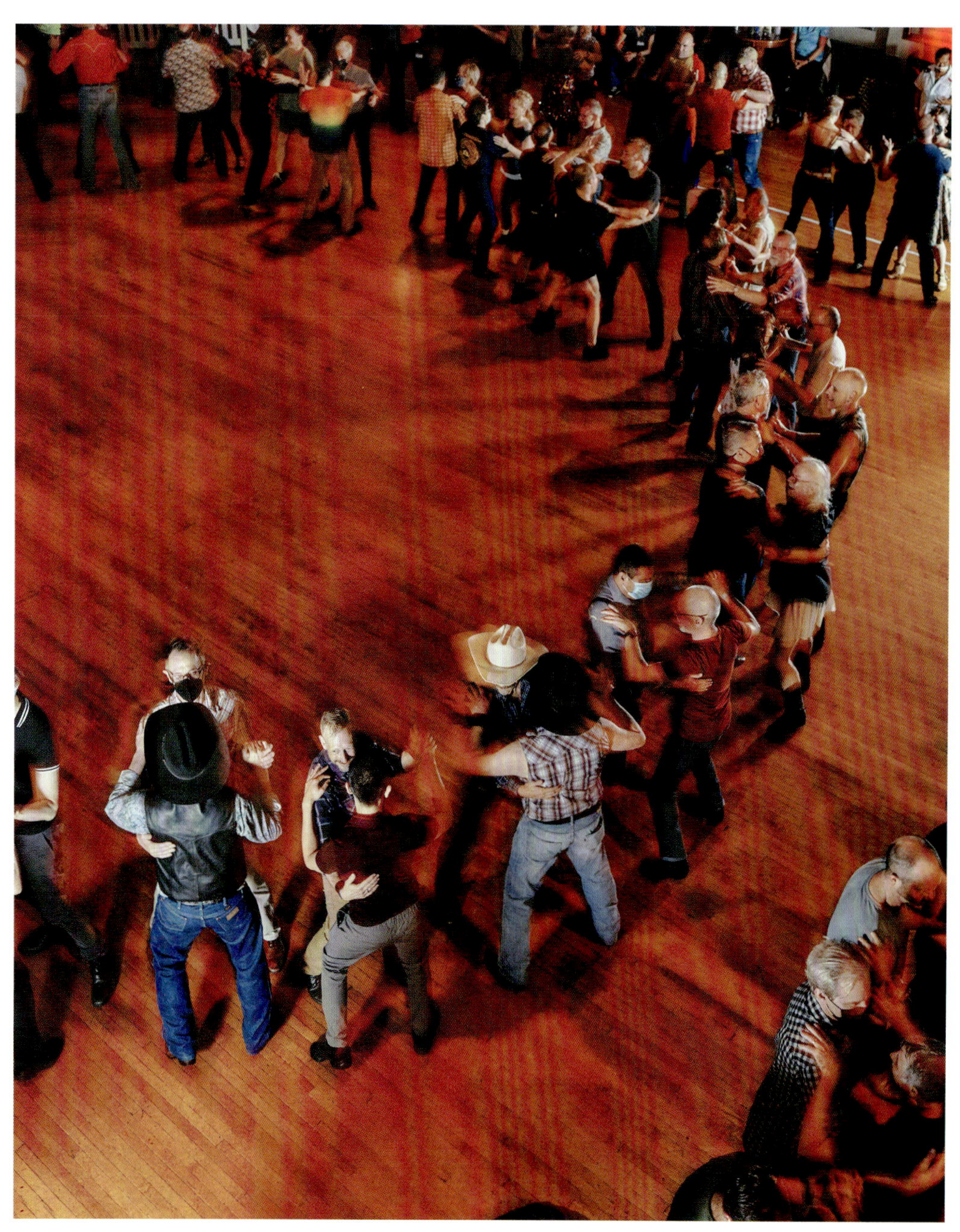

organizer, found a space, and Sundance was formed."

Hayes, a jovial fellow with a thick white beard and a bearlike hug, discovered country-western dancing in 1993. On the back patio of a leather bar, the former Full Moon Saloon in Orlando, he witnessed the joyous yet then-unfamiliar sight of men lovingly dancing with other men. It sparked a revelation for him. He had danced in clubs before, but the intimacy offered by country western's various partnered techniques was instantly more enticing. "It's one of the dance styles that provides the most connection, even over ballroom," he says. "You're holding each other very close."

Hayes began teaching dance workshops in Florida, and later Texas, in his spare time. Meanwhile, he was also becoming familiar with the Sundance Association through frequent visits to the Bay Area. When he moved to San Francisco in 2002, he plunged into the community, starting out as a volunteer coordinator. In the two decades since, he's watched the Stompede grow from a small gathering in the back room of a club to an extended weekend loaded with programming. In 2022, an estimated 600 people attended the Saturday-evening festivities alone, and this popularity has inspired similar events in other cities around the United States.

"I came to Stompede and fell completely in love with it," says Mary Bulgarelli, who performs with a line-dancing troupe called the L.A. Wranglers. Bulgarelli first attended the Stompede in 2014 and, in 2022, coordinated a three-day spin-off conference in Southern California called the Wrangler Weekend Los Angeles. It has been running for over a decade. "We all move together to the sound of music, so it's very unifying."

The crown jewel of the Stompede is the Saturday-night hoedown. When the afternoon's workshops wrap up and the evening approaches, eager dancers pour into the Regency Ballroom wearing all manner of colorful

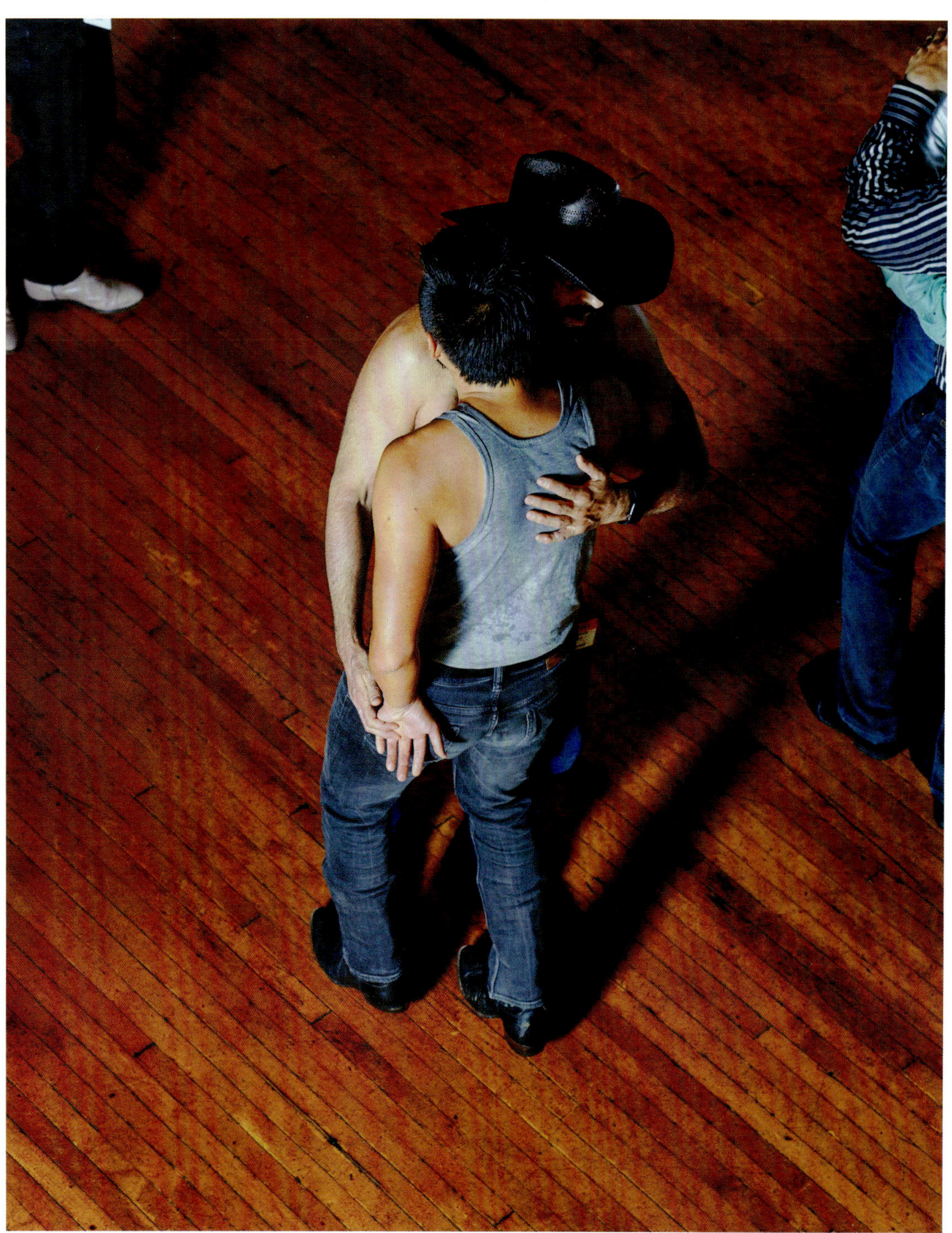

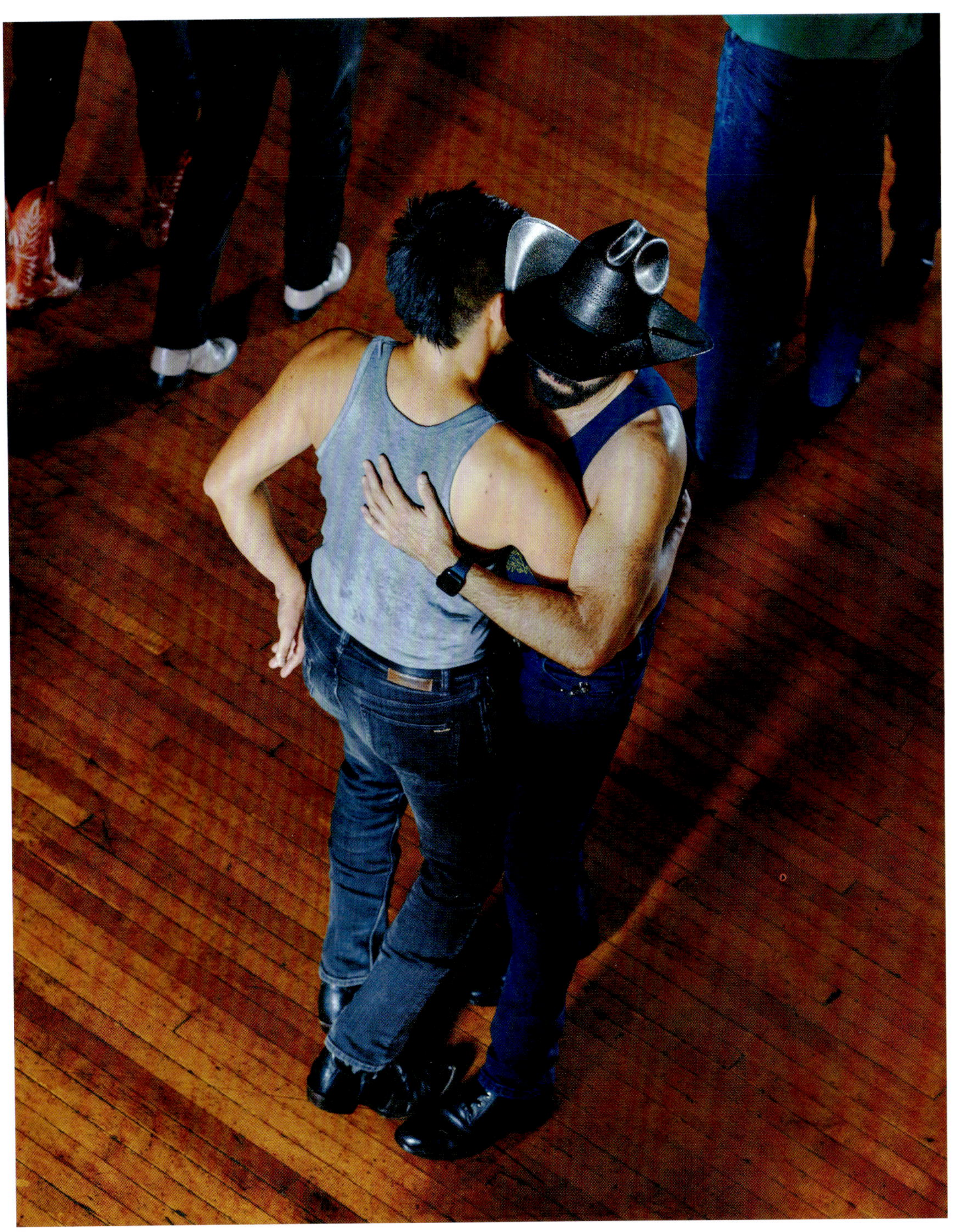

Western wear. The year Yael and I attended, there were ten-gallon hats, bright plaid tops, and plenty of hip-hugging Levi's. One couple debuted a matching set of suits to which they had spent the past year hand-gluing gems in elaborate patterns. Hayes arrived in a striped navy shirt, unbuttoned down to his belly and tucked into a pair of blue jeans. He was right on time for the show to begin.

A series of exhibitions kicked off the evening. Bulgarelli moved to the middle of the space to perform with the L.A. Wranglers, who all sported towering black caps. They were followed by an extravagantly dressed ensemble known as the Manhattan Prairie Dogs, who make the trek from New York City every year. Then the floor gave way to hours of open dancing, which is when attendees get to step up and show off. When a line dance is called, the entire room is engulfed in parallel rows of neat choreography, done to pop country, if not outright pop, and at one point spilling over onto the sidewalk outside. Cowboy boots are optional, but staying engaged for the length of the song is a must.

Country-western culture and LGBTQ+ identity might seem like contrary concepts. In some ways, they are, or at least they have been. Until recently, coming out could harm or even end a country musician's career. Even as some of the genre's biggest artists—like Brandi Carlile and the Brothers Osborne's T. J. Osborne—speak openly about their sexuality today, the industry is still dominated by straight men. The image of the cowboy too (whom some of the Stompede's patrons draw aesthetic inspiration from with their denim slacks and leather accessories) is a fraught symbol of masculinity, almost always portrayed as white and heterosexual.

Yet some dancers view their co-opting of Wild West aesthetics and rituals as a triumphant, healing

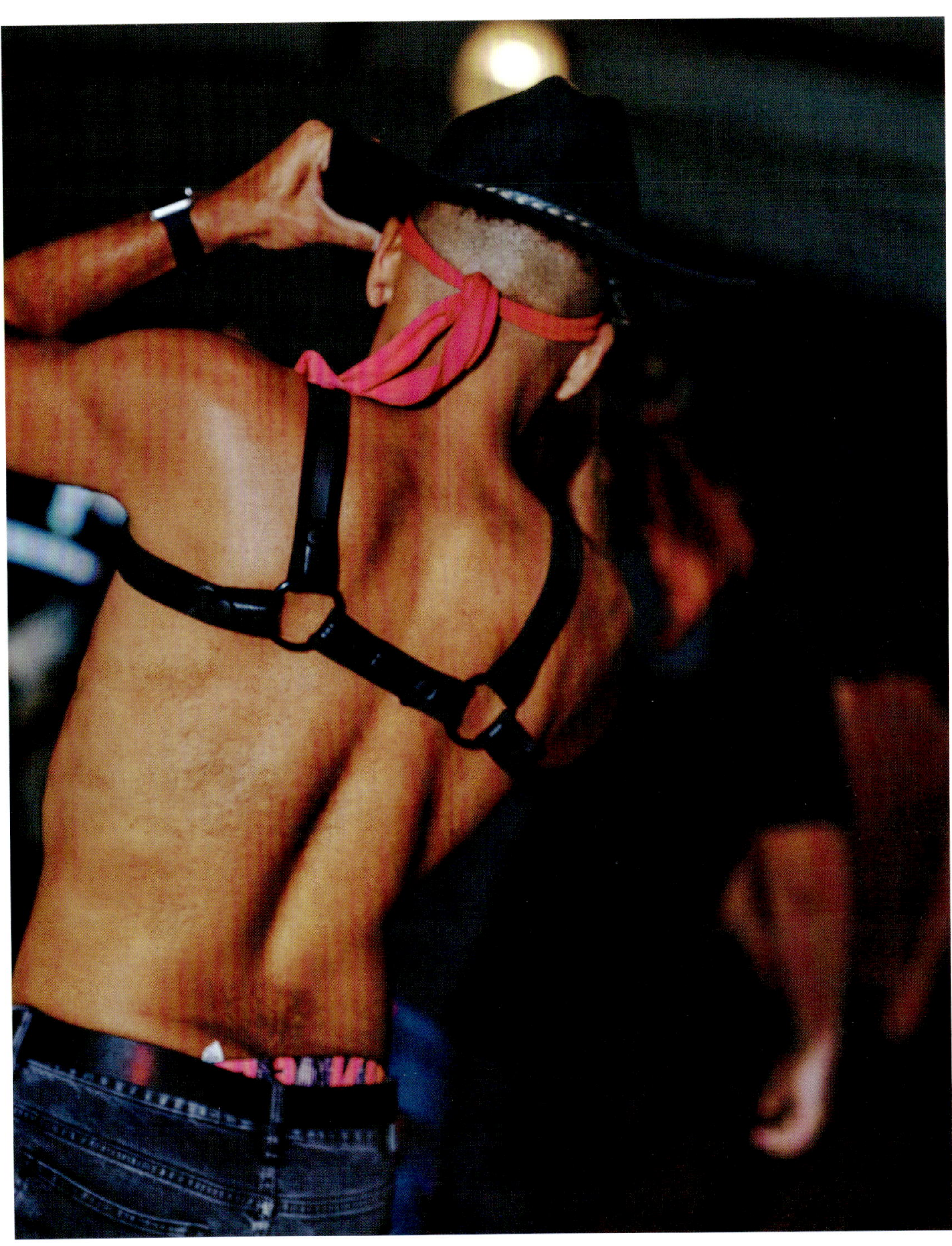

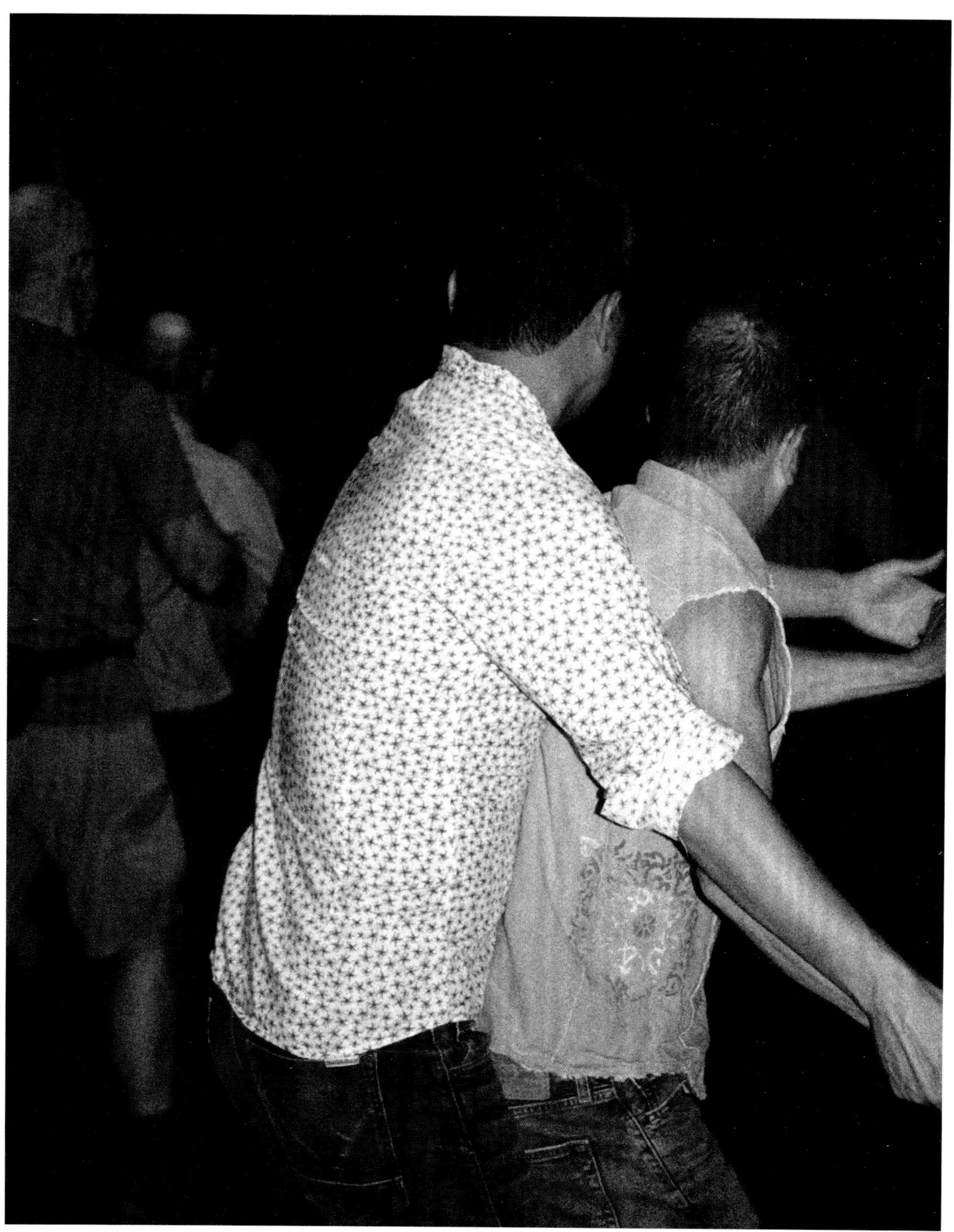

act. For many people, as first-time Stompede-goer Cecil Whitney puts it, "It's a reclamation of a piece of culture they haven't been able to connect with since they were a kid."

Whitney began dancing in 2019 at the Cuff Complex, a leather bar in Seattle, and says they were drawn to country western for the inherent power play involved in leading and following. "In queer country-dance spaces in particular, folks get really switchy," they say. As the roles' traditionally gendered associations break down, it makes for "a really fun exchange."

As of this writing, 2023 was scheduled to be the Stompede's last year, but hopefully it will continue in a new form after that. For now, near the center of the dance floor, two men seem to be connected at the arm. They whirl across the room and around each other, wearing button-down shirts with the sleeves ripped off. The taller of the pair, boosted by the height of his square Stetson, guides his partner in a relaxed swing dance, pushing him away and pulling him back, until they swap, and the other takes control.

As the song ends and the dance pauses momentarily, the Larsons find a seat at a table to the side of the dance floor. "Back when we were going three times a week, we'd do all the line dances, and now we're winded walking up to here," Dawn says with a laugh. "We're just so grateful to be able to get back." She says it feels like a family reunion.

The Larsons were married in 2016. Tonight, Dawn wears the same shoes she wore on her wedding day, a striking pair of brown leather riding boots with her initials pressed onto the heel in Swarovski crystals, right beside Kris's. She's taking a quick break for now, but when she gets back up to dance with her wife, close as ever, they'll sparkle once again.

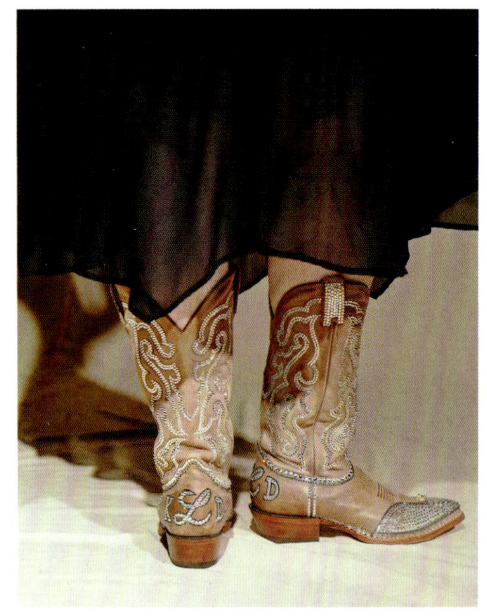
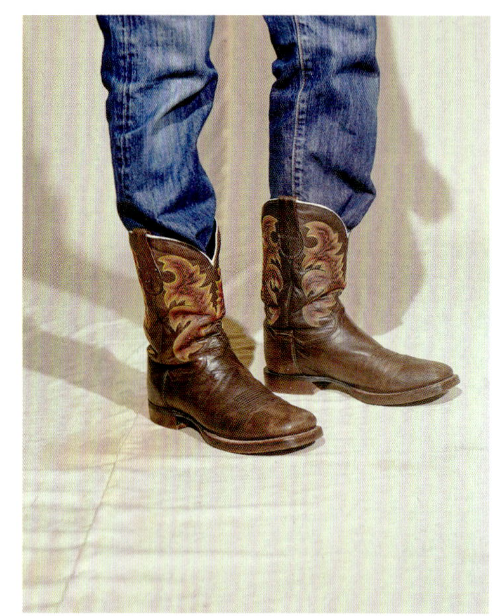
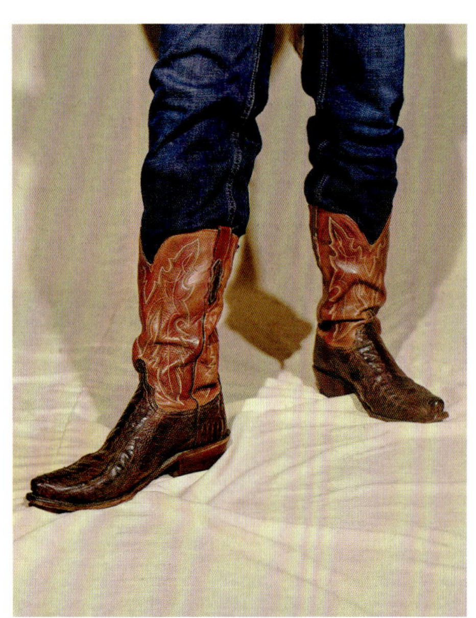
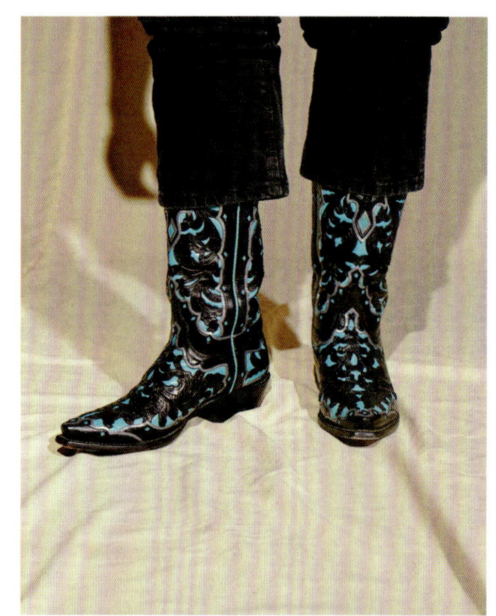
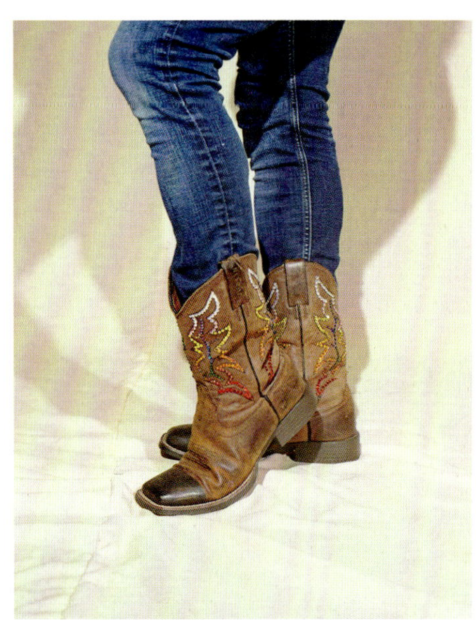
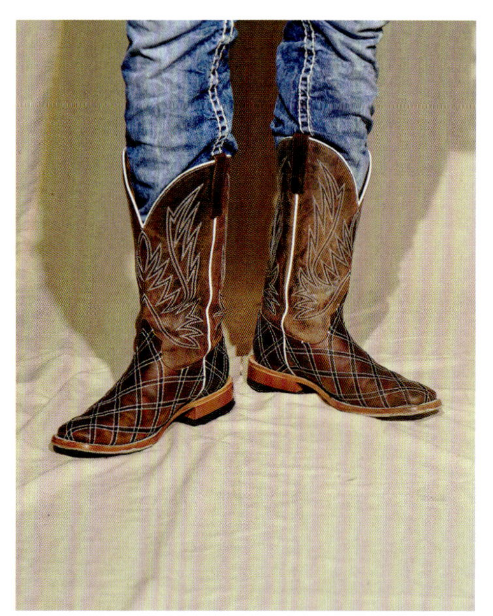

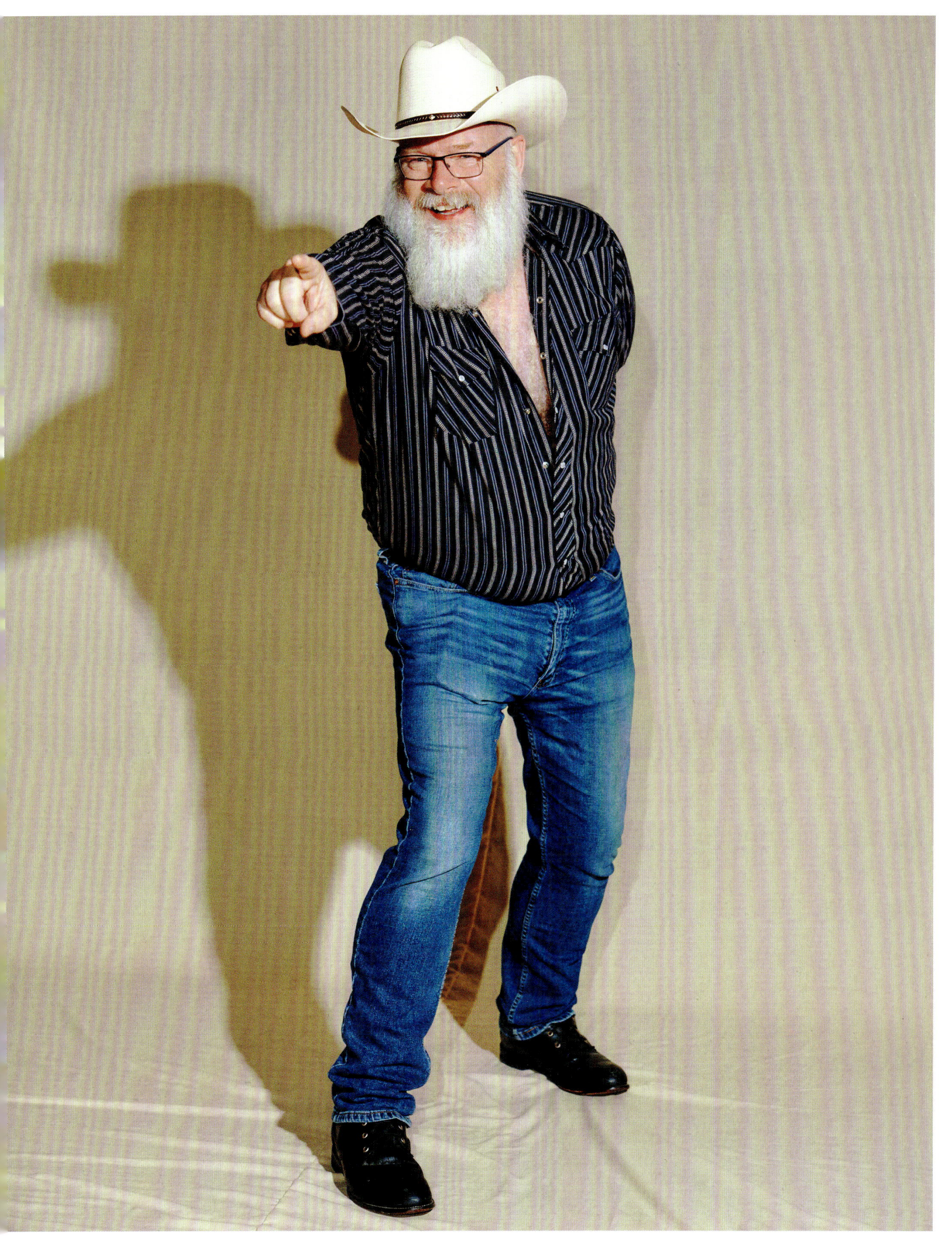

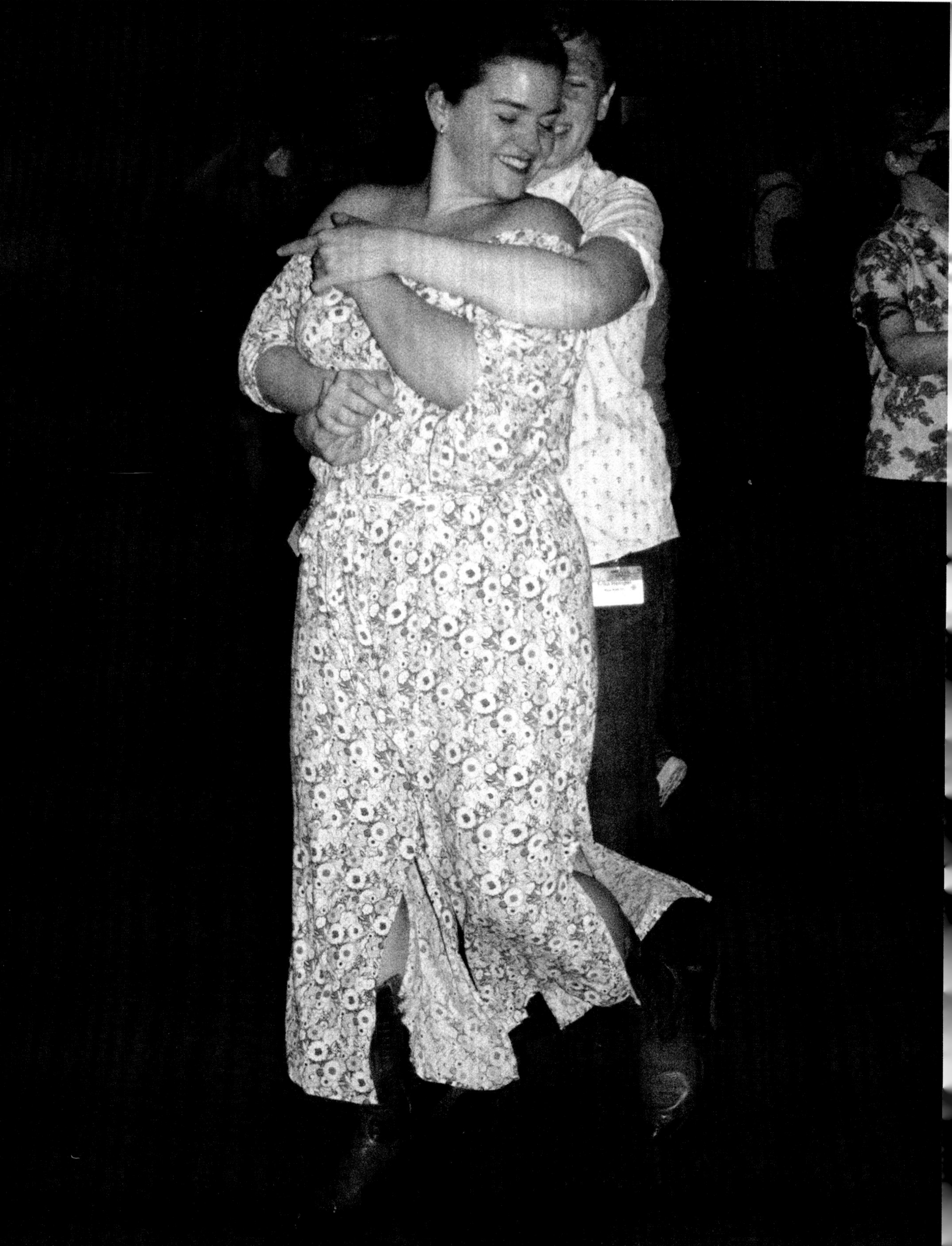

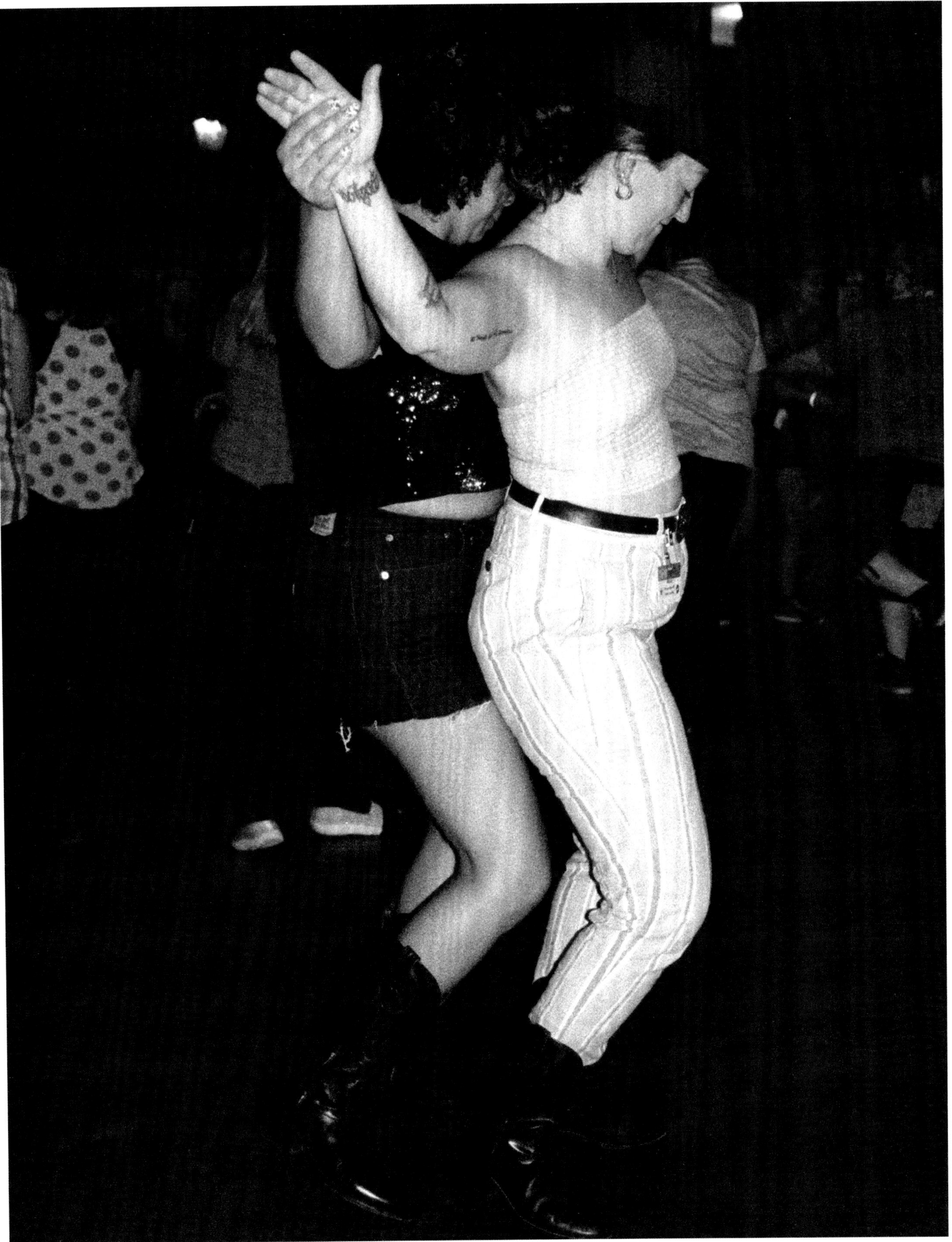

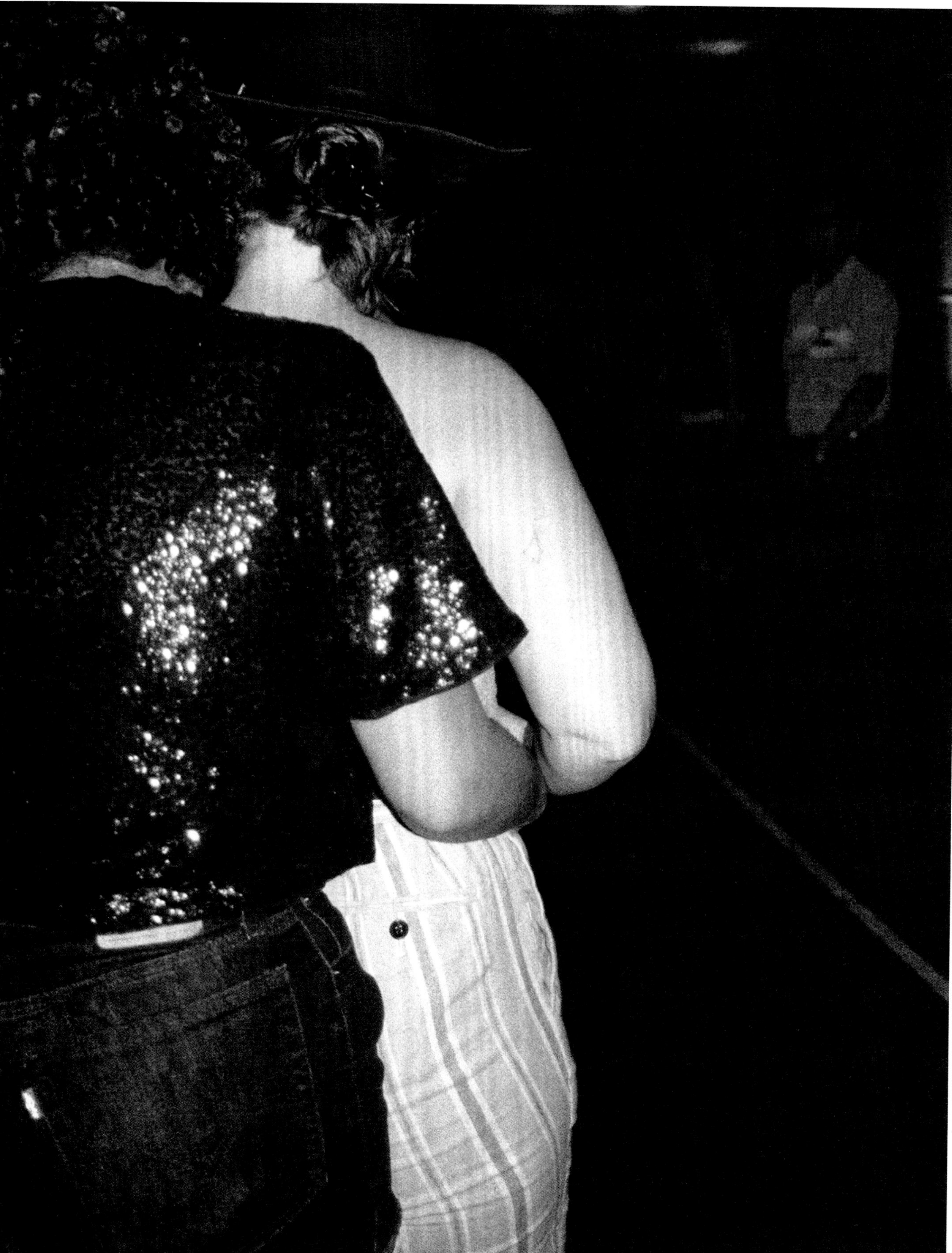

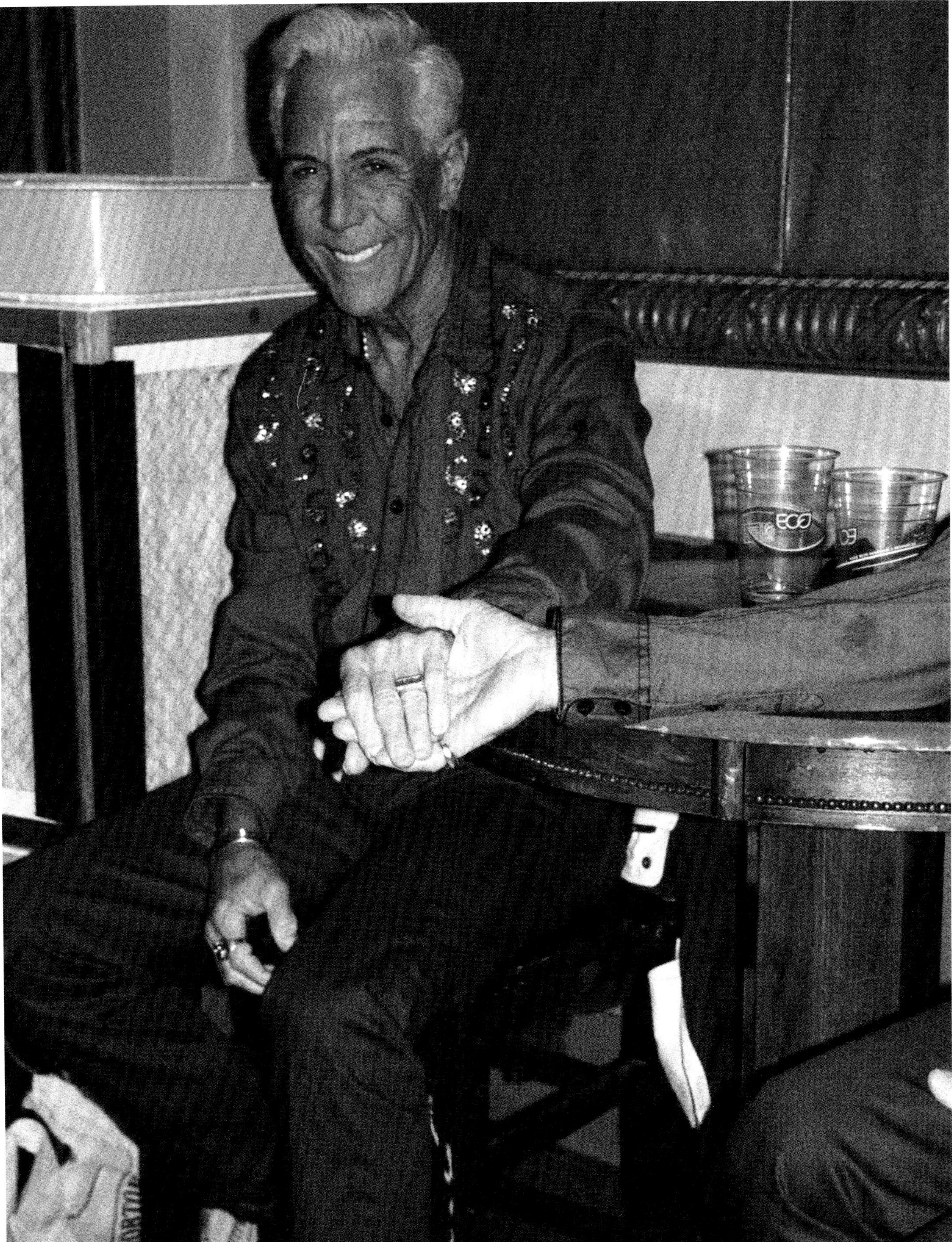

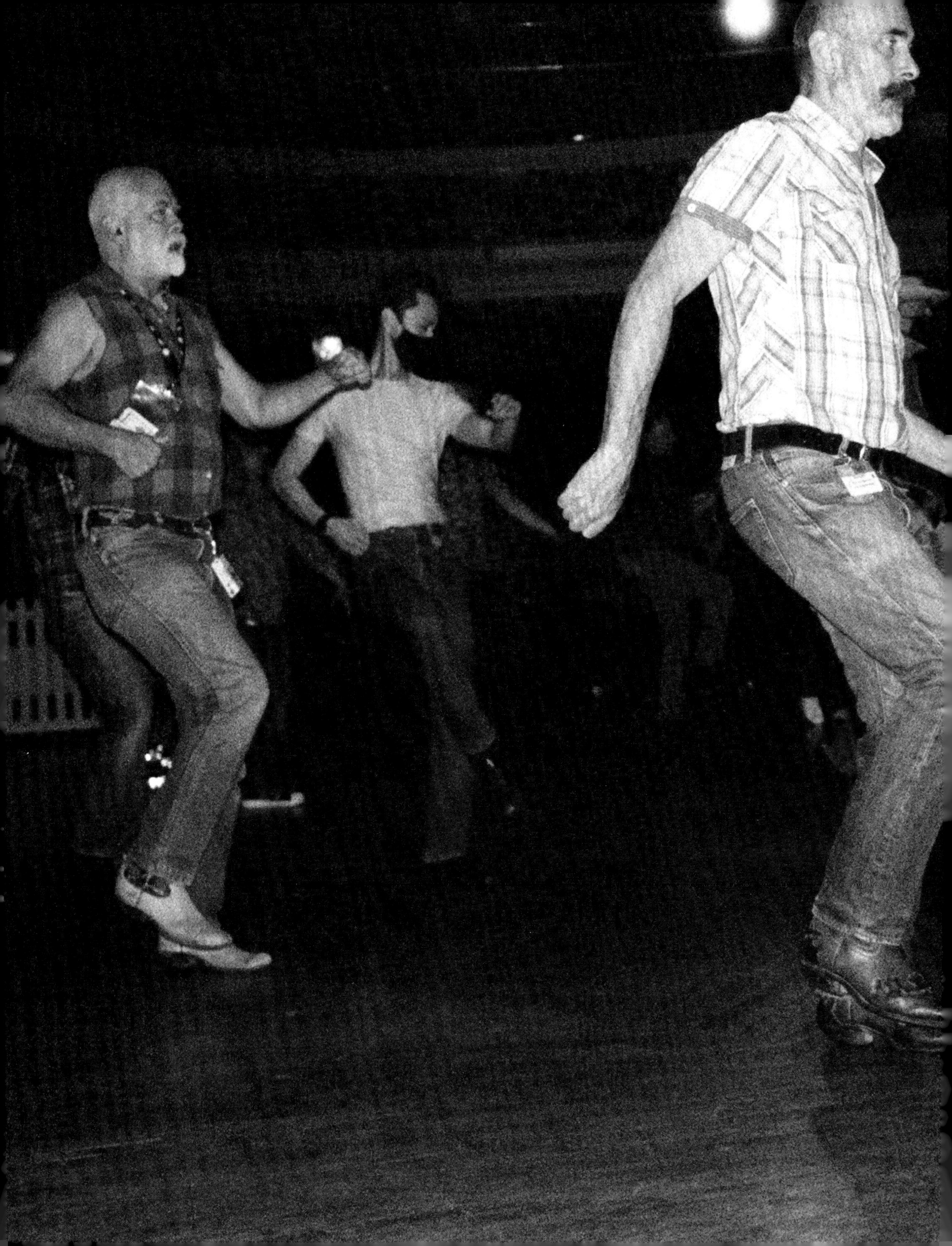

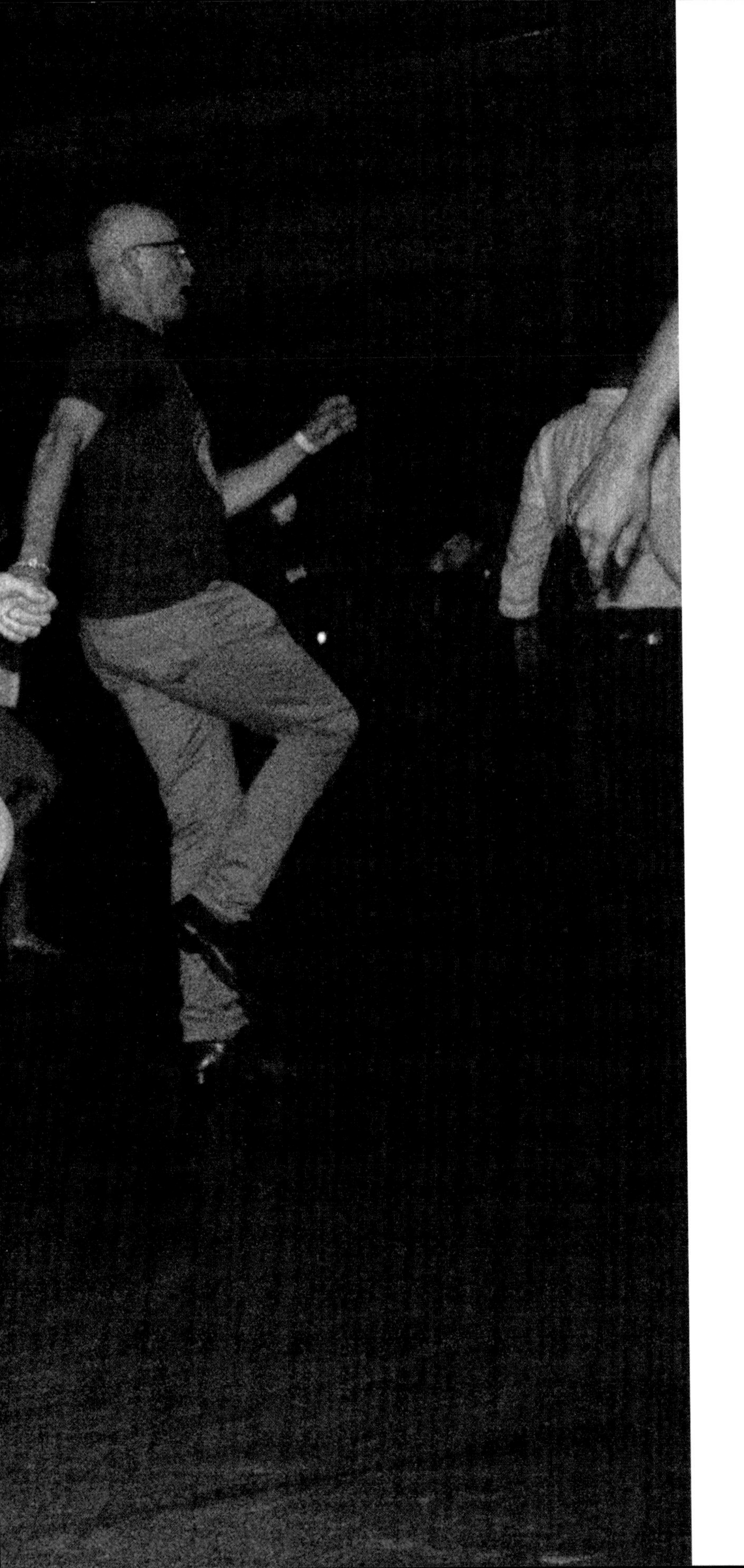

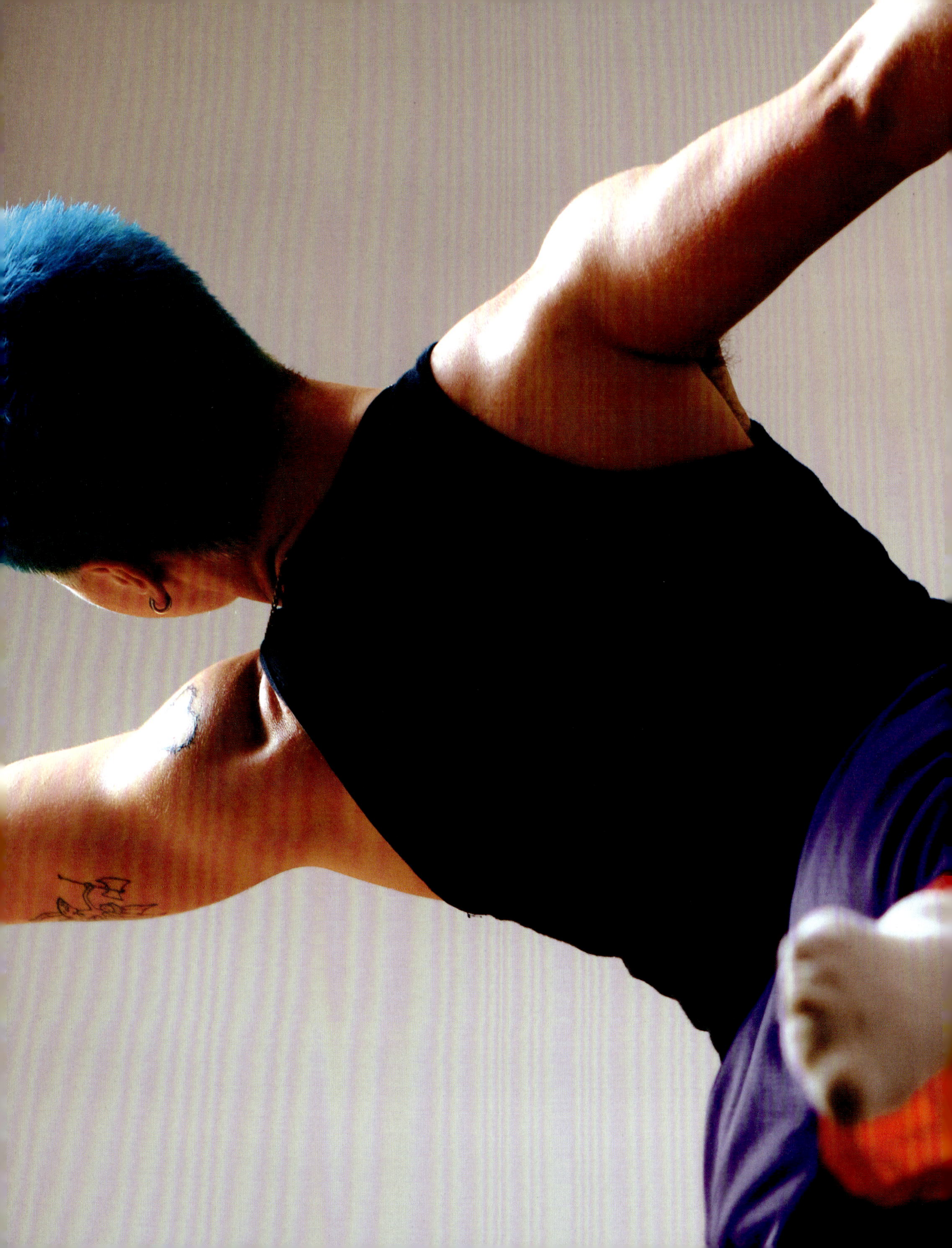

BALLEZ

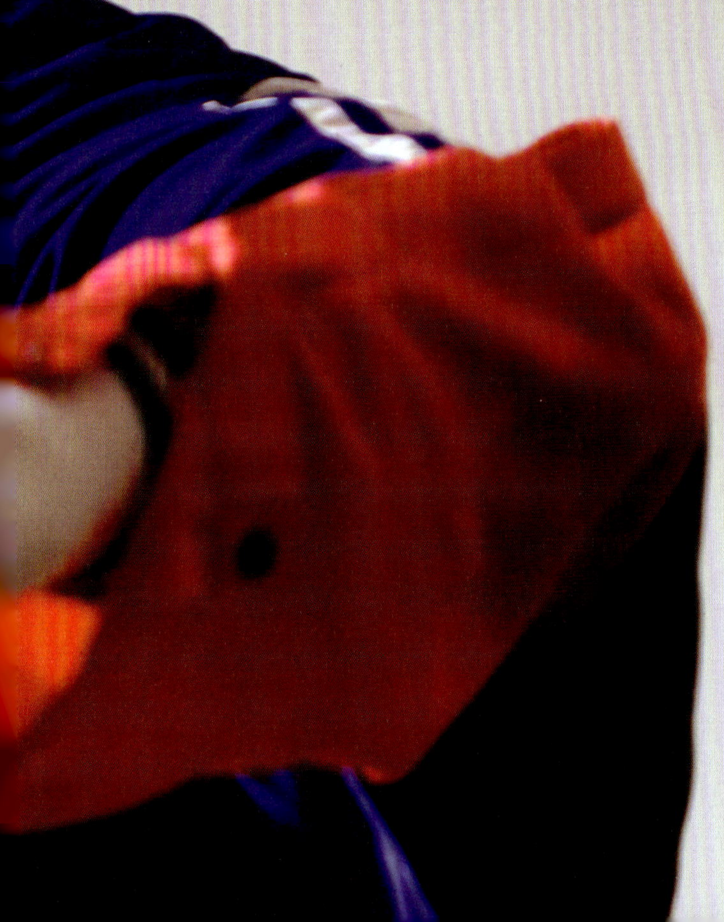

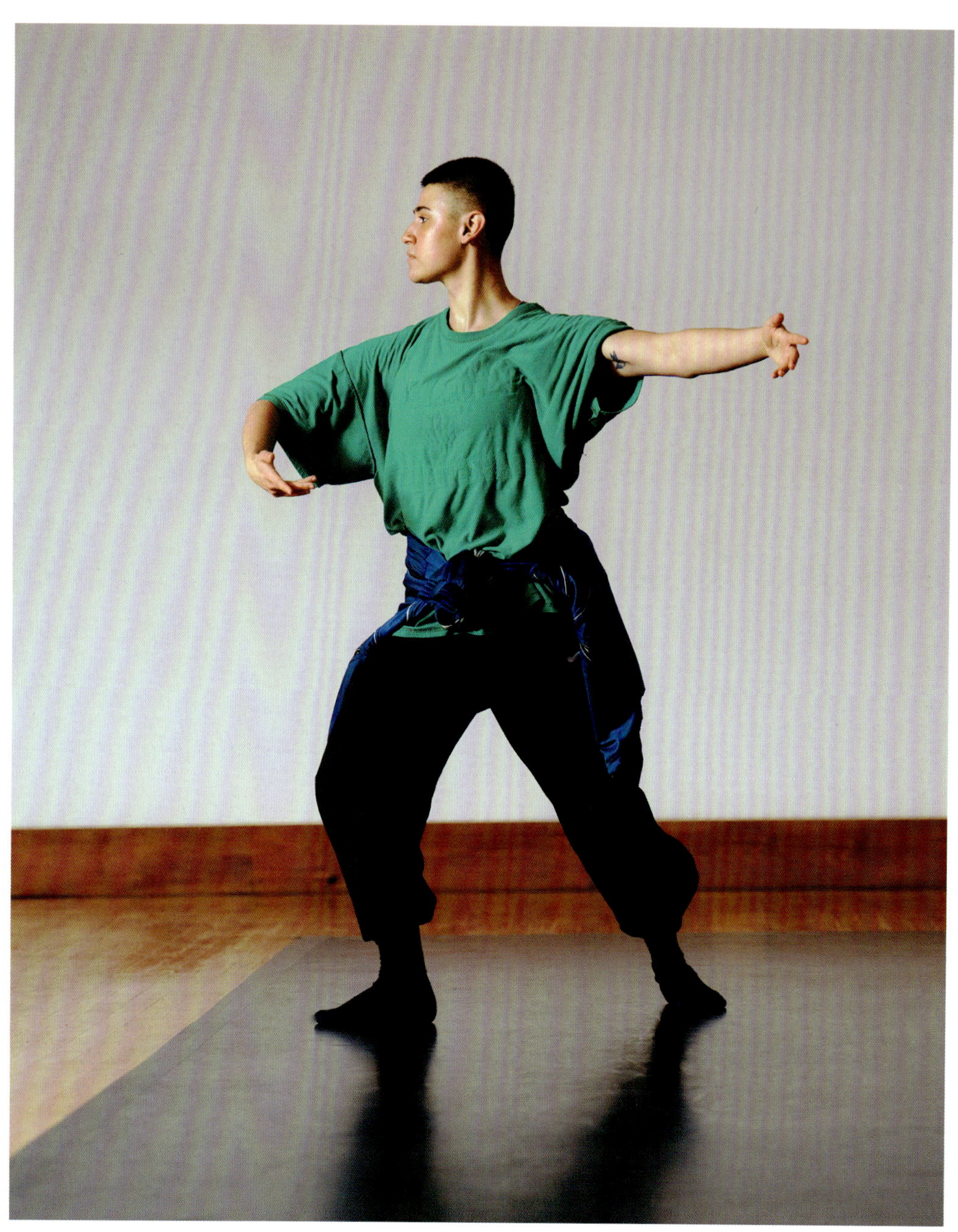

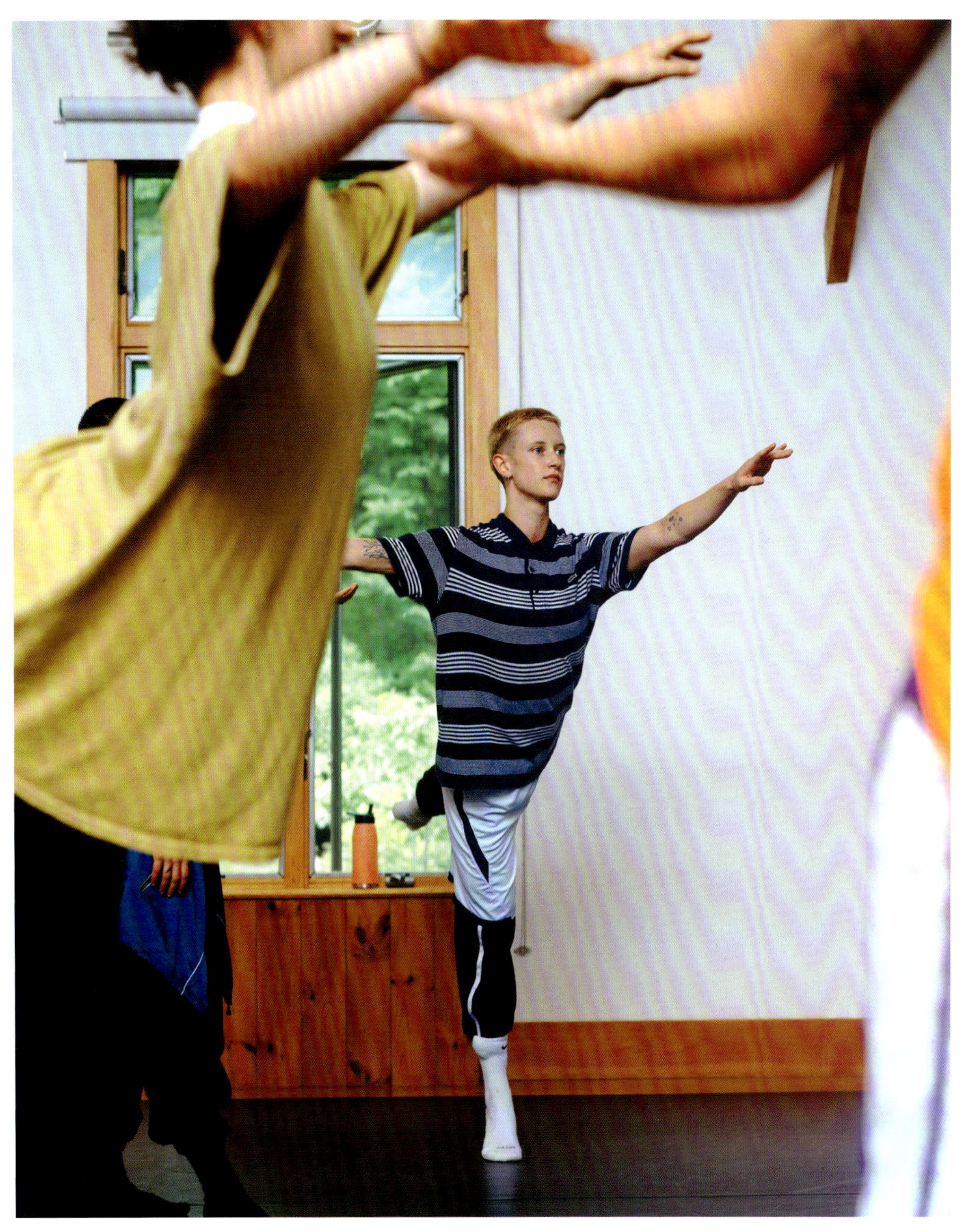

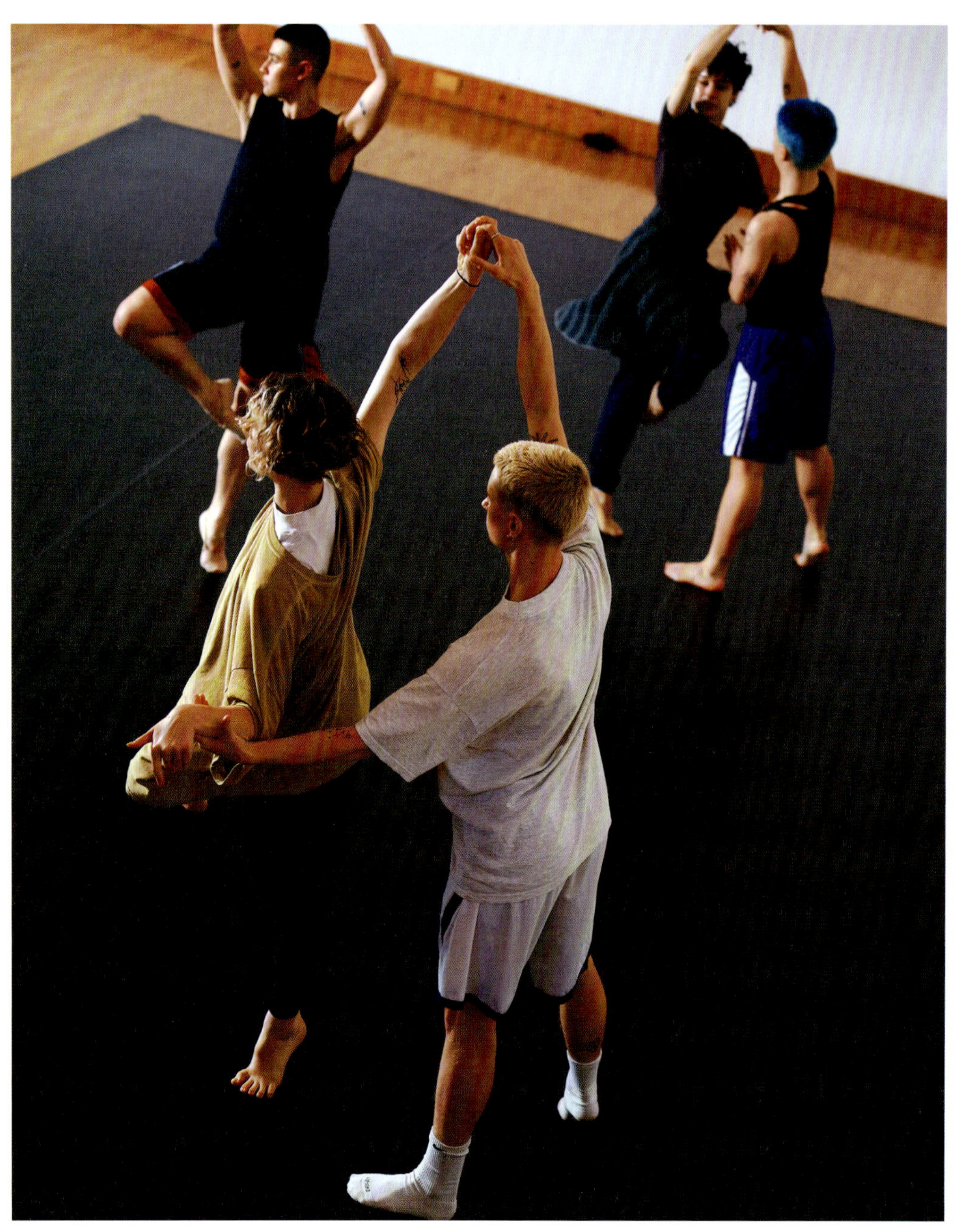

THE COMIC BALLET *COPPÉLIA*, A ROSE OF THE ROMANTIC ERA, IS propelled by the unwitting passion of its handsomely gullible lead, Franz. Perched on a balcony overlooking his rural village's harvest celebrations is the titular mechanical doll. So realistic is she that, spying her from below, the young hero mistakes the puppet for an impossibly beautiful human girl and falls in love. Taking advantage of this infatuation, the doll's maker, a cunning alchemist named Dr. Coppélius, attempts to siphon Franz's soul to give life to his beloved creation, only to be tricked and thwarted by Swanhilda, Franz's fiancée, hidden by a clever disguise.

The dancer who originated the lead role at the Paris Opera in 1870 was not a man at all. Rather, the renowned danseuse Eugénie Fiocre, then the theater's principal, slipped into sleek white tights and became the sprightly Franz. The part would solidify Fiocre as one of the most celebrated dancers ever to perform *en travesti*, a theatrical term for portraying a character of the opposite sex. This was the convention of the ballet throughout much of the nineteenth century, a time when the rigidly perfect, aesthetically pure movements of ballerinas ruled the stage. Men performed mimed or comedic roles, while the dancing roles, regardless of their identities, were reserved solely for women.

In some ways, the codes of the ballet have not changed tremendously since the nineteenth century. The medium remains divided along gender lines. With few exceptions, plots follow heteronormative scripts. Dancers' bodies are strictly policed, and those who deviate from established norms are punished, forced to choose between having a career and expressing themselves fully. That's why the dancer and choreographer Katy Pyle, founder of the ballet company Ballez, was drawn to *Coppélia*. Perhaps this tale of mistaken identity and disguise, complicated by questions of gaze, offered an alternative vision for the art form, one where beauty and destiny could be self-determined.

"If I had been a ballet dancer in that era, I would've been so psyched to get to do male roles," they say, "and to get to perform my masculinity and have it be appreciated and valued."

Pyle's own experience dancing ballet has been a yearslong process of learning, unlearning, and searching for their own worth within the genre. They began studying at the age of three and left their family home in Austin, Texas, at fourteen to train at the University of North Carolina School of the Arts. They showed remarkable talent early on, but they recall being consistently chastised for the strength of their movement. "I tried to make myself appear more delicate and feminine, to look shy and coy and cute," they say. "I was performing a self that didn't align with who I am."

Despite Pyle's dedication to the art form, they were not immune to the pressures of the industry. They left the program a few years later, sure that they would never again perform ballet. Yet as time passed, and as they performed new genres and tried on new identities, their body still yearned for ballet, which they describe as their "first language."

So in 2011, Pyle started Ballez as a response to the industry's archaic standards. The company works within the recognizable structures of historical story ballets but gives the spotlight to lesbian, trans, and queer people. In *The Firebird*, which debuted in 2013 at St. Mark's Church in New York, Pyle played a lesbian princess opposite a high-femme dominatrix sorceress and a "Tranimal" phoenix with precious feather earrings. In 2021, Ballez's *Giselle of Loneliness* took the problems of ballet itself as its subject. The audience watched faux auditions and was asked to decide which dancer best aligned with the medium's fraught ideals.

Underscoring these shows is Ballez's mission to bring queer bodies into the traditional ballet canon, a reparative act. It returns the art form to those whose love for it persists despite having been ostracized by it.

***

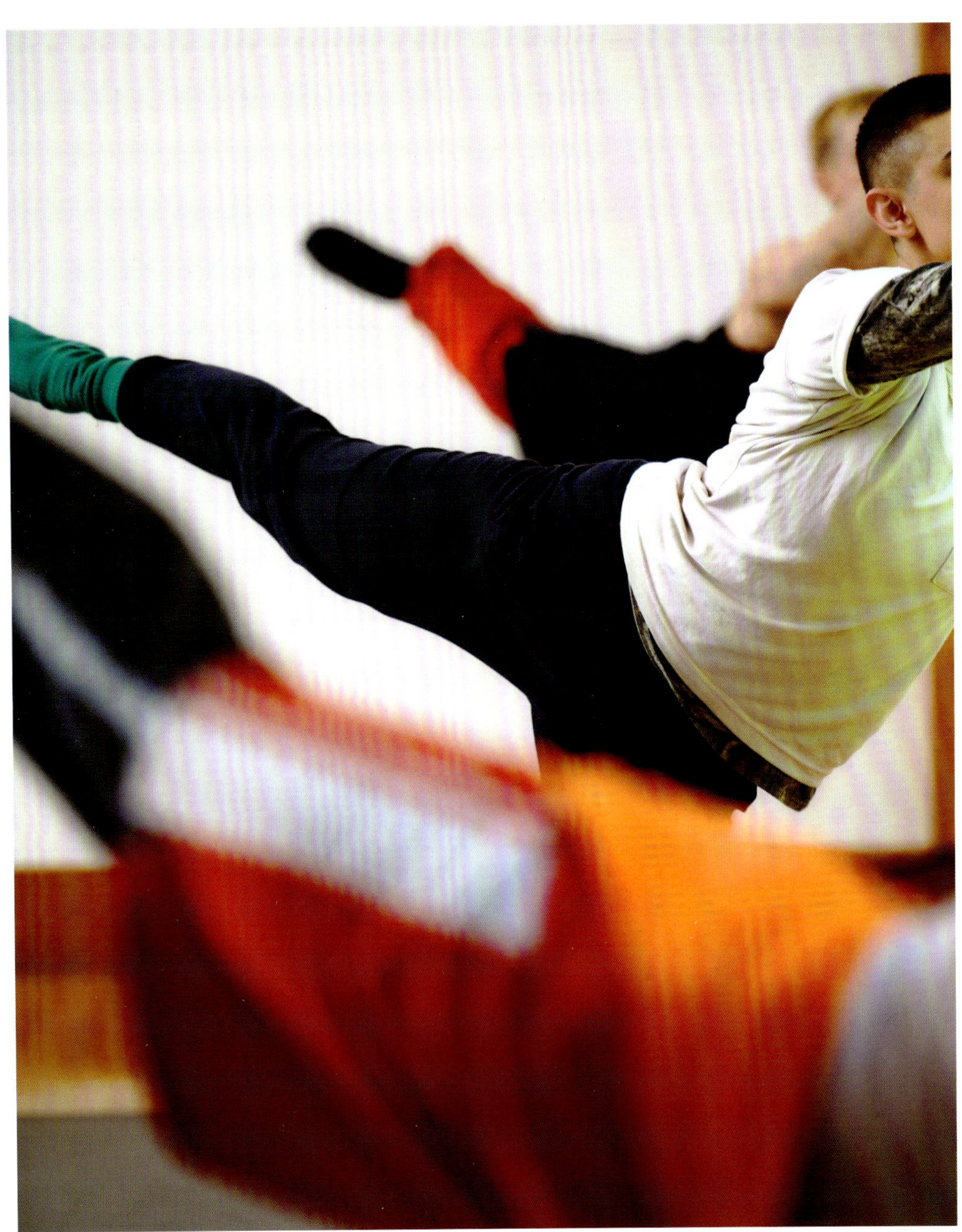

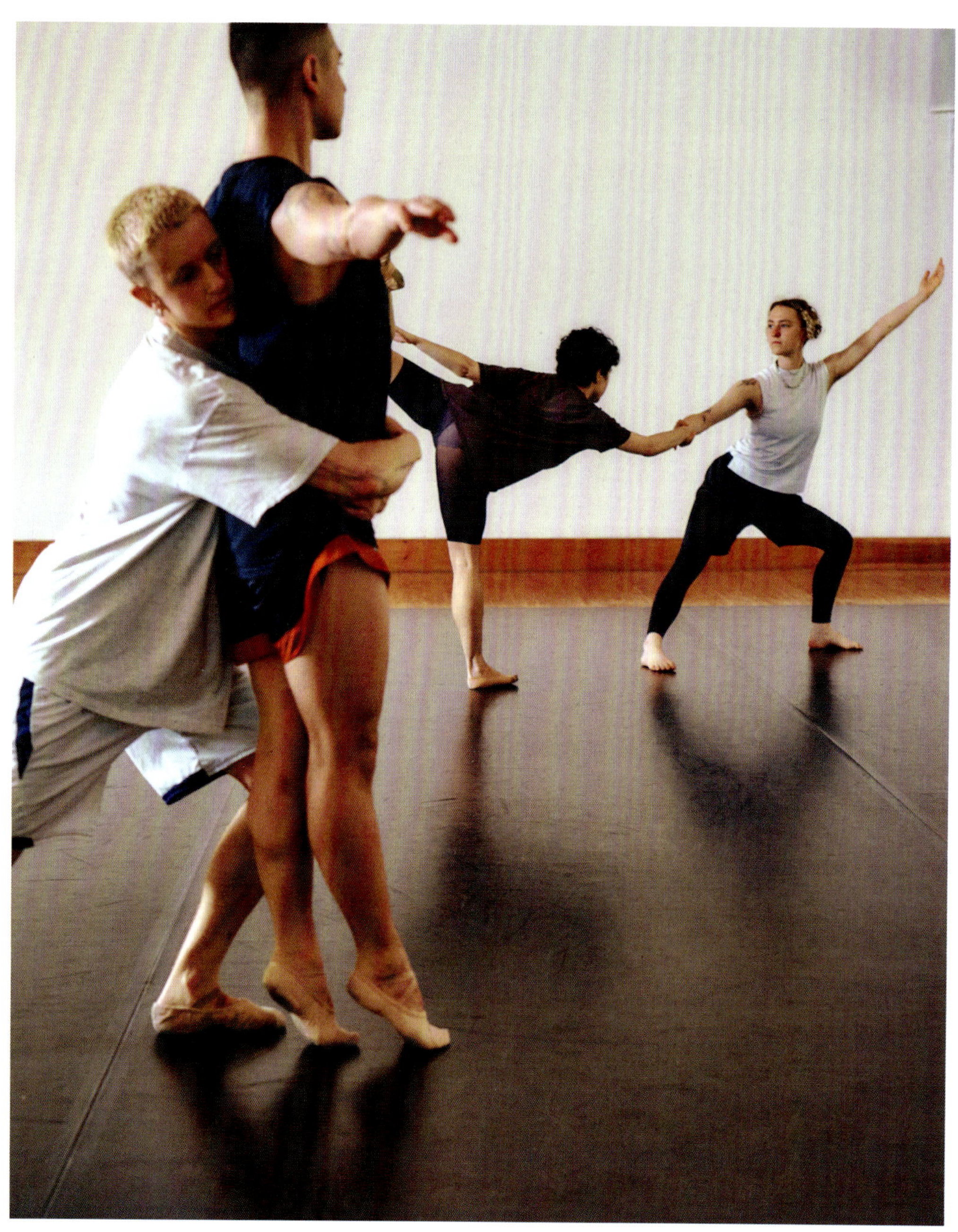

When we visit Ballez at a serene plot of land in Mount Tremper (a tiny town nestled within the dense greenery of the Catskill Mountains), Pyle has gathered five dancers: Arzu Salman, cove barton, Jay Beardsley, Jules Assue, and MJ Markovitz. Over the course of a week, the group will begin picking apart and rethinking *Coppélia*, a radically reimagined version of which, *Travesty Doll Play Ballez (after Coppélia)*, Ballez will debut at the Joyce Theater in New York. Going into the residency, Pyle's vision for the show is hazy, but by the end, after close conversations with the performers and illuminating daily rehearsals, it will start to take shape.

The dancers stay in an old farmhouse, where each day begins and ends with preparing and enjoying a collective meal. This ritual brings the artists, some of whom have only recently met, closer together. "You don't get that in daily life, and you're just able to understand each other more," observes Beardsley, a graduate of the dance program at Virginia Commonwealth University in Richmond. "It lends itself to the quality of what we're doing."

After a quick breakfast of drip coffee and fried eggs, the dancers make the short walk up a dirt road to a large red barn with a sloped roof and three tall windows on each side. Here, around 10:30 a.m., a ballet class kicks off the workday.

Each dancer takes their place beneath a window, holding the sill for balance in lieu of a bar. Pyle stands at the front of the pack, hovering over a computer from which they sound off brief spurts of pop songs by Lil Nas X and Robyn, demonstrating each position with ease. Plié. Tendu. Arabesque—stretched as the twinkling sounds of SOPHIE's "It's Okay to Cry" blast from speakers attached to beams overhead. You won't find the slick buns or blush-colored tutus of a ballet performance in a class like this; these dancers wear their hair buzzed and their basketball shorts loosely layered over sweatpants.

The scene is much the same in the weekly classes Pyle teaches in

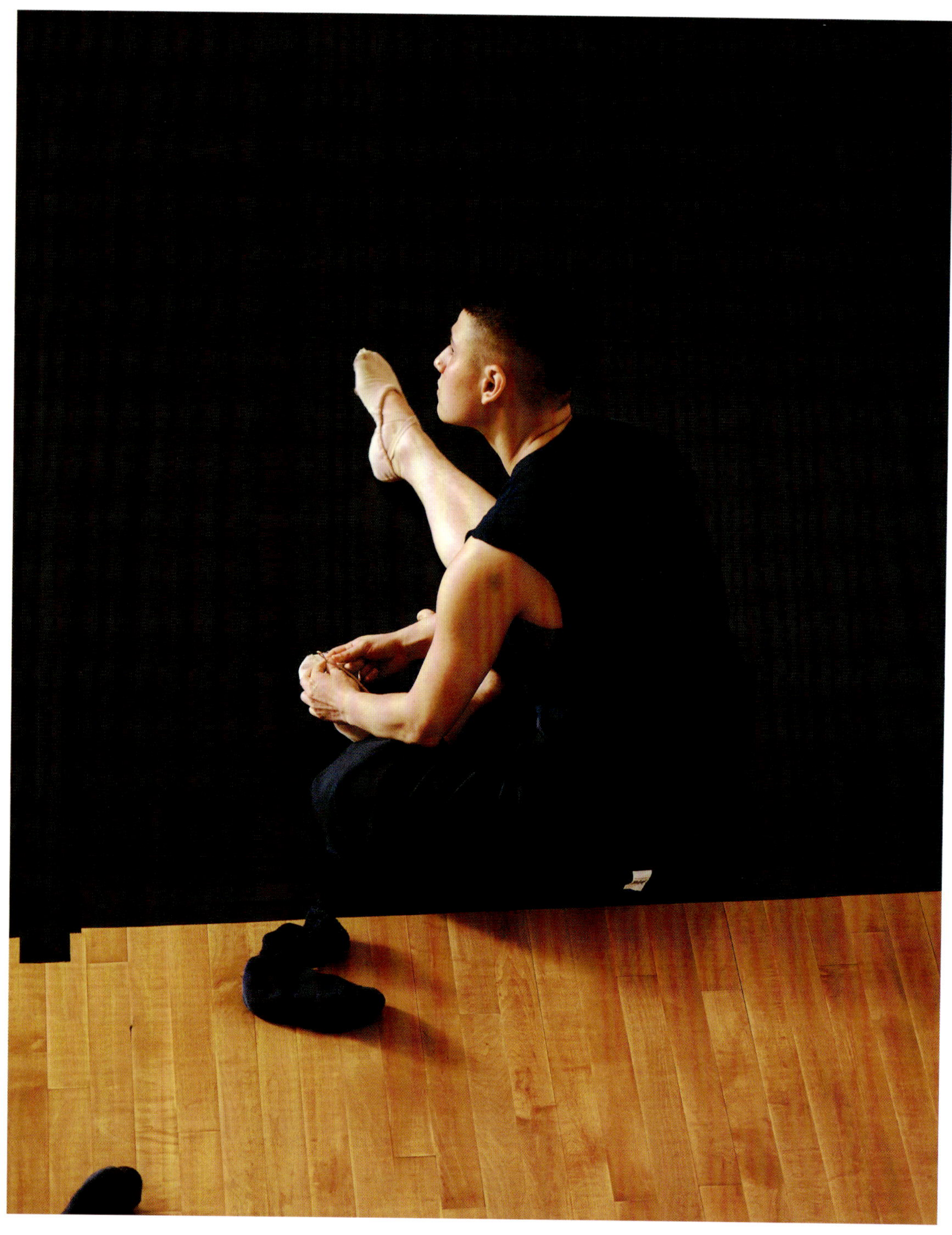

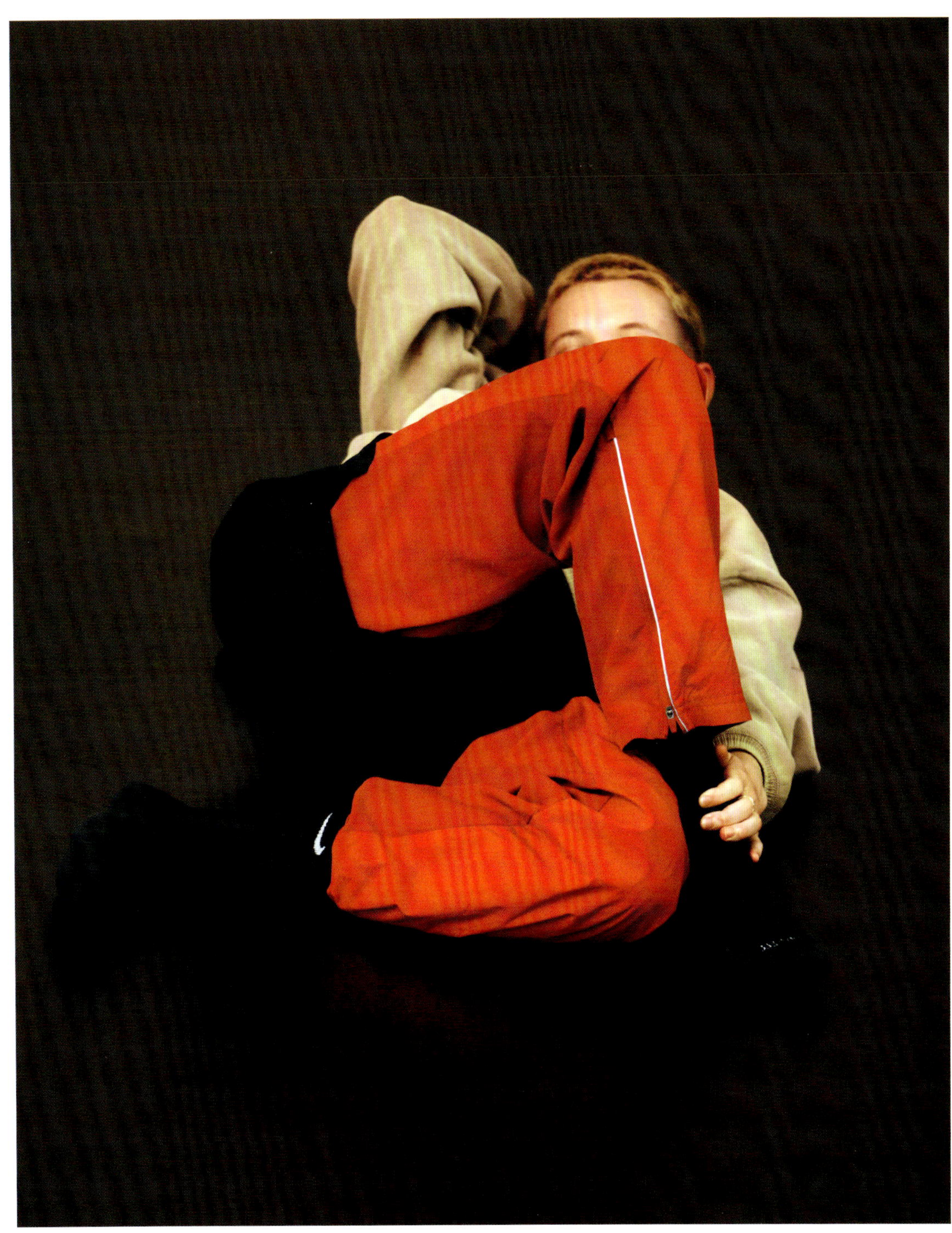

New York at a studio near the Flatiron Building. These classes offer the entry point for many of the company's members, with dancers seeking them out for their "flirty and fun" atmosphere, as well as the comfort of collaborating with others who share one's history and experience.

"In school and in dance, I'd never been in circles of all trans and nonbinary people, and that's something I feel so lucky to be experiencing," says Assue, an Ailey/Fordham-trained dancer. "It's a safe space to explore these skills and workshop with one another," adds Salman, who also studied at Ailey/Fordham. "We understand each other."

"Living as a queer and trans person and having a relationship with ballet, it's a constant negotiation," says barton, a graduate of the dance program at Cornish College of the Arts in Seattle. "Ballez is unpacking it. It's like this unveiling of ballet as a very heteronormative, gendered thing—and flipping it upside down."

***

After the dancers pause for an hour-long lunch, the rest of the afternoon is committed to *Coppélia*, beginning with the mazurka. Set to composer Léo Delibes's joyous score, this freewheeling folk dance functions as an interlude during which a crowd of villagers gathers to celebrate in the town square. In Ballez's rehearsal, the upbeat energy of the music also provides an opportunity for the dancers to showcase their flashiest lifts, spins, and jumps. At one point, barton flings himself across the floor in a jump so high, he seems to float above the group. Markovitz follows shortly after with another great leap toward the opposite end of the mat. The next moment, the group is positioned center stage, lifting Salman by the arms high overhead as he kicks his legs straight out in either direction.

The mazurka is a tremendous contrast to the ballet's doll dances, the motions of which are robotic,

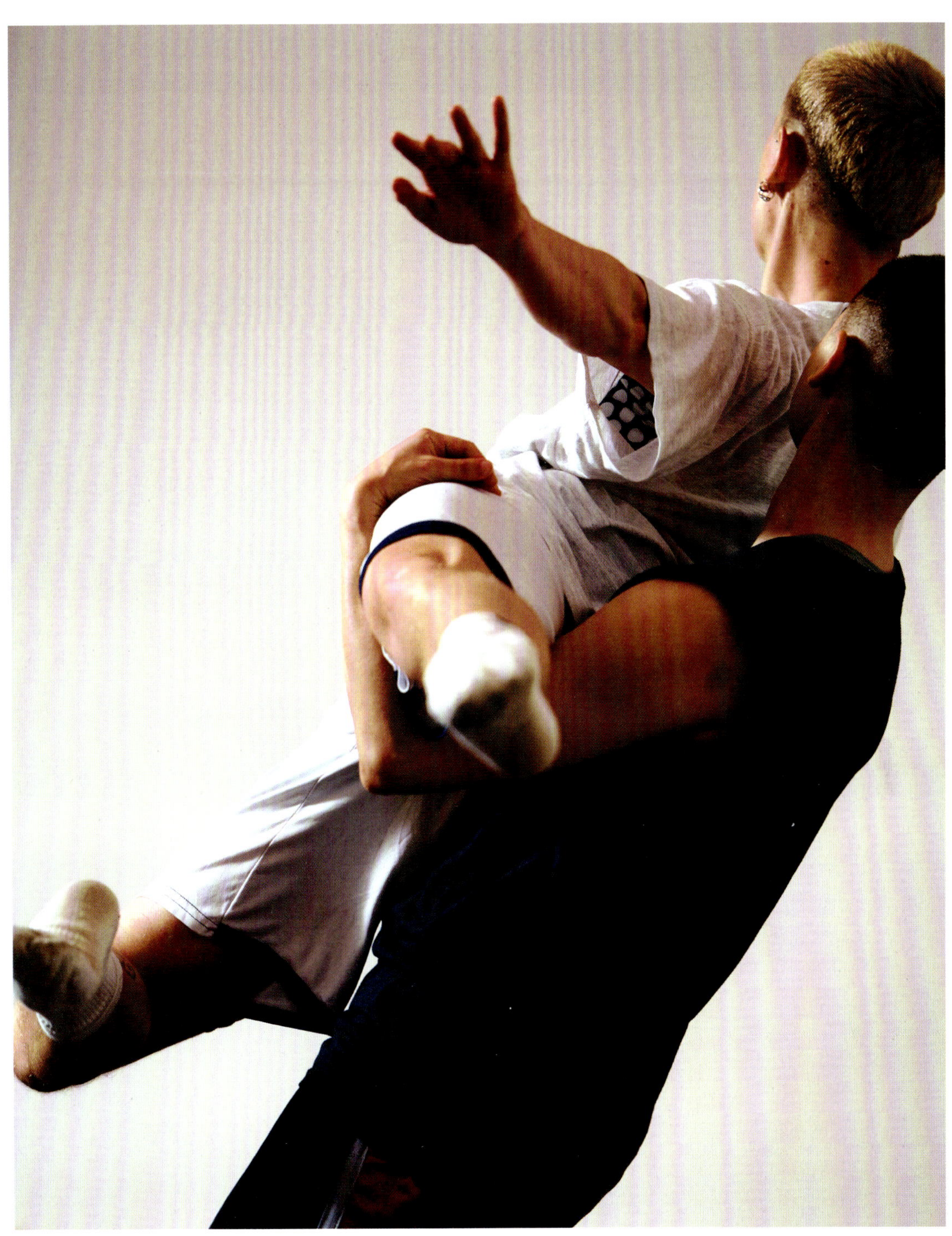

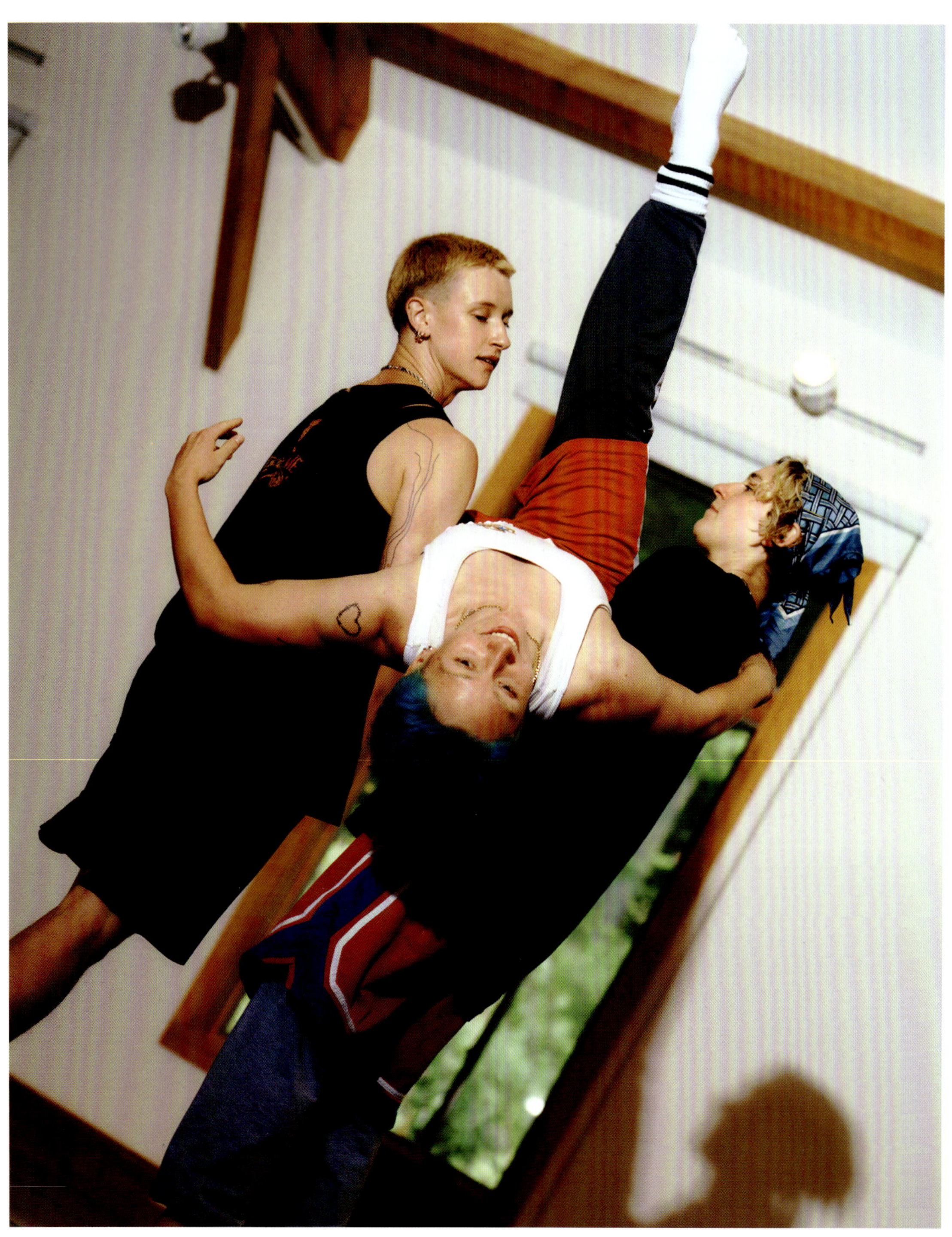

choppy, and even limp at times. One leg pointed upward behind them, Assue's head falls to Beardsley's arm, and they bob over it slowly like a drinking-bird figurine. Then they both step back, stretch their arms toward the ceiling, and switch, repeating the motion once more. Pyle's reference for the dolls is the artwork of Greer Lankton, whose eerie soft sculptures, some miniature and some life-size, resemble celebrities and subcultural figures like Divine, Diana Vreeland, and Candy Darling. The sculptures' exaggerated, occasionally harsh features make them appear at once grotesque and impossibly glamorous. "I feel connected to these fears and fantasies about my own body," Pyle says. "And I'm very into dress-up."

As lifeless objects, dolls might seem like peculiar vessels for a company whose core mission is to return agency to the artists not often afforded it. Yet dolls are made to be played with. They can be altered, dressed up, or torn apart; just like identities, they might be exciting, ever-changing sites of experimentation and transformation. Pyle considers restructuring the acts of *Coppélia* to make their message clear. Will they move the mazurka, with all its free-form flamboyance, from the first act to the end of the show or swap Delibes's music with a contemporary pop song? This is what Ballez is all about: twisting the structures of the ballet to make it work for the dancers themselves.

On the final day of the residency, the group improvises a new scene: Dr. Coppélius bringing his puppet to life. The dancers take turns posing their colleagues, moving their limbs into various frozen positions. Pyle pulls Markovitz's bent knee upward; barton shapes Assue's arms into an overhead oval. Then, standing upright, Assue spins and spins and spins, continuing the motion on their own. For a moment, master and marionette seem to trade places, and the dolls are brought to life not for the pleasure of another's eye but by their own power.

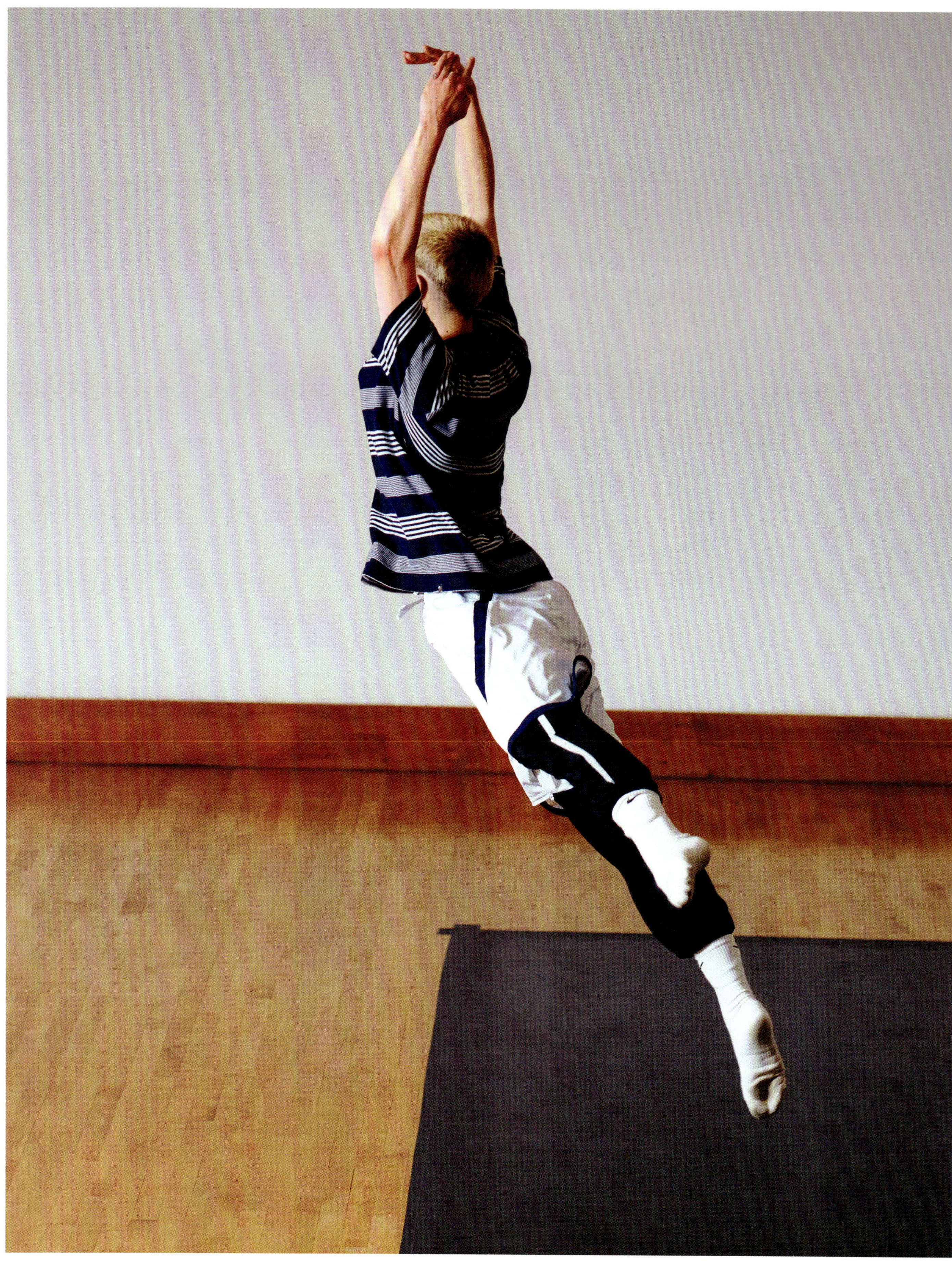

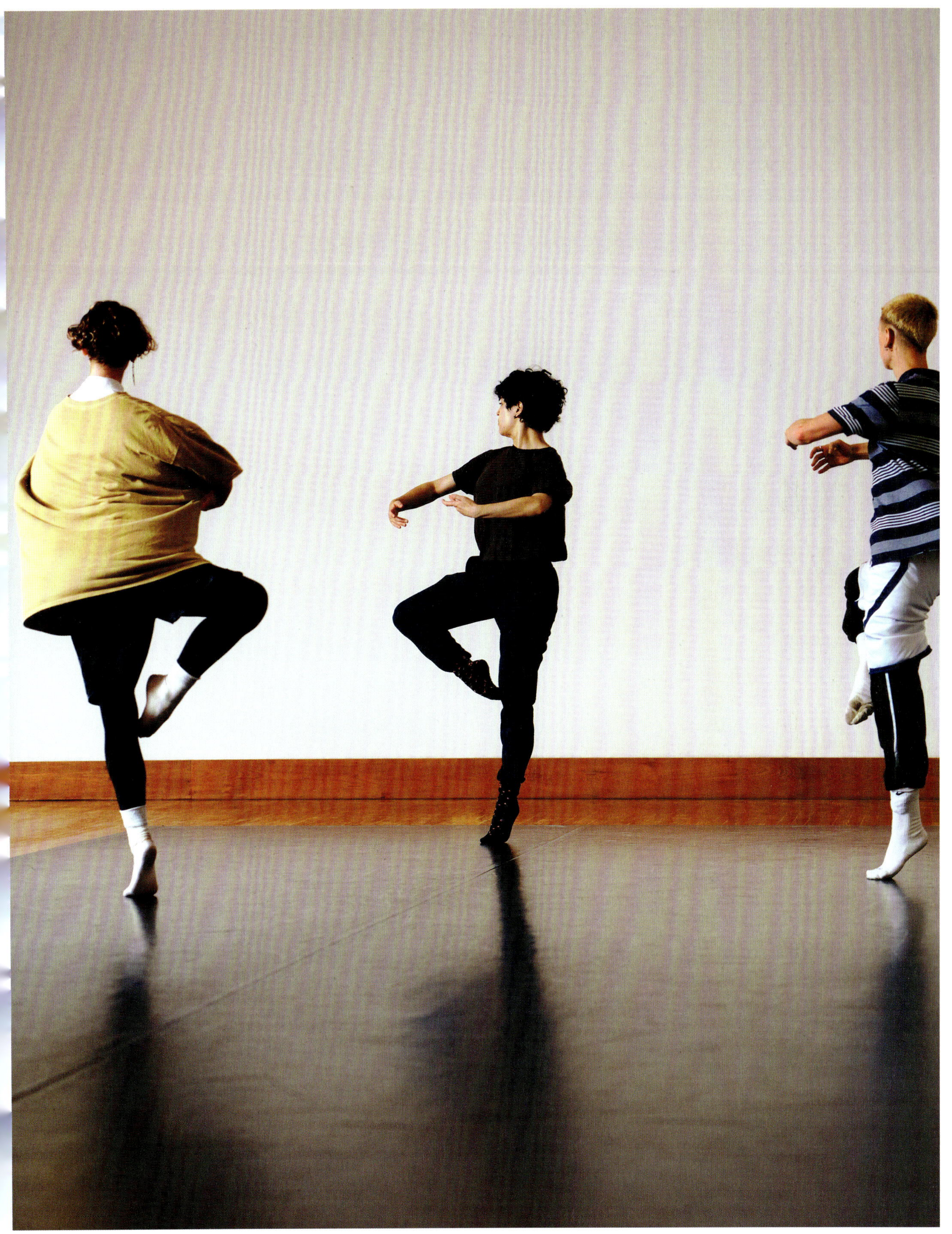

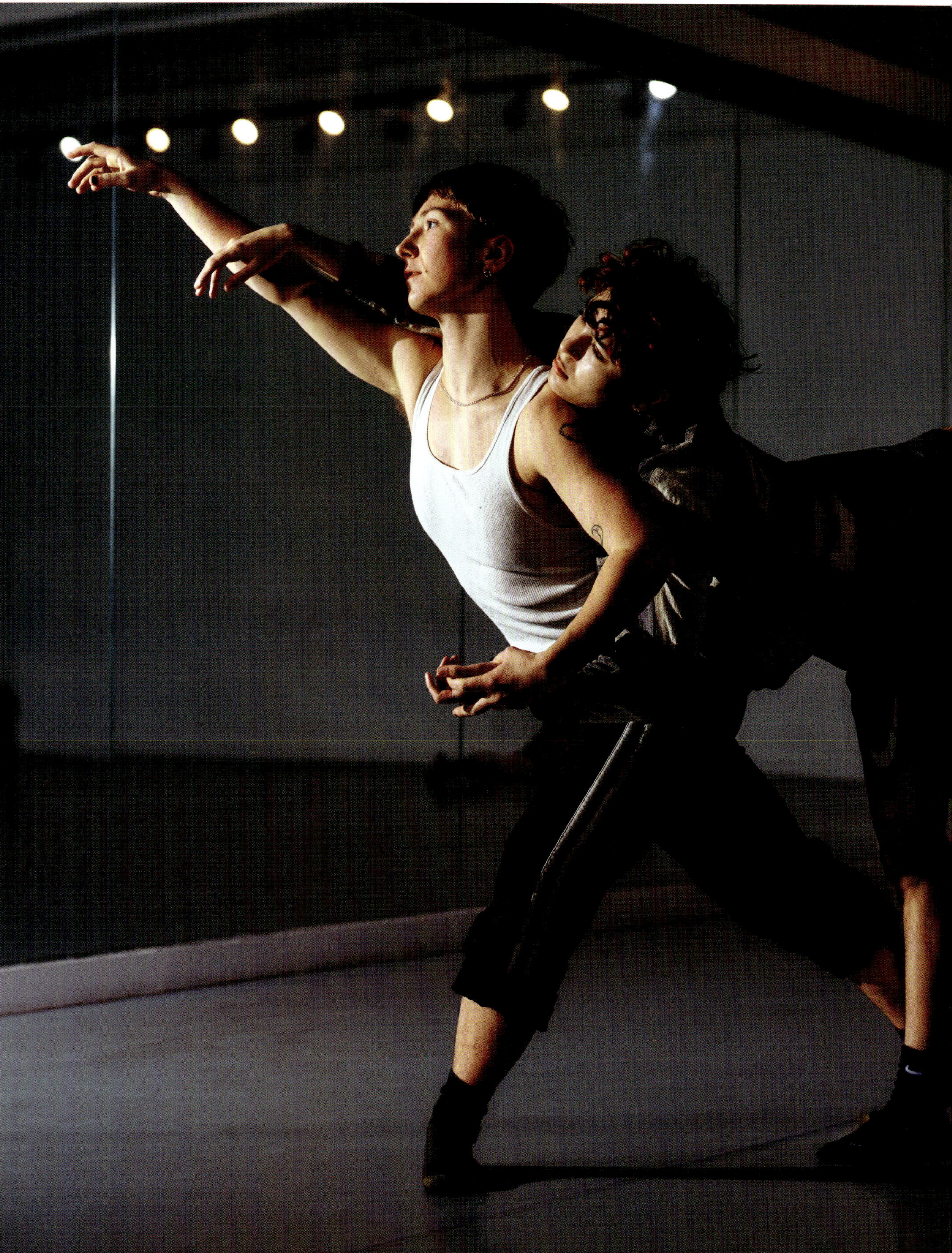

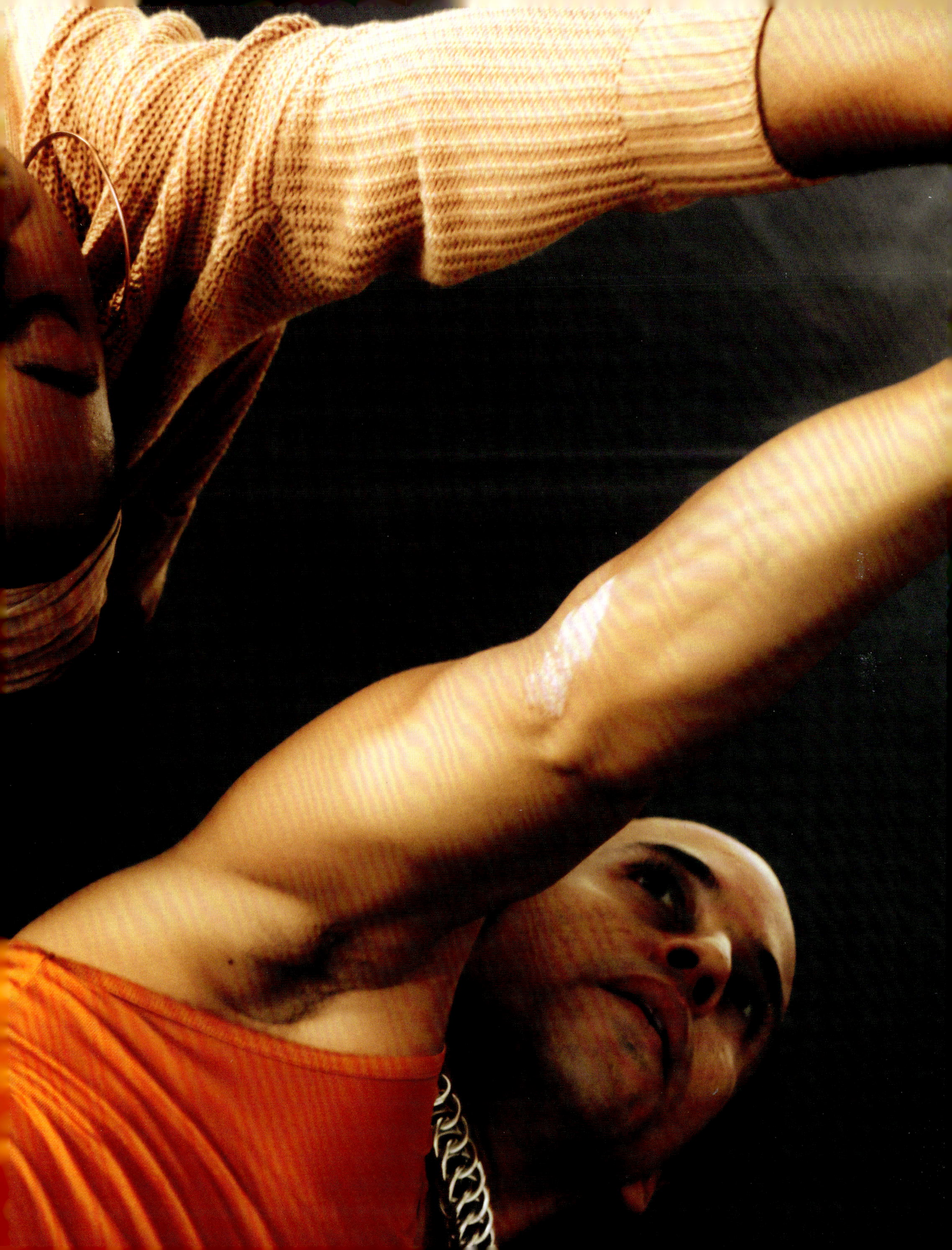

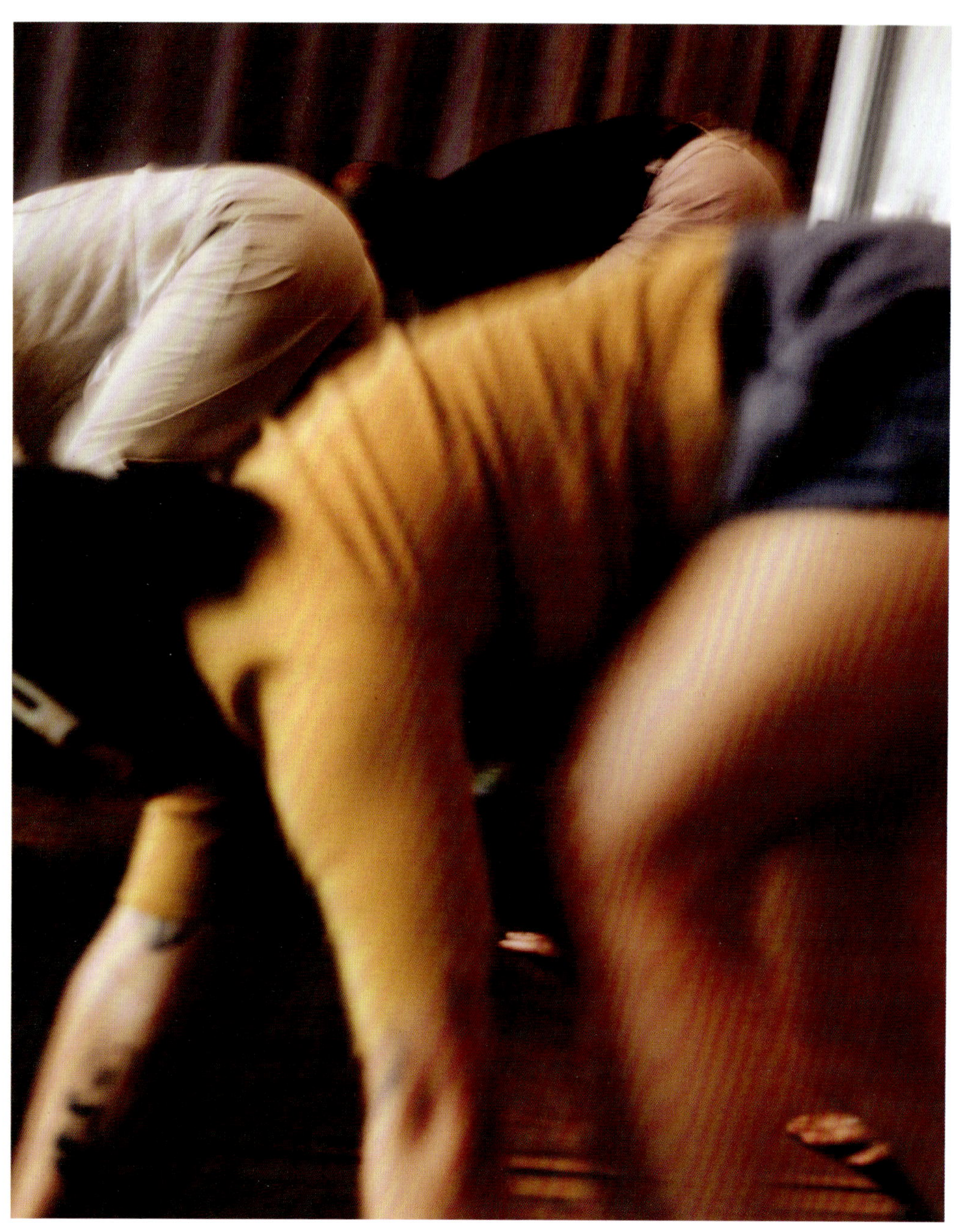

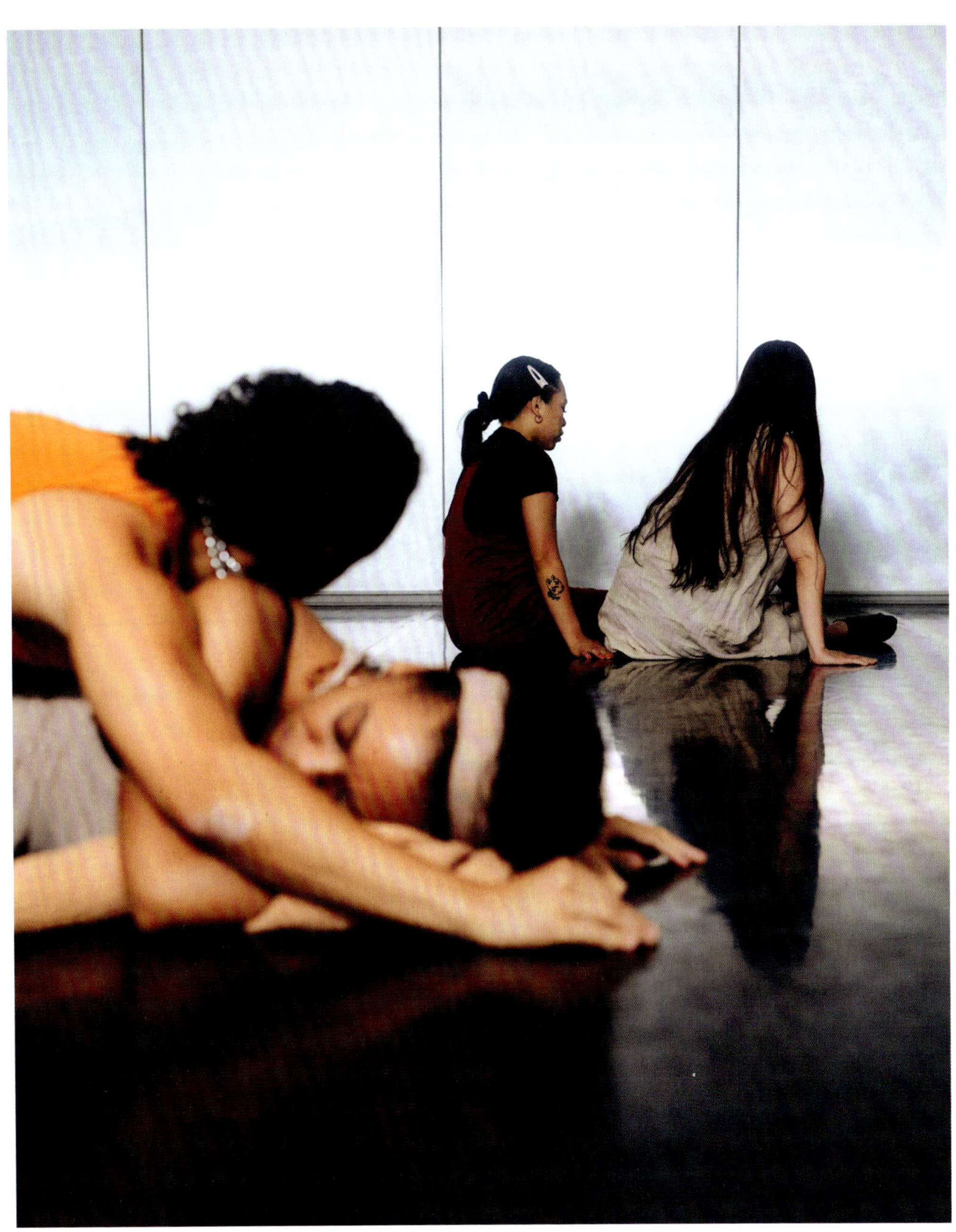

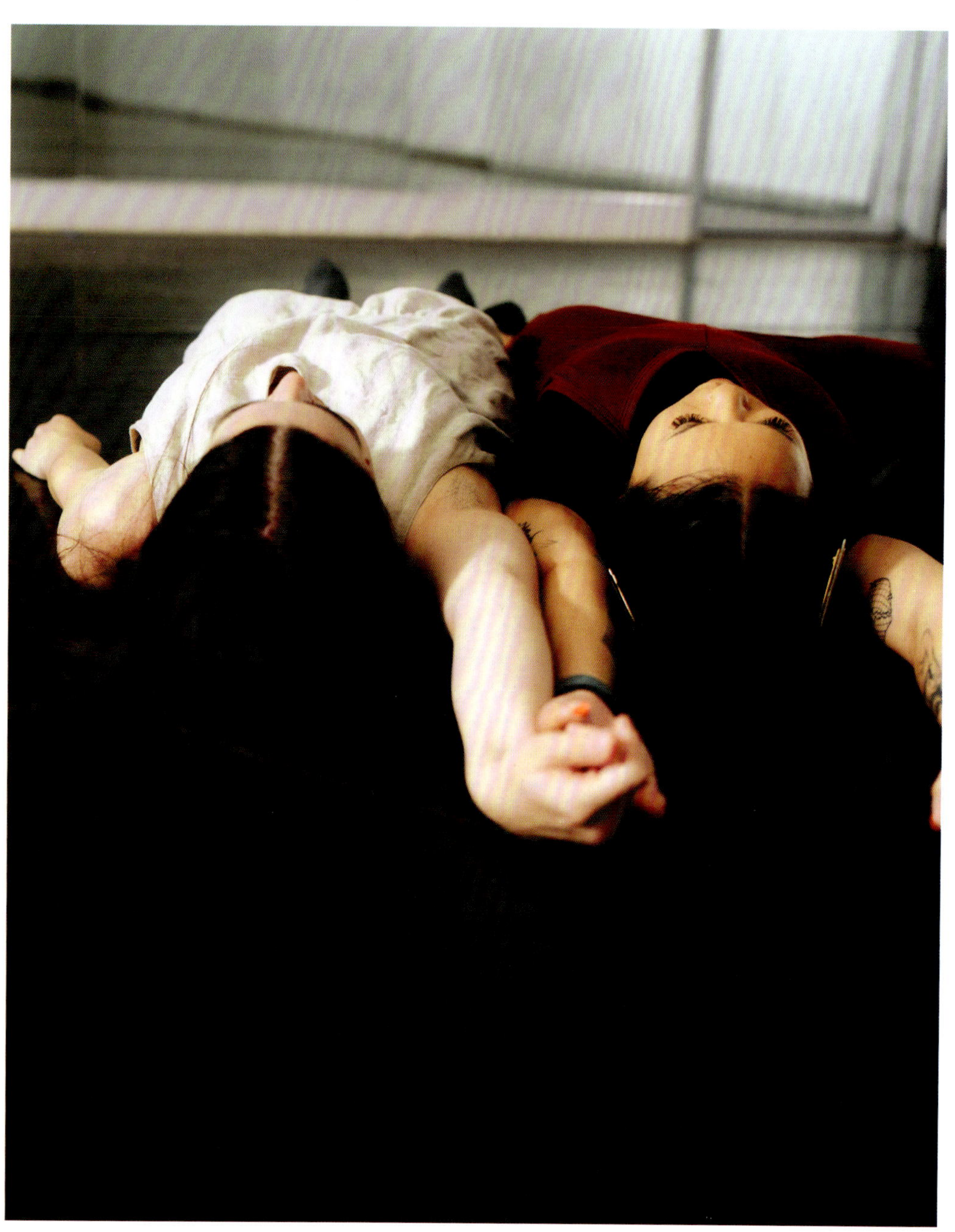

IN DECEMBER 2021, THE COMPANY FEATH3R THEORY PREMIERED *WEDNESDAY*, an experimental stage retelling of the 1975 film *Dog Day Afternoon*. The movie is a favorite of the group's artistic director and choreographer, Raja Feather Kelly. It's a queer love story starring Al Pacino as the bank robber Sonny Wortzik, and it was derived from the true tale of John Wojtowicz, who attempted a heist to fund a gender-affirming surgery for his lover.

Yet as with any product of Hollywood, *Dog Day Afternoon* took several liberties with its plot for the purposes of entertainment and mass legibility. One of its fictions is the portrayal of Wortzik's partner, Leon Shermer. Appearing only briefly and played by a cisgender man, Chris Sarandon, Shermer was loosely based off a real person named Elizabeth Debbie Eden. Her perspective was largely left out of the film and sensationalized; she was another trans woman stamped out from her own history in favor of furthering another's narrative.

Despite some of their clear differences, Kelly, a queer Black man, could relate to Eden. He knew what it felt like to minimize parts of himself, lest his existence to be turned into a spectacle for others to see. After growing up in Fort Hood, Texas (now called Fort Cavazos), where his mother was in the military, he moved to New Jersey. Though Kelly felt fortunate to land his first job performing with David Dorfman Dance before graduating from Connecticut College in 2008, he kept his identity separate from his work for many years. Even as storylines diversified in film and television in the late aughts and 2010s to include more Black and LGBTQ+ characters, Kelly rarely felt adequately represented.

"I didn't see myself. And when I would claim myself as a Black queer person, I saw others box me into a certain idea of what that meant," he says. "My queerness, it's alien to everyone else's queerness."

Nonetheless, Kelly has a keen grasp of the screen's power to shift minds and bend hearts; it is a looking glass reflecting deeply held notions of who we are and what we aspire to be. This idea is the basis for the feath3r theory, which Kelly founded in 2009, the year he moved to New York City. Though he has become known for the subtly stirring choreography he develops for Broadway and off-Broadway productions, his own shows are often cutting examinations of pop culture that mix incisive theater and virtuosic dance. *UGLY Part 3: BLUE* was the final of a trilogy of solos considering depictions of Blackness in popular culture, which Kelly performed at JACK in Brooklyn in December 2022. For this performance, he sauntered onstage wearing a full-body cobalt catsuit, trimmed with a cropped bob wig, glittering barn-door eye shadow, and a cascading tulle train. A "glamour alien," as Kelly described the persona.

With *WEDNESDAY*, he was aiming to right the wrongs of *Dog Day Afternoon* by shifting the perspective from Wojtowicz to Eden. After all, he thought, if he didn't do it, who would?

Ultimately, Kelly's take was a display of his connection with Eden's story. It was as much about his own experience, and those of his dancers, as it was about Eden's. The show operated like a staged documentary, looking inside the company's process, with the performers occasionally breaking the fourth wall to explain how they would react to the scenes being acted out. The question of ownership, of who should be allowed to tell another's story, became central to the work—and to the public's perception of it.

Not everyone agreed with Kelly's vision. The response to *WEDNESDAY* was polarizing both outside the company and within it. Some felt they could learn a lot from the piece; others believed Kelly wasn't the right person to tell Eden's story. "They were like, 'As a Black queer man, you should not be telling the story of a white trans woman. It just doesn't work,'" Kelly recalls. Perhaps he felt a little like Icarus

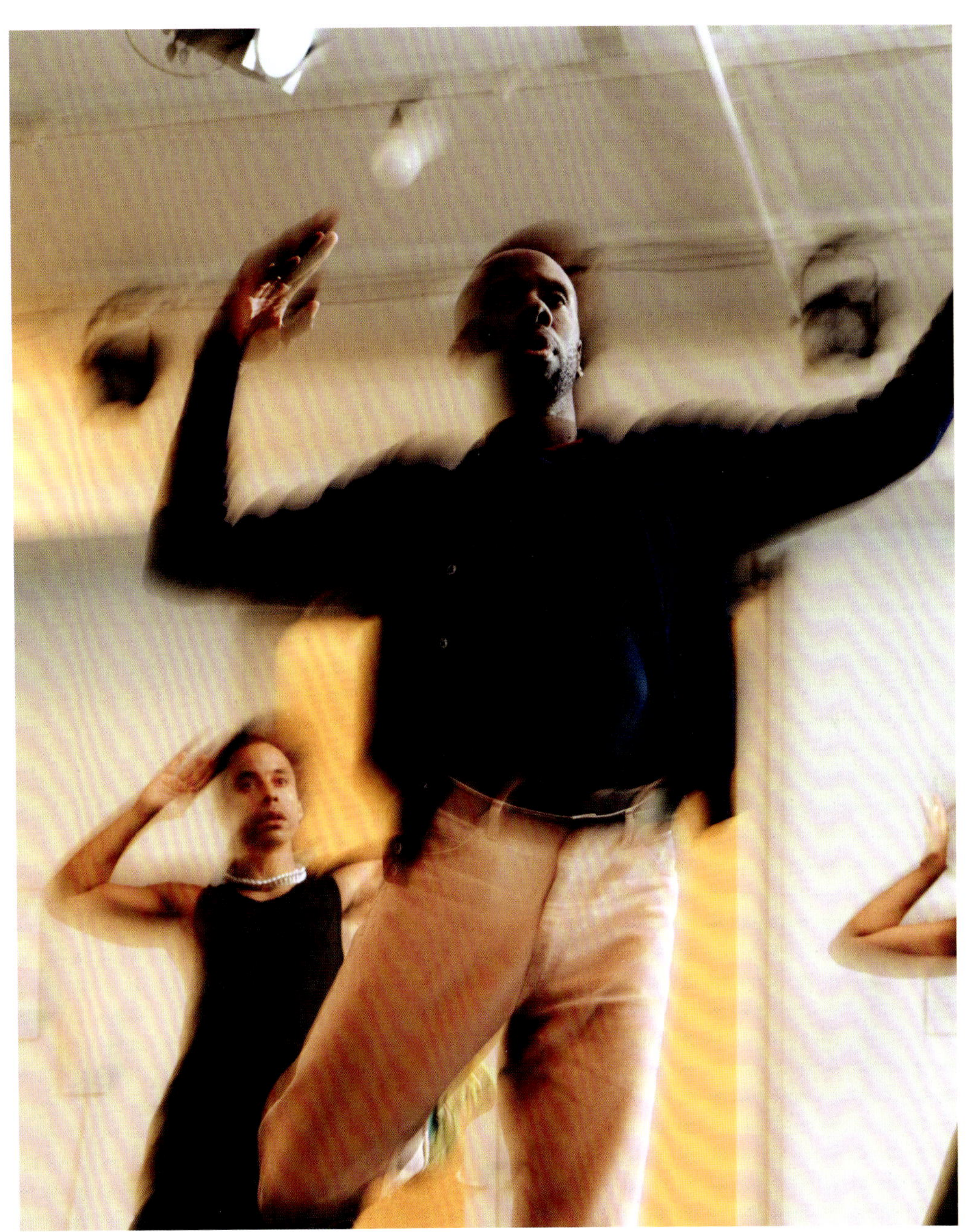

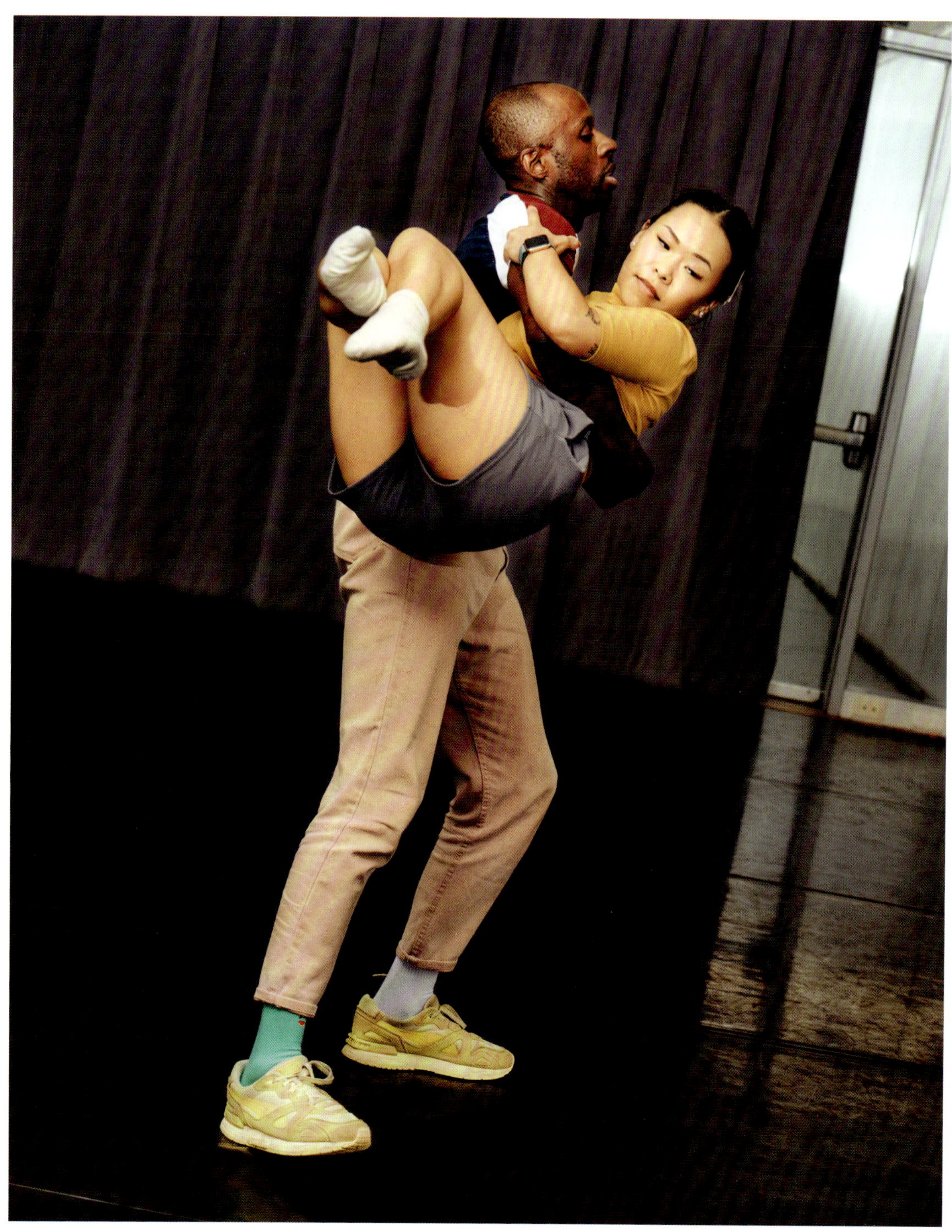

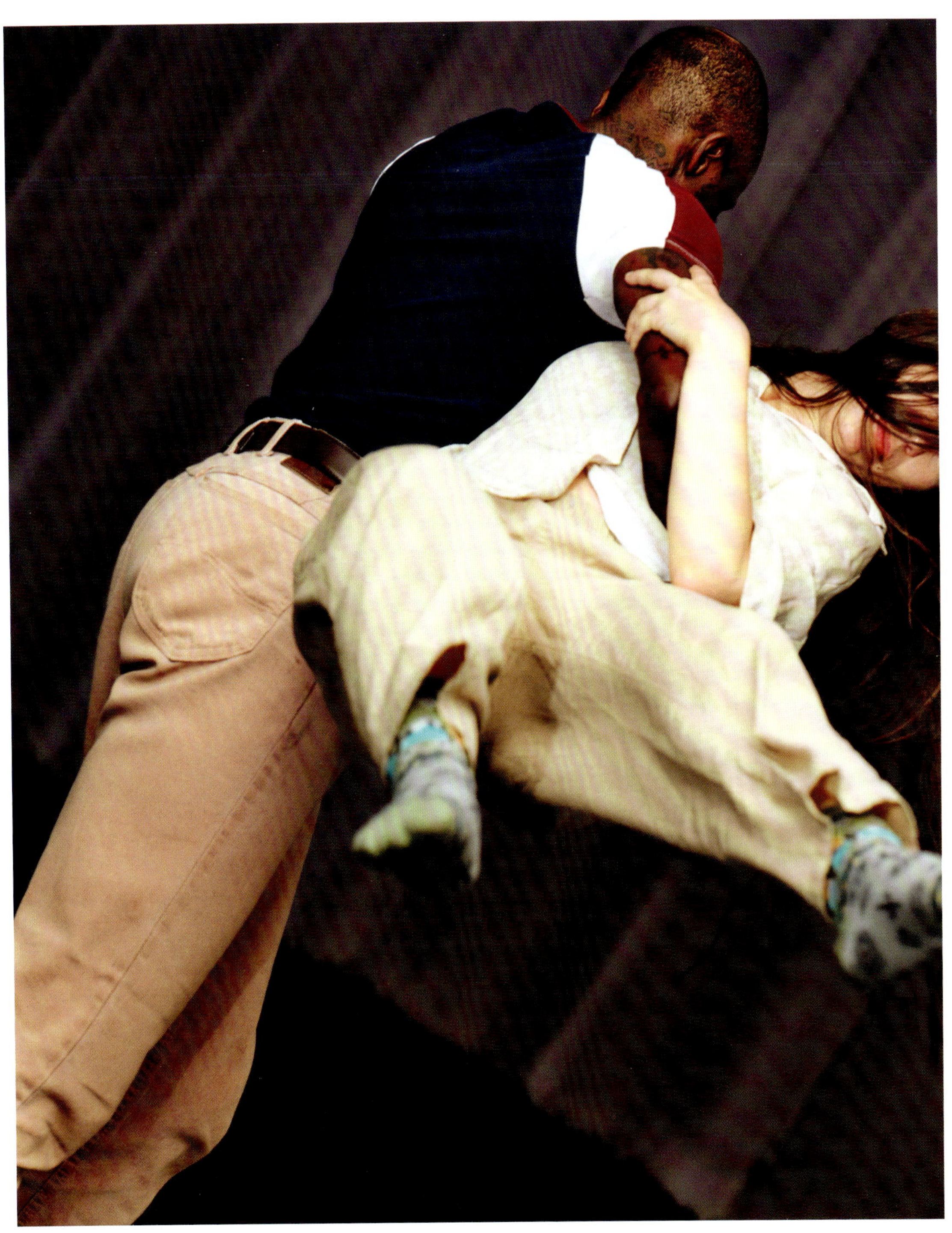

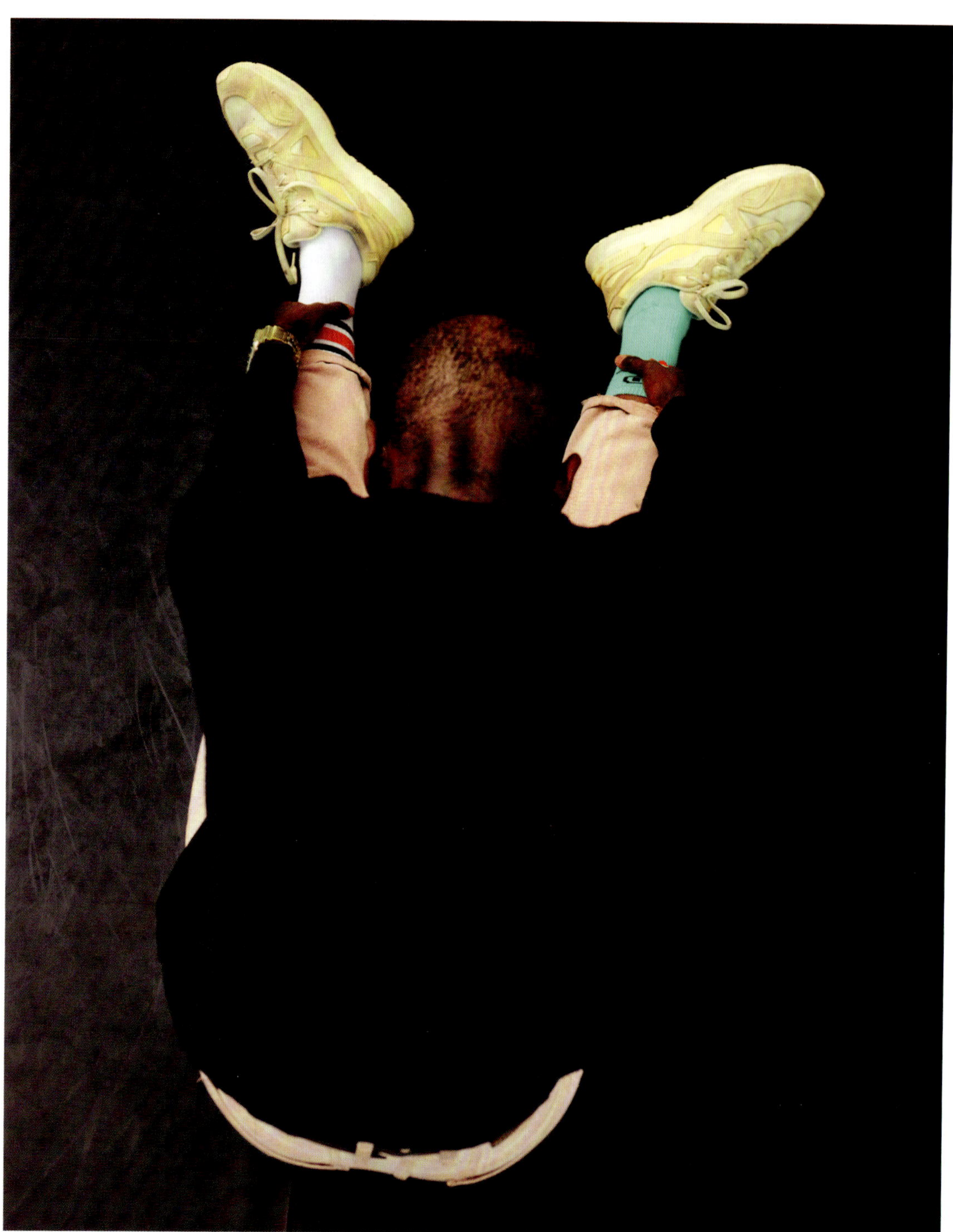

flying too close to the sun. The experience left him disheartened but not uninspired.

The Greek myth was one entry point for one of the feath3r theory's latest works: *Death, Loneliness, and THE ABSOLUTE FUTURE of the Multiverse, or How to Cover the Sun with Mud*. Kelly considered the image of the sun, how its rays can burn but also give life, and it reminded him of his own resilience. "There are good queer people and there are bad queer people, but I still believe they are a light in the world. And that light cannot be covered," he says. Though the subject of the show has since expanded to highlight social media and its dual ability to connect and isolate, with plans to boil down dialogue from various accounts' posts, Kelly notes that "it started with my needing just to find the courage to make something again."

The first rehearsals began in July 2022 inside a modest studio with a wall of windows overlooking a rain-drenched street in Chelsea. Kelly had enlisted five performers to develop the framework of what would eventually become *THE ABSOLUTE FUTURE*—"the scaffolding of a fictional world," as he puts it. He offered his collaborators open-ended prompts, such as to create, on the spot, either a dance that explained what the multiverse is or a dance for a lonely person. From there, meaning was up to the performers to prescribe.

As they took a few minutes to jot down their thoughts and plan out their steps, Kelly played the prologue to *Little Shop of Horrors* from a laptop and flitted about the perimeter of the space, brushing up on a brief blip of choreography he would later show in *BLUE*. As he moved, the colors of his mismatched socks flashed at his ankles, one lavender, the other dotted with pictures of Mickey Mouse. About thirty seconds in, Kelly, a mischievous collaborator, stopped the track and restarted it from the beginning. After at least six rounds of this, he called on the performers to step up and showcase their solos one by one.

Their responses, seemingly raw reactions when severed from the prompt, would be refined and would eventually inform some aspect of the show.

Kelly's way of working is constant across his endeavors, whether he's developing a new performance for the feath3r theory or a blowout Tony-winning show. His first Broadway project was choreographing Michael R. Jackson's musical *A Strange Loop*, about a queer Black writer wrestling with his inner thoughts, each with its own persona embodied by six actors. Much of Kelly's work for the play went into fine-tuning the thoughts' personalities through their minute gestures and overall mannerisms—a limp wrist here, some swinging hips there—which emerge in numbers like "Inner White Girl." Rather than lifts and jumps, Kelly opted for restrained motions in the shoulders and fingertips to convey the big emotions burbling forth from the shy protagonist, Usher.

As always, he offered the performers assignments, working closely with each person to discover and solidify choreography that fit them and their character. The result was movement that felt distinctly personal to each performer, alive and organic—what Kelly describes as "heightened behavior." Yet creating such idiosyncratic choreography comes with its own set of difficulties, particularly in its replication by subsequent performers.

"I've run into a little bit of trouble now that *A Strange Loop* is something that is commercial or marketable, because I made so much of that material on the person," he says. "Sometimes I would just be talking to them, and I'm like, 'You should do this and you should try this,' or 'You should behave this way.' But then that all has to be recorded in a way that someone else can do it, and that's not always easy for me to do."

So, had Kelly flown too close to the sun? When we left the rehearsal for *THE ABSOLUTE FUTURE*, that remained to be seen. But flying, falling, and rising again, light as a feather, would surely make for a compelling story.

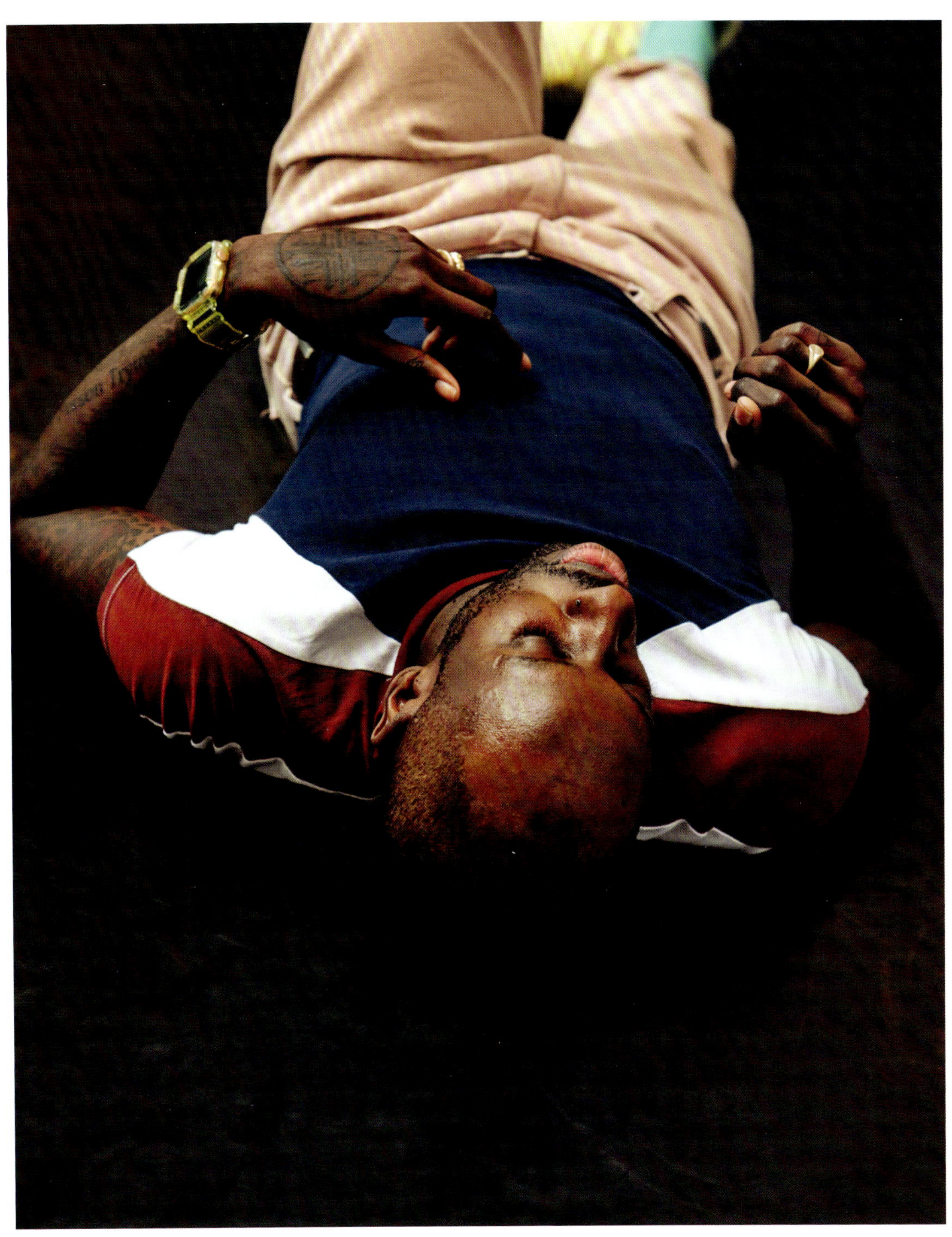

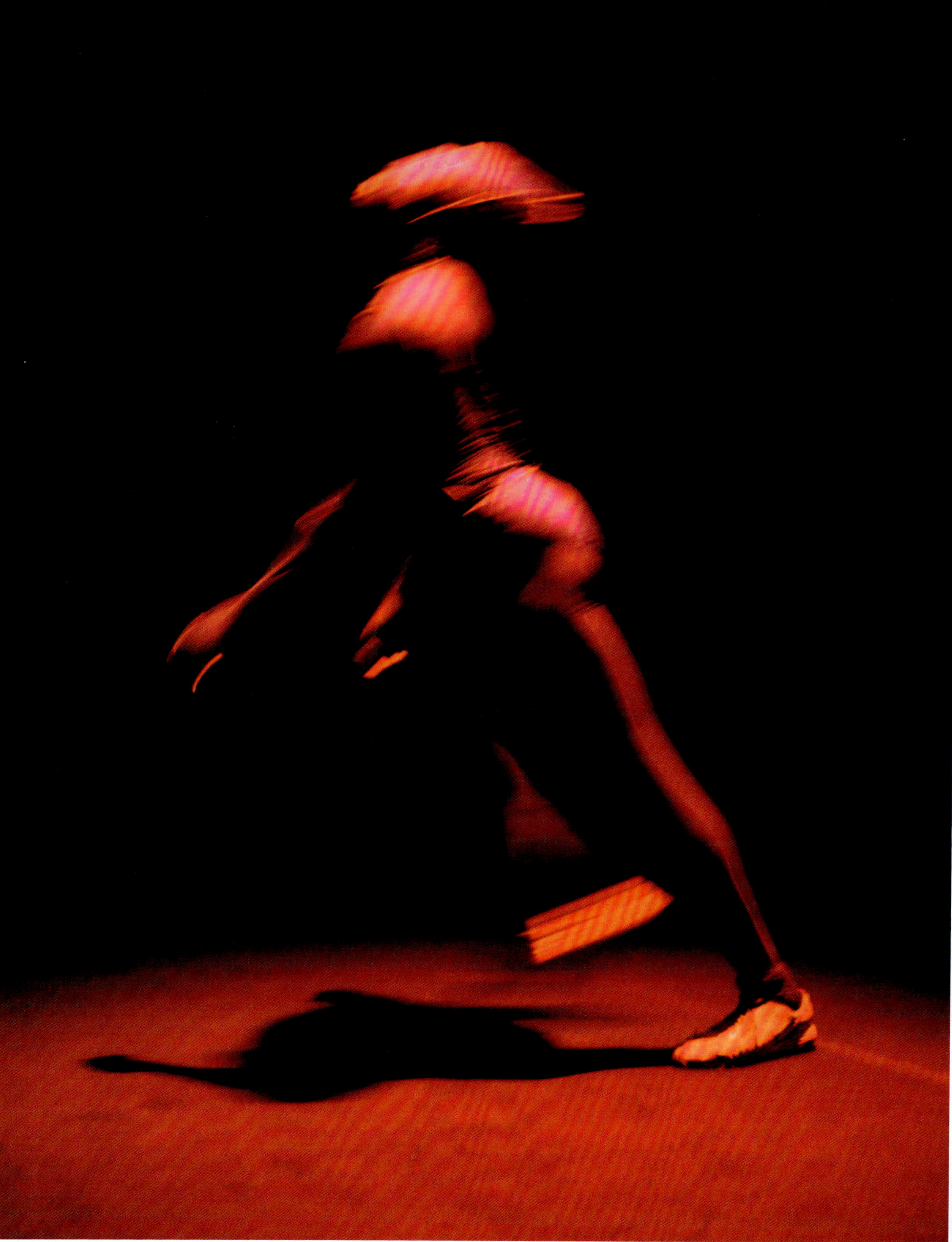

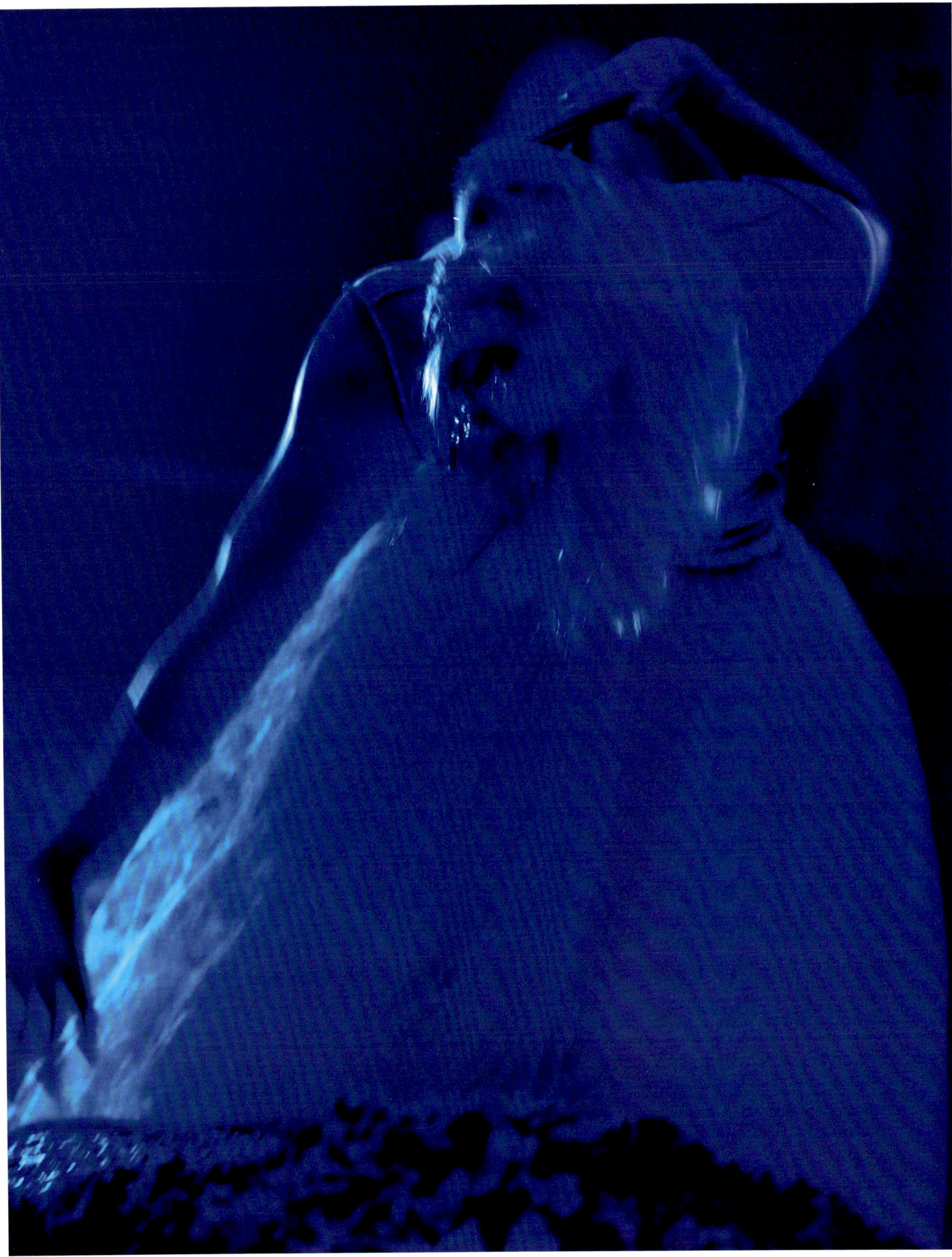

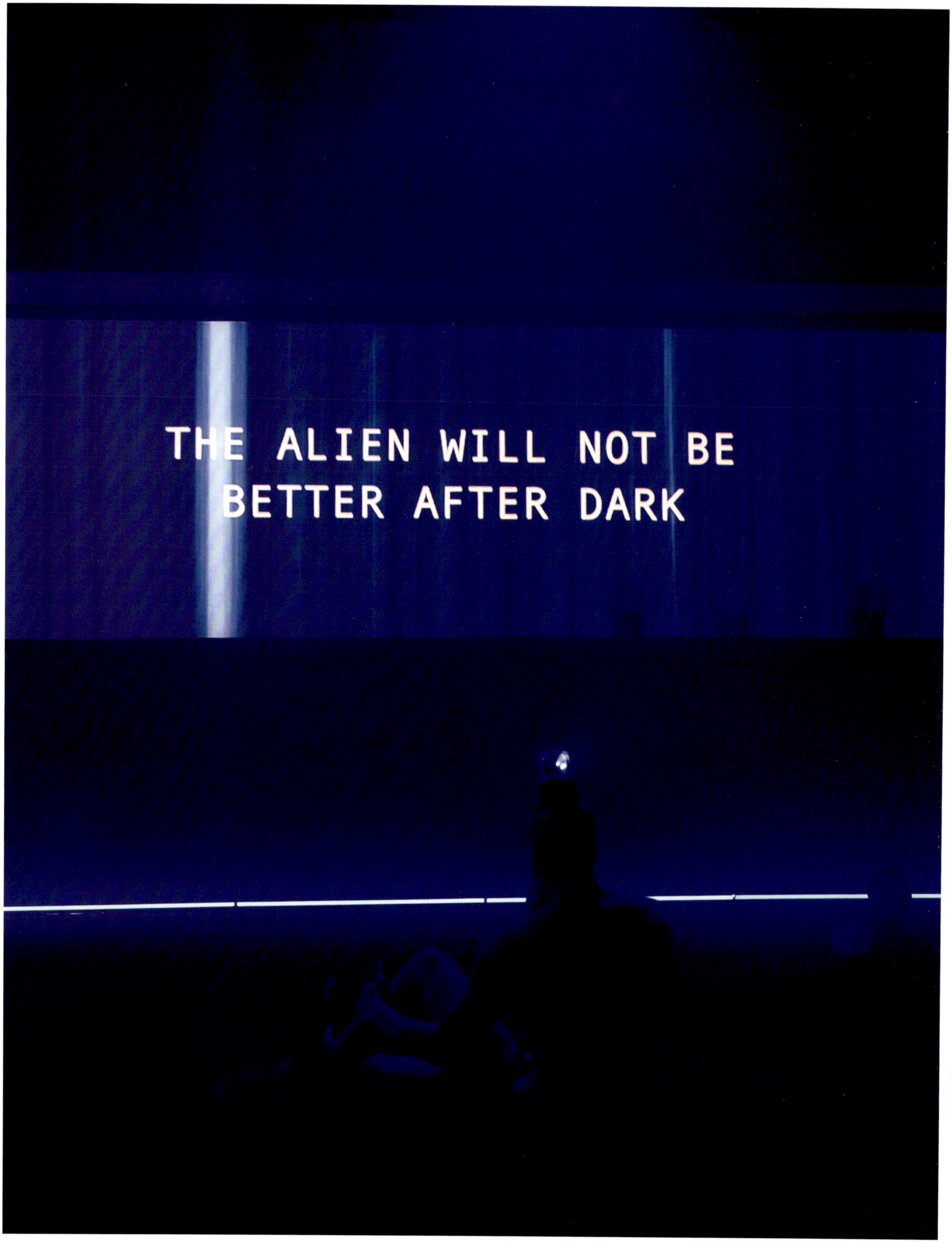

THE ALIEN WILL NOT BE
BETTER AFTER DARK

WILL NOT PERFORM

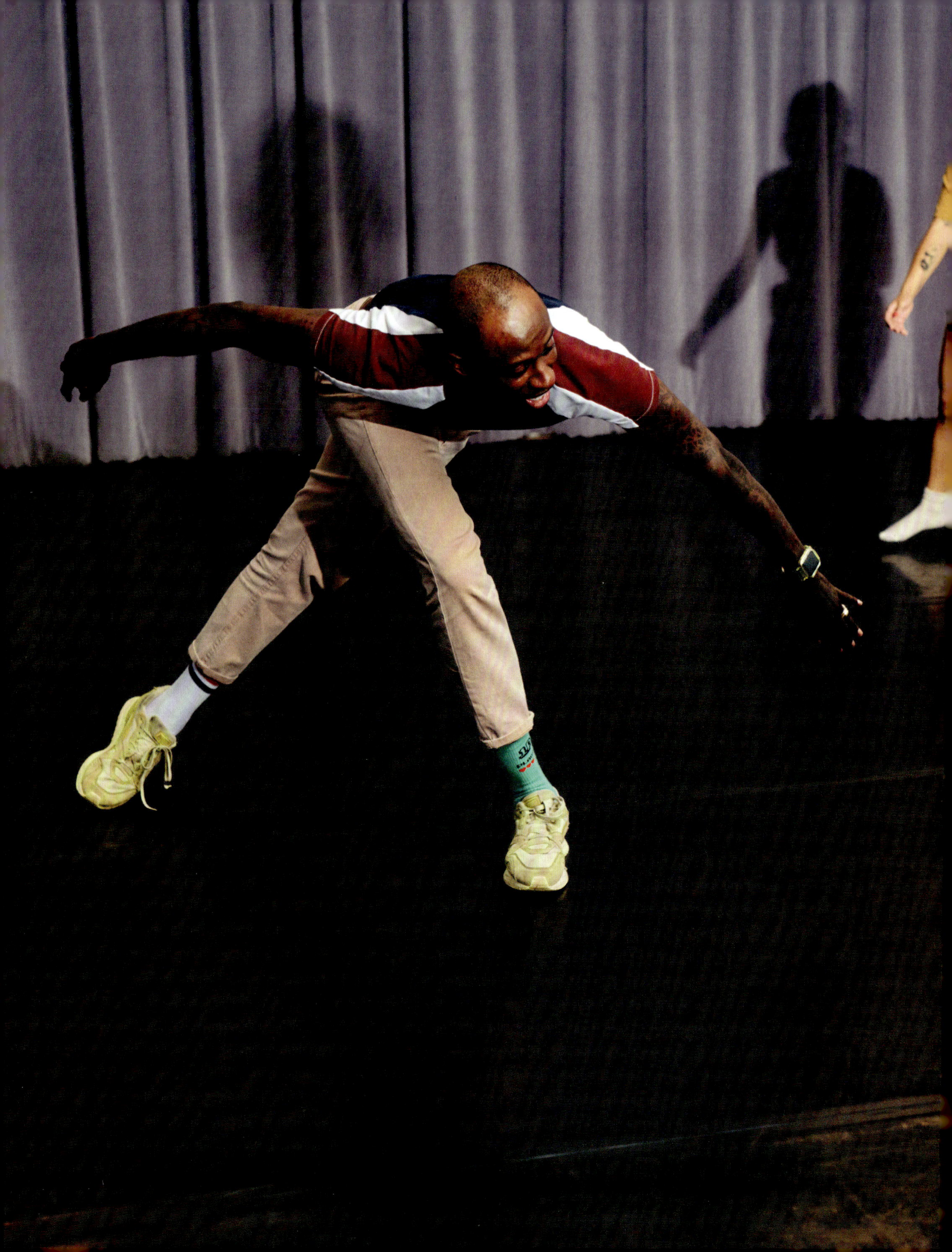

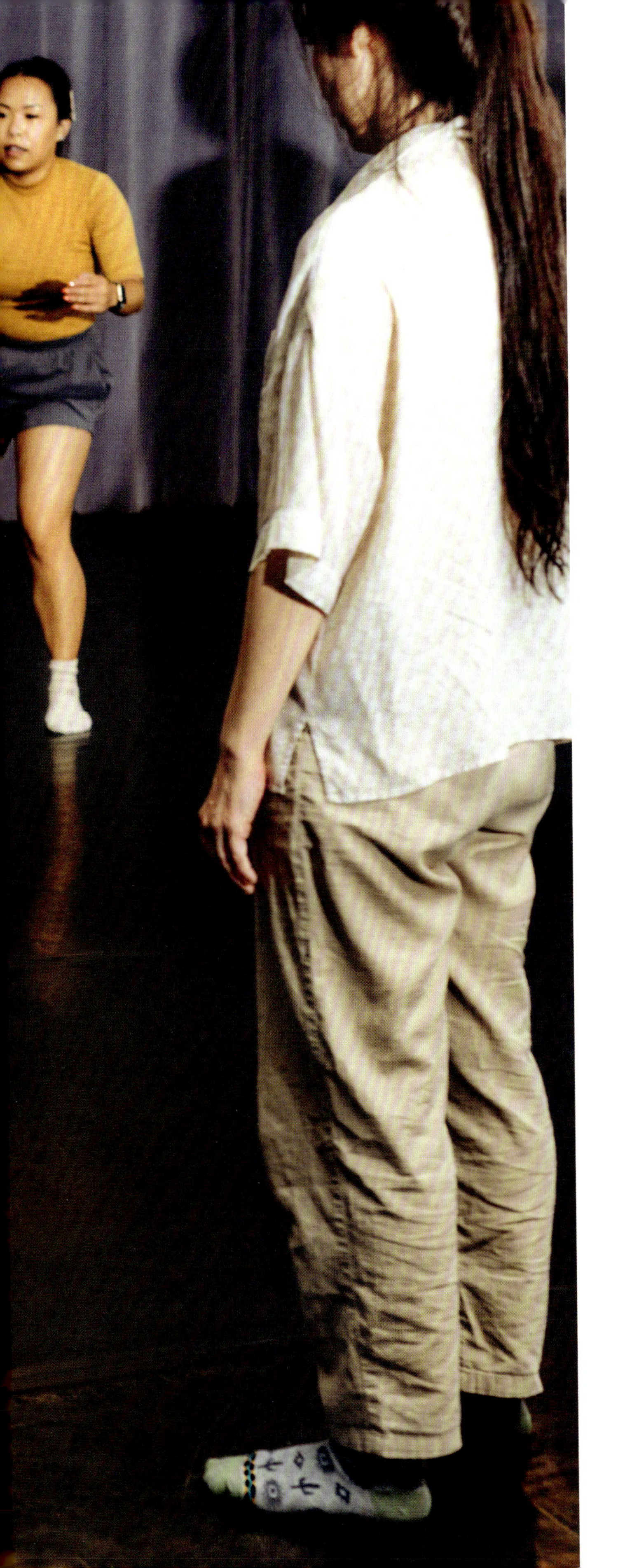

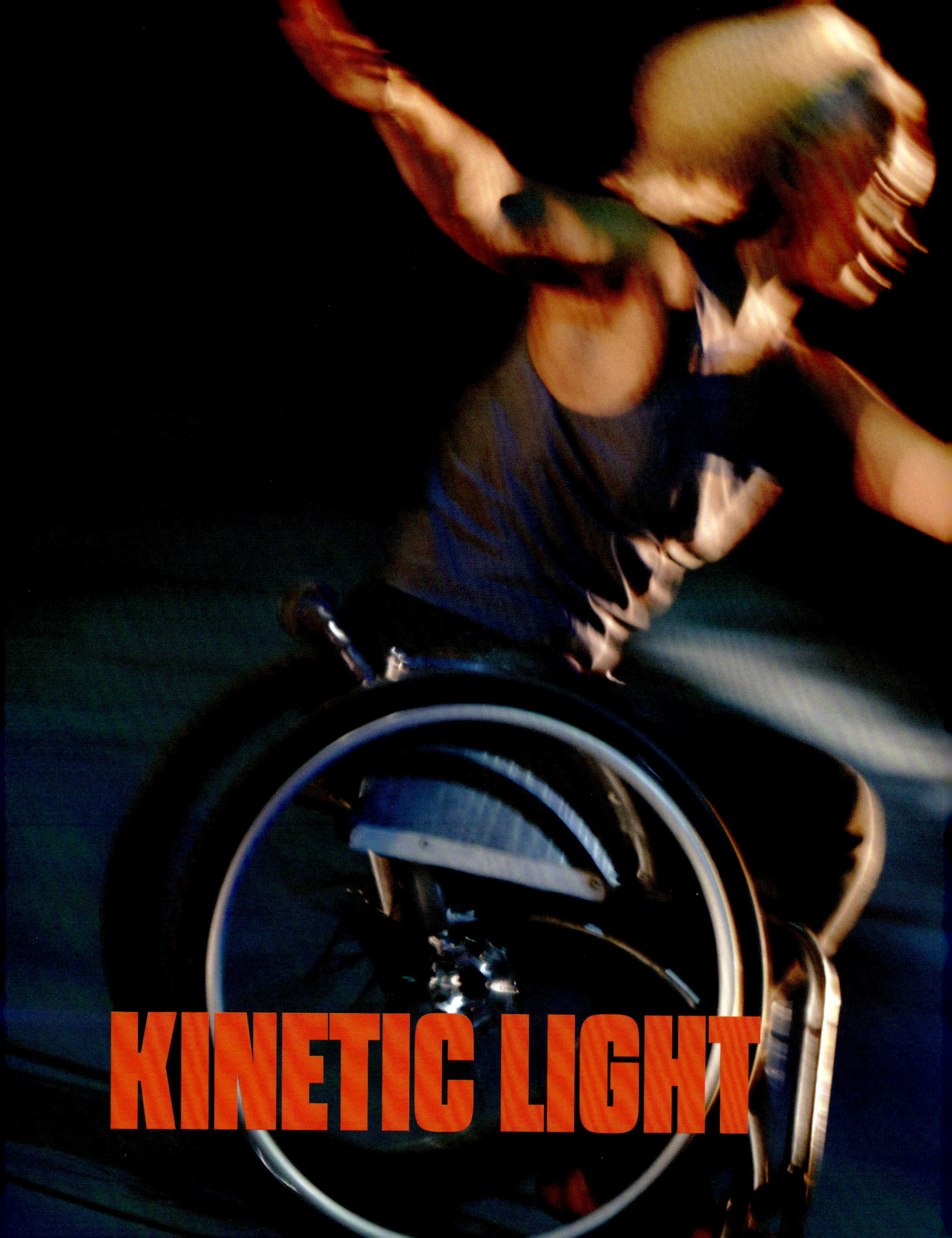
KINETIC LIGHT

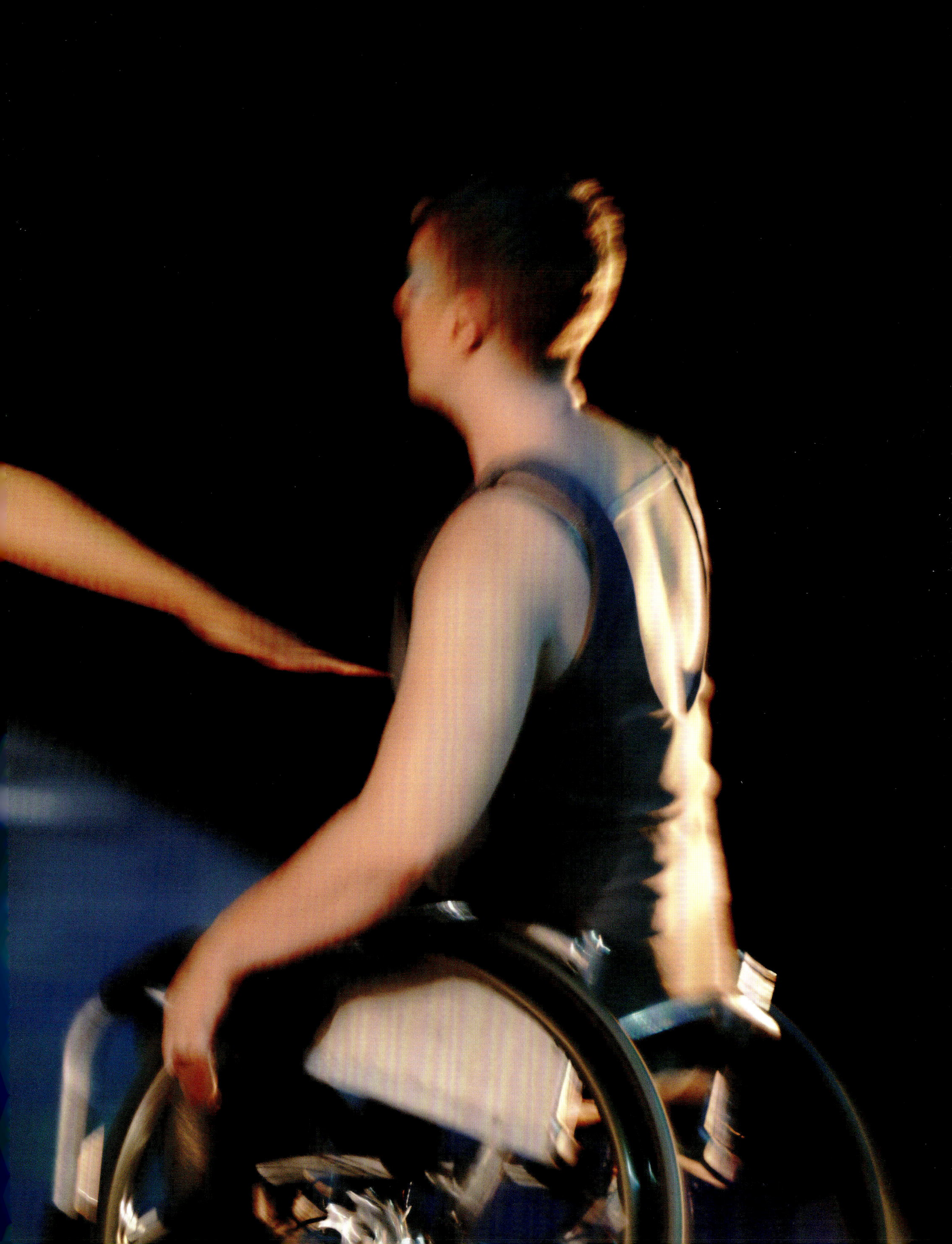

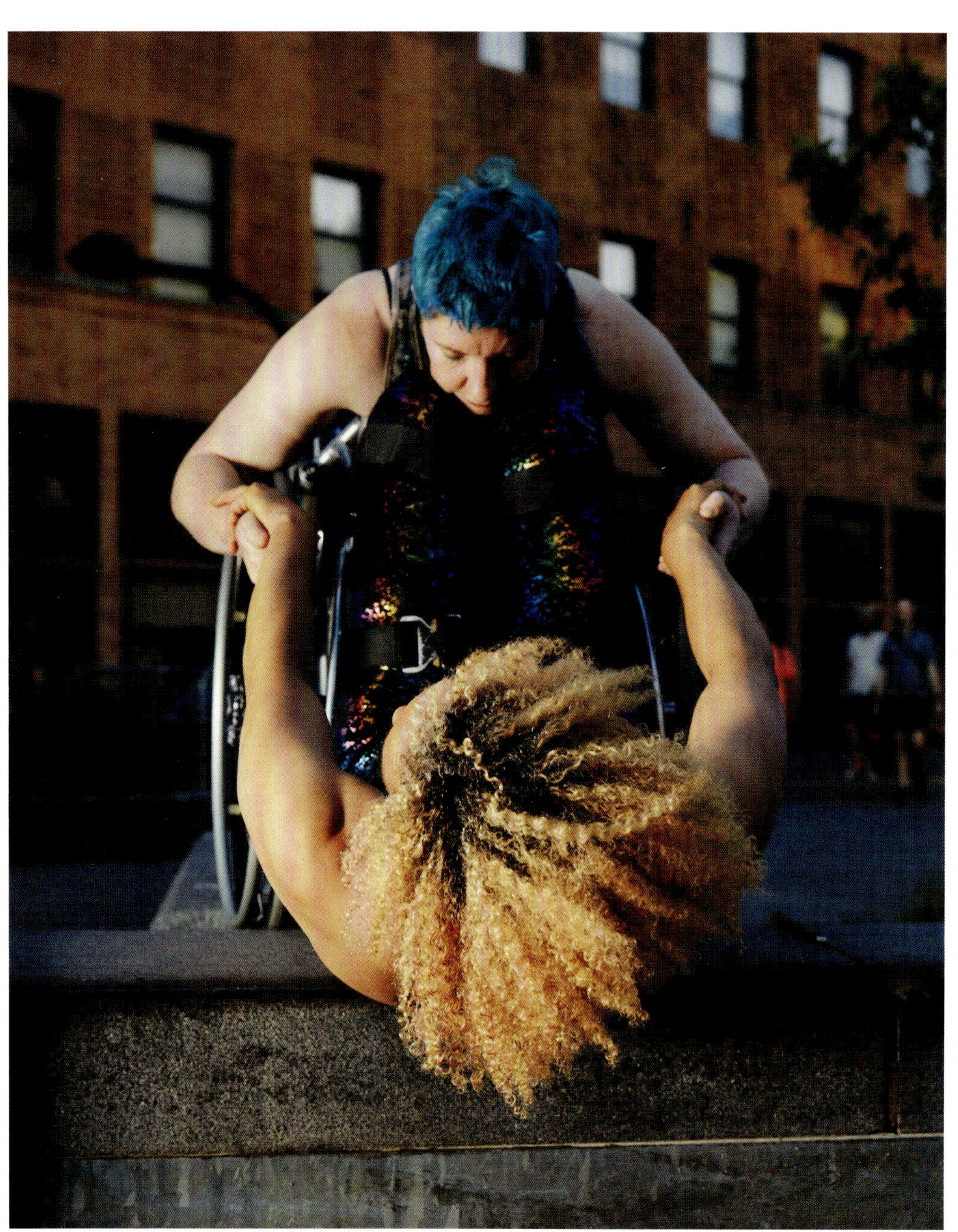

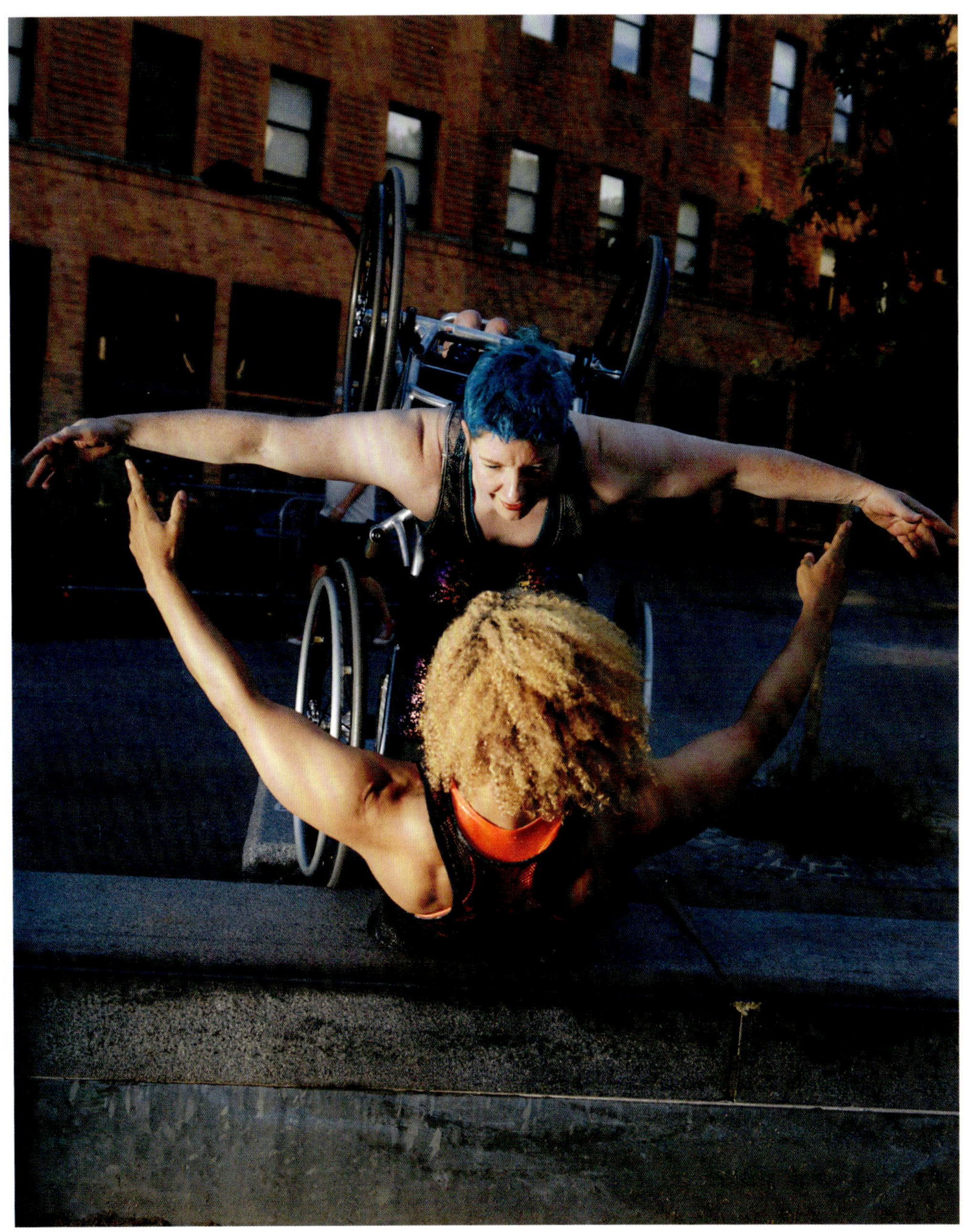

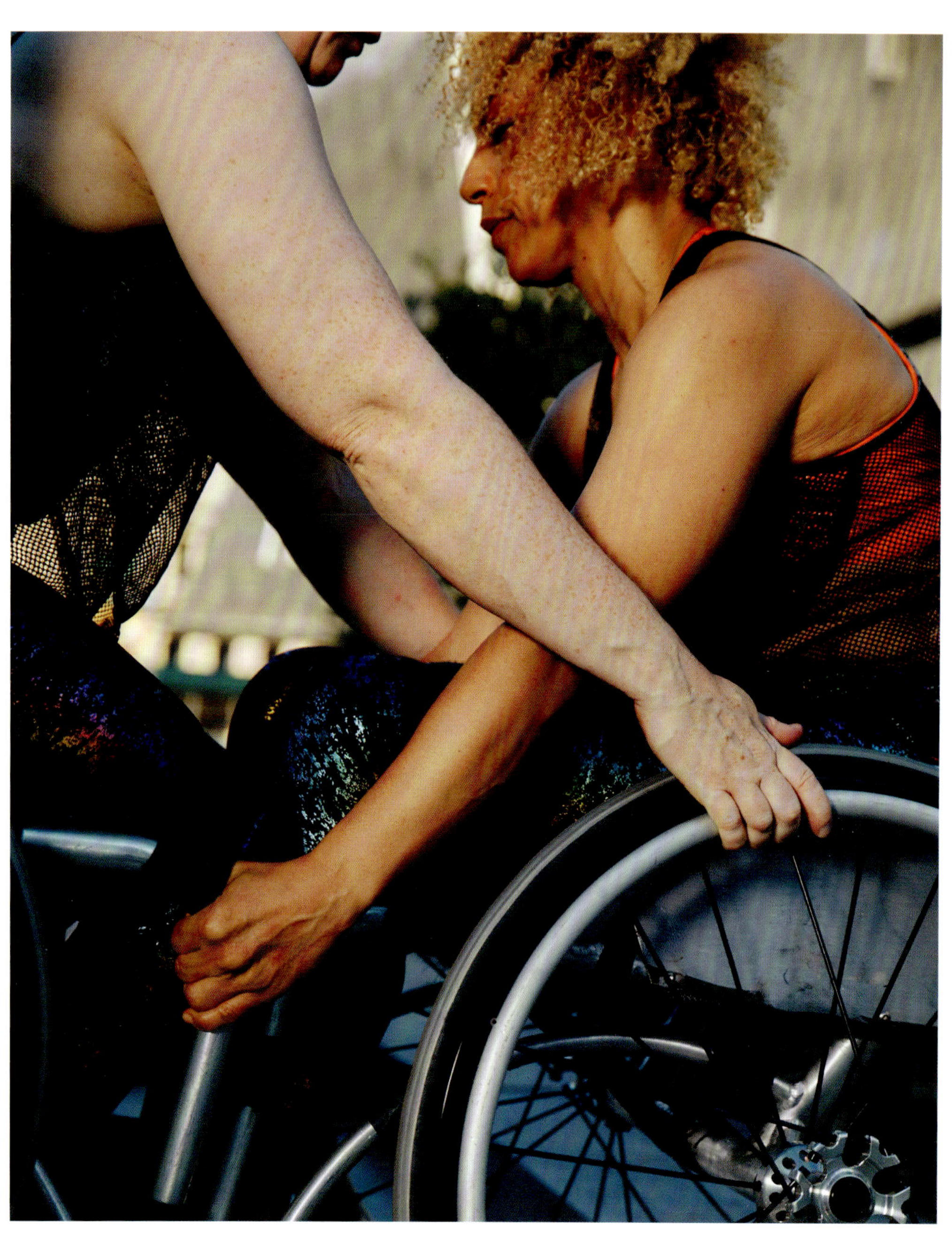

WHEN I ATTEND A PERFORMANCE OF DANCE, THE FIRST ASPECT I register is what I see. The shapes an artist creates with their body. How their movements interact with those of other performers. What, if anything, these express about a particular plot line or an overarching theme. Vision is the sense that I, a sighted person, am most conscious of informing my understanding of the world. And certainly, when I visit the New York premiere of *Wired* at the Shed—a series of vignettes about barbed wire and the complex histories and associations it ensnares, concocted and staged by the disability arts ensemble Kinetic Light—there is much to behold.

The group's dancers include Alice Sheppard and Laurel Lawson, both of whom use wheelchairs. They begin the show dangling above a dark stage. A soft light, designed by founding scenographer Michael Maag, glimmers off their spokes and over their frames, and the ethereal sounds of a cappella vocals grow louder as the dancers inch toward the vinyl floor. Just a few minutes after they reach the ground, they return to the air, soaring and swinging like pendulums through another scene. Later, Jerron Herman, a dancer with cerebral palsy, appears onstage wrapped in a restrictive spiral of sharp brambles. His tense choreography ripples with quiet energy.

Everything that contributes to this rich atmosphere seems carefully considered—the sparkling lamé costumes worn by the performers, the somber glow that bathes them. And yet the visuals are but one way of experiencing Kinetic Light's performances. Some of the theater's seats are outfitted with technology that allows them to react and tremble to the music, while an exhibition preceding the performance lets attendees get to know the props through touch. Kinetic Light also uses the app Audimance, which they developed as a "choose your own adventure" approach to audio description. It is loaded with various interpretations of the show, ranging from plain language to erotic verse, that can be switched or mixed at any point according to how an audience member wishes to encounter the performance.

For this collective of disabled artists creating dance with disabled audiences in mind, access is not an afterthought or merely an ADA requirement but a seismic creative force informing every dimension of a piece. "It's everywhere all the time," says Sheppard, who is also the group's founder and artistic director. "Every time we do something, it increases and it grows, and it is messy and complicated and beautiful." Nor is disability a deficit to Kinetic Light's practice. It is something to be celebrated, an experience, a culture, and a perspective without which the unique, transcendent worlds they conjure could not exist. This outlook intrinsically challenges limited ableist understandings of dance performance as a primarily visual output and expands the potential of what the medium can and should do.

"The work is inherently accessible," Lawson says, "because we're thinking about many points of entry and many valid ways of experiencing it without prioritizing this nondisabled set of assumptions about how you come to the work. Dance is a kinesthetic art. Dance is the art of embodiment. So, who better than disabled artists to blow this shit up?"

Kinetic Light is part of an accelerating movement of disabled artists working to transform the creative fields—television, theater, fine art, and, yes, dance—from the inside out. By sharing their art and pushing for equitable access, they can make disabled audiences feel cared for and represented or illustrate entirely new modes of thinking and making. In the excellent essay "Our Work Is Working," which assesses the state of the disability arts movement for the October 2022 issue of *Art in America*, the critic Emily Watlington recounts how impairment has long been a catalyst for innovation. The contributions of disabled

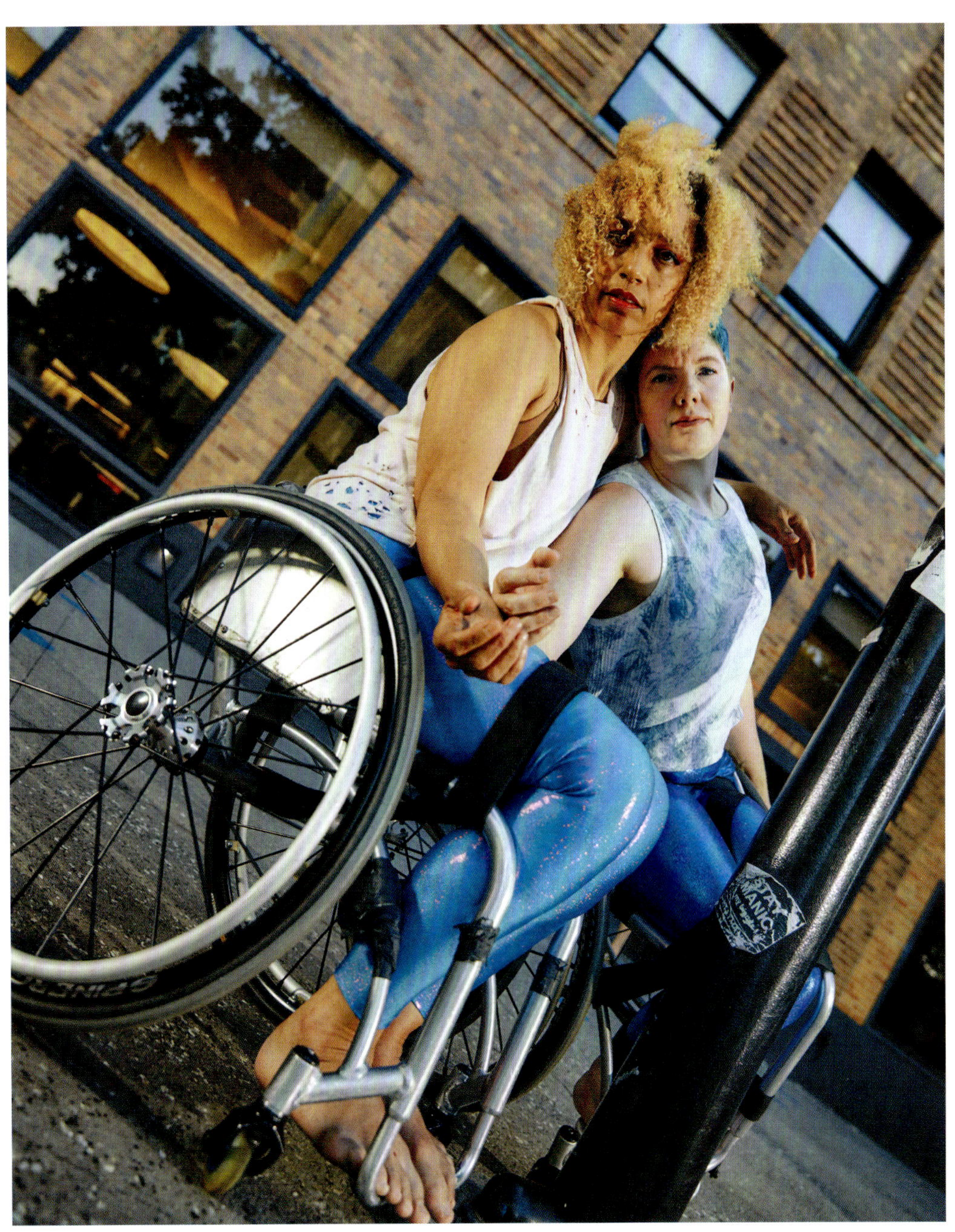

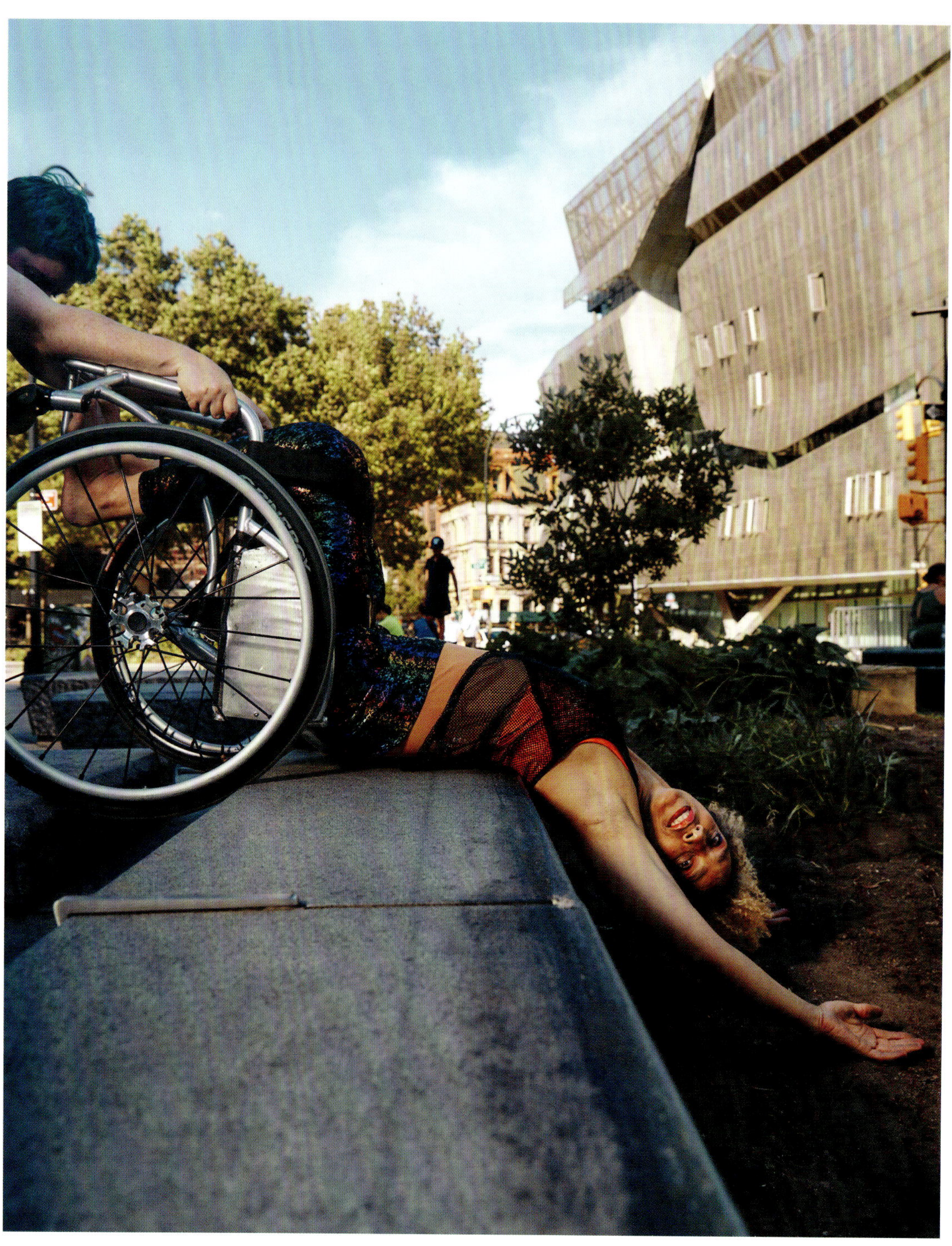

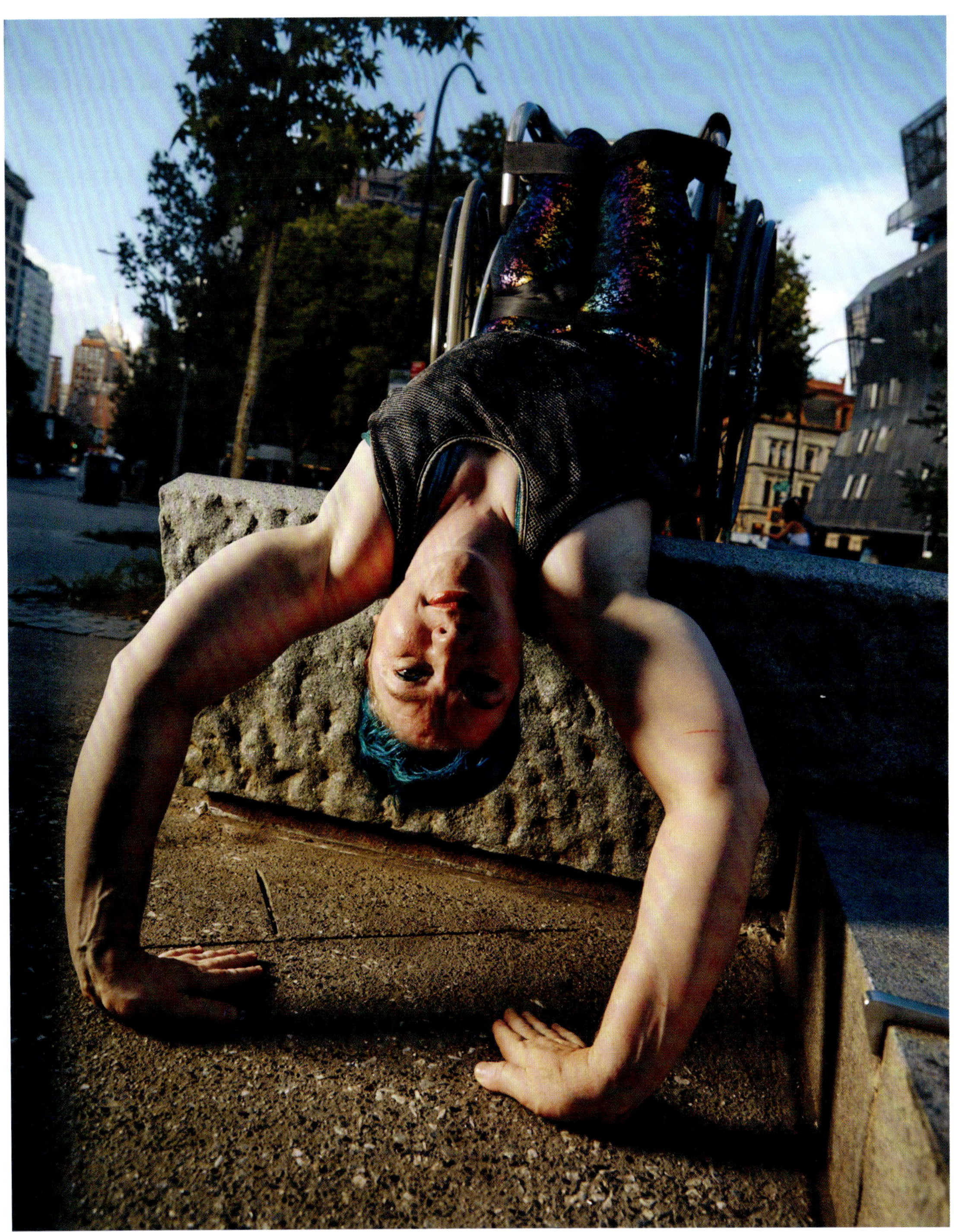

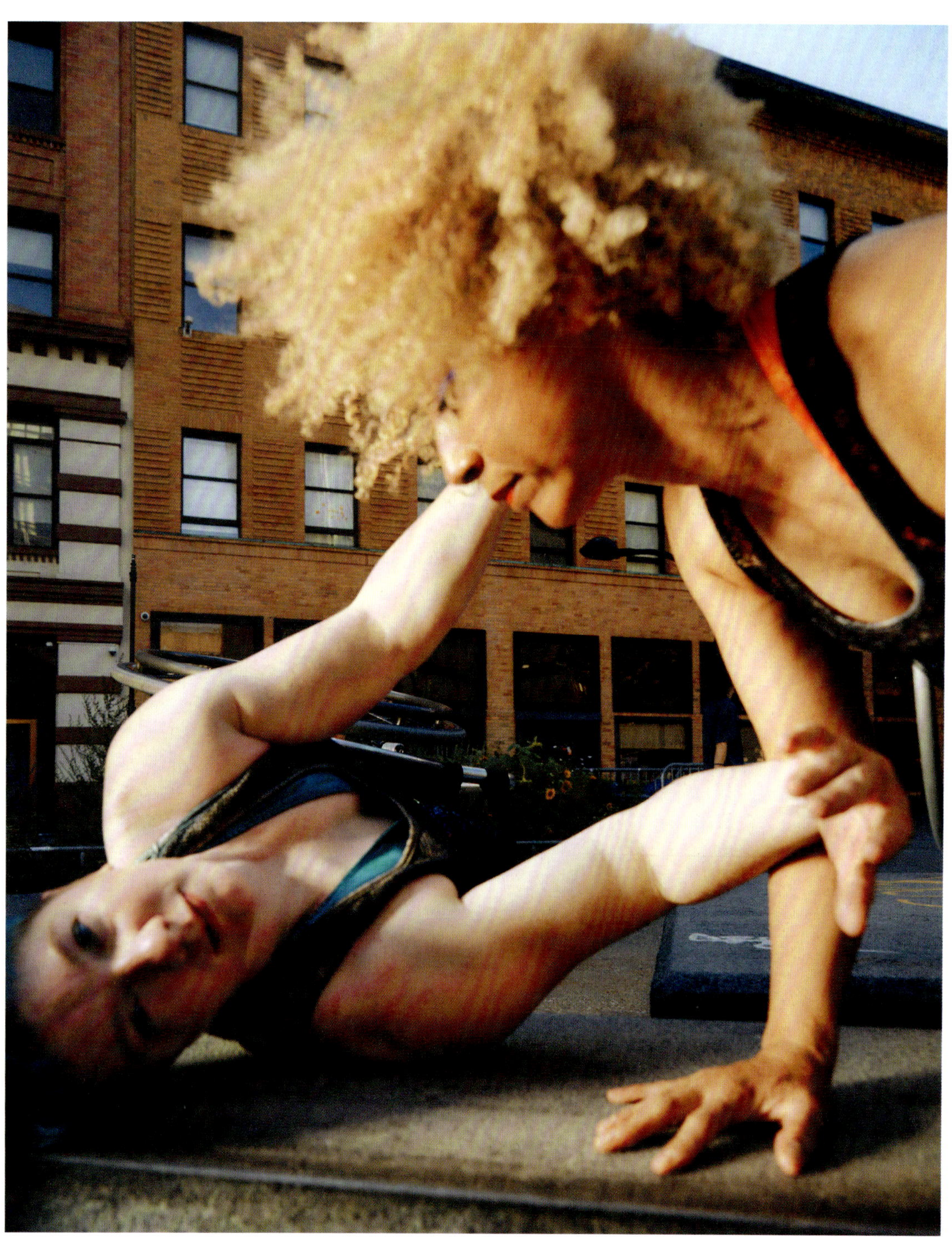

activists and thinkers, though, often go unrecognized by history:

> Alexander Graham Bell's invention of the telephone was rather incidental: He was (not unproblematically) trying to create a tool that might enable his Deaf mother and wife to communicate as a hearing person would. The curb cuts that abound on sidewalk corners, where they are enjoyed by stroller pushers, bicycle walkers, and suitcase draggers, were brought to us by disabled activists who smashed pavement with sledgehammers.

The artists of Kinetic Light are both building off this work and pushing it forward, and they have been for many years. After leaving her career as a medieval studies professor, Sheppard trained under the ballet dancer Kitty Lunn and debuted with Lunn's physically integrated company, Infinity Dance Theater. By the time she began touring with AXIS Dance, one of the United States' most celebrated physically integrated ensembles (disabled and nondisabled performers dancing together), she had become familiar with Lawson's work in the same field. The two choreographed their first duet together for the Atlanta-based company Full Radius Dance under the direction of artistic director Douglas Scott, with whom Lawson had performed since 2004. The piece "Minsky's Burlesque," a section of Scott's work *Snapshot*, featured close partnering, an element that persists in the gravity-defying bird lifts performed by Kinetic Light today.

In 2015, Sheppard met Maag at the Oregon Shakespeare Festival, where he worked as the resident lighting designer, and eventually the three creatives all came together in a "ratty little studio," Lawson recalls, in Oakland, California. That was 2016, at which point Kinetic Light was formed. Today, they rehearse in studios wherever their tours find them—San Francisco, New York. The trick, Sheppard notes, is finding spaces with ceilings tall enough to accommodate their increasingly skyward aerial explorations.

Queer themes have been present in the ensemble's work since its formation, often explicitly but not always so. The troupe's debut piece, *DESCENT*, takes inspiration from Auguste Rodin's sculpture *The Toilette of Venus and Andromeda*, one of many in which the famed French artist depicted lesbian subject matter. The performance takes the epic interracial romance between the two mythological deities whom Rodin cast statically in bronze and transposes it into movement.

Andromeda is freed from her chains in her portrayal by Sheppard, whose identity as a multiracial Black woman returns the princess's original racialization as Black. She glides gracefully across a sculpted plywood ramp. Onstage, she meets her star-crossed lover, Venus, who, thanks to Maag's painterly lighting design, also appears *star-drenched*. The backdrop of constellations shifts to unfurling florals to signal one especially tender moment, a sex scene. In a seemingly mundane yet deeply intimate action known to many wheelchair users, Venus is unstrapped from her chair—has the sound of crunching Velcro teeth ever sounded so hot? She takes a seat atop Andromeda's lap. The two face each other, embracing.

Sheppard and Lawson have been surprised to discover the scene is not always read as depicting gay love, as they intended. "It is amazing what people will refuse to see," Lawson says. Still, a queer perspective remains present across Kinetic Light's practice, even in pieces like Wired where the subject matter is less clearly so. Rather, Sheppard says queerness can be traced in how their work "analyzes and strategically

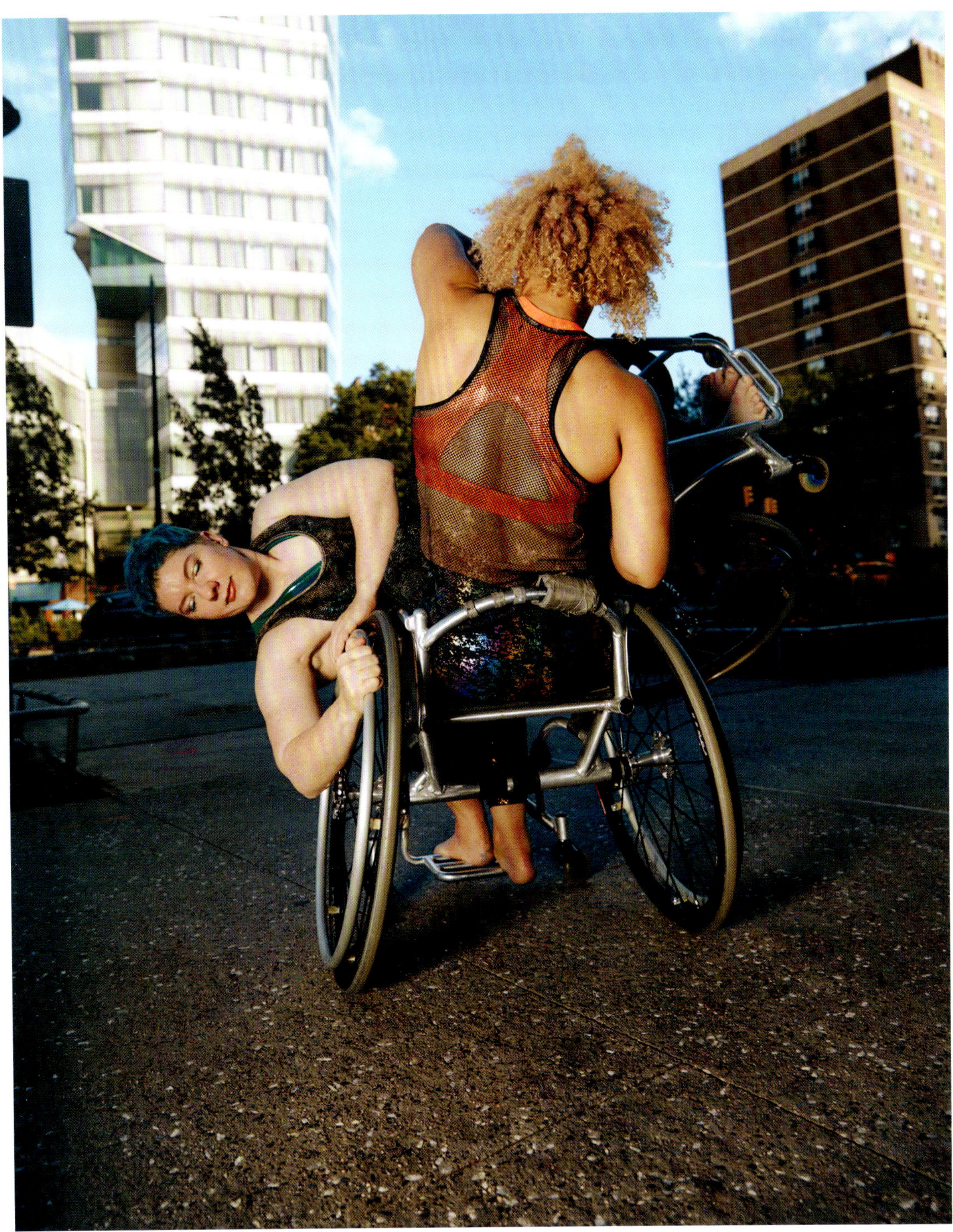

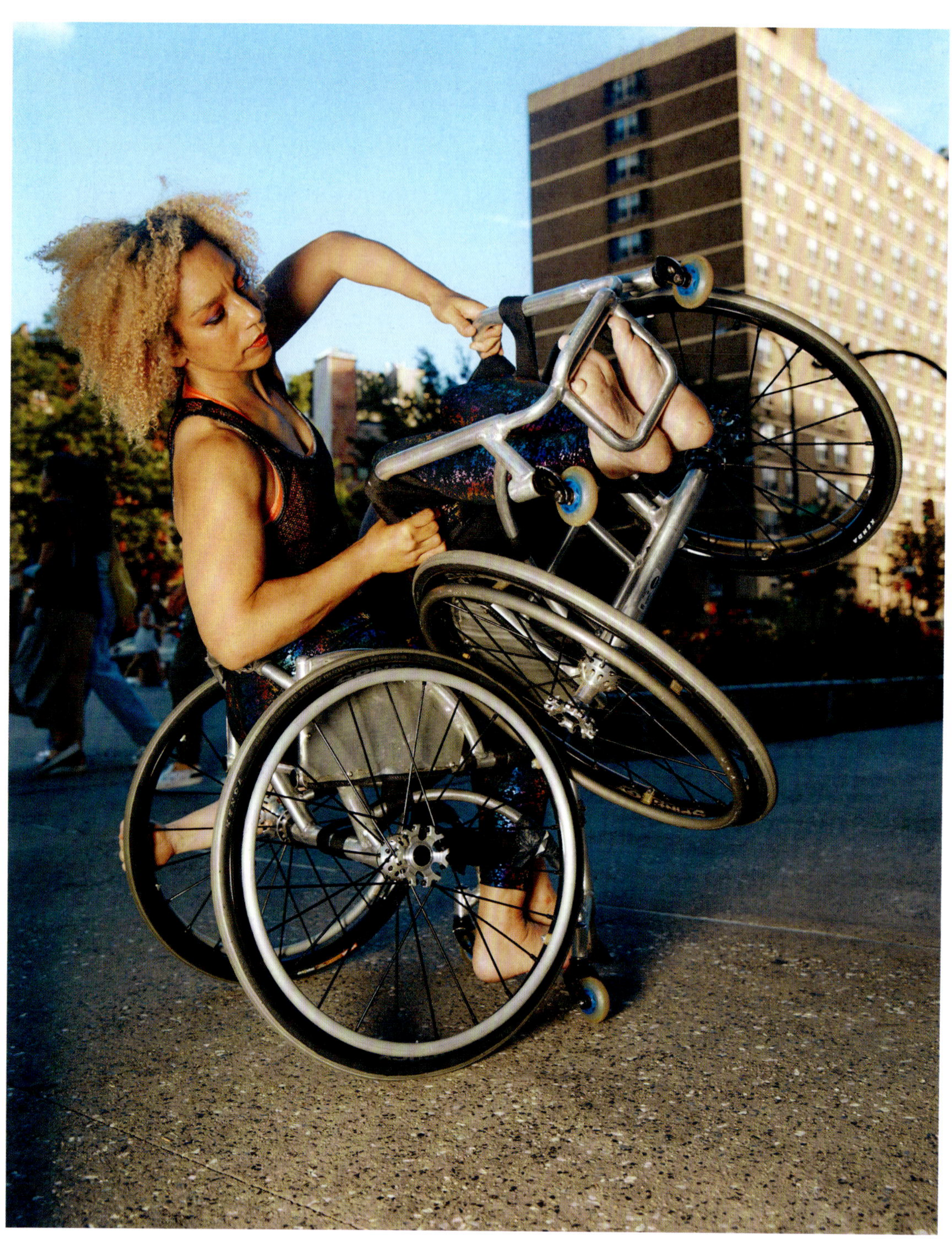

places itself in relationship to certain mainstream concepts." Its markings, like those around disability, might not always be apparent to outsiders, and yet in both arenas, dance has the power to change how we see and what we experience.

"It's also about what queerness reveals. What does queerness surface in some ways?" Sheppard probes. "What does it nest with? As an aesthetic, what does it mess with?"

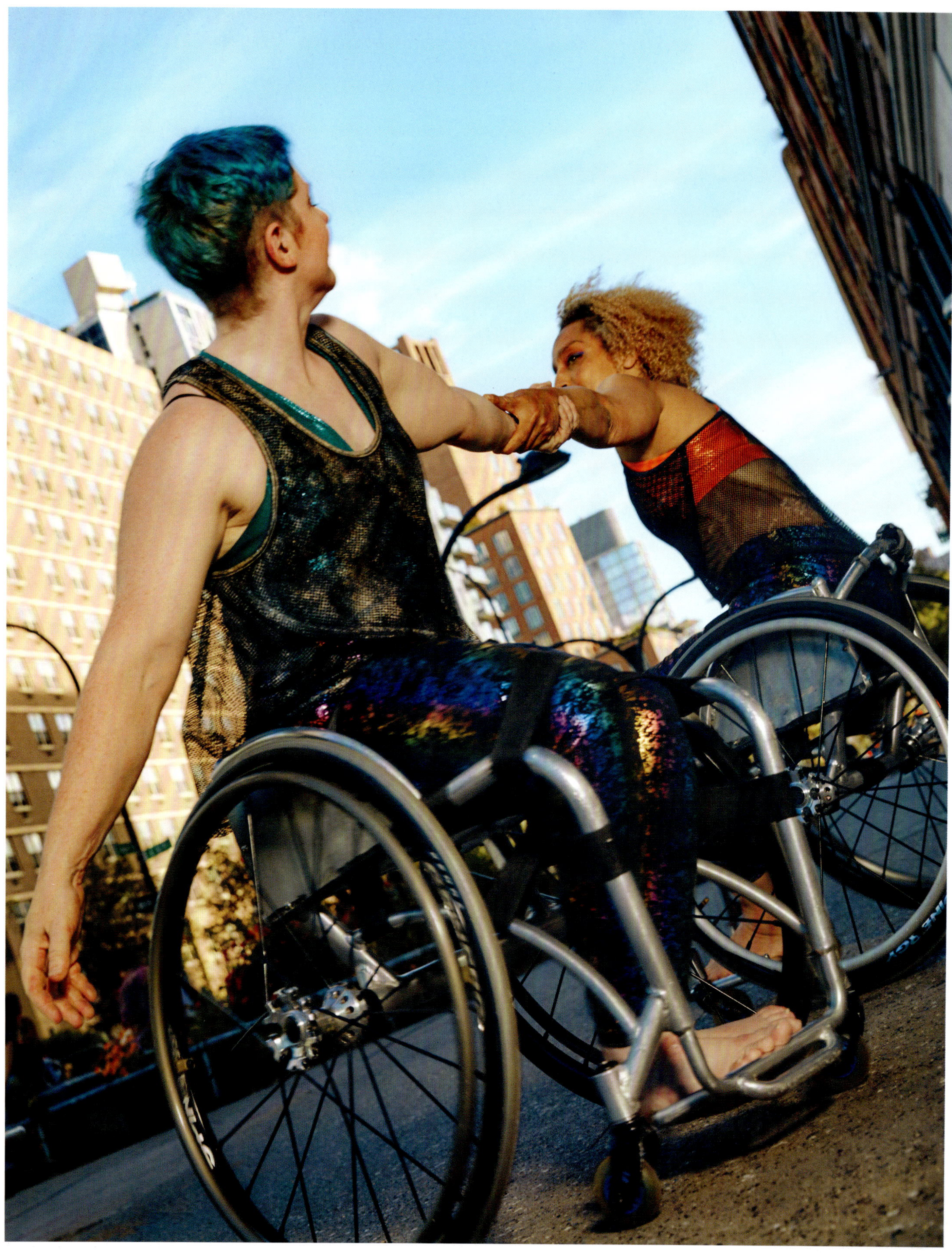

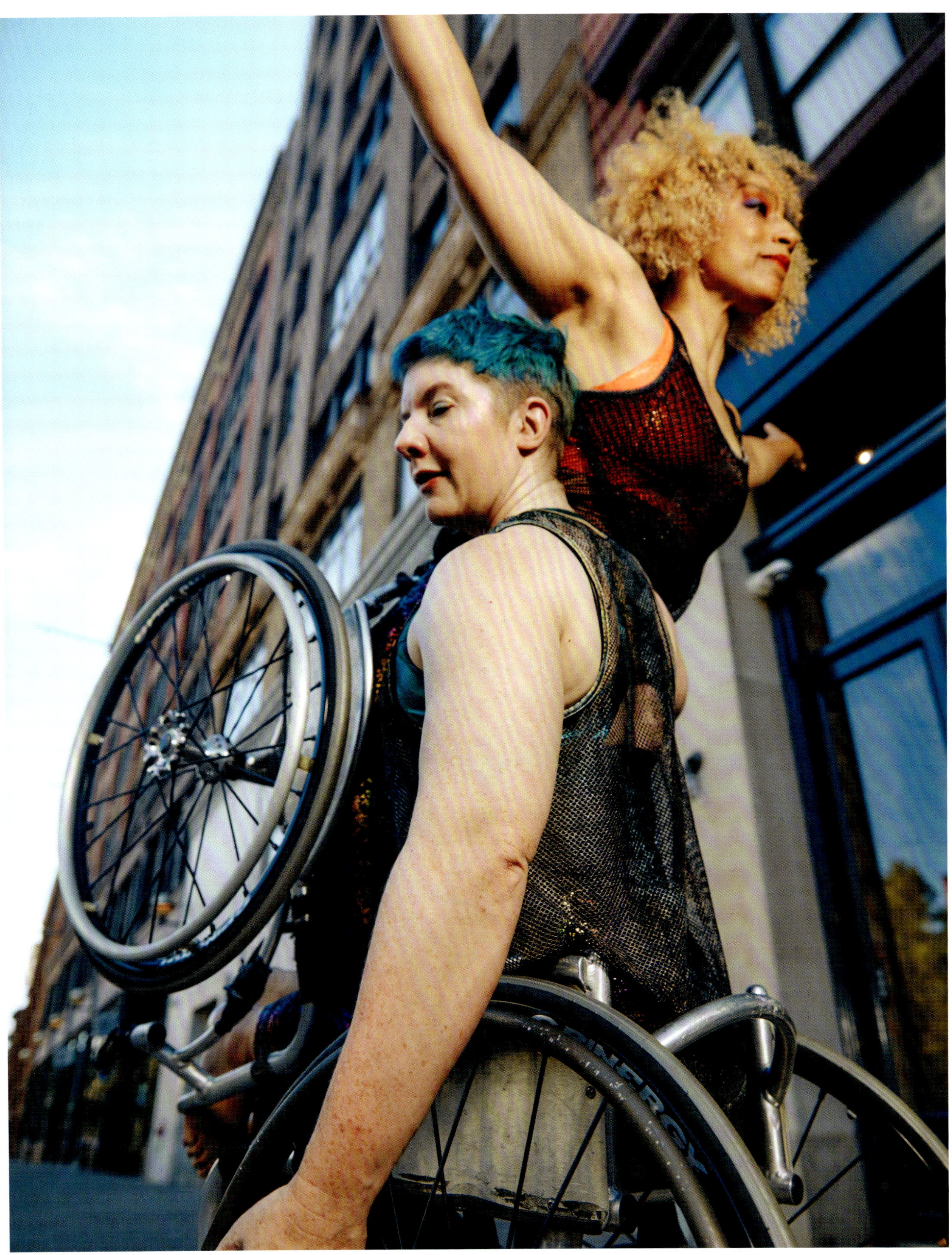

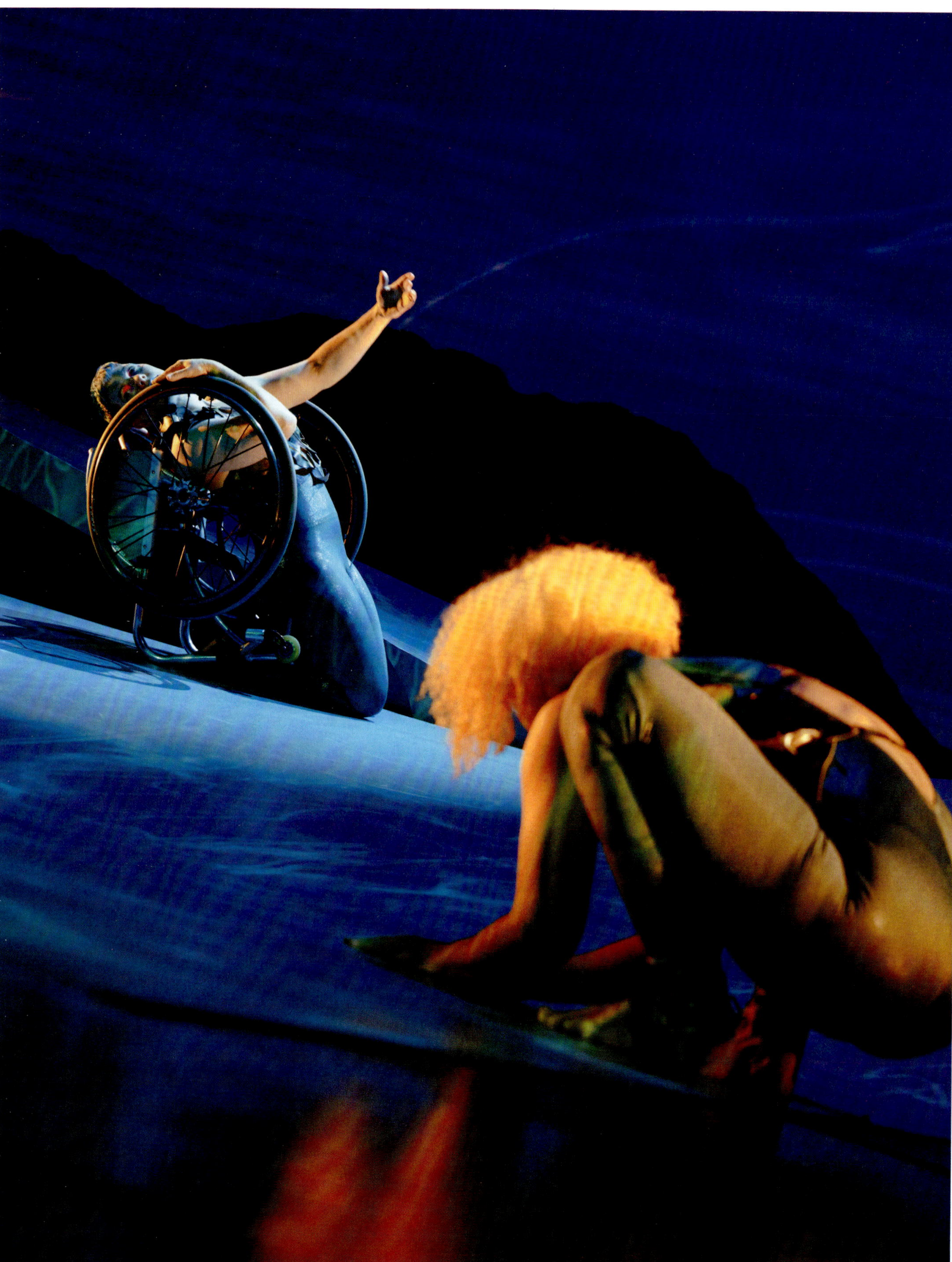

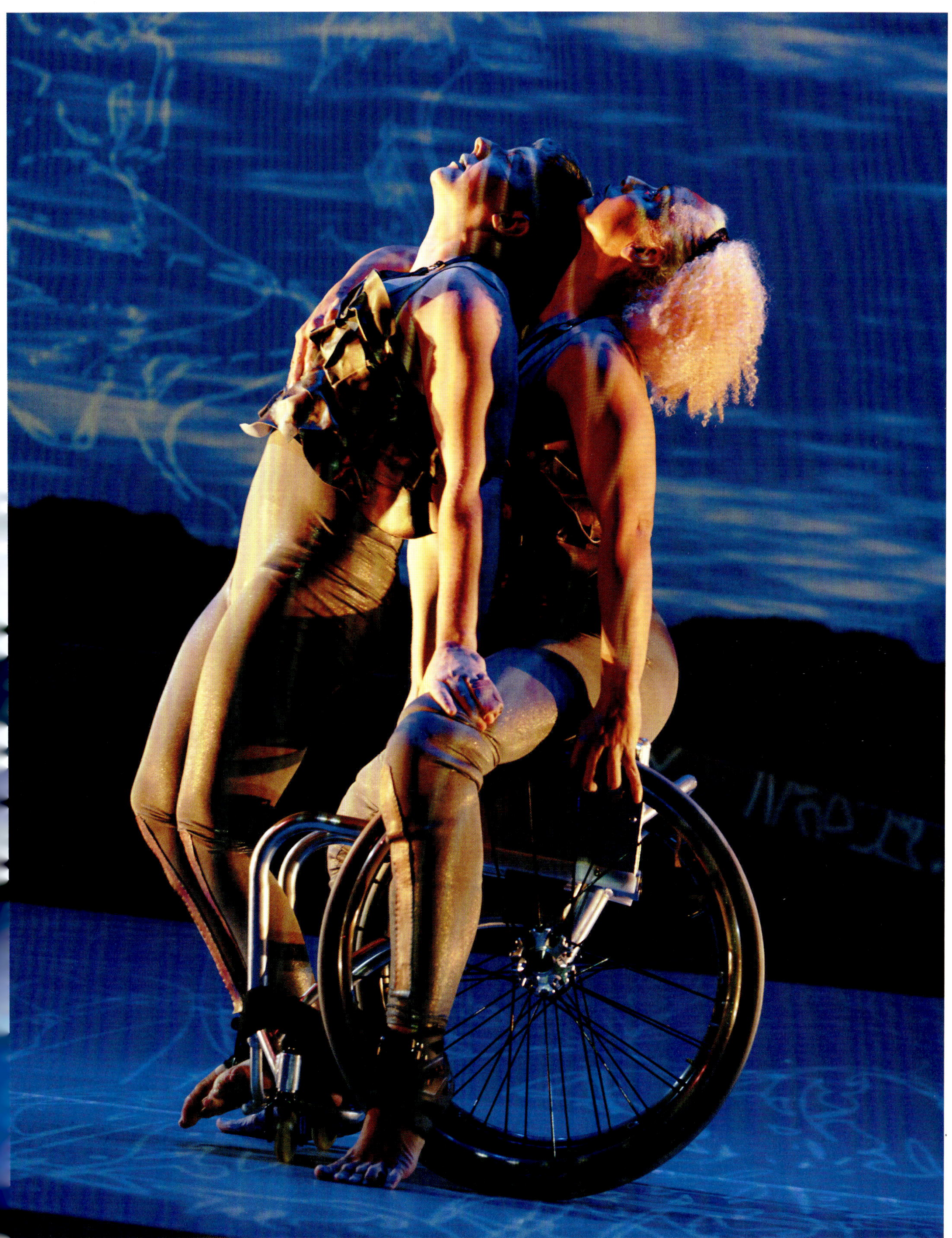

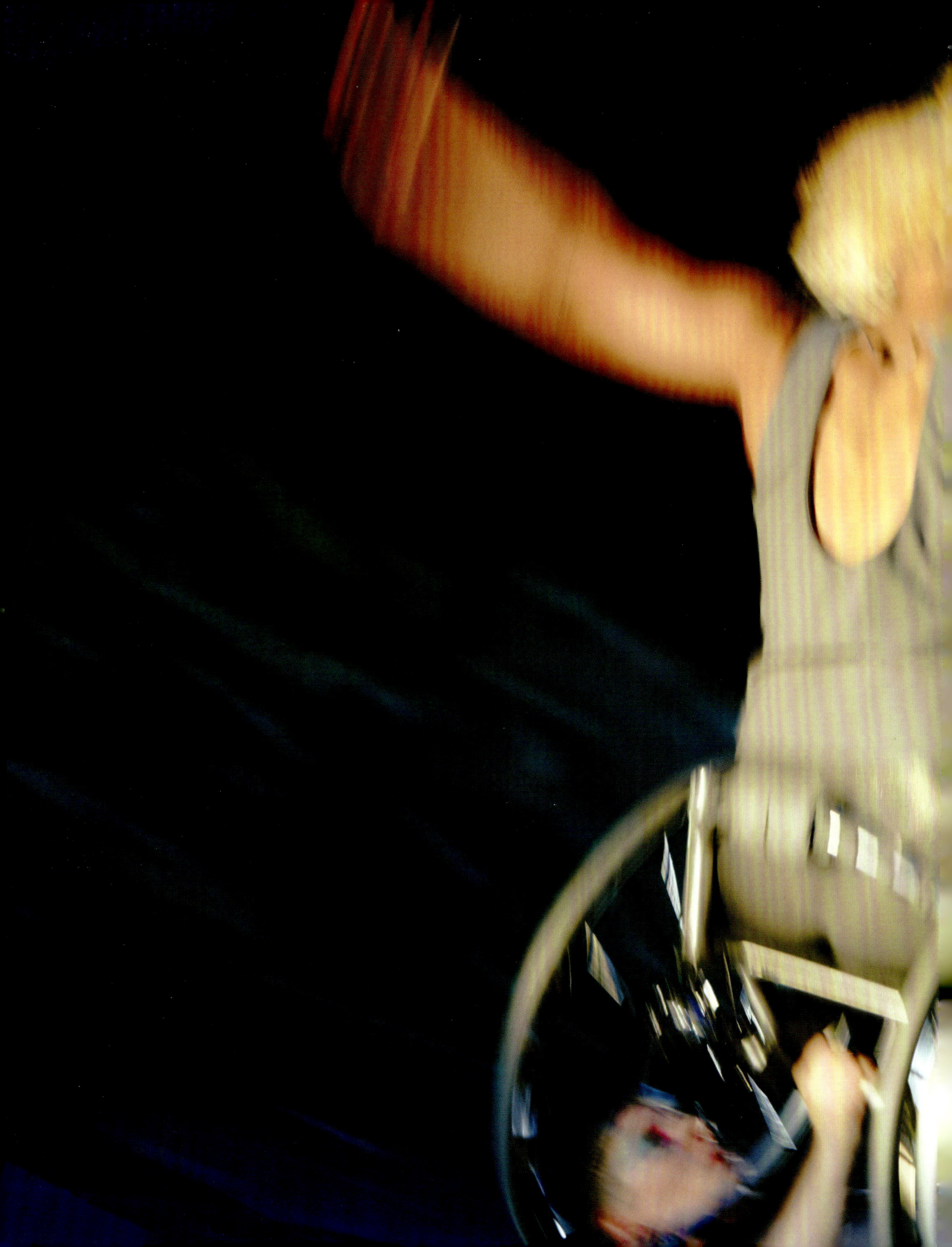

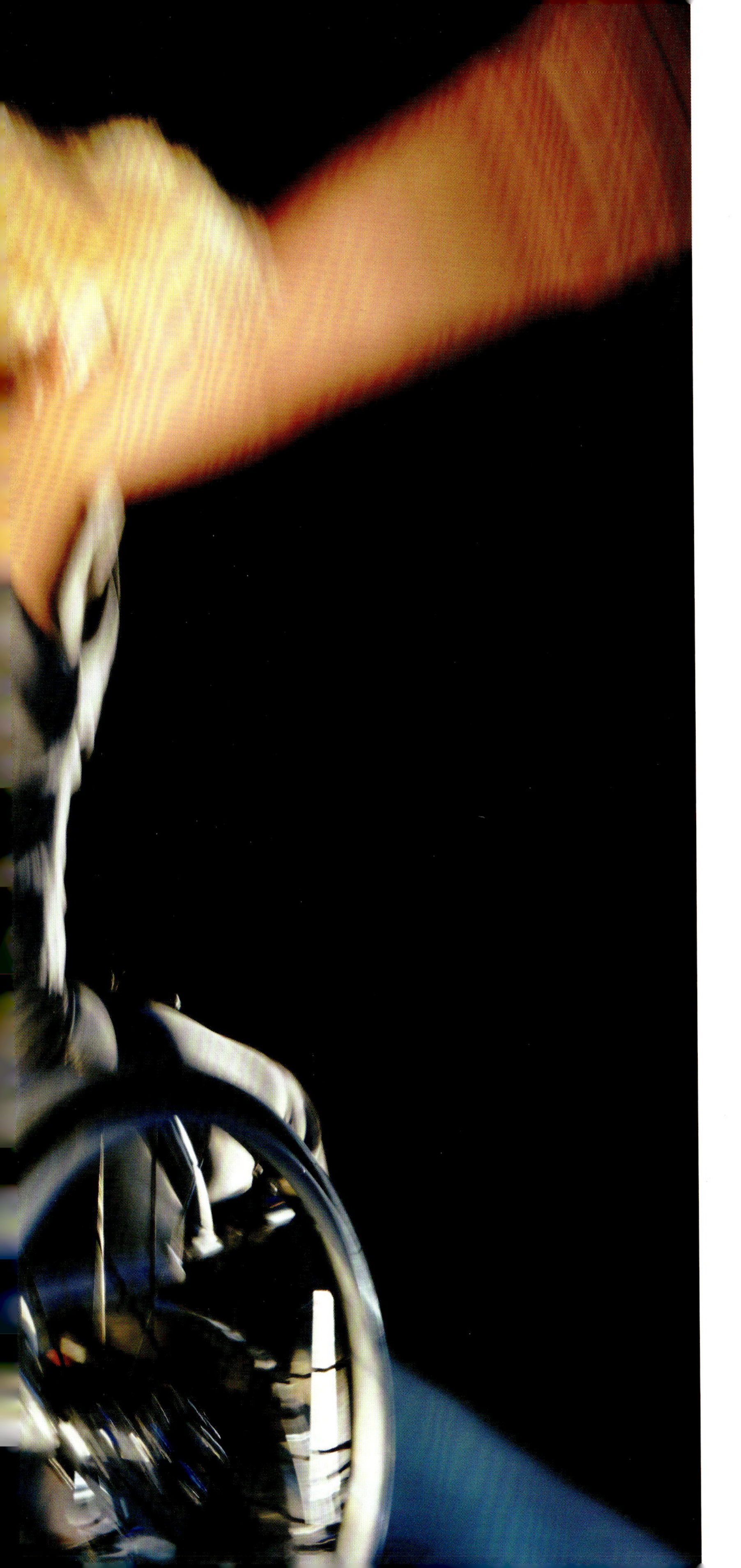

VANGELINE THEATER/NEW YORK BUTOH INSTITUTE'S *QUEER BUTOH*

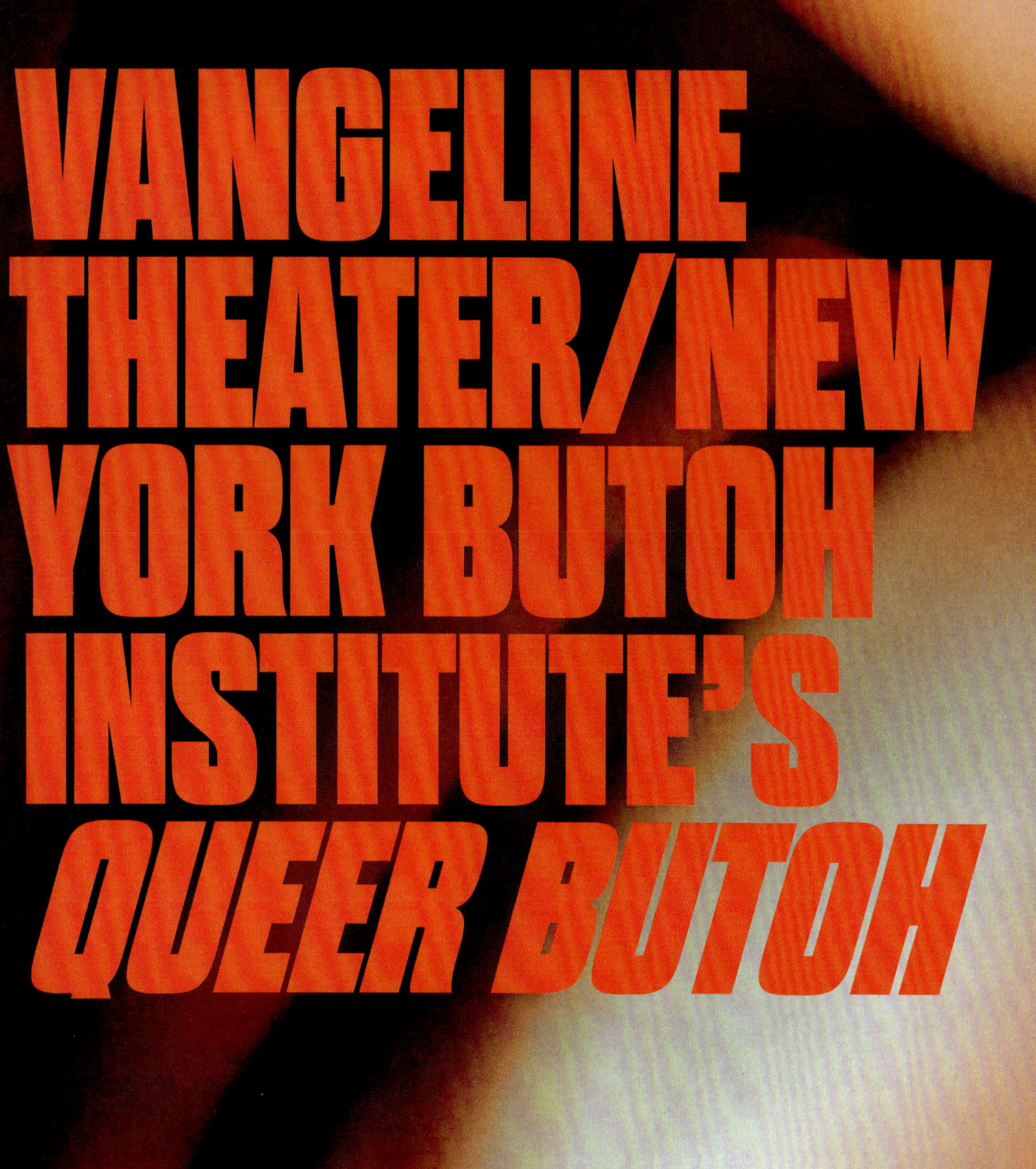

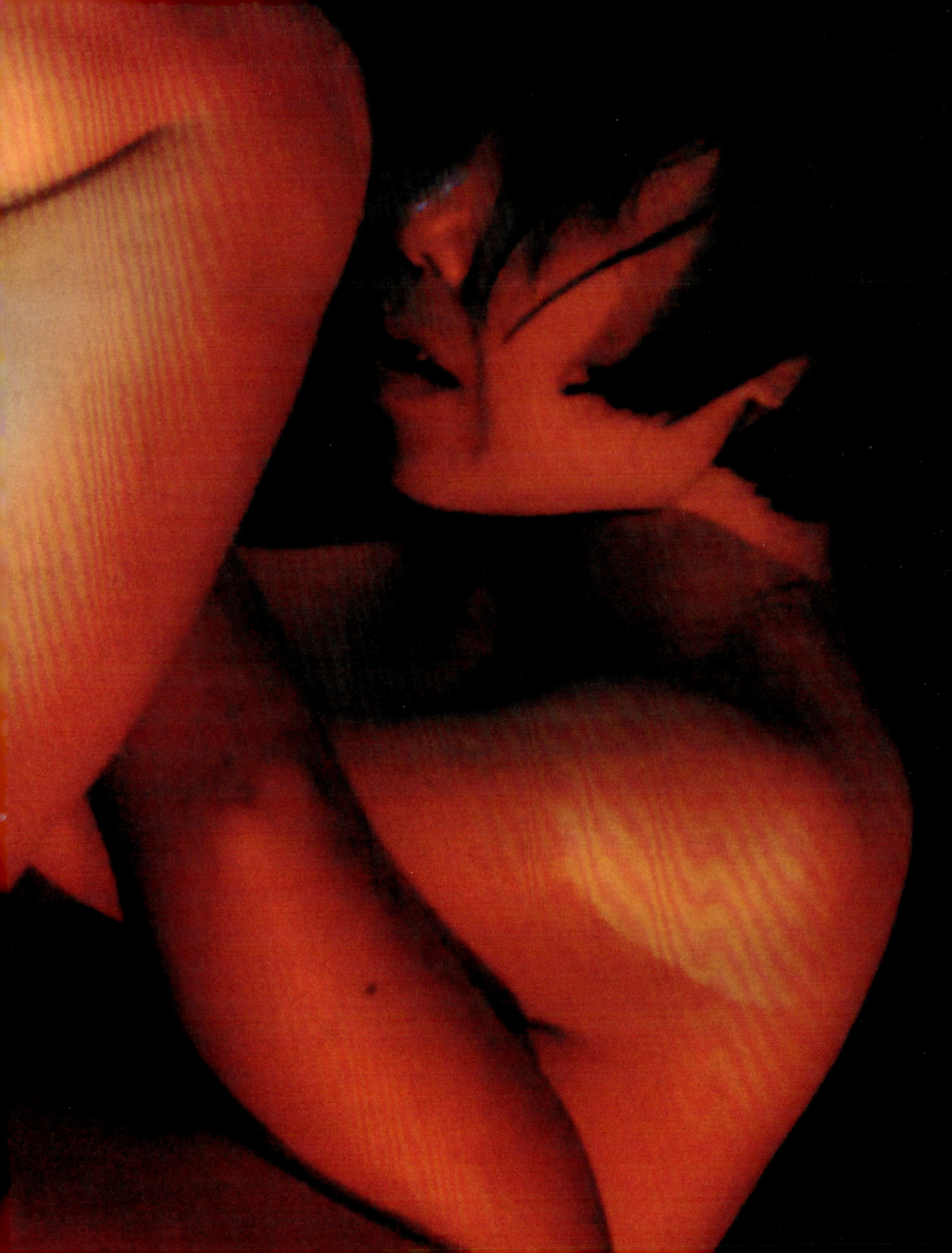

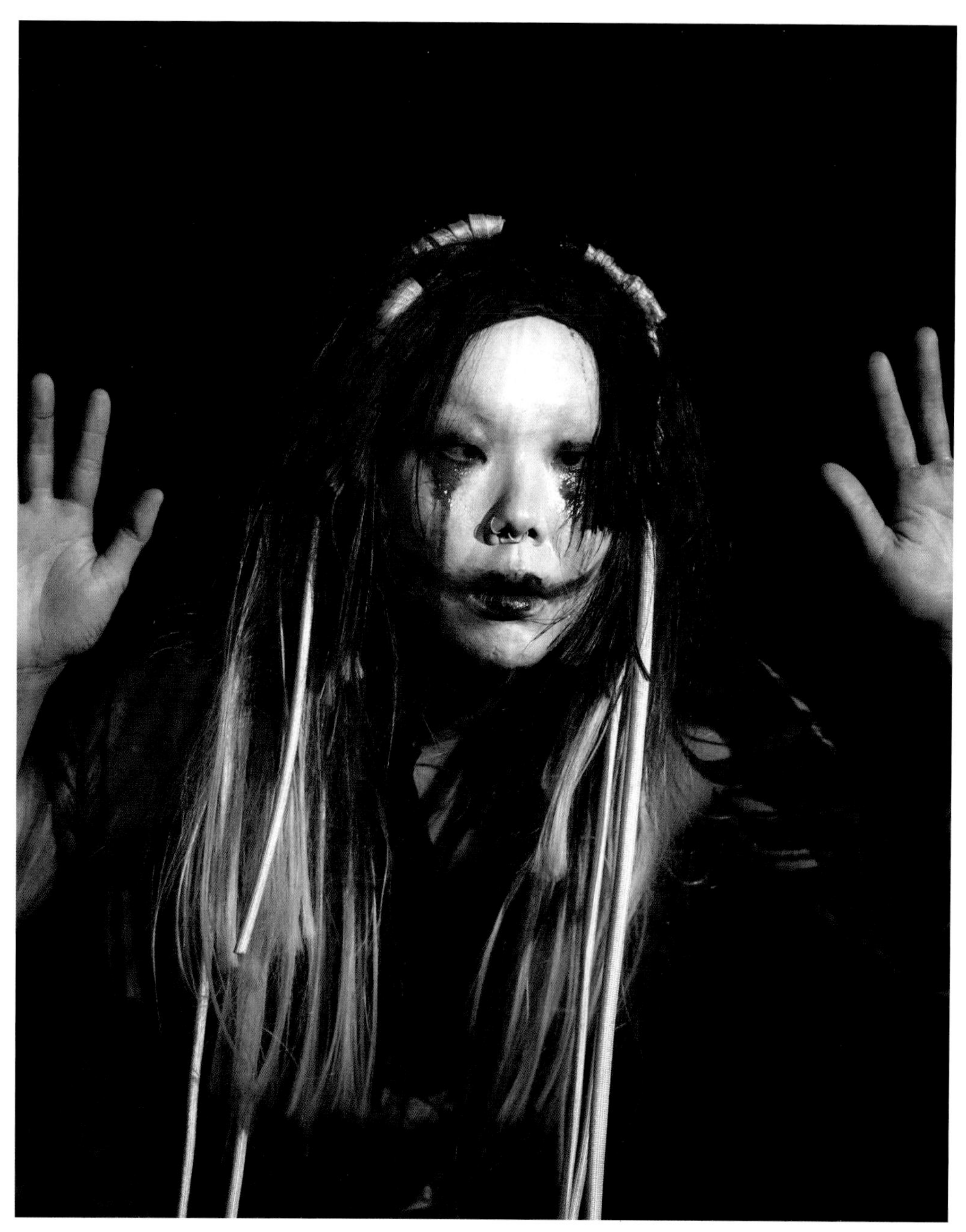

IN 1959, A PERFORMANCE AT THE DAI-ICHI SEIMEI HALL IN TOKYO began entirely in darkness. The disembodied sounds of footsteps could be heard emanating from the stage as the director of the work, Tatsumi Hijikata, chased down the dancer Yoshito Ohno, son of Hijikata's longtime collaborator Kazuo Ohno. This fifteen-minute work, *KINJIKI*, or *Forbidden Colors,* was adapted from the novel of the same name by Yukio Mishima and depicted a relationship between two men. The noise became heightened with moans and finally, at the climax of the show, the frightened screams of a live chicken, presented as a token of love, then suffocated between one of the dancer's legs.

Hijikata's performance was considered so extreme at the time of its presentation that he left the All Japan Art Dance Association and became an outcast within the country's contemporary dance community. However, *KINJIKI* would also give rise to a potent new form of dance theater, teeming with morose themes and occultic imagery, that Hijikata would come to call *ankoku butoh*, or "dance of darkness." As difficult to classify as it is perplexing to behold, butoh, as it is commonly known today, embraces and explores fluidity and otherness, making it a welcome refuge for many LGBTQ+ artists. It asks the performer to dig below the blood of the body to uncover and make visible the truth of their soul, however frightening or sublime. Queerness, ambiguity, and an antiestablishment spirit have been hallmarks of the genre since its founding.

Critical of the American values seeping into Japanese culture after World War II, Hijikata turned inward, toward his birthplace in Akita Prefecture in northern Japan. Images of muddy rice paddies and farmers hunched over fields lingered in his mind as he sought to craft a new style that was largely free from

Western influence. The movements he generated were typically low to the ground, flickering between painstaking slowness and spurts of frenzied gestures, which are still seen in contemporary butoh. Where ballet might deal with the precision and strength of the body's movement, butoh is frequently concerned with its frailty—weighted by illness, crumpled in death—and transformation. By summoning these harsh realities, and meeting them, the dancer might come away with a greater sense of self-understanding.

"It's a way of looking at the world, of looking at yourself, of looking at community," explains the butoh dancer and instructor Vangeline, founder of the New York Butoh Institute. "Butoh opened up a new vista for me in terms of exploring gender and my gender identity and exploring other facets of myself as a performer."

Having trained in jazz and gotten her footing within New York's underground burlesque scene in the '90s, Vangeline often felt relegated to sexualized or aesthetically pretty roles. Her introduction to butoh came in 1999, when she attended a haunting performance by Sankai Juku, a Japanese troupe that smatters their bodies with white powder—an image sometimes conflated with the genre as a whole. She felt an instant, electric connection. "They were so androgynous," she recalls. "It felt spiritual. There was a darkness underneath, a light and a darkness. It seemed to me that there were a lot of possibilities for myself."

Some of Vangeline's most celebrated works have delved into such dueling ideas as light and darkness, masculinity and femininity, beauty and the grotesque. For the duration of her hour-long solo *Butoh Beethoven: Eclipse (Admiring Tatsumi Hijikata)*, she sustained precise, subtle motions.

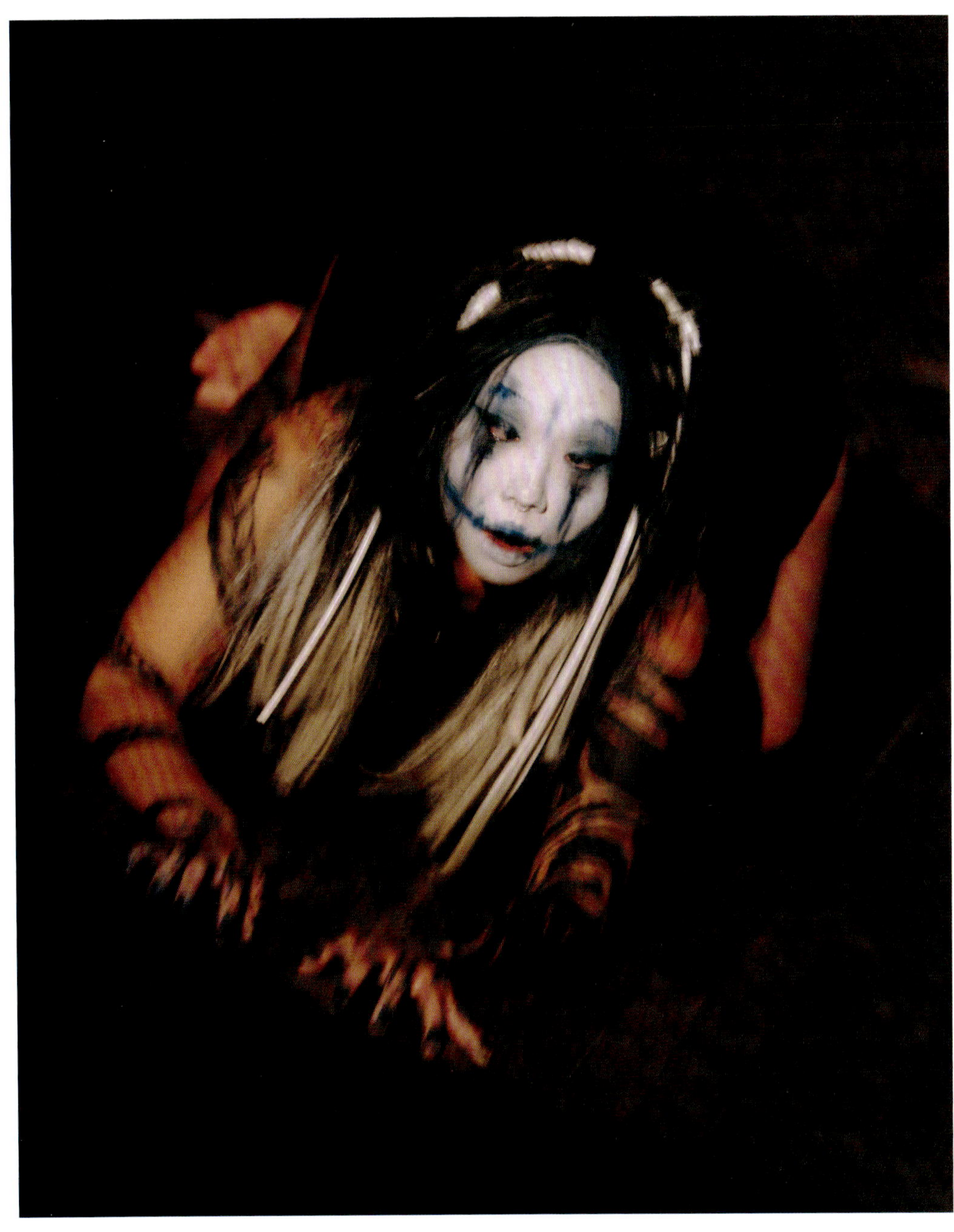

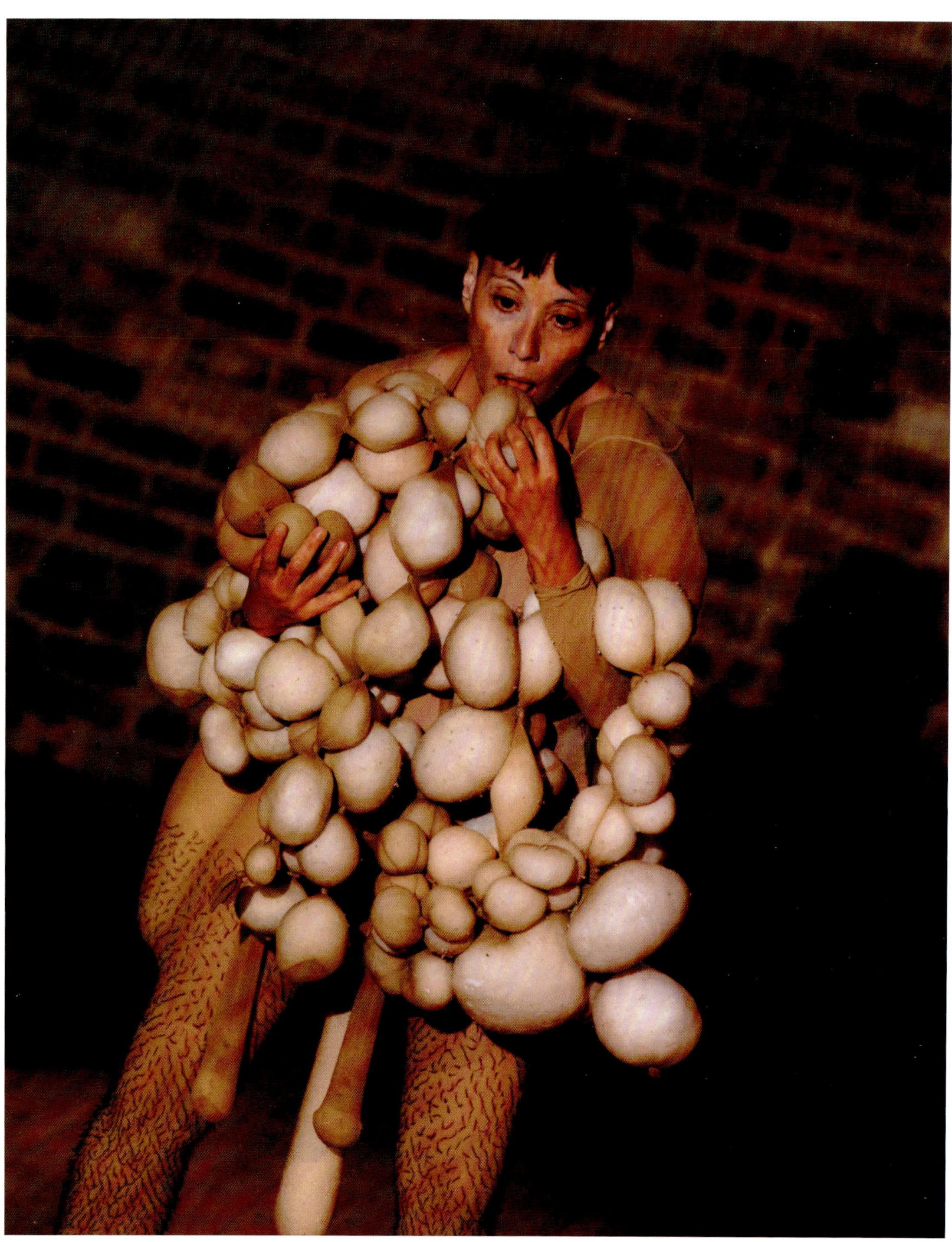

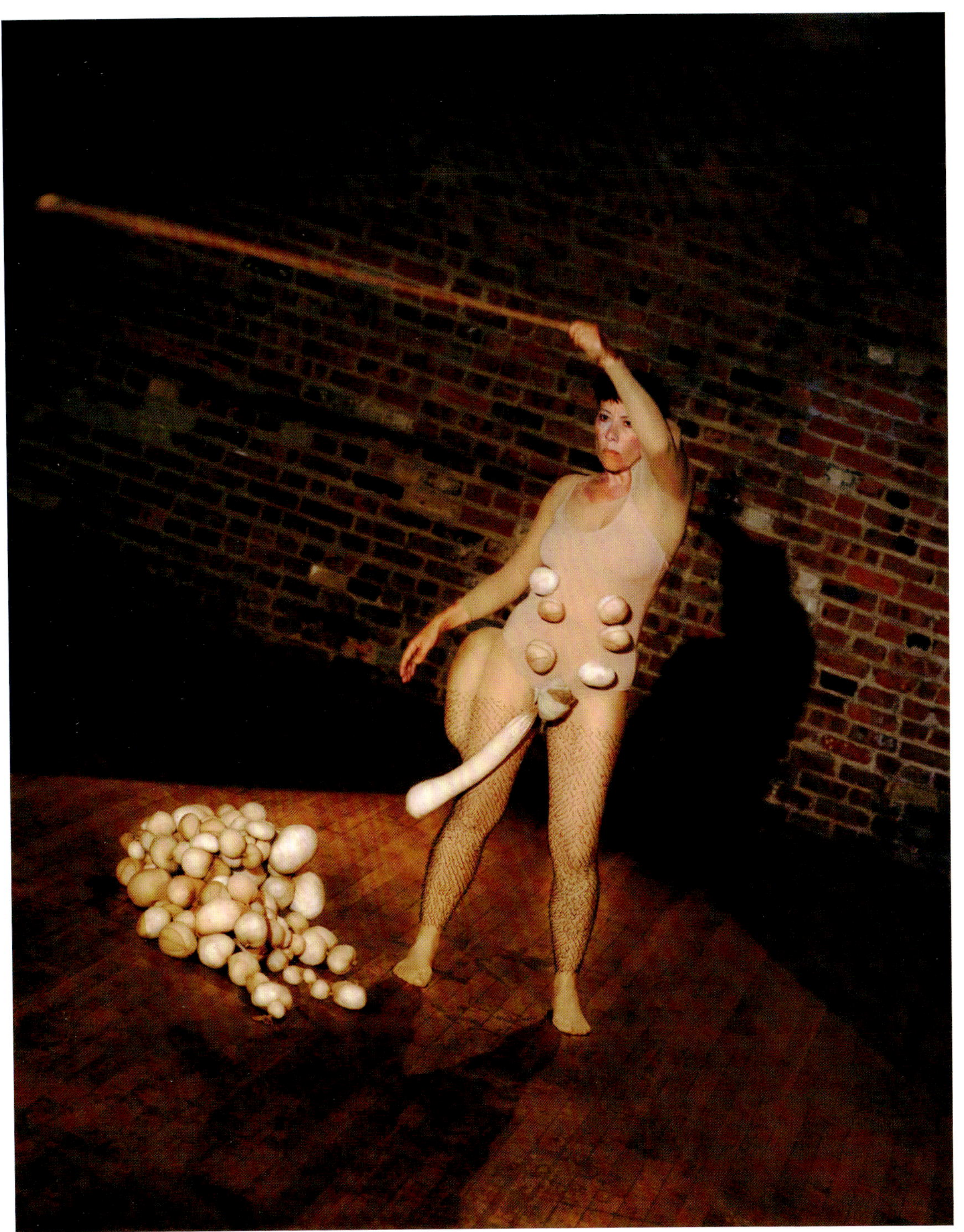

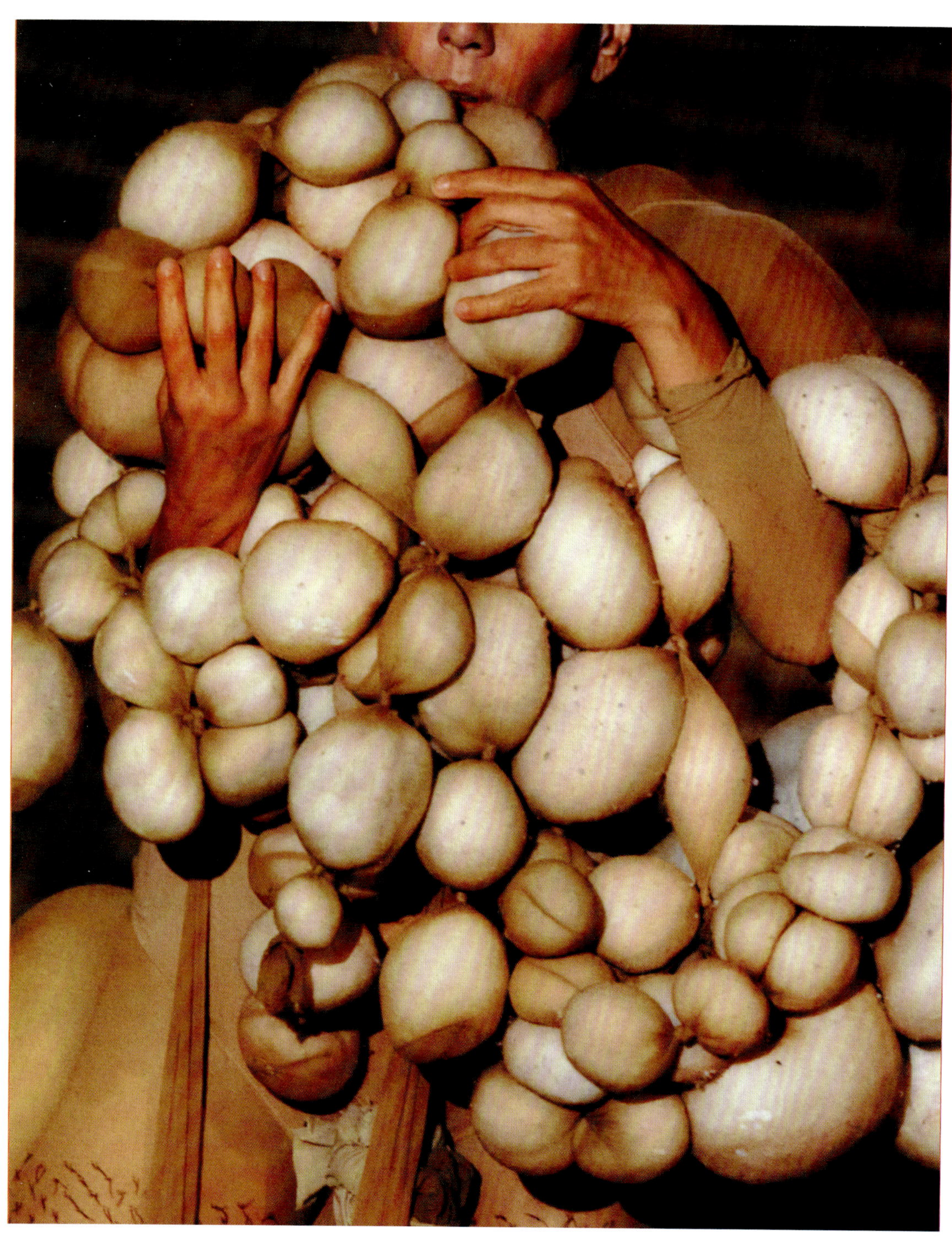

With her cheekbones painted to appear skeletal, she clutched a conductor's wand, motioning as if two great artists, butoh's founder and the German composer Ludwig van Beethoven, were resurrected and collaborating within her. Lilting and soft at times, then thunderously harsh at others, the dance reflected the myriad expressions inside the performer herself. It toured internationally in 2016 and made her a star.

That same year, Vangeline staged the first of a performance series highlighting butoh's close relationship with queerness. In 2022, for the sixth annual showcase, performers from varying backgrounds and regions—dustin maxwell from the United States, Xue from Singapore, and Hélène Barrier from France—brought their own interpretations of this prompt to the Brick, an intimate nonprofit theater in Brooklyn's Williamsburg neighborhood. The performances they showed there were mesmerizing and meditative, often leaving the audience with more questions than answers.

The show opened with a dim haze, smoke dissipating into the corners of the redbrick room, as if nighttime had just slipped over the sun. Two figures wrapped in black, dancers Tomoe Mae and Kavya Yang, stood at either end of the stage, their backs to the audience. As they inched forward, their robes slid to the ground and they began crawling about each other, seemingly shape-shifting. Then maxwell emerged from beneath a golden cover and began navigating the space, at one point rolling across the ground, raising his behind sensuously toward the audience. By the end of the dance, the three characters had found one another, heaving and melting into one fleshy mass.

One critic likened the piece to a creation myth, part of "a queer history of the universe." Maxwell, a visual artist and a student of Vangeline's, compares some of his

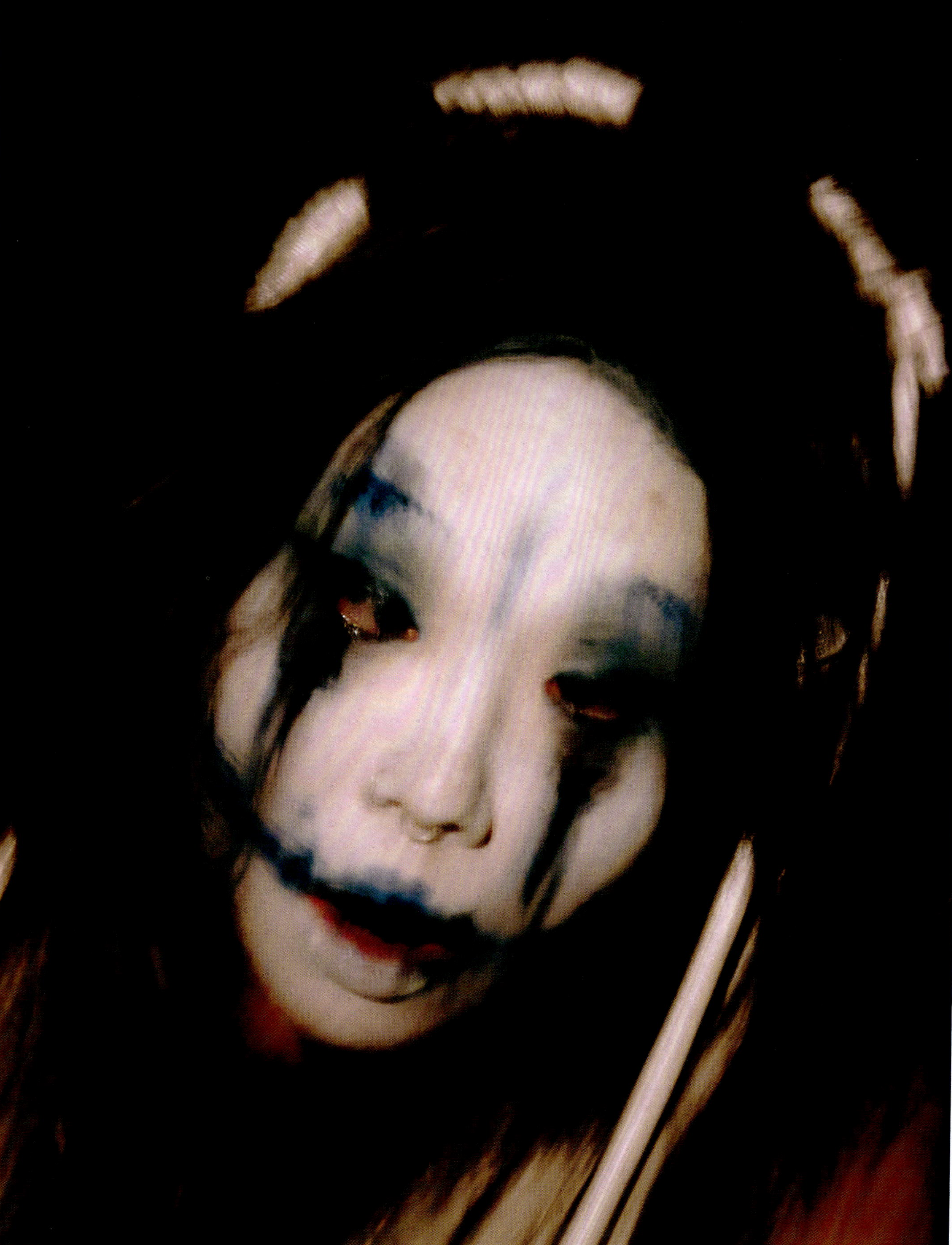

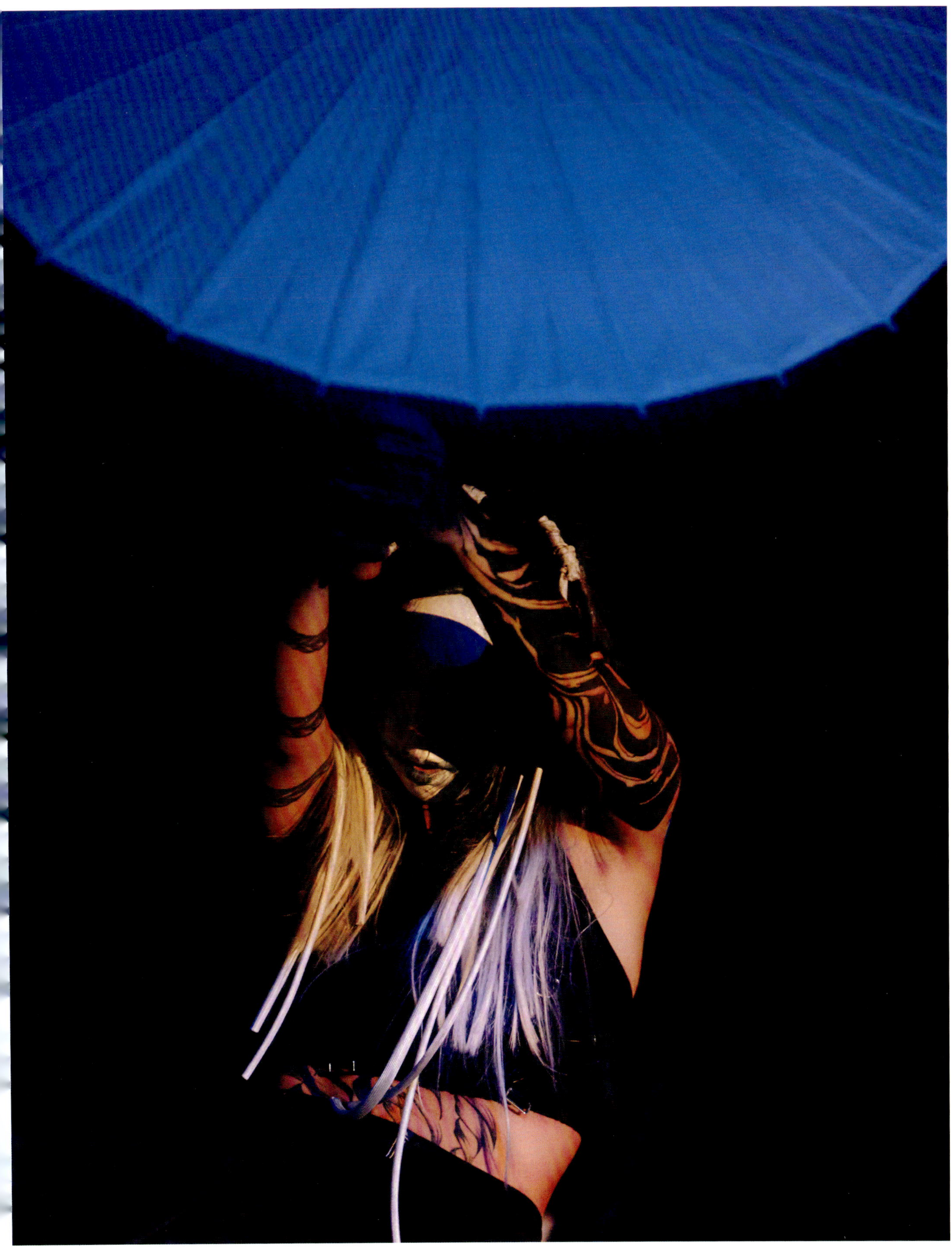

movements to the quality of "light slipping"—slow and steady—while others are wild spasms that evoke a community of insects scurrying out from under a rock, a metaphor for the revelation of difficult truths. The idea resonates with maxwell's own coming-out experience; the devout Mormon community where he was raised didn't easily accept his identity as a gay man.

"Butoh has an honest way of letting something come forward. It's never constructed. It's never really conceptualized, even. It's just something that's pure and raw that comes forward from the darkness of the body," maxwell says. "Queerness is the same way where it's like, 'These outer forms don't fit me. There's something else within me that doesn't fit in these boxes that have already been premade.'"

Some butoh teachers instruct their pupils to leave their identities behind when practicing—their sexuality, their race, everything they believe defines them—in pursuit of discovering something deeper, some universal truth, perhaps, that tethers them to the universe. Vangeline speculates that this might feel like a relief for dancers who often bear the weight of others' prejudice and preconceptions. Drag, with its transportive gender-irreverent magic, is also commonplace in butoh. Barrier, for example, slips into a drag king persona with a skin suit made from sheer tights and speckled with yarn to give her the appearance of having dramatically hairy legs. During her performance, a bulbous nylon testicle hanging between her thighs is stretched to extremes and swung in circles overhead.

When Xue dances, everything dissolves. They say that in the process of "emptying out" that their butoh practice demands, they occasionally meet other entities whom they later inhabit during performances. Gahara, an impish figure they describe as a "cosmic schoolgirl," was summoned onstage

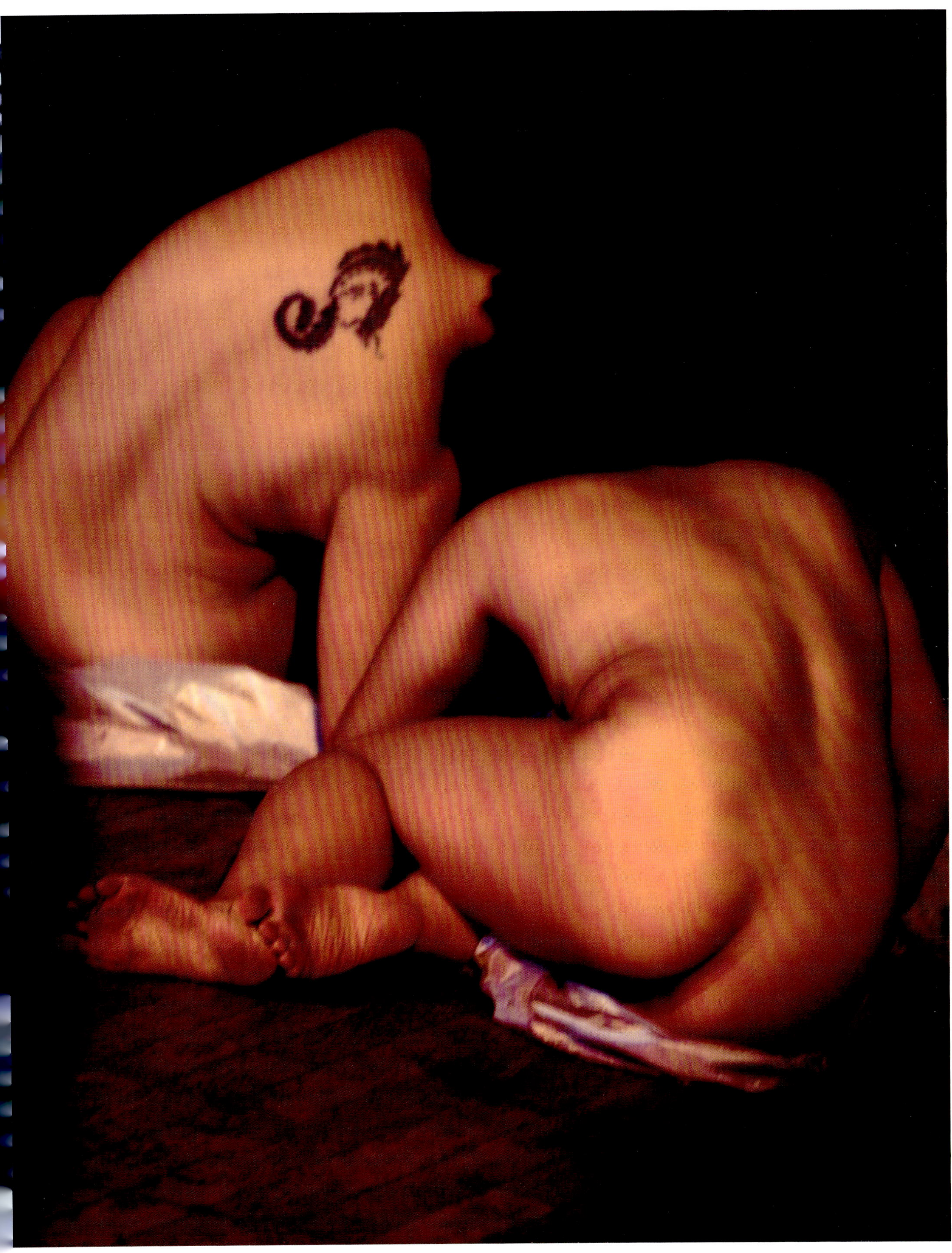

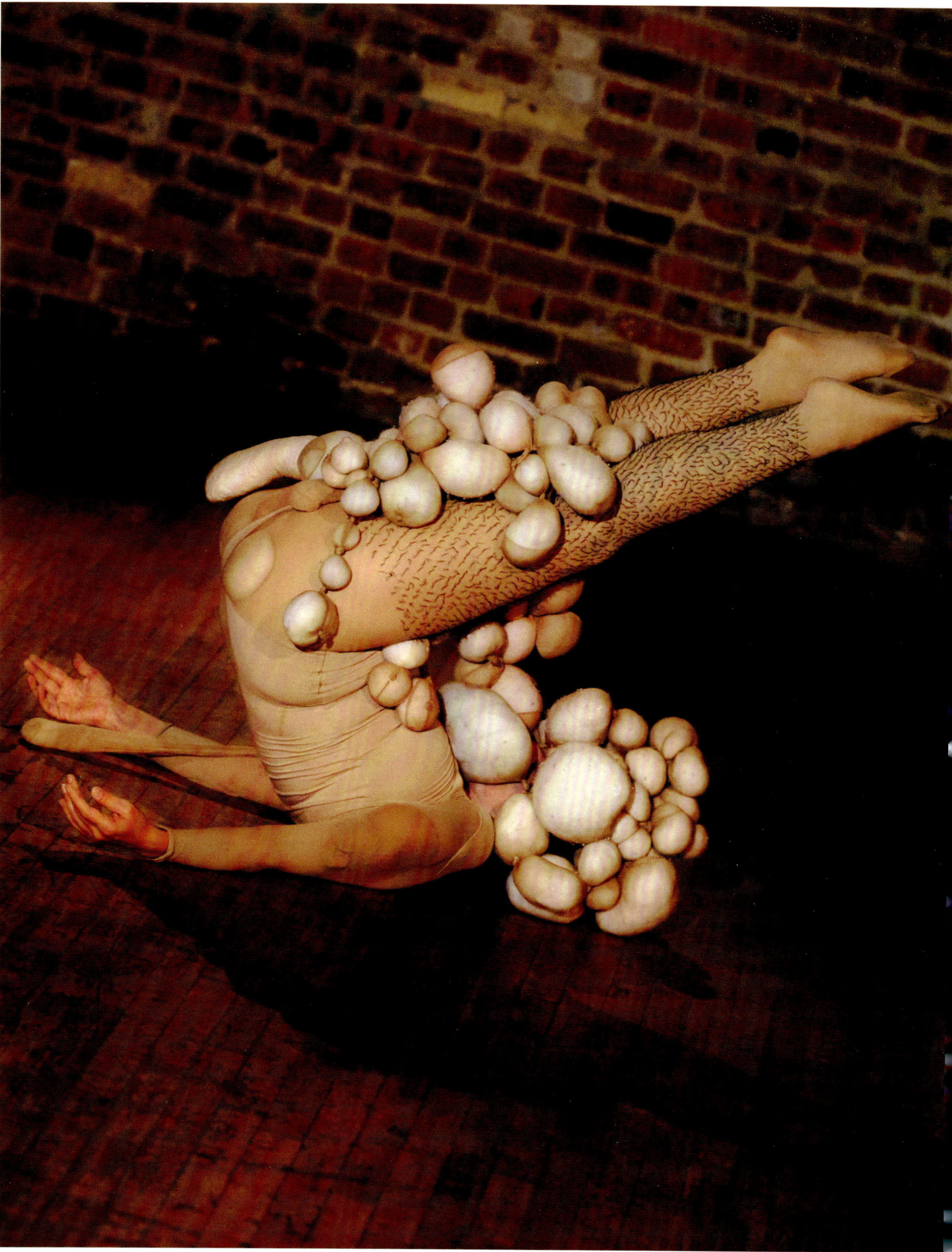

with frizzy black hair and her face painted white. Xue's performance was accompanied by the musician Merwin Wong, who only left his post behind an audioboard once to wander the space with an electric violin in hand. To this soundtrack, Xue rose, shuffling their feet. Their mouth grew into a wide-open grin, a silent scream dotted with blacked-out teeth. As the sounds of thunder ricocheted from Wong's speakers, Xue's frame convulsed wildly—were they writhing in fear or quivering with childlike glee? The sensations, one gathered, can be difficult to detangle.

Xue mostly improvises their movements so that each resulting performance is unique. Their style is "activated in real time and space" and subject to present-day conditions. They teach workshops at an arts space called the Glass Hut in Singapore, which they describe as a "techno-capitalist city" where everything is "built to have a reason and a purpose." When they were growing up there, and when they recently returned, speckled with tattoos after years spent living abroad, they felt that their difference was not always welcome. Now they help others to unlearn those expectations they feel are particularly present in their culture. "When I first started doing butoh, I would describe it as unscripting the socialized body—rewriting a lot of these codes and modes of understanding that we've inhabited," they explain.

Though the approaches to butoh highlighted at the Brick differed greatly, each dancer emphasized the art form as a meditative space for honest exploration and discovery. Xue suggests that the darkness of butoh is less about evoking fear or horror and more akin to the nothingness you encounter when you close your eyes, an immersive empty oblivion where everything is possible. "That's the magic of butoh, that it allows you to dream," they say. "I think that's what queerness is as well: tapping into this other sort of state, this sense of shifting and being able to transform infinitely."

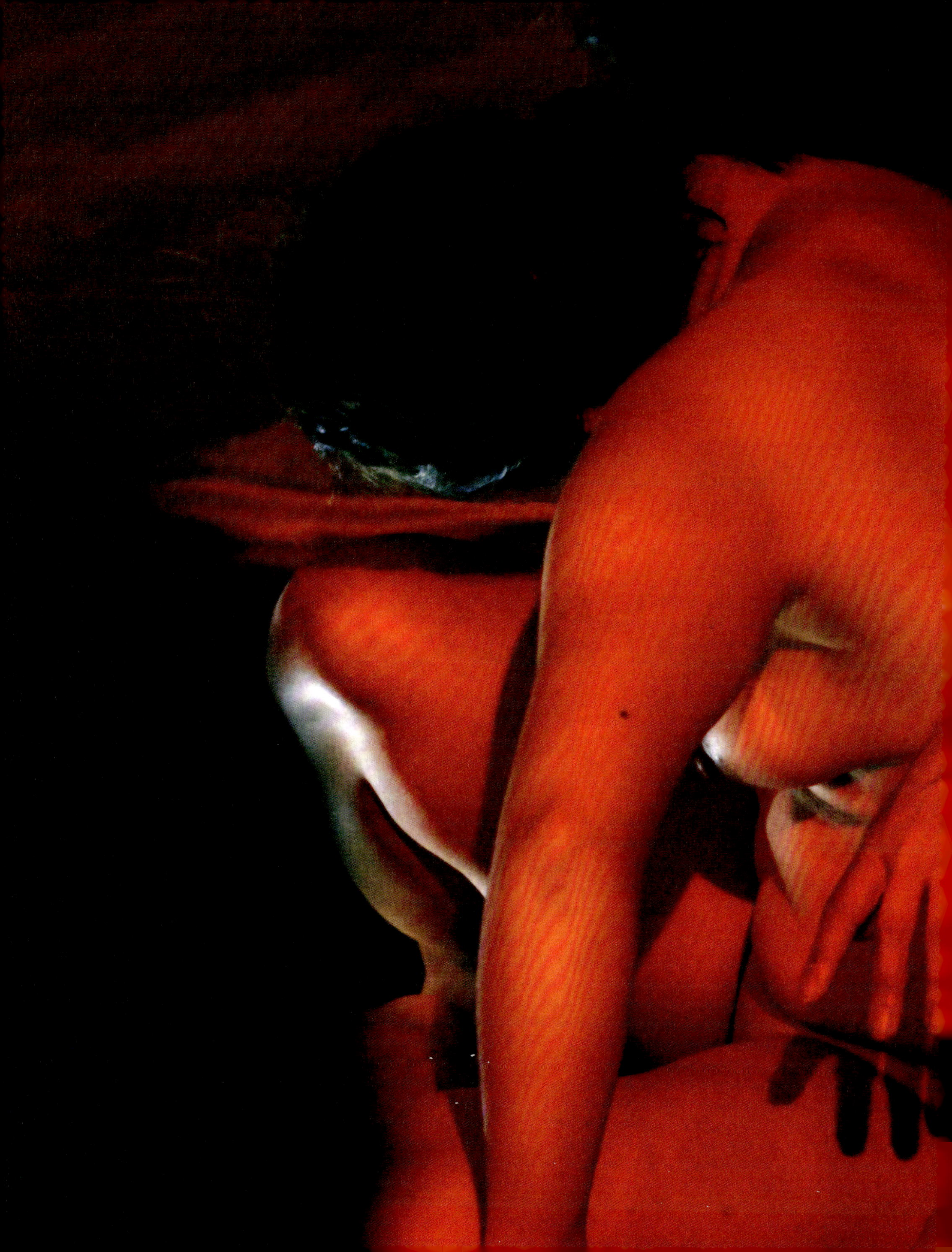

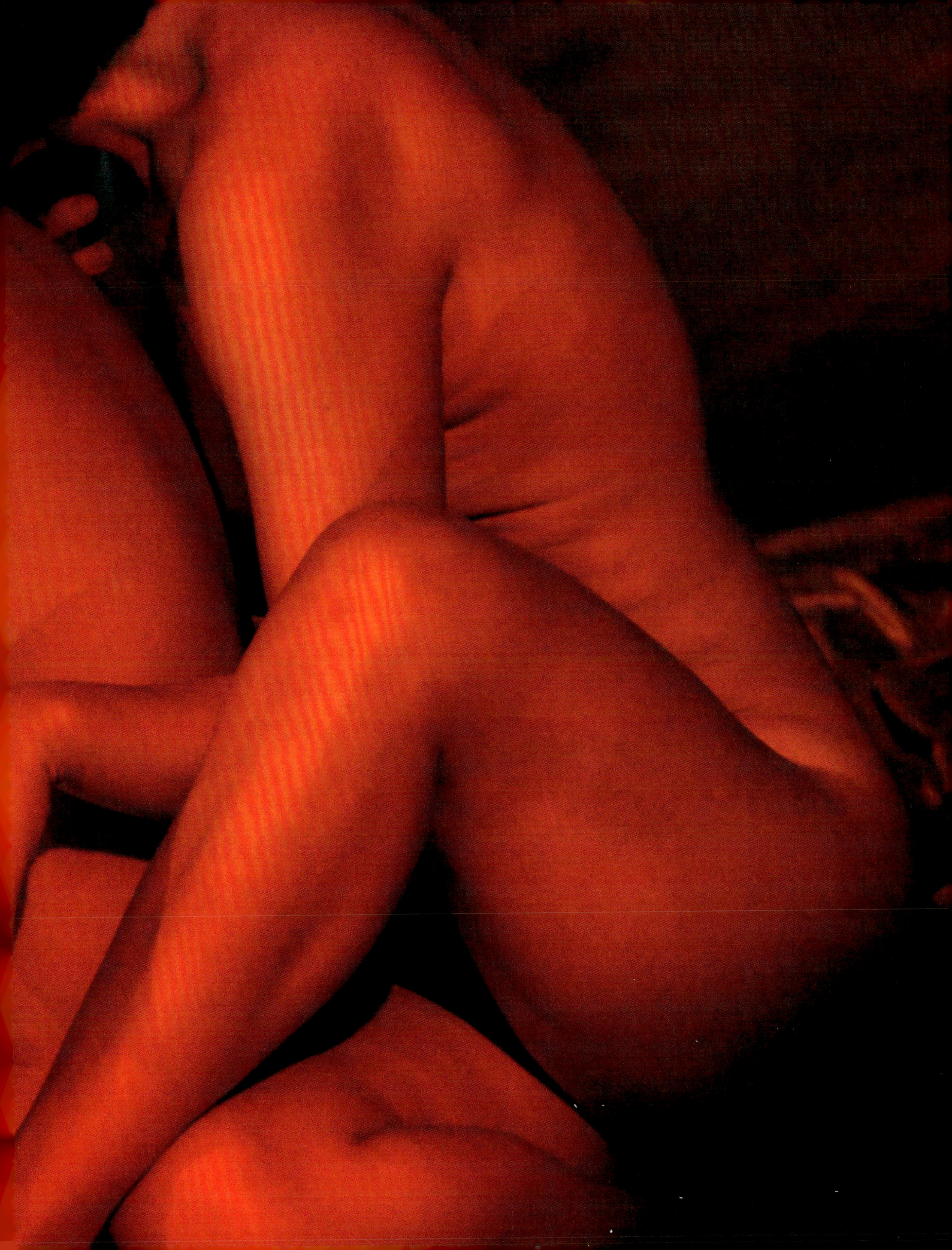

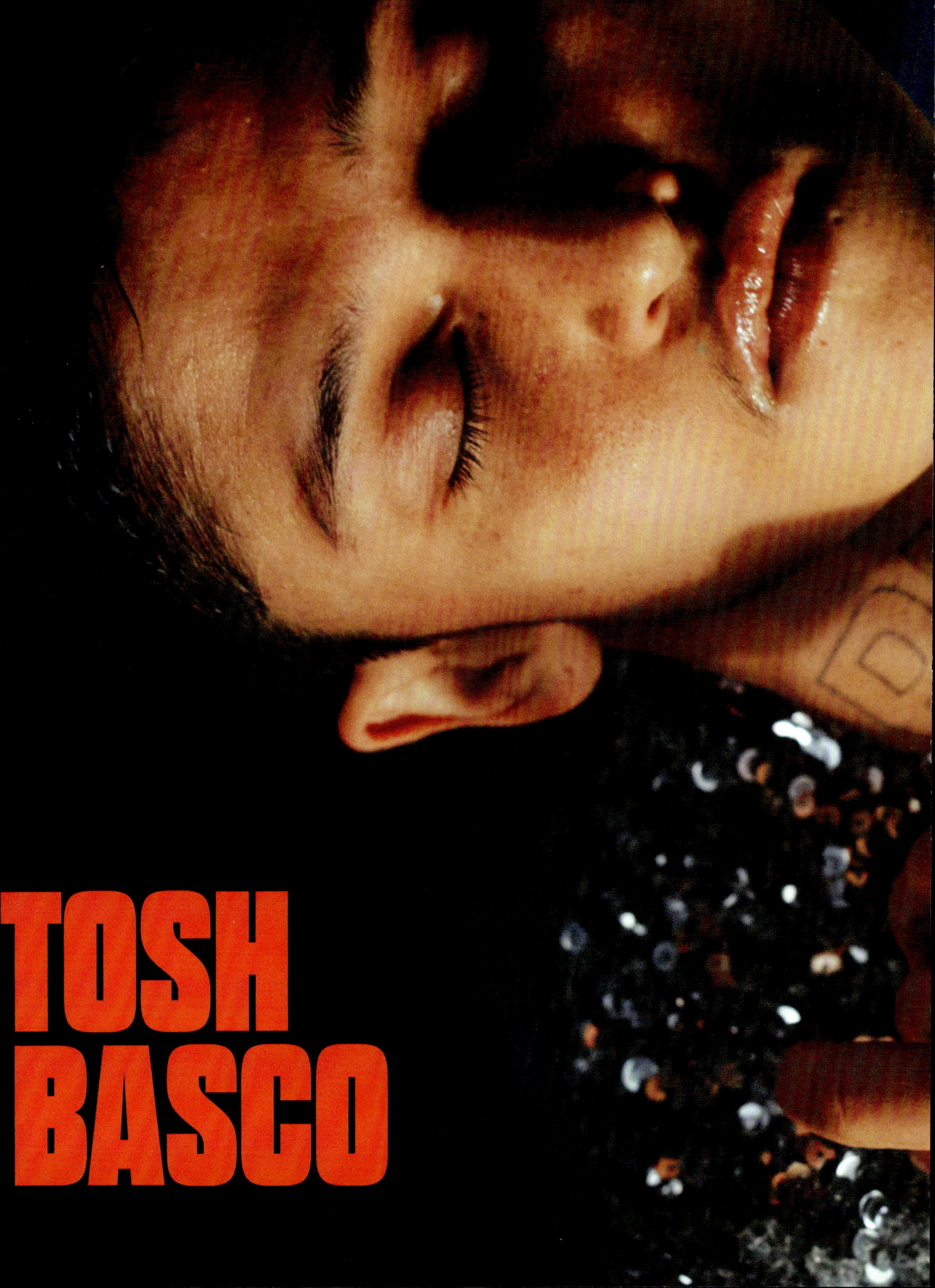

TOSH BASCO

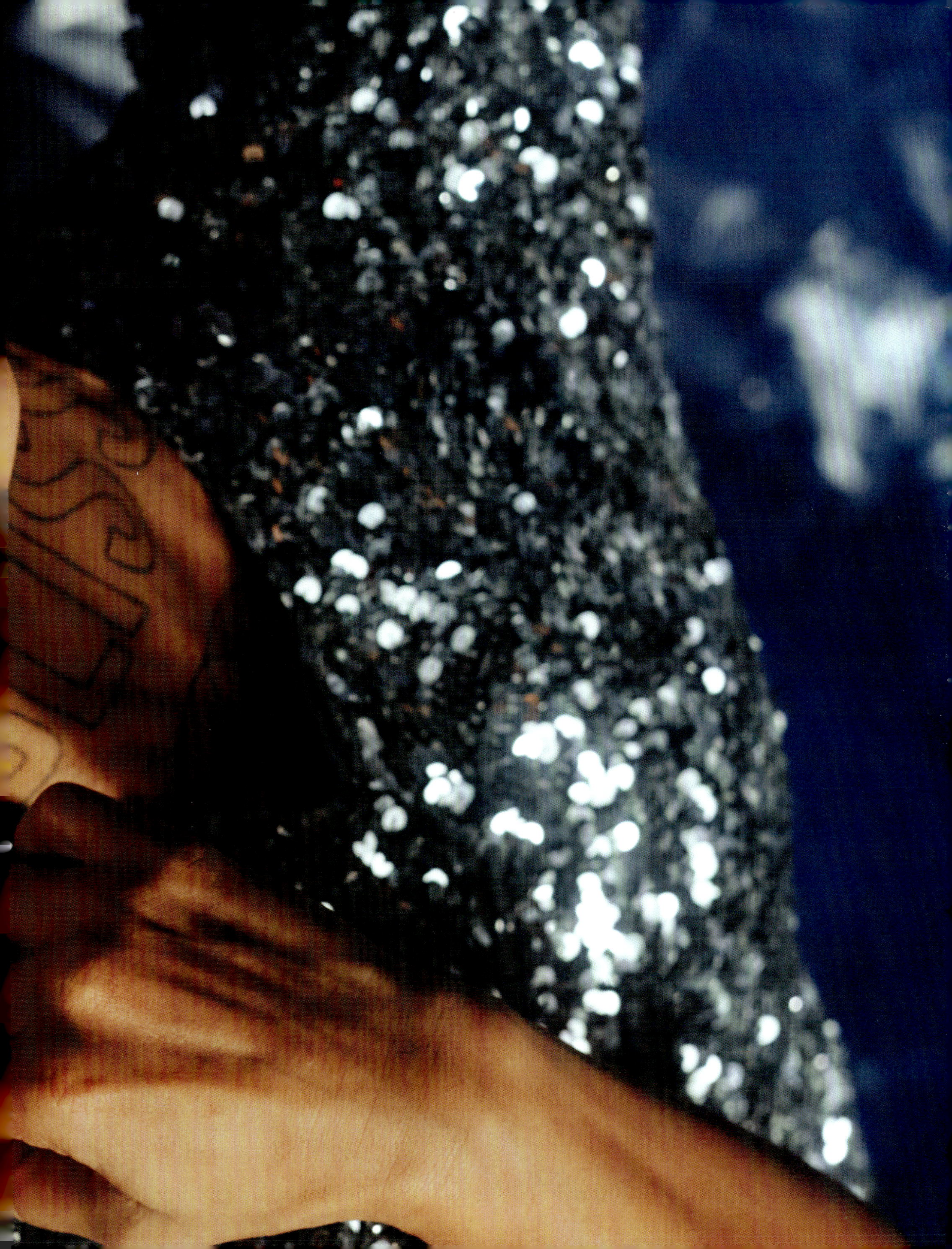

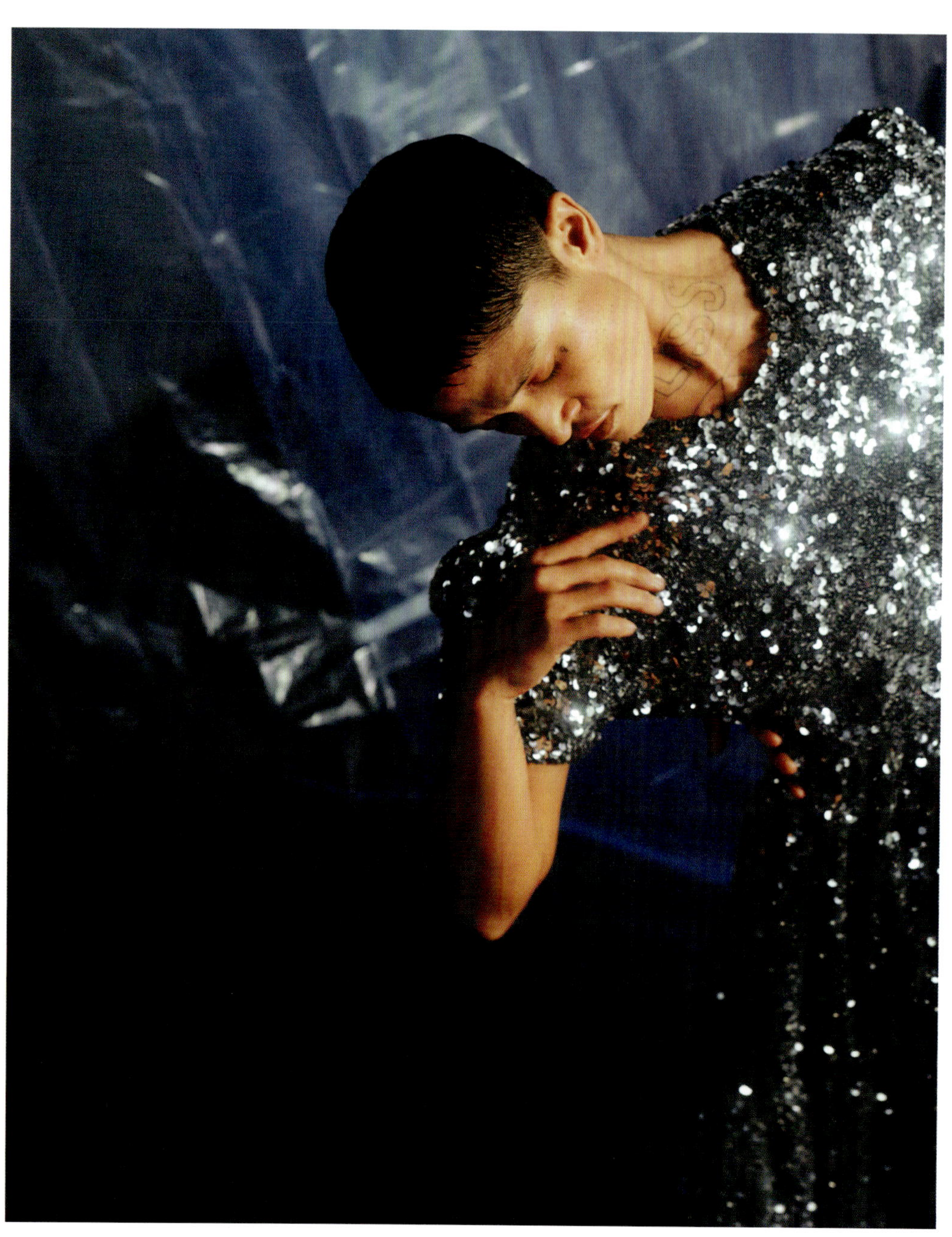

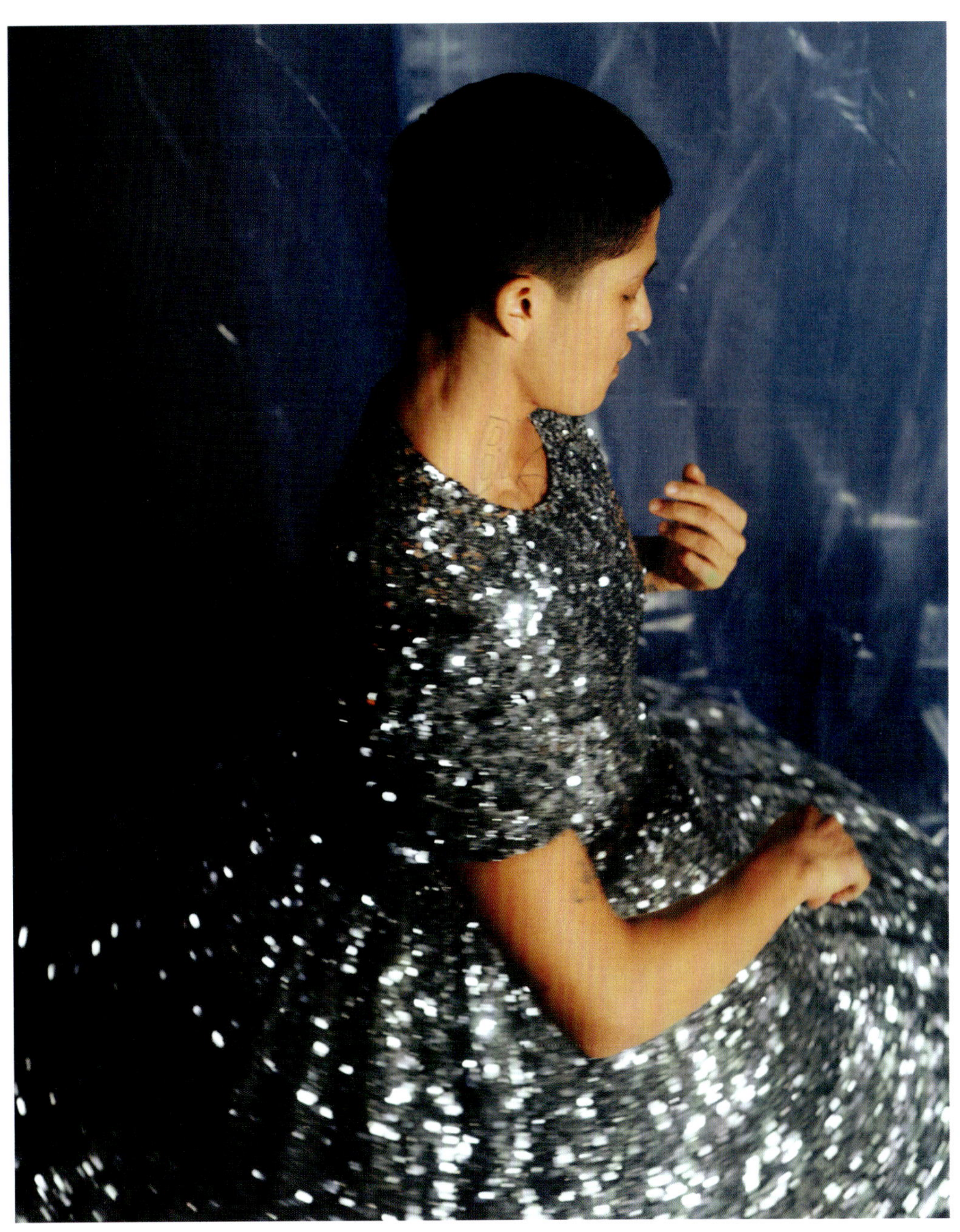

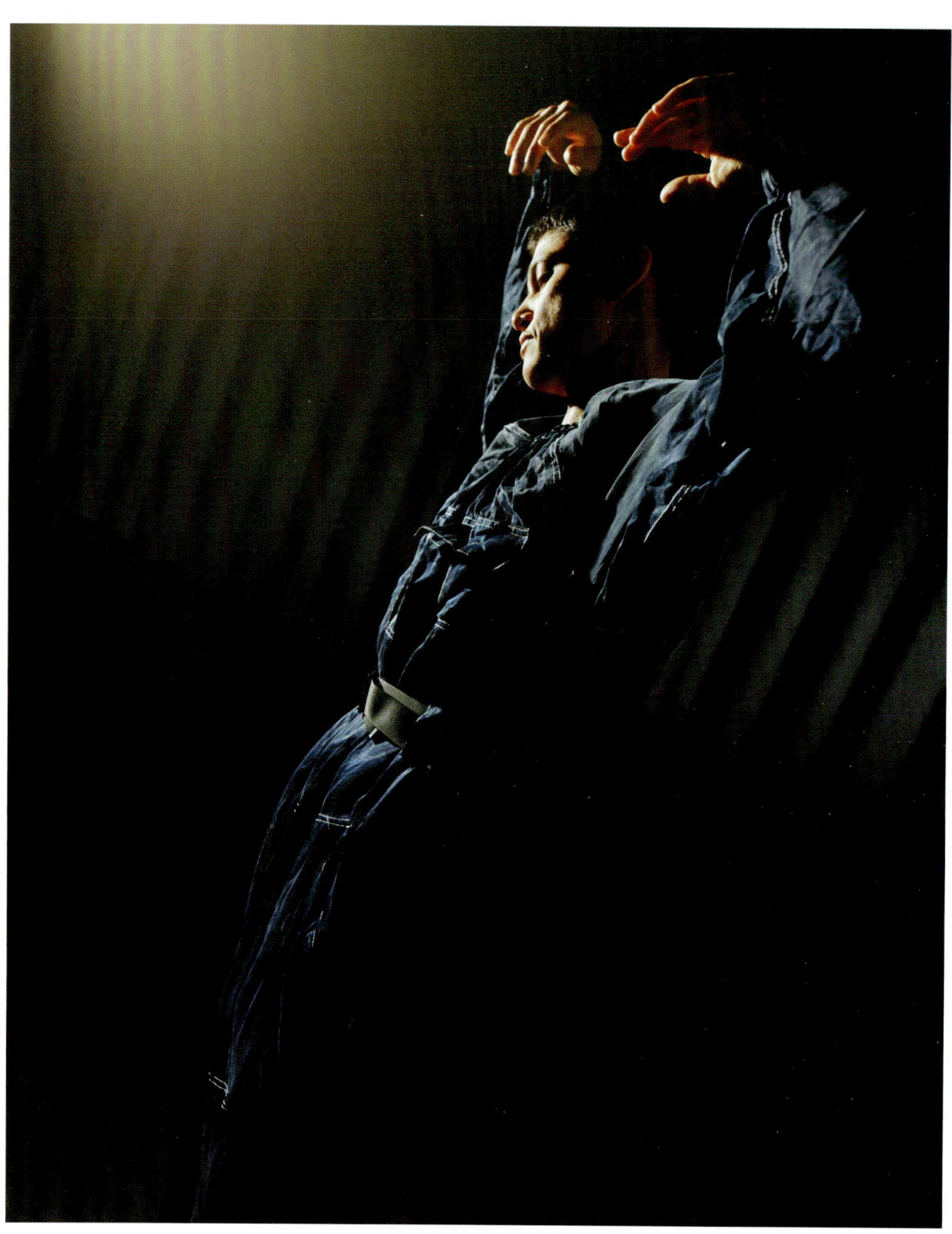

WHEN TOSH BASCO WAS INVITED TO PERFORM AT THE VENICE Biennale for the first time in spring 2019—a career high for an artist in any medium—she turned away from the grand, white-walled galleries with their constructed sense of neutrality. Instead, she decided to debut her piece *Untitled Hand Dance* on a platform erected atop a grassy knoll in the Giardini park. There, the performance would be at the mercy of its surroundings. She wore a simple black pantsuit and a white button-down shirt. There was no soundtrack for her movements, just silence cut with the whispers of birds nesting in trees above. When, on one day of the festival, it began to rain, she continued to dance through the drops.

Three years later, in November 2022, Basco attempts to recreate fragments of this and other recent performances in a small black-box studio inside the Schiffbau outpost of Schauspielhaus Zürich. She's been an artist in residence here since 2019, as part of Moved by the Motion, the interdisciplinary ensemble she formed with her creative partner, the film-maker and visual artist Wu Tsang. For our photoshoot, Basco puts on the same black suit, dancing once again in near silence, though rather than the sweet chatter of birdsong, there is the frantic clicking of a camera's shutter. Her palms are flattened and pushed outward, as if defending her core against a great invisible force. Then she knots her arms behind her back, her fingers fluttering, before unwinding them into a flurry of harsh jabs.

This performance—particularly the simple outfit—is a reference to a piece by Kazuo Ohno, cofounder of butoh (for more on that art form, see the previous chapter). Ohno, in his ninth decade and partially immobilized, danced with his arms and upper body while seated in a chair. Much as the butoh master did, Basco sometimes communicates through furrowed brows and pained facial expressions, and like Ohno's, her movements are extracted from a deep, unseen place.

Basco's multidisciplinary and often collaborative practice is rooted in vulnerable performances that are largely improvised. No two dances will look the same; each is subject to the conditions of the present. Still, the exercise of attempting to recreate a previous performance points to the nature of improvisation itself, which Basco sees as a "mode of survival." She developed this philosophy based on the writing of the scholar Danielle Goldman, author of *I Want to Be Ready: Improvised Dance as a Practice of Freedom*. To improvise is to respond in hostile environments and within constraints, one framework for struggling against power.

"I don't have control over how people encounter me. They're going to see what they see. I can dress more formally rather than in sweatpants or something, but at this point, I can't hide my brownness, I can't hide my transness," she says. "Being forced to encounter how people want to see me in their desire and their violence, to me, that's how improvisation carries out into the world."

Improvisation has given Basco the tools to navigate an astounding variety of venues and interactions, from the airy halls of the Museum of Contemporary Art in Los Angeles to the cavernous belly of the techno-fueled nightclub Berghain, a former heating plant located in Berlin's Kreuzberg neighborhood. She's toured with the rapper Mykki Blanco and collaborated with the cult-favorite street-wear label Hood By Air. And in November 2022, Moved by the Motion's surreal stage production of *Pinocchio*, for which Basco contributed movement direction and starred in the title role, premiered at Schauspielhaus Zürich before an enraptured audience of local children. As the show closed, some kids stood up to dance while others swayed elatedly in their seats.

***

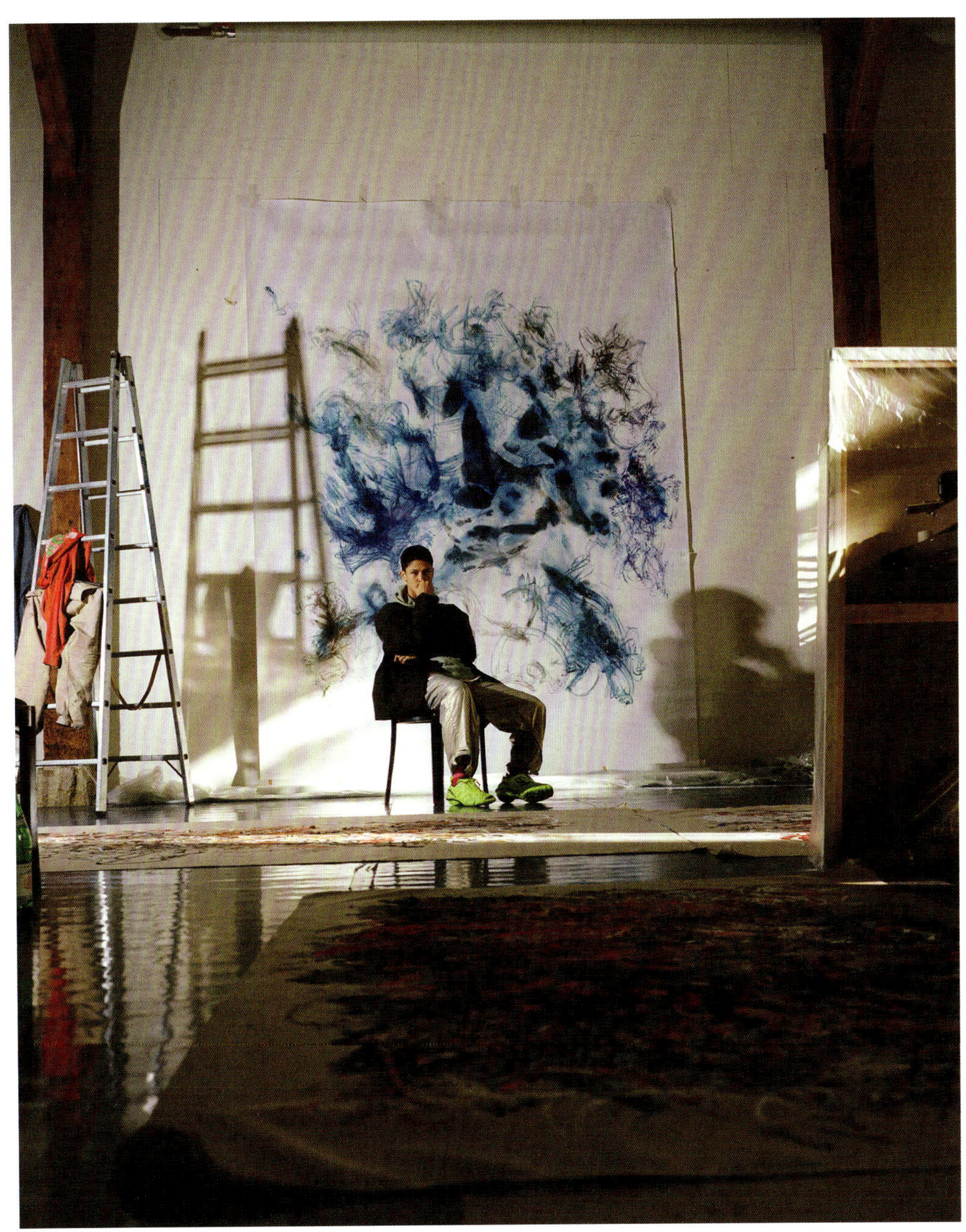

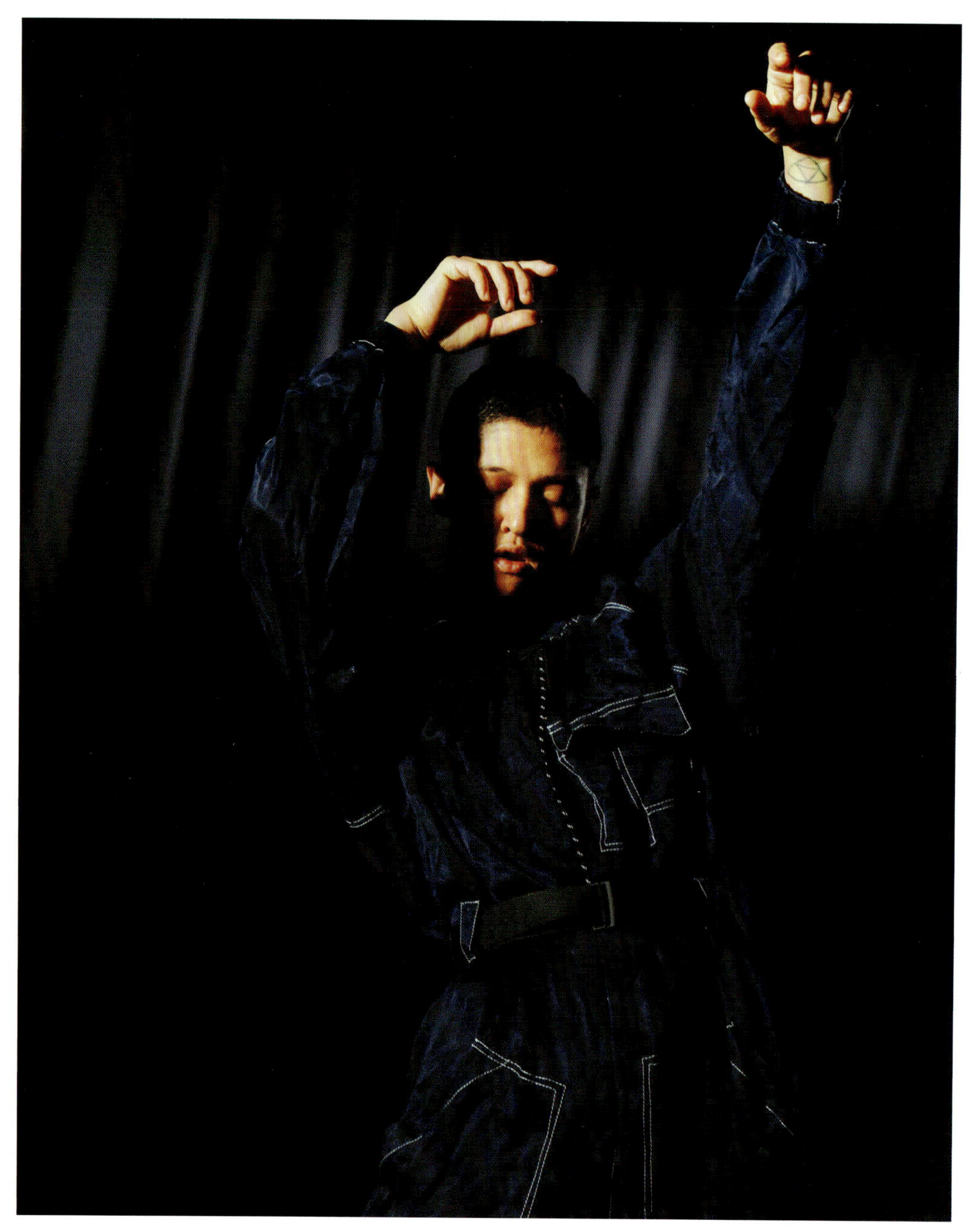

Much of the way Basco thinks about performance today can be traced back to the nightlife of San Francisco, where she grew up and staged the early pieces that would establish her name. As a young trans and Filipino person, immersing herself in the city's queer underground became a vital lifeline, "a way of finding my people," she says. She had recently dropped out of college when she was invited by her friend, the dancer Justin F. Kennedy, to create and perform a character as part of his thesis. Though that piece never materialized, the invitation led to Basco lip-synching in drag for the first time at the erstwhile Stud bar. It was a way to test the waters when dancing before an audience still felt frightening. "In doing so, I found this insatiable feeling of clarity," she says. "It caught fire in me. It ignited something that I was otherwise unable to touch."

In place of a formal dance training, drag became Basco's lineage. She would often appear in clubs with her chest bared and painted with white circles, or drenched from head to toe in sparkling gold glitter, and perform shamanistic lip syncs over house remixes of Rihanna or Destiny's Child. Sometimes the incessant flashing of an LED bulb would glow from behind her teeth as she mouthed a song's lyrics, an eerie trick that gave her the appearance of something beyond human, even robotic, and that she recently resurfaced for her turn as the fibbing puppet. She adopted the moniker boychild in the early 2010s, a name that encompassed her critical attitude toward gender as well as, perhaps, the potential for growth.

Though she no longer creates under that pseudonym, the lip sync remains a key prism through which she considers performance. As performed by drag artists in gay bars, lip-synching is a sacred art, a process of interpretation, not unlike translating a text from another language. Through the

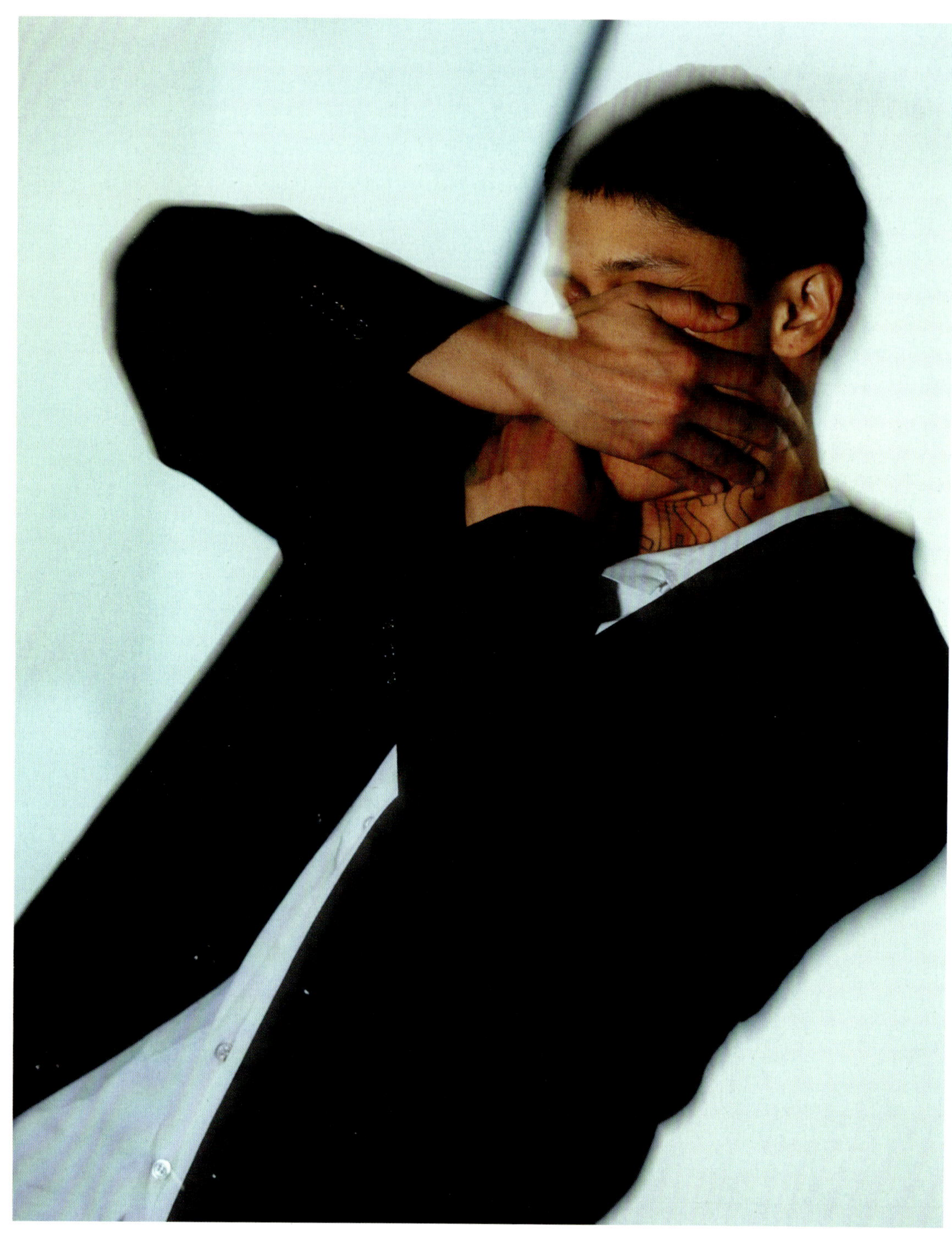

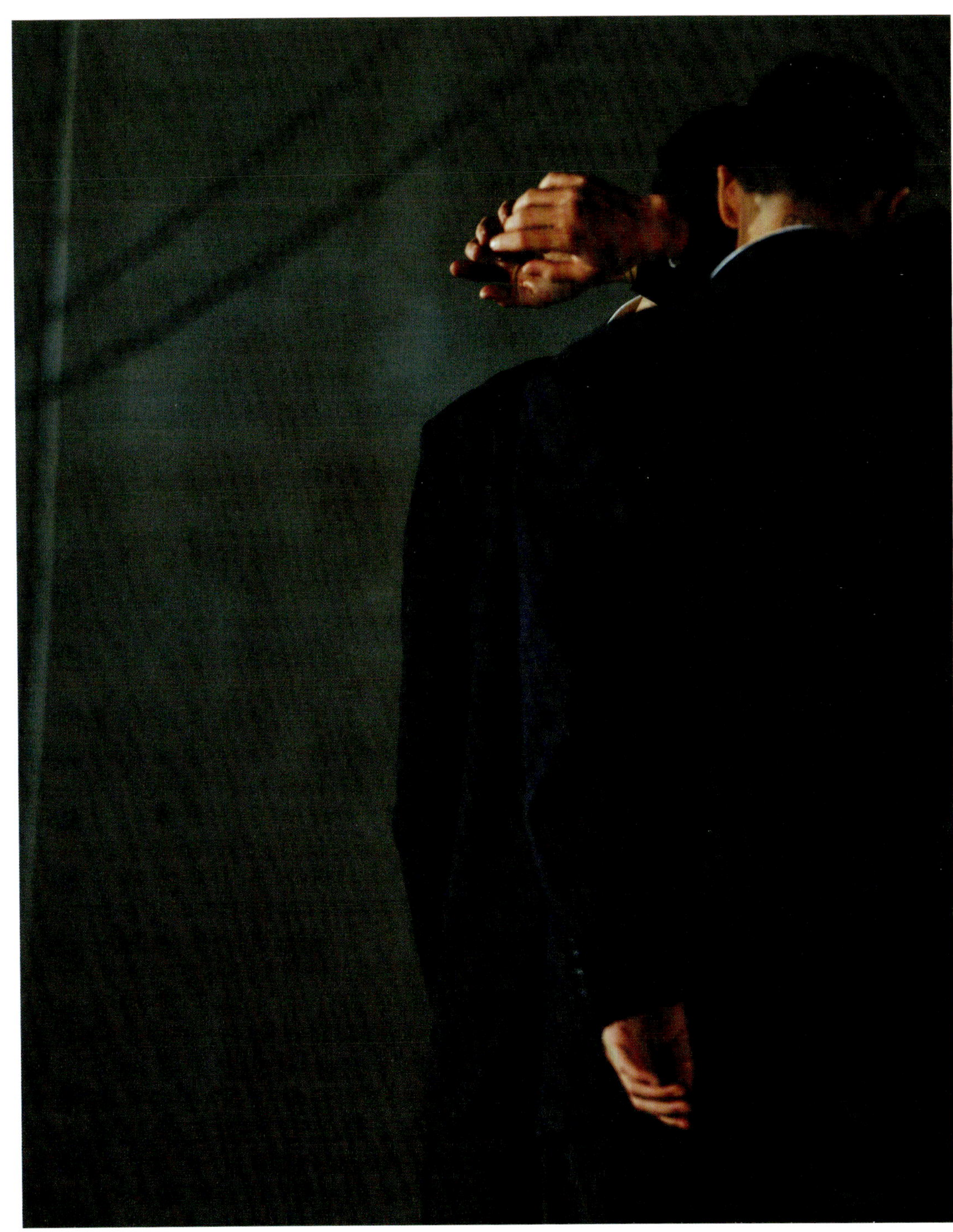

body's motions, a performer gives new meaning to a track's words and sounds. Today, rather than reinterpreting a pop song, Basco might employ lip sync to revisit an artwork or examine a collaborator's writing. *Untitled Duet (the storm called progress)*, a September 2022 performance at Berlin's sprawling exhibition hall Gropius Bau, took the Swiss-German artist Paul Klee's 1920 drawing *Angelus Novus* as its subject. Accompanied by the dancer Josh Johnson in a vast dark room, Basco was cast under a spotlight. Its glow pierced the sheer fabric of her gown, and the dance took her into an instinctual trancelike state.

In these moments, her thoughts tend to collapse away from any sense of linear time, into an internal void that Basco describes as being at once liberatingly empty and "very full."

"Like outer space," she probes, "is it empty or is it full?"

***

After years of touring from one nightclub or gallery to the next, Basco has appreciated the opportunity to settle in Zurich, at least for now, during Moved by the Motion's residency. When it's warm outside, she swims with the locals in the Limmat river. For a cooler autumn evening, she recommends a visit to Seebad Enge, a public sauna floating on the edge of a lake. For the first time, her schedule has been stable enough to make renting and maintaining a studio feel worth the cost, and she's found a one-level space with blue marley vinyl floors; it's housed within a former military stable. In that room, and out of this relative calm, her practice has been permitted to grow in exciting new directions.

A flood of morning light illuminates several paintings in progress that cover nearly every surface of Basco's studio. One work hanging against the wall is a torrent of blue pigment scribbled on white paper, stretching more than eleven feet on

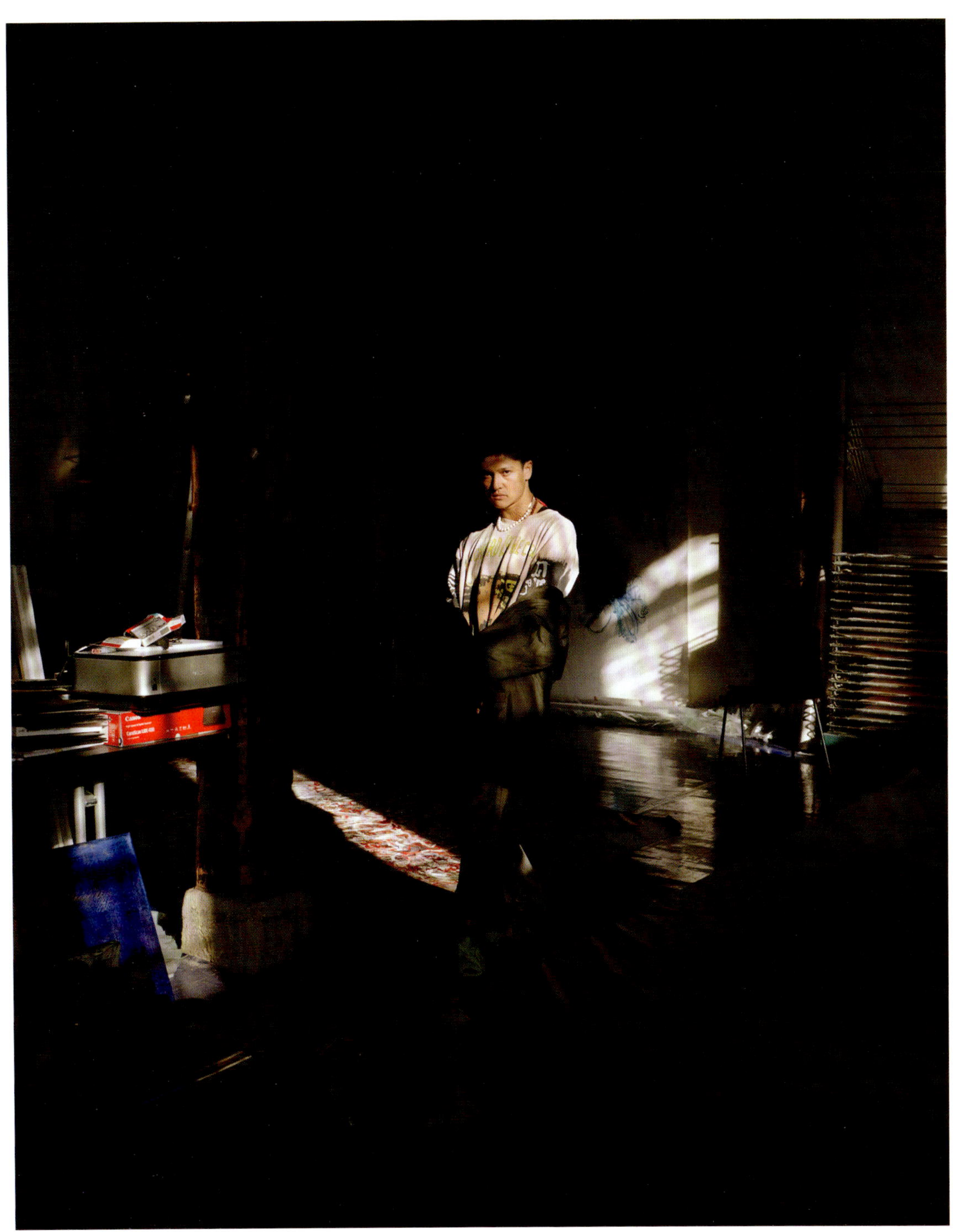

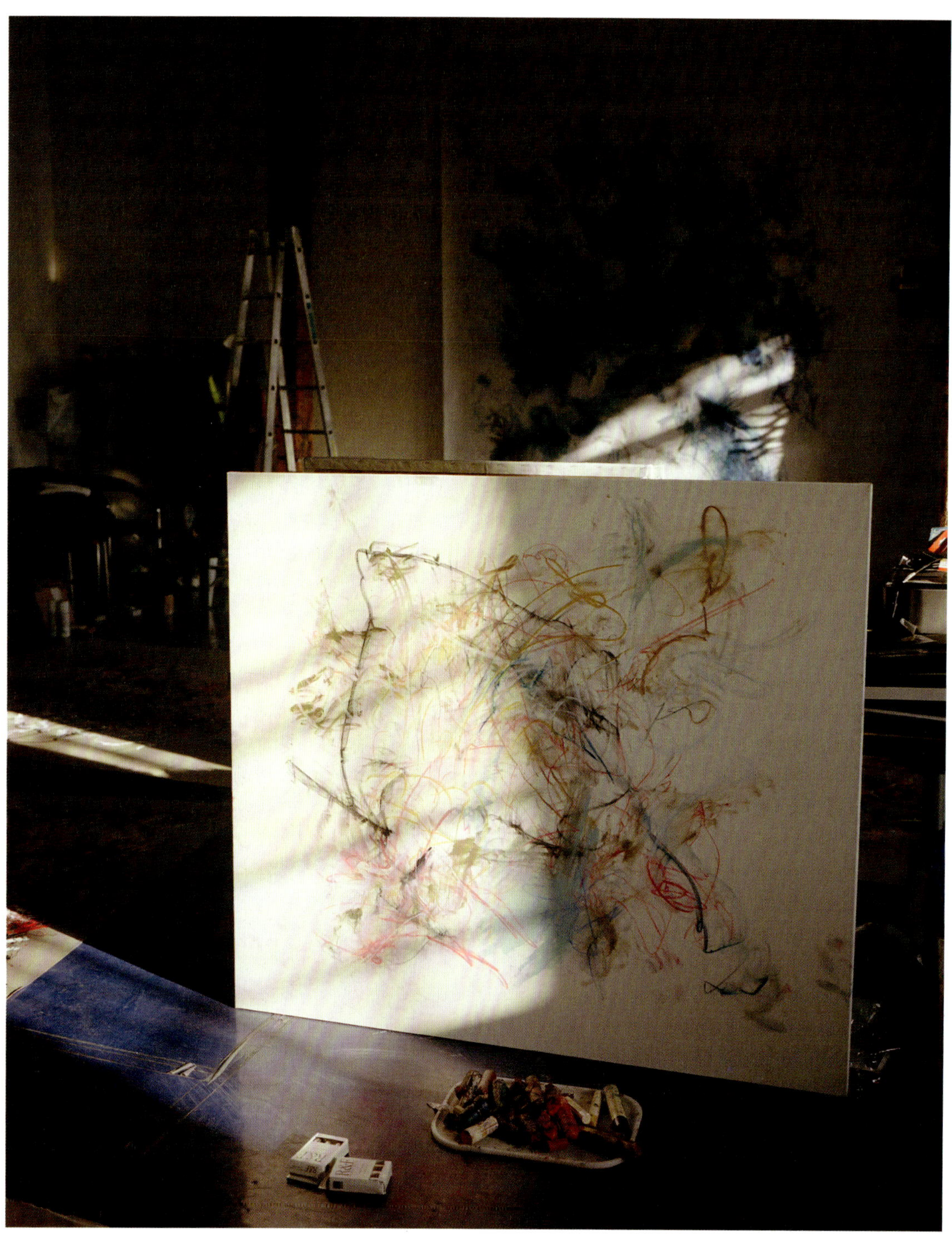

its longest side. Other pieces on canvas, sprawled across the floor, display layers of yellow, black, and red acrylic, with brambles of thin lines that congregate around hefty dollops of paint. She produces these paintings much like her performances, as improvisational reflections of her inner world.

"It's a way for me to transmit and transmute things that I'm thinking about that my brain literally cannot handle. It's something that thinking can't do in and of itself," she says. "The painting and the drawings are my own sense of catharsis, a way of expressing the performance."

Basco has often struggled with seeing photographs of her performances, feeling in photography the desire of capture. The most important thing she learned from performing in nightclubs, she says, "is to connect with the audience"—a rule to which she still adheres. Of the hundreds of live pieces she's staged over the years, many were never recorded, their potential to live on outweighed by the urgency of being present. She sees her paintings and drawings as a natural extension of her movement practice, an alternative form of documentation in which the dance lives past the moment of performance, its energy still visible once the body has gone.

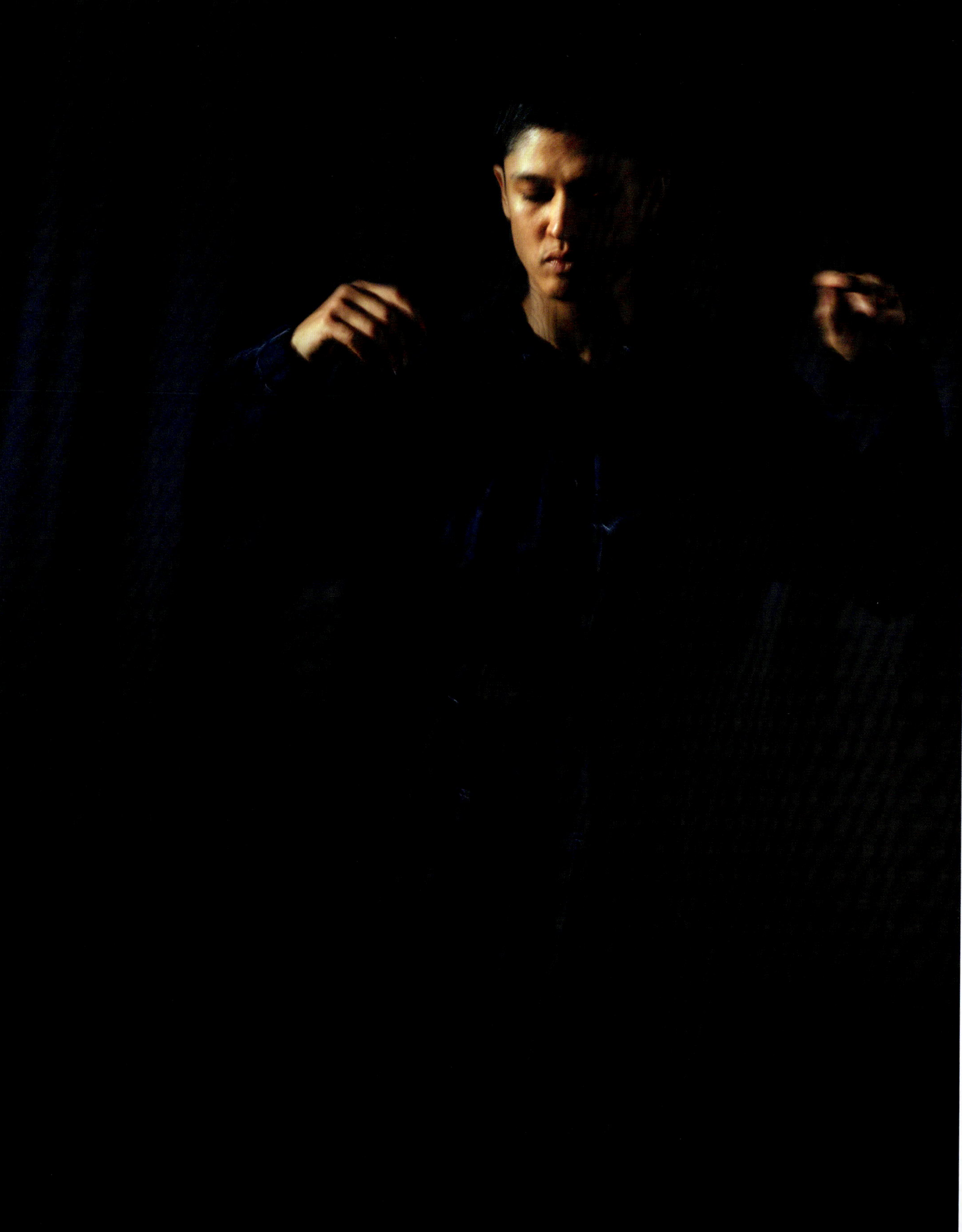

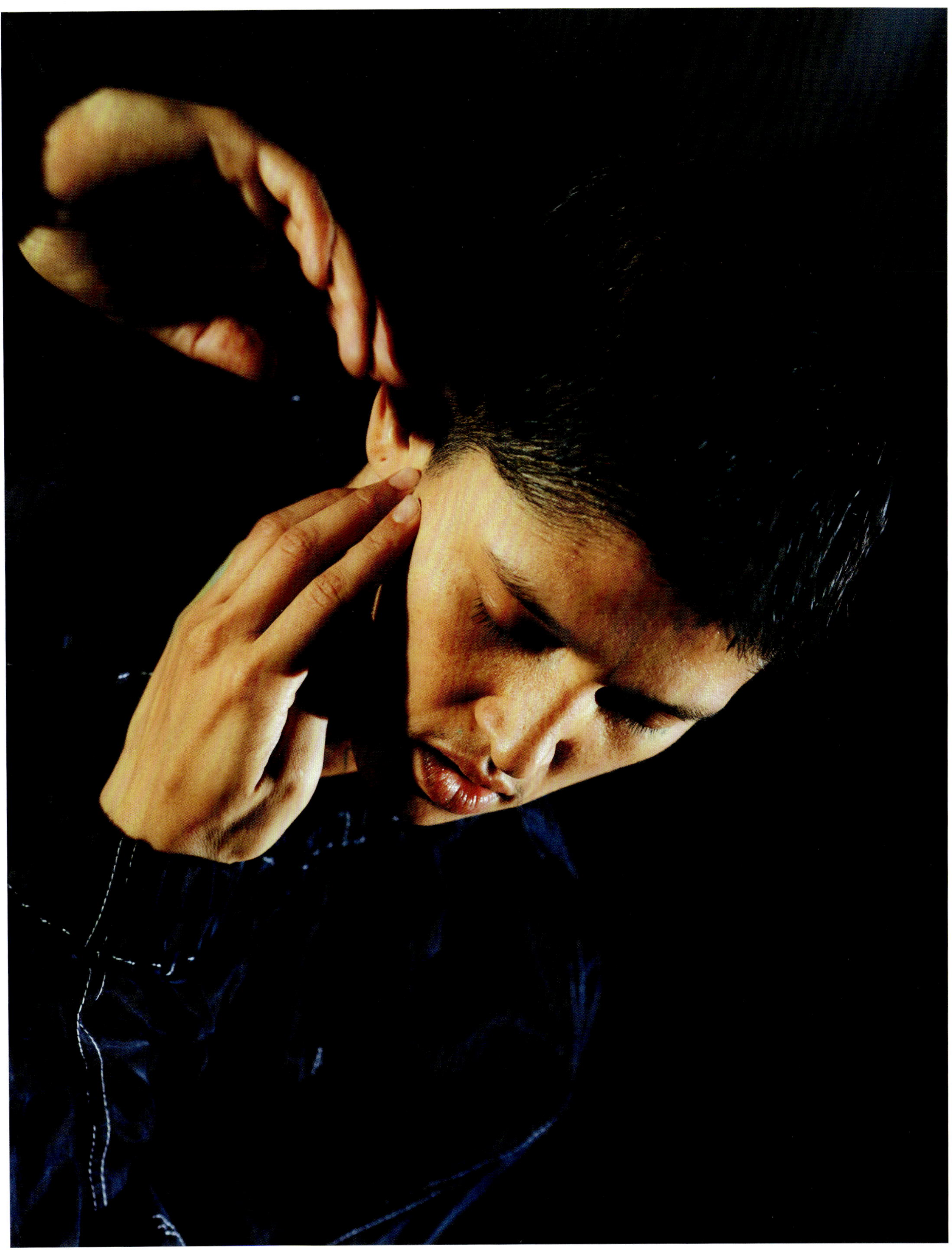

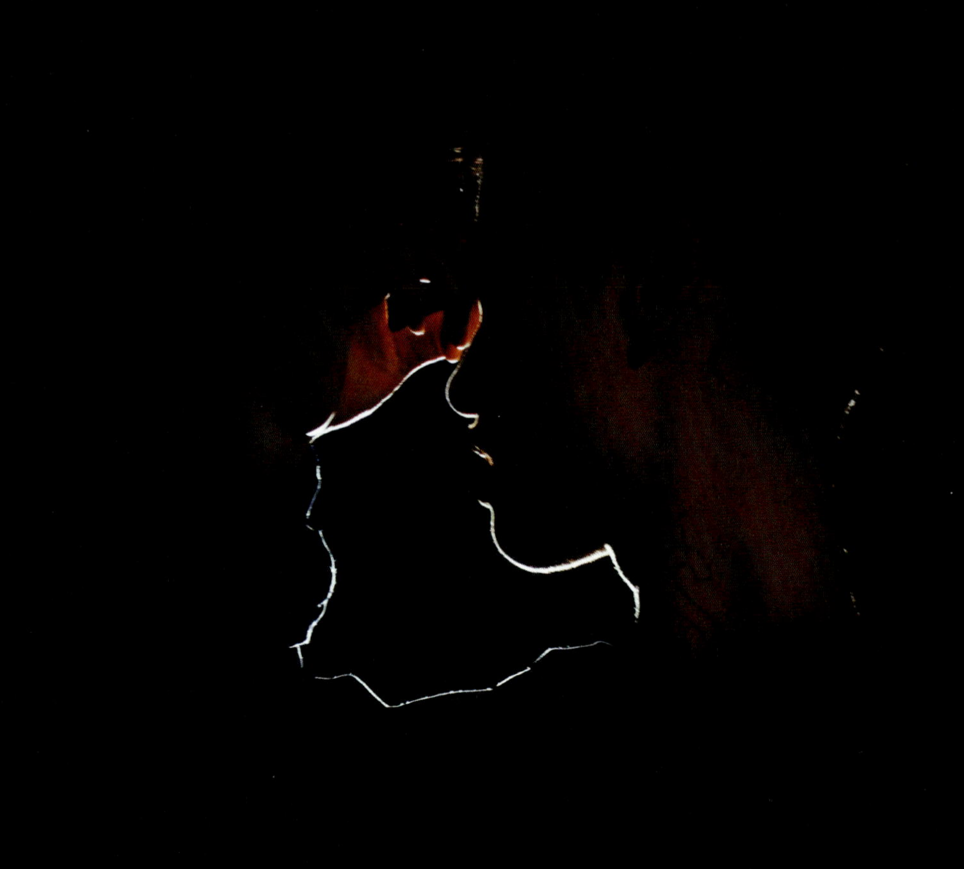

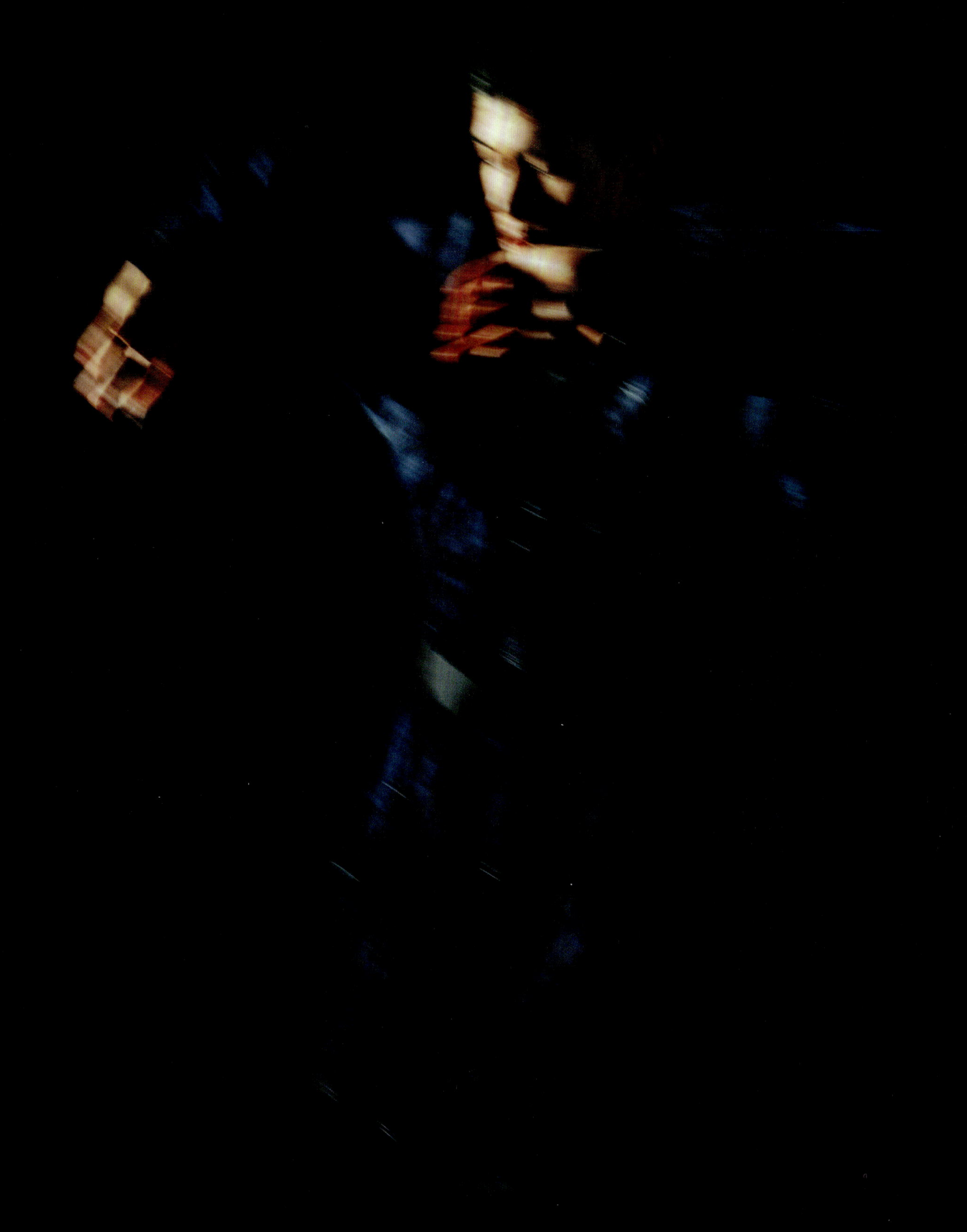

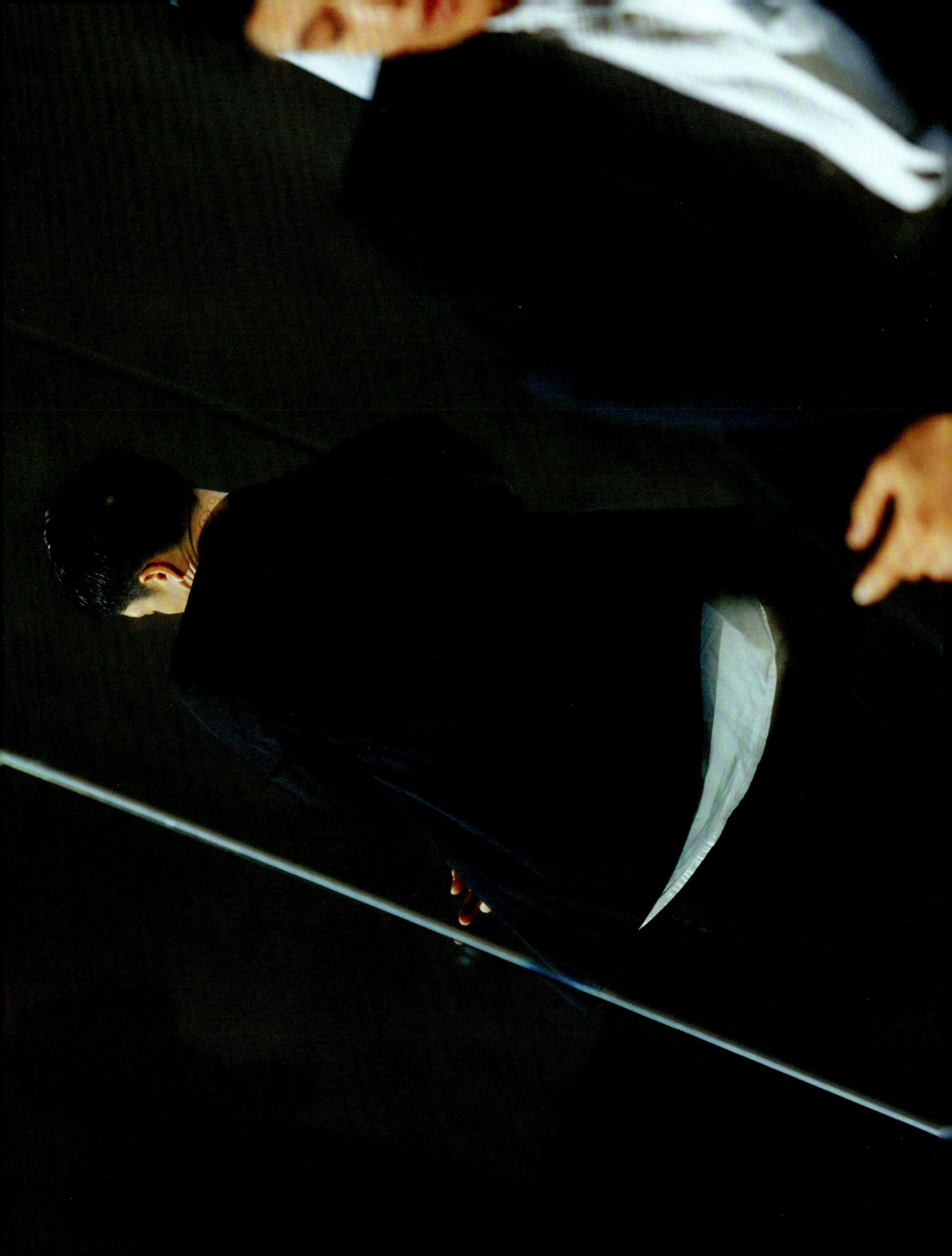

COMPAÑIA MANUEL LIÑÁN

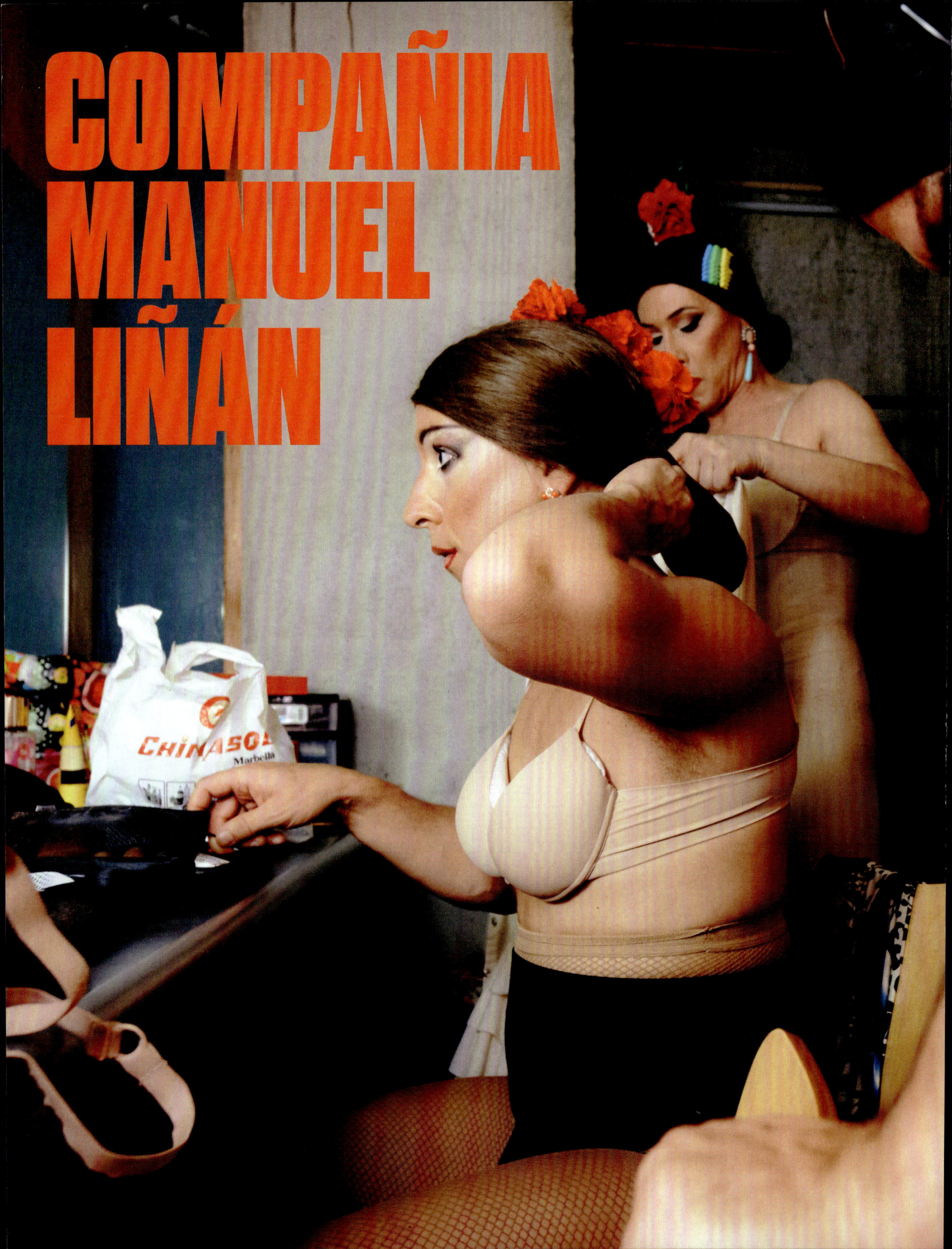

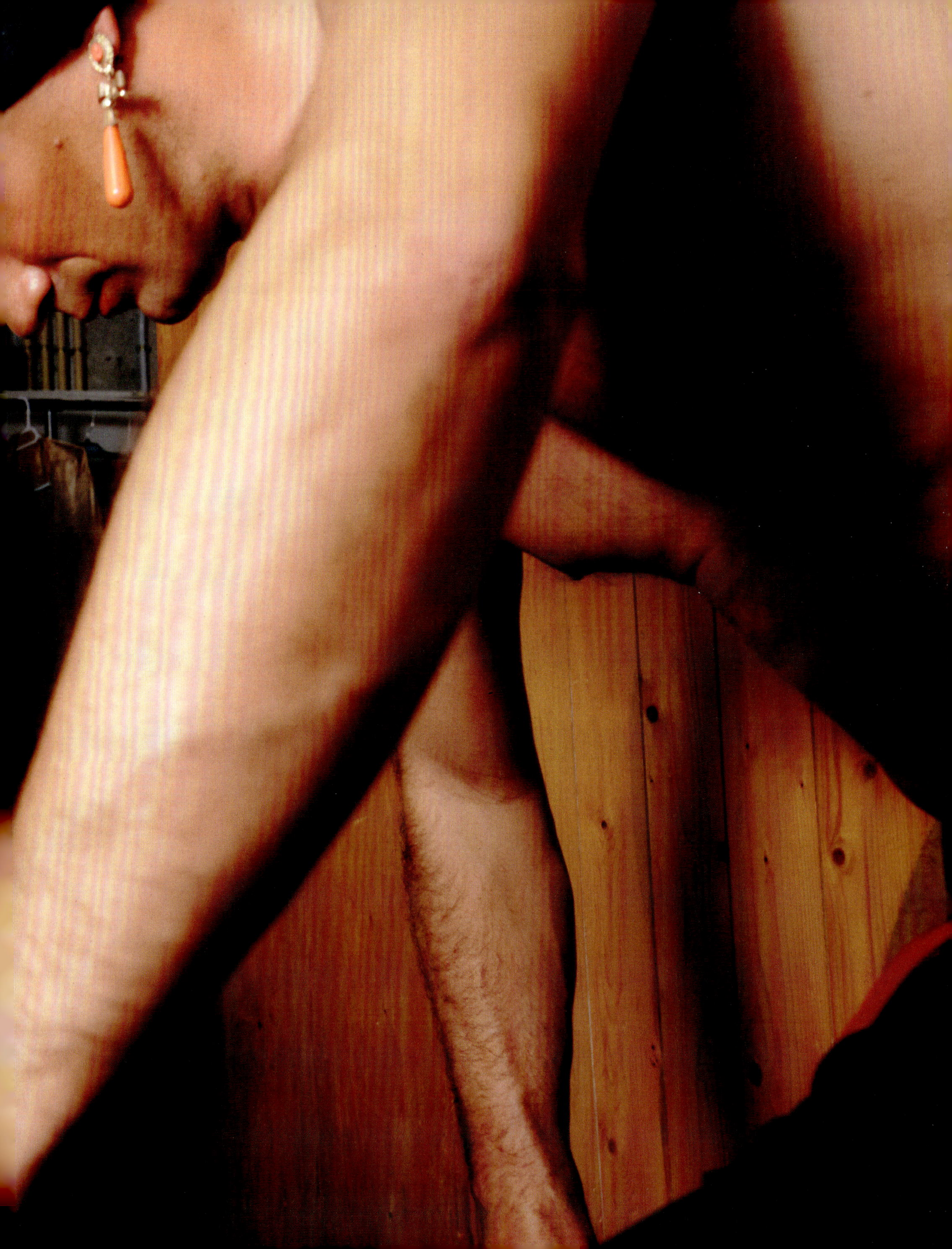

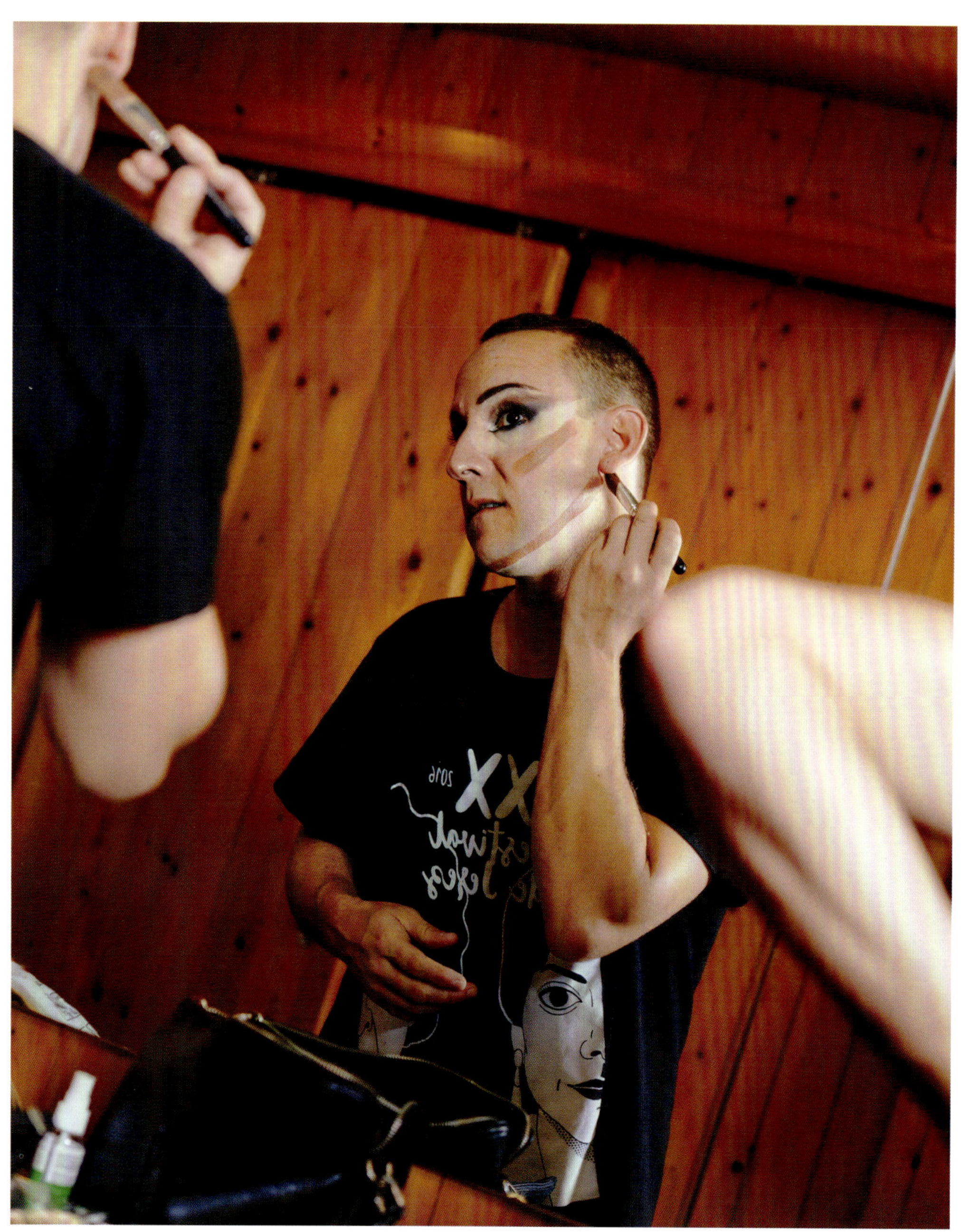

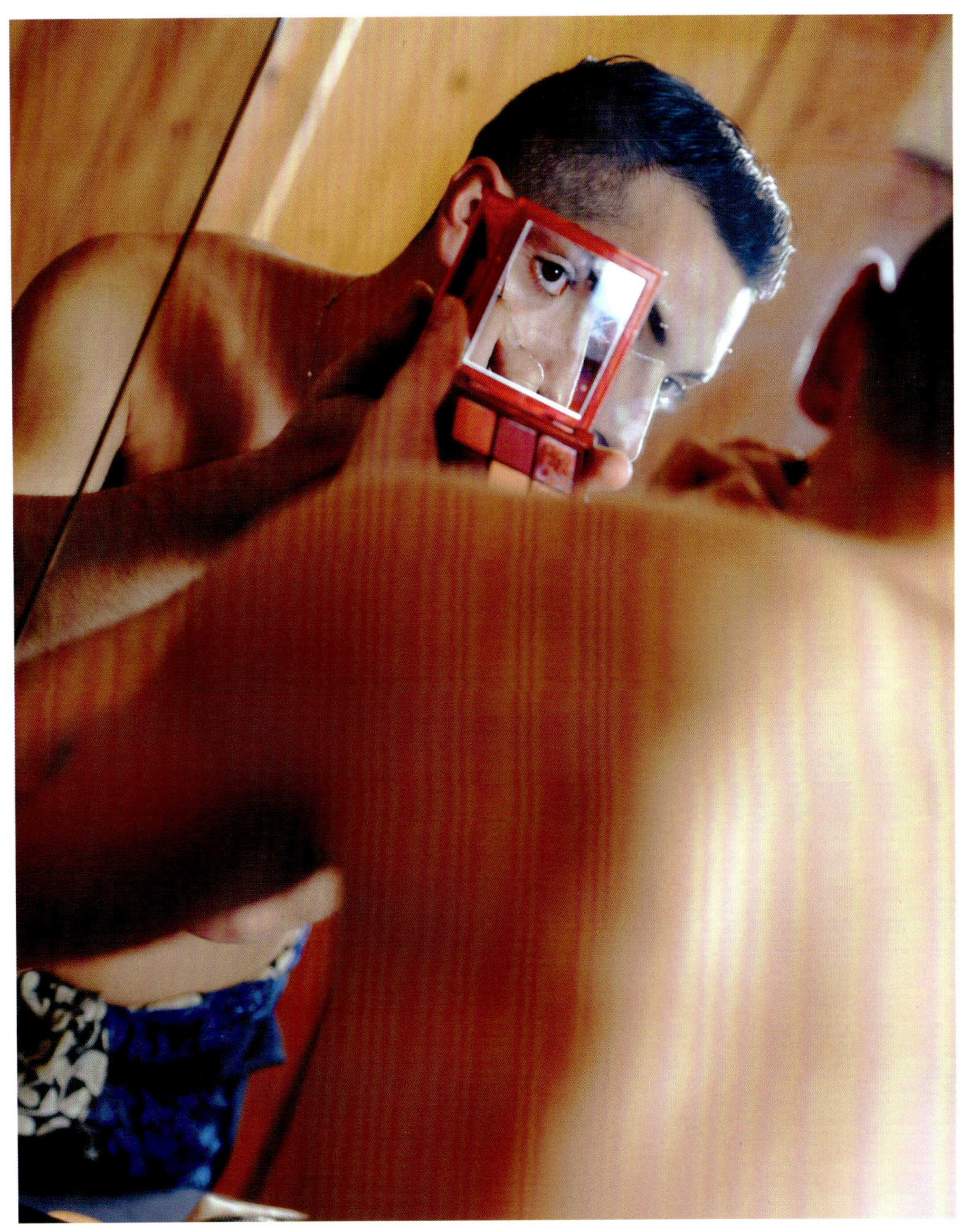

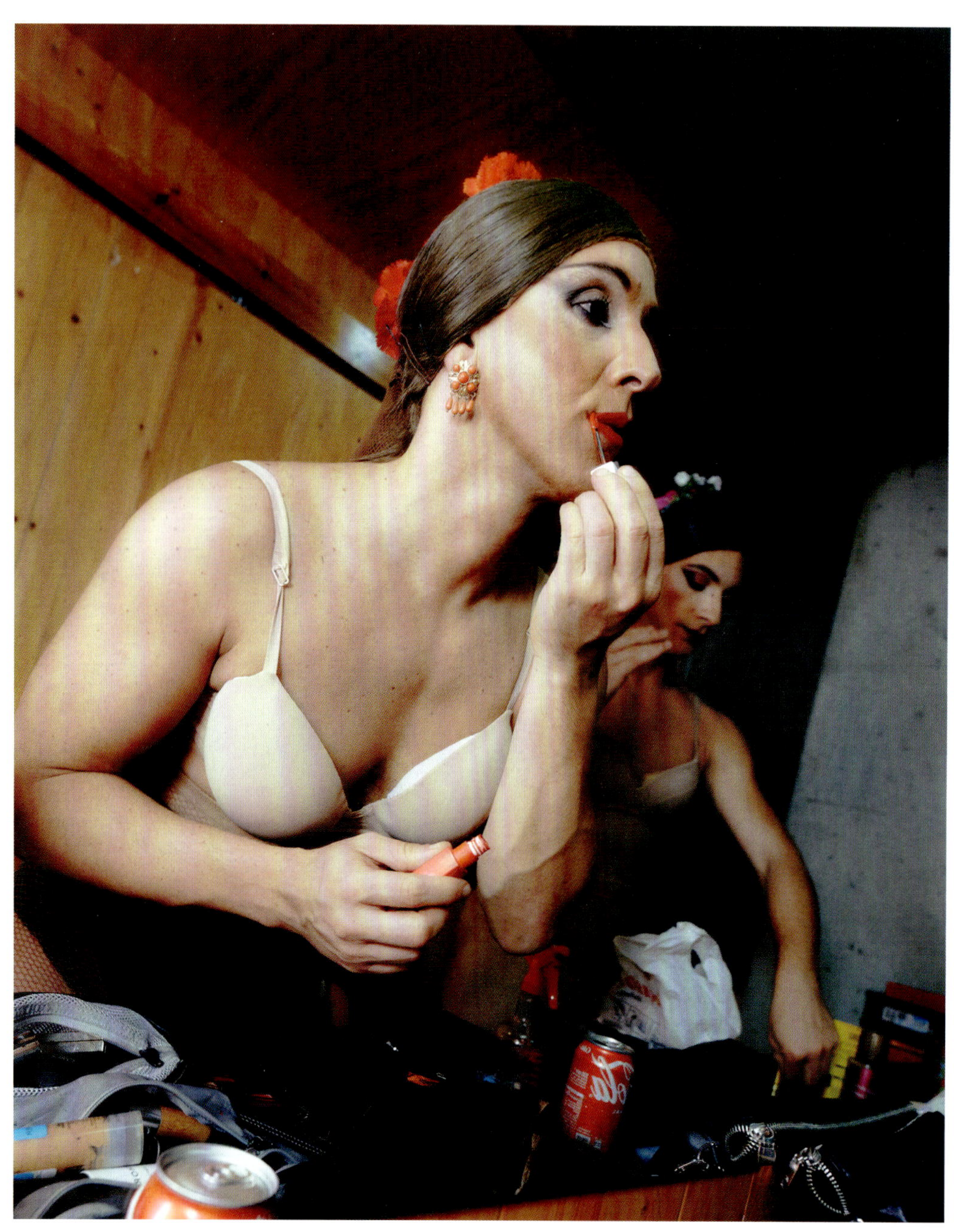

MANUEL LIÑÁN WAS BORN TO BE A BULLFIGHTER. NAMED AFTER his father, Manuel Arroyo—who once competed as the fierce torero El Extremeño—he was the youngest of three children growing up in Granada, a city in the hilly Andalusia region of southern Spain. After a car accident halted Arroyo's career in the ring, Liñán, the only son, was encouraged to follow in his father's footsteps. From an early age, he put on the traditional *traje de luces*, the matador's skintight and lavishly beaded ceremonial garb, and, with his family, observed the bloody brawls from the high-up stands of an arena. "Olé," the crowd would shout as the fighter narrowly dodged the creature's horns with his glorious red cape. "Olé! Olé!"

But to Liñán, learning to fight felt like an unwanted responsibility. The brutal sport was mired in a rigid concept of how one should be a man, and Liñán, a small and shy child, fancied softer art forms. He admired the flamenco dancers in his hometown, with their flower-adorned hairdos and extraordinary polka-dotted dresses. He noted their fearsome beauty and the tenacity with which they moved—"the silhouette of a woman with the long skirt with lots of volume." Watching them perform, he recognized that, though bullfighting was in his blood, it was dance that moved his heart.

He began studying flamenco while still in kindergarten and, by the age of thirteen, was performing professionally in local *tablaos*. However, his training came with its own set of restrictions about what he could wear and how he should behave. "It was clear that you could not do the woman's movements," he recalls. "I felt restricted in different parts of the body: in the arms, the head, the hips, and most of all, the hands." While his father was out of the house, he would steal away into his mother's closet, a treasure trove of beautiful dresses and silken skirts that beckoned him inside. His mom kept watch as he performed in secret, parading in her clothes with his cheeks kissed by blush. Arroyo didn't approve, so when Liñán began his dancing career in earnest, he took his mother's surname.

Today, Liñán is a celebrated performer and choreographer of vanguard flamenco. He moved to Madrid in 1997 to continue his training and, over the years, performed as a soloist in various respected companies, such as those of Merche Esmeralda and Teresa Nieto. *NOMADA*, a show he debuted at the 2014 Jerez Flamenco Festival, marked a pivotal moment. Though he had occasionally incorporated the *bailaora*'s dramatically tailed and ruffled skirt, the *bata de cola*, here it became a staple. "It was a fantasy, a dream come true," he describes. He also appropriated the classically feminine movements that were previously forbidden to him. Instead of moving two fingers, as is typically allowed of men in this style, he granted himself permission to twist his wrist and flourish his whole hand.

This has since become his signature. Now heading up his own company, Liñán creates shows that reflect his personal journey to regain that childlike freedom he experienced when he first stepped into his mother's wardrobe. His performances express a deep passion for flamenco in its fullest expression, with little regard for the gendered impositions that hinder a complete exploration. As a gay man showcasing the beauty and joy of his identity through the medium, Liñán is a living testament to flamenco's foundational outsider spirit.

Mixing wailed poetry and intricate guitar playing with rhythmic dancing featuring claps, snaps, slaps, and stomps, flamenco is an intricate art form with mysterious roots. It emerged centuries ago out of the Andalusia and Murcia regions of southern Spain. Scholars have speculated on its compounding of influences, though few agree on the origins of the term flamenco itself. It has been co-opted as a national symbol, yet it was once reviled by Spanish elites and condemned by the Catholic

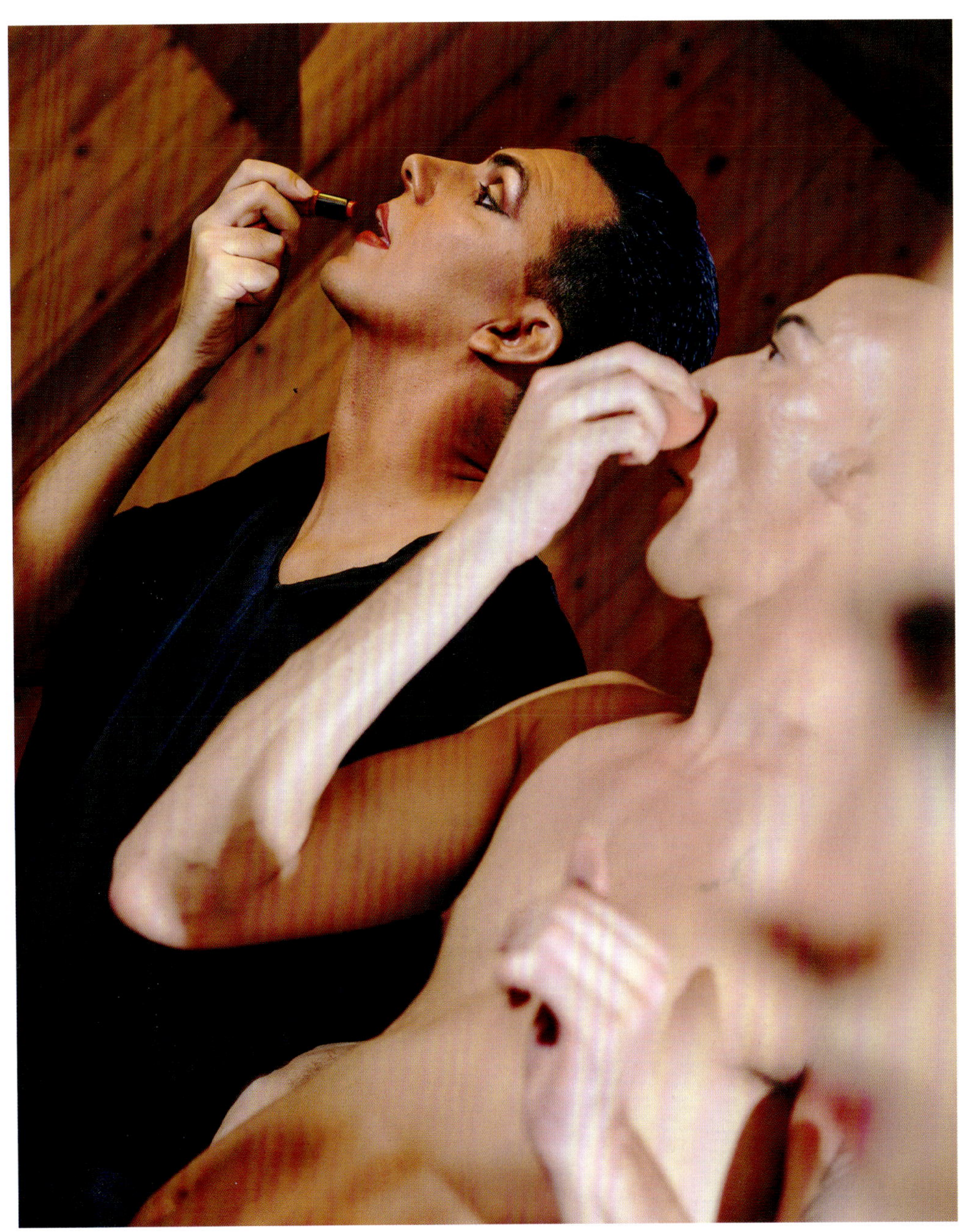

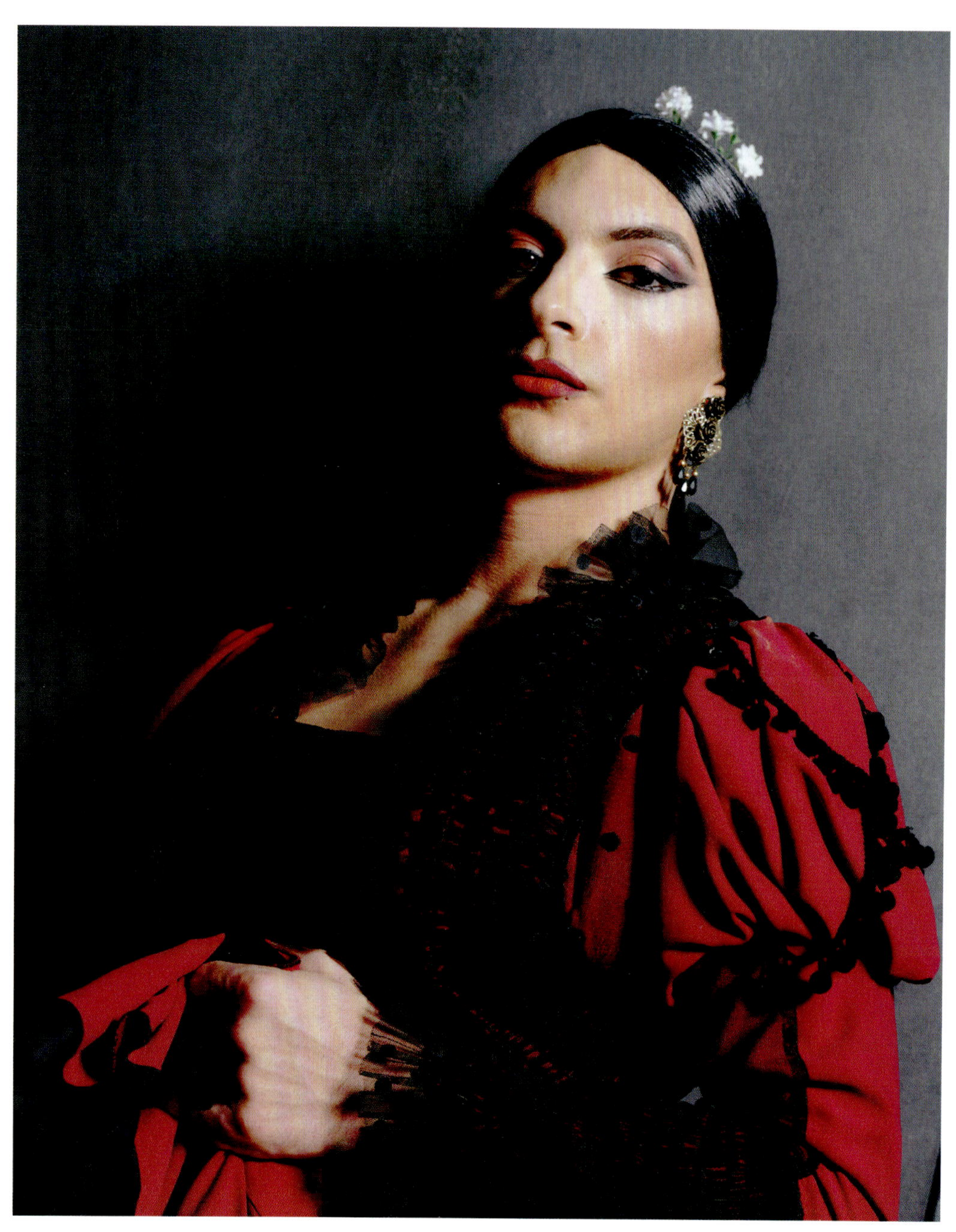

church, in part for its association with the country's spurned Roma people and its tendency to be performed in urban venues. Though contemporary flamenco has its own conservative strands, in its purest form, it was a dance created by and circulated among outcasts.

Liñán's ultimate love letter to the flamenco of his childhood imagination is his show *¡VIVA!*, which doubles as an invitation for others to indulge their own colorful fantasies. He is accompanied by six dancers—Manuel Betanzos, Jonatán Miro, Hugo López, Miguel Heredia, Víctor Martin, and Daniel Ramos—all men who perform traditional alegrias and bulerías wearing pinned black wigs and heavy *mantones* (shawls) that drip with fringe. The show premiered at Madrid's Teatros del Canal in 2019, but most of its subsequent tours were put on pause due to the COVID-19 pandemic. When performances eventually resumed, the work was suddenly enlivened with vital new energy, as if it were being danced for the first time. In November 2022, the troupe arrived in the sunny seaside port of Cádiz for a sold-out, one-night appearance at the Real Teatro de las Cortes, a theater of over 400 seats.

As the somber whinnies of a tuning violin filled the auditorium during the sound check, the dancers arrived at the theater one after another. They crammed into a dressing room barely big enough to fit all seven bodies, let alone the metal racks that shouldered the weight of their hefty costumes. Bags of makeup and hair were spread across a table before a wall-to-wall mirror. Nude tights were stretched over muscular thighs. Wigs were pinned tightly to hairlines. The air in this tiny room became so hot and thick with hair spray that, had a match been struck, the whole building might have ignited on the fumes.

Liñán cast *¡VIVA!* with dancers he already knew and whom he sensed "were people who had the same fantasies," he says. However, none of

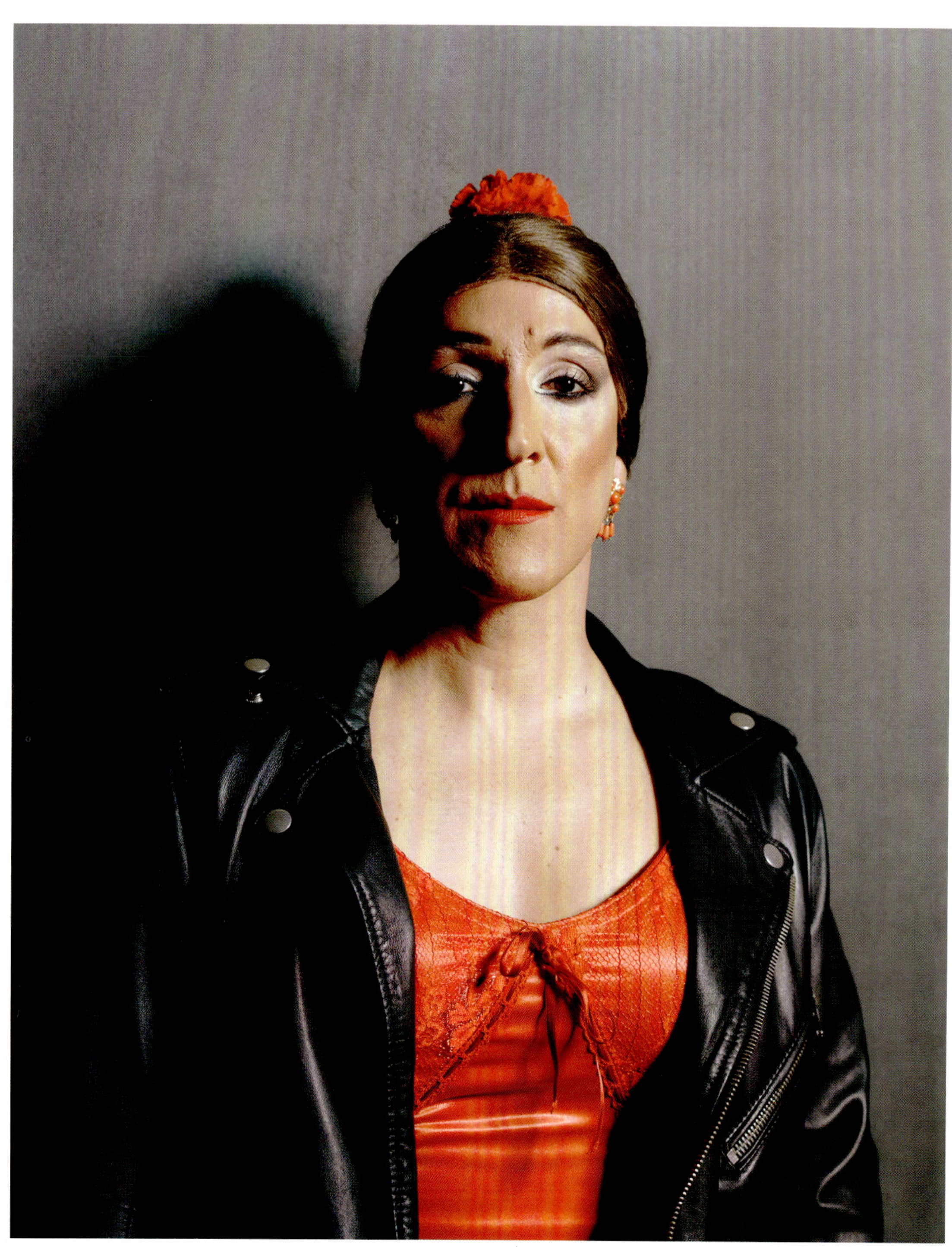

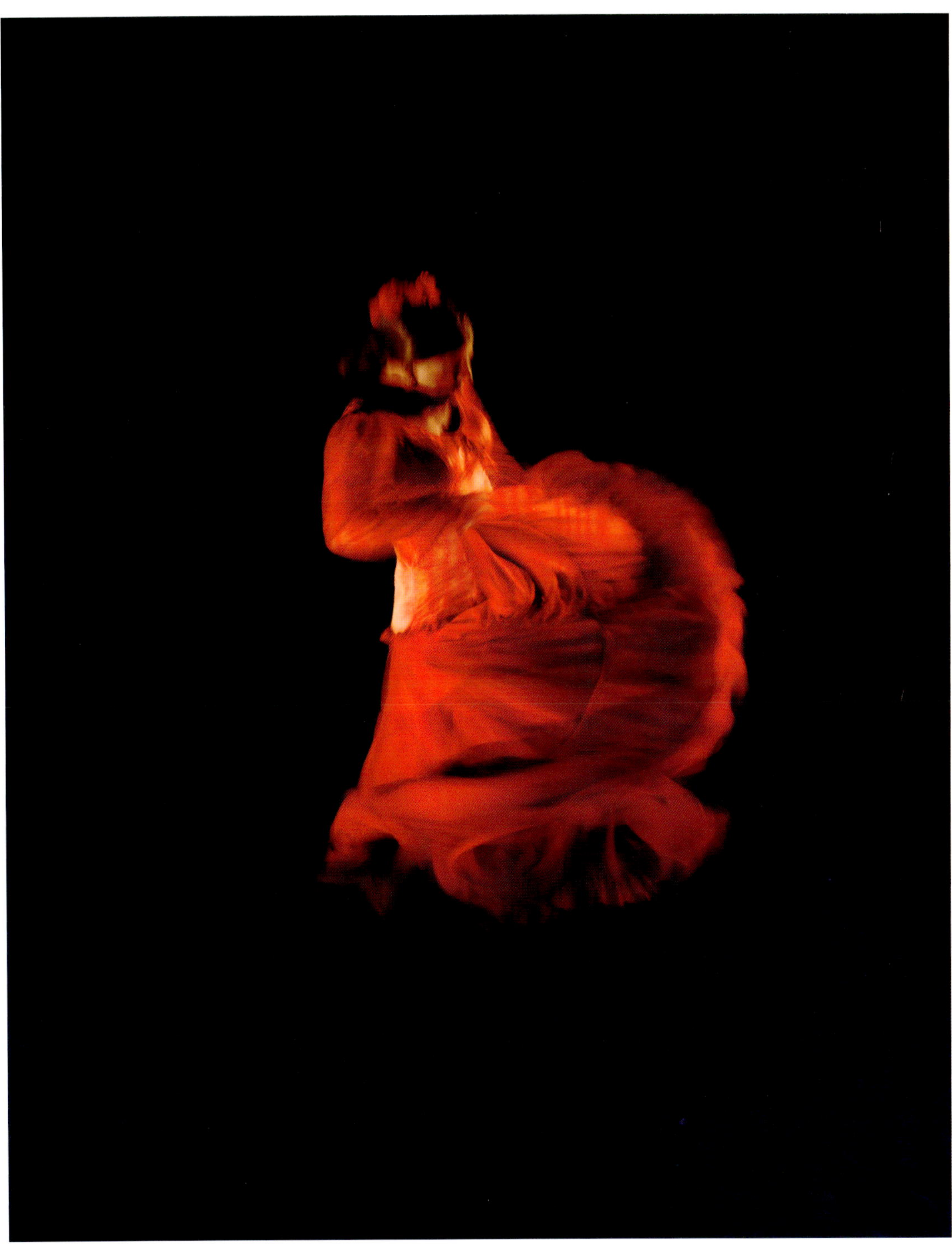

them had any prior professional relationship with drag. As they got into character, they offered each other makeup tips, like how to properly draw an eyebrow or line a lip. The tallest of the bunch, López, who had previously performed under the choreographer Javier Latorre, stood at the edge of the room, shaving every hair that had sprouted on his head and chin since the company's last stop. Despite this new challenge—and the nicks the razor left on his cheek and ear—he described his tenure with Liñán as a wholly transformative experience. "Manuel's vision is genius. It's gold," he says. "It's woken up something in me that has made me fall in love."

***

When the curtains rise, a lone dancer in a brilliant red dress is revealed. She looks away from the audience, slowly swaying with a braid hanging at her back. A singer's voice cries out from somewhere unseen—who could she be, we wonder, this rose with her geranium-stained garb, the picture of flamenco itself? Her hips begin to move and her hands curl, followed by her arms. When she suddenly flips around to face the crowd, all is revealed: She is he, Liñán, the star of the show. *¡VIVA!* continues like this throughout the evening, teetering among moments of surprise, delight, sadness, and humor. During one vignette, the company chases López about the room, attempting to lift his bright blue skirt. He shoos them away with stomps that, slamming into a microphoned stage, reverberate throughout the room. Martin's long dress, as he spins across the platform, unfurls like blossoms at the height of spring.

For the finale, the dancers don a set of extraordinary white *batas de cola* decorated with green polka dots—the colors of Andalusia—and take their turns leaving the stage. When they reappear, it is without their

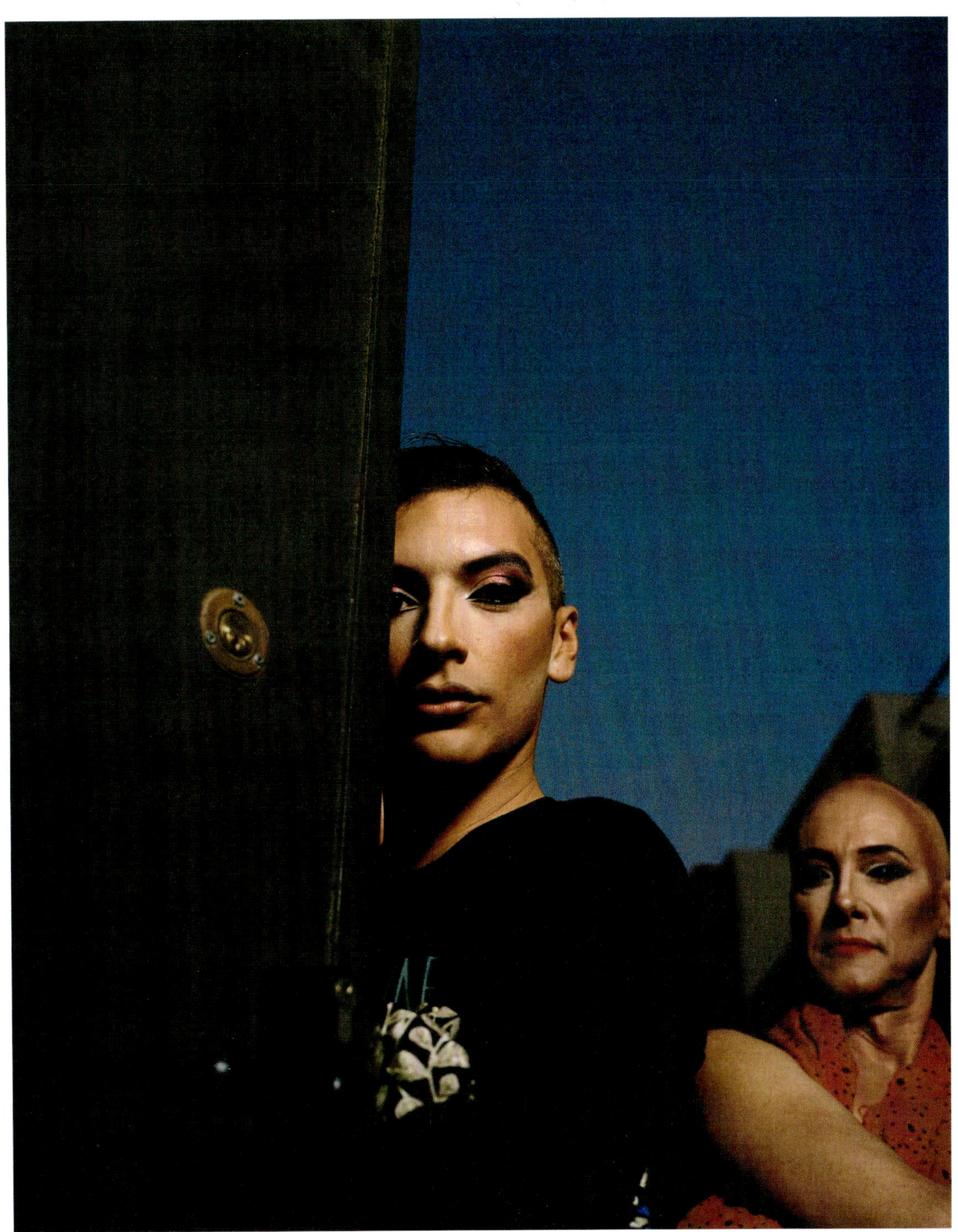

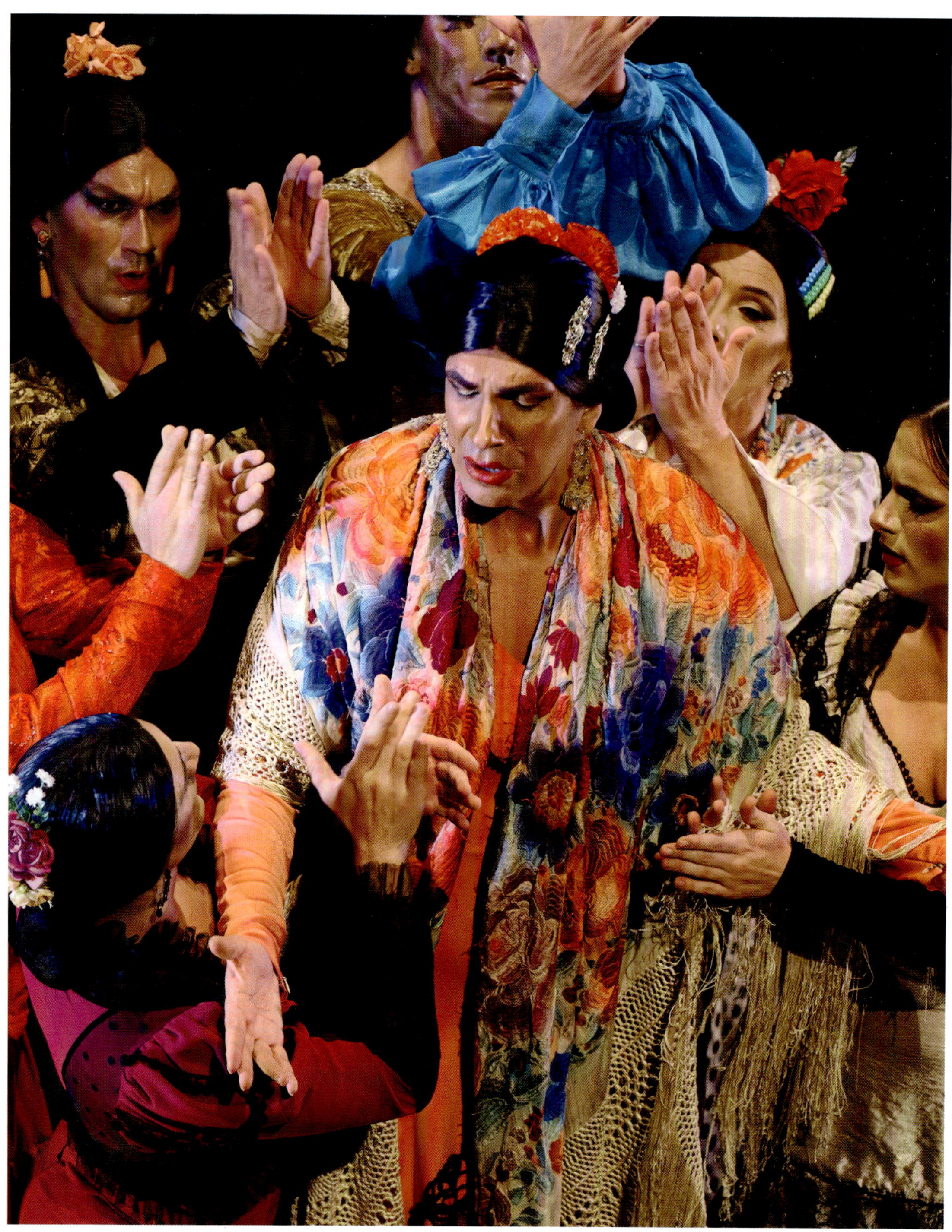

gowns, in just undershirts, socks, bras, and nylons. The jarring effect of the change seems to point to the fact that the weight we give to a piece of clothing, a mess of stitches, is much like the rule about who can perform the moves of a *bailaora*: entirely of our own making. "It's just them being them, men, but dancing with dresses and with wigs," Liñán says, "and just being free to represent every movement they want."

The dancers exit the stage, leaving Liñán standing alone in a button-down shirt and tall socks. He rips his hair from his head and falls to his knees. After a brief pause, the curtain drops to the floor. The crowd rises, erupting with cheers. "Olé," they shout as Liñán takes a bow, his lipstick smeared with sweat. "Olé! Olé!"

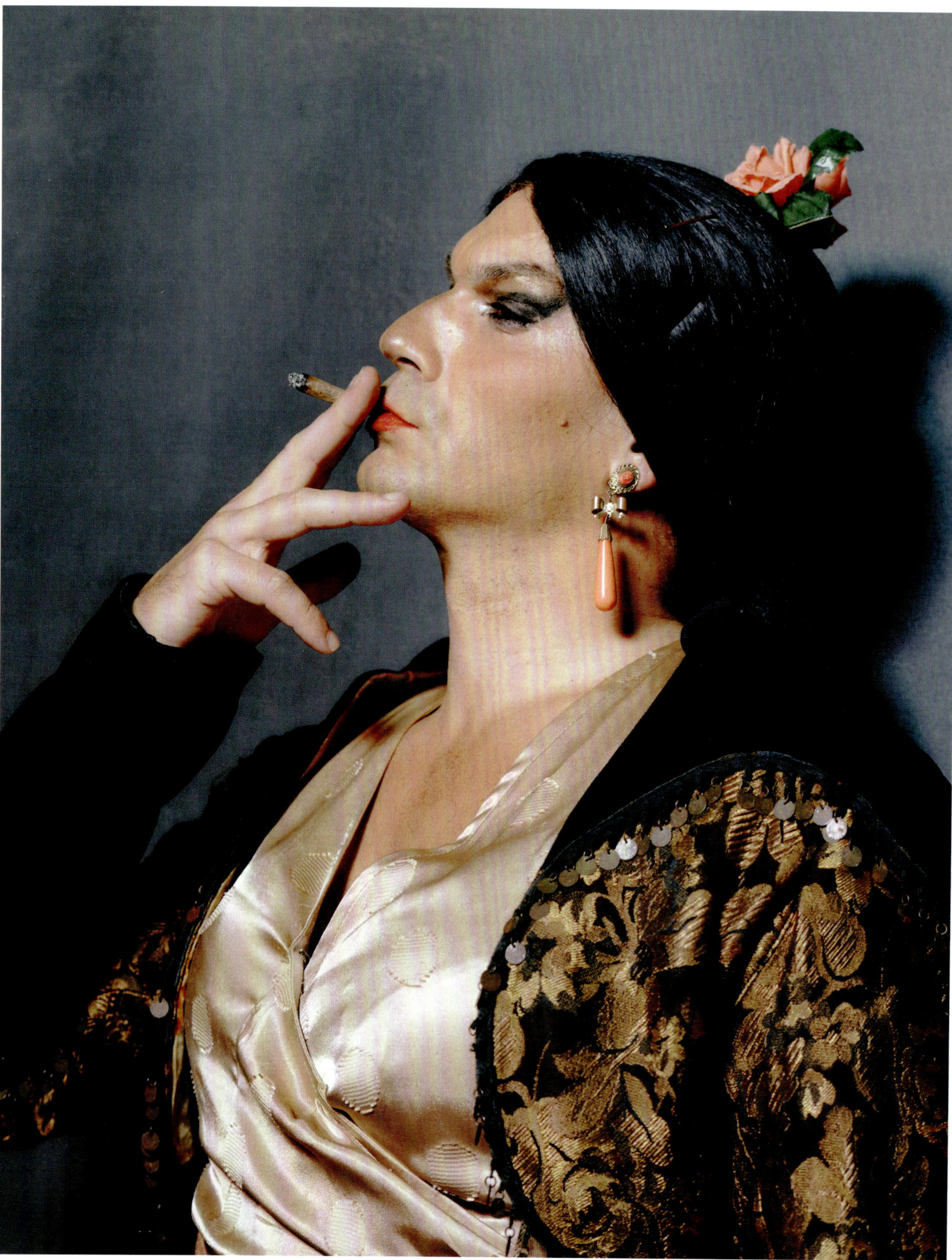

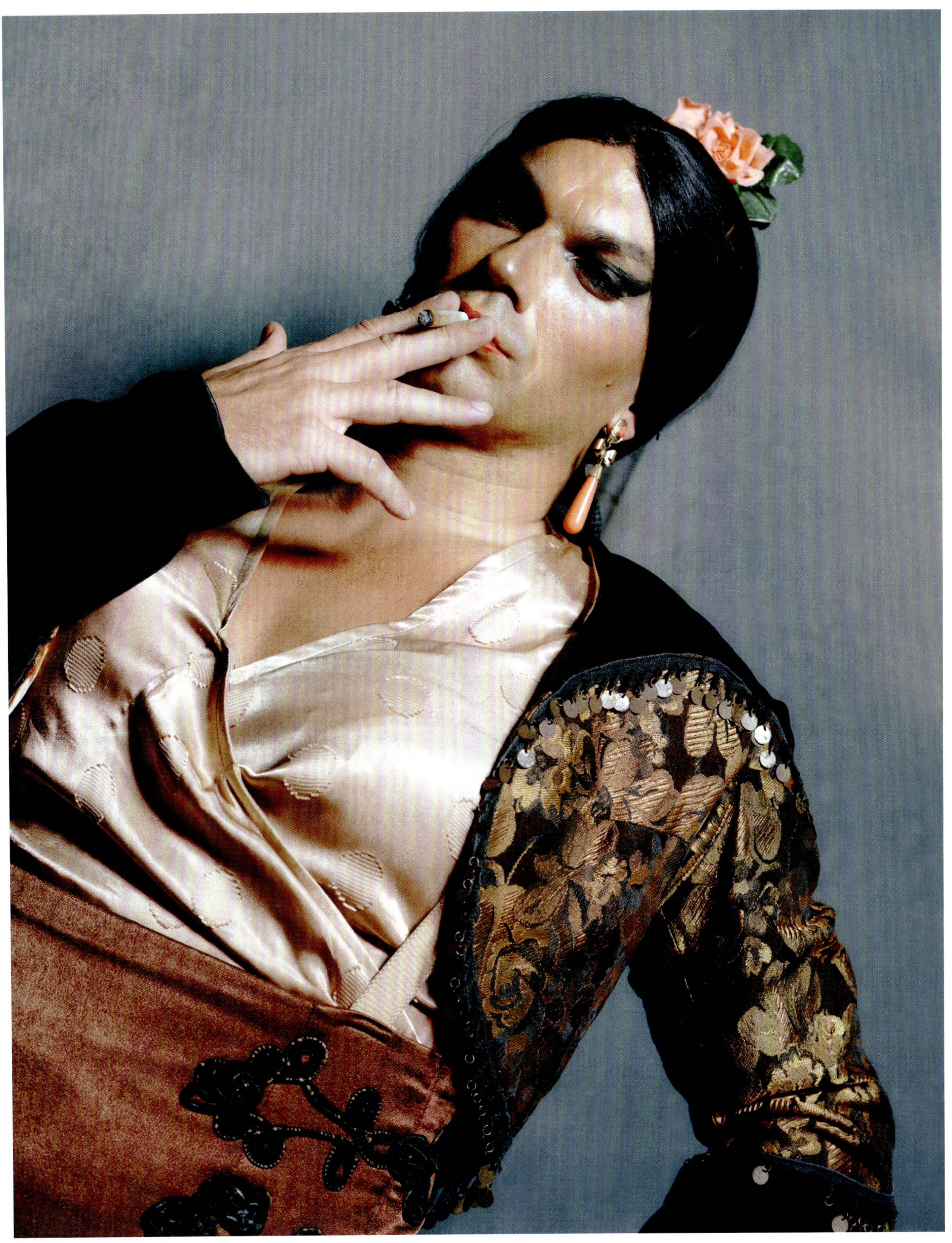

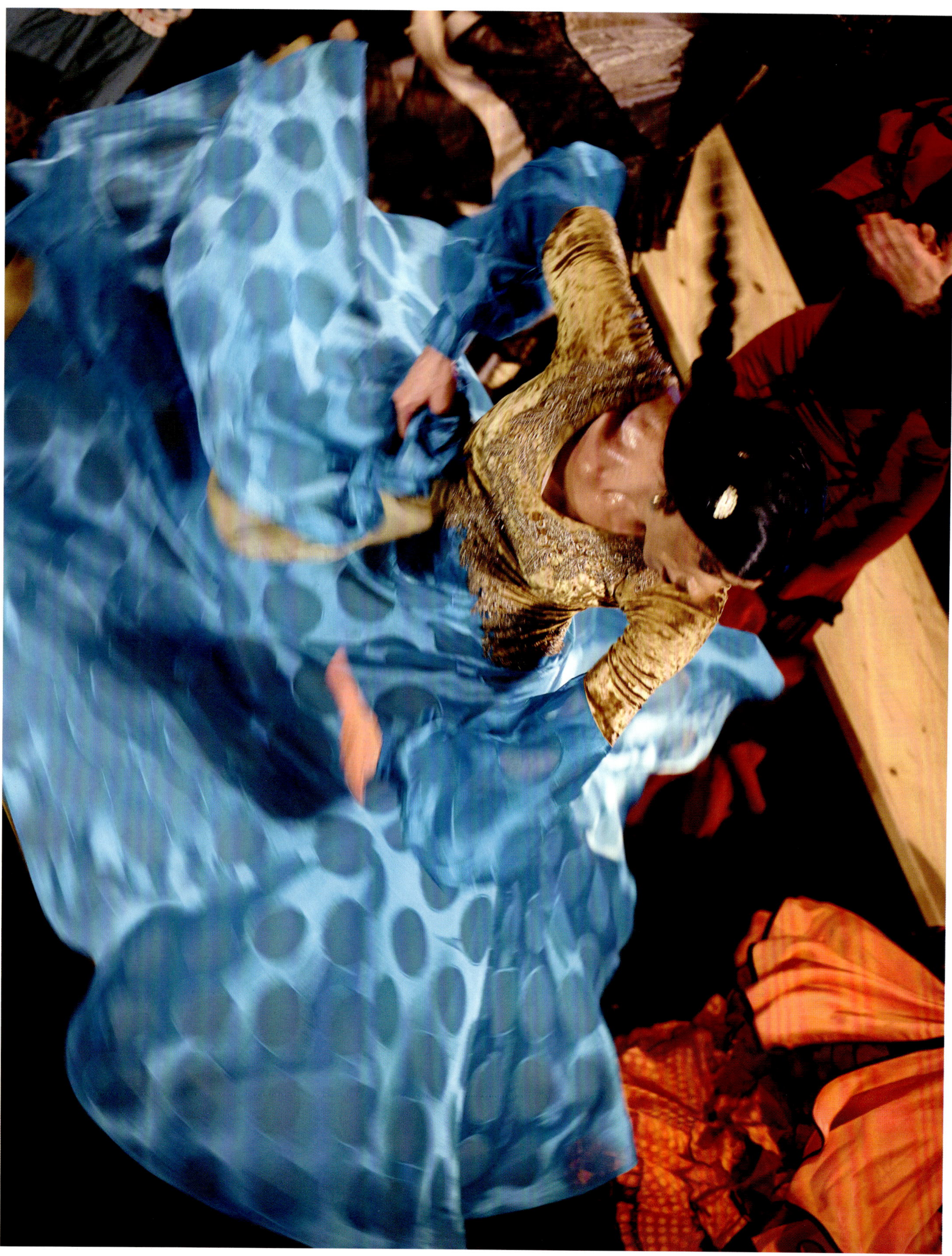

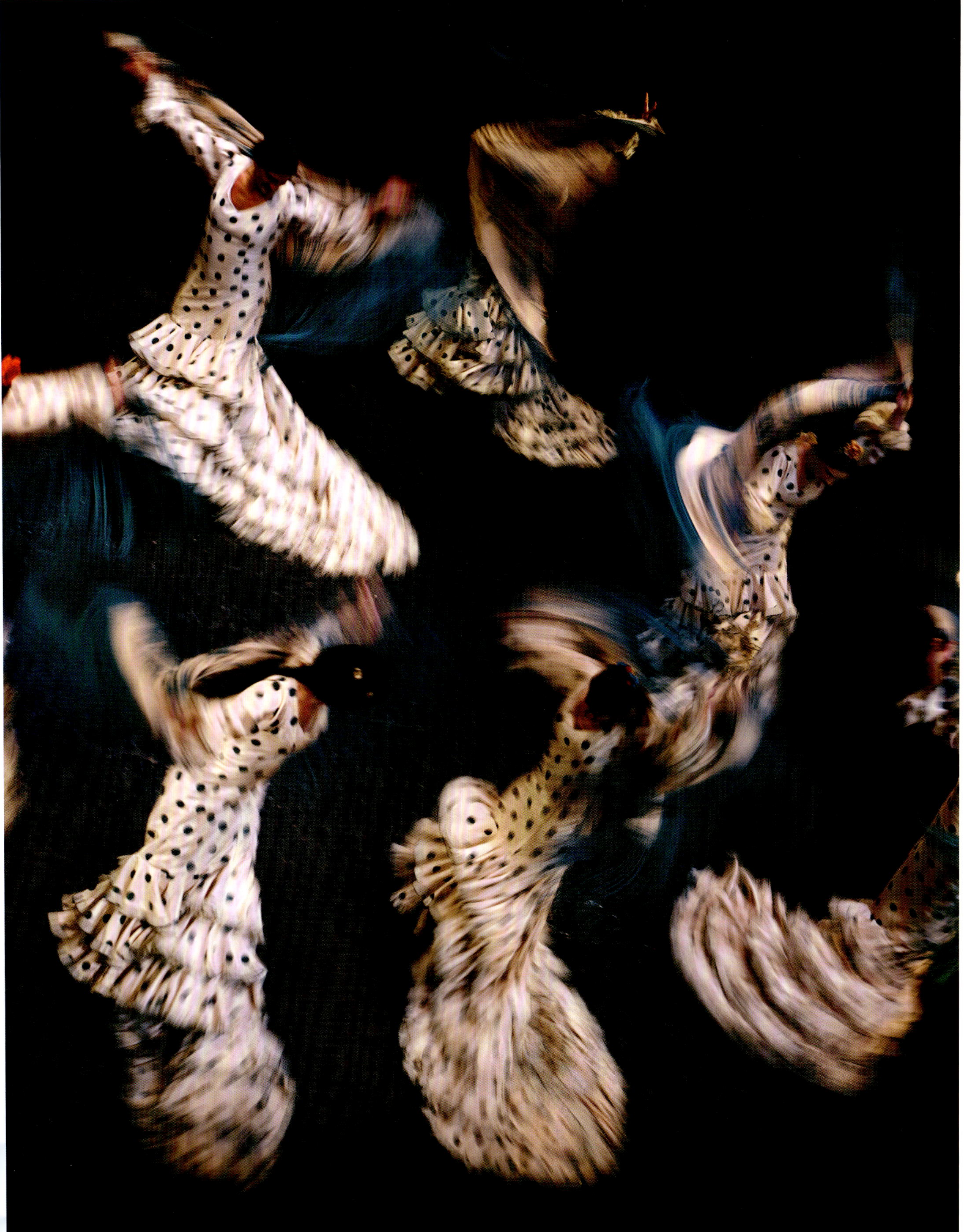

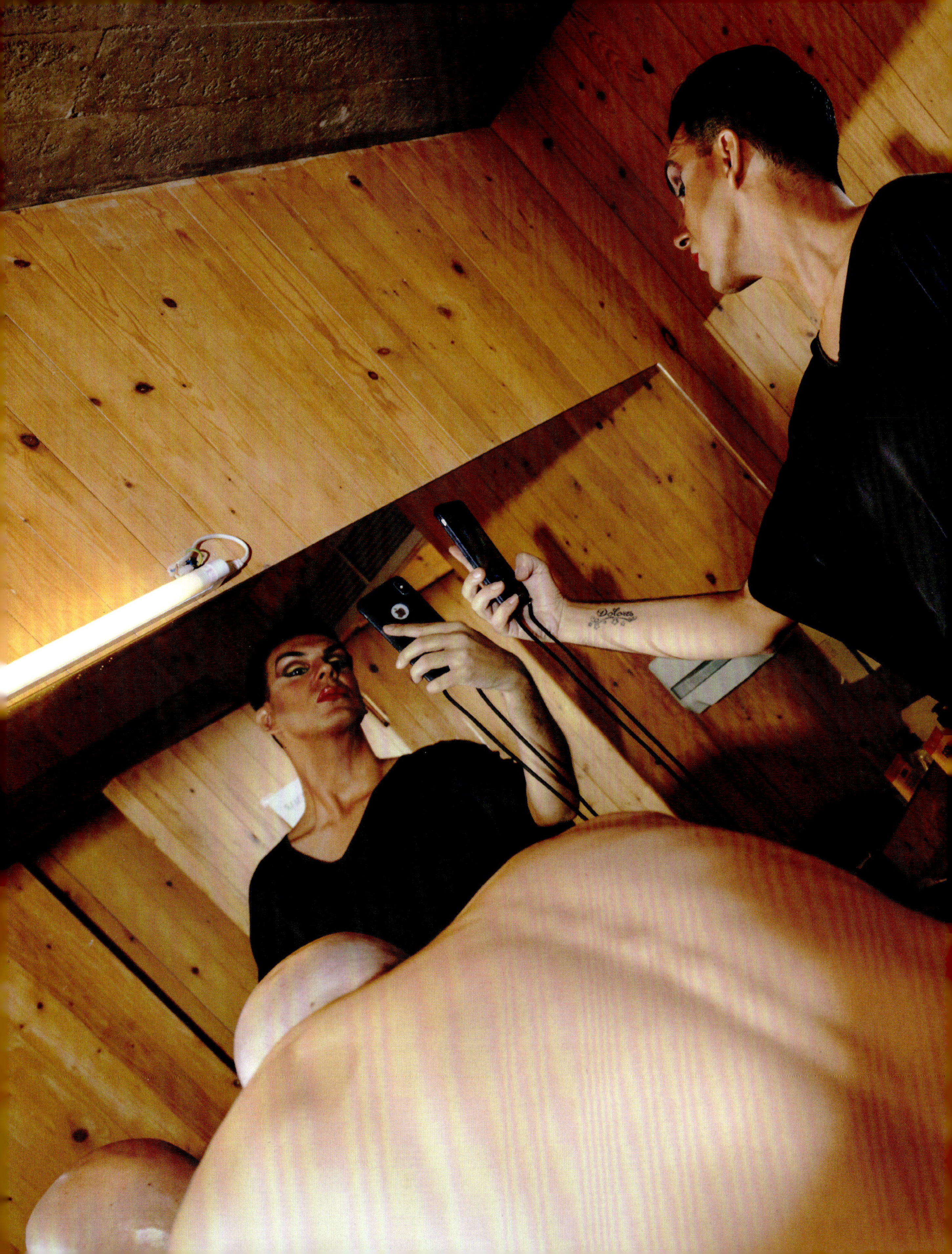

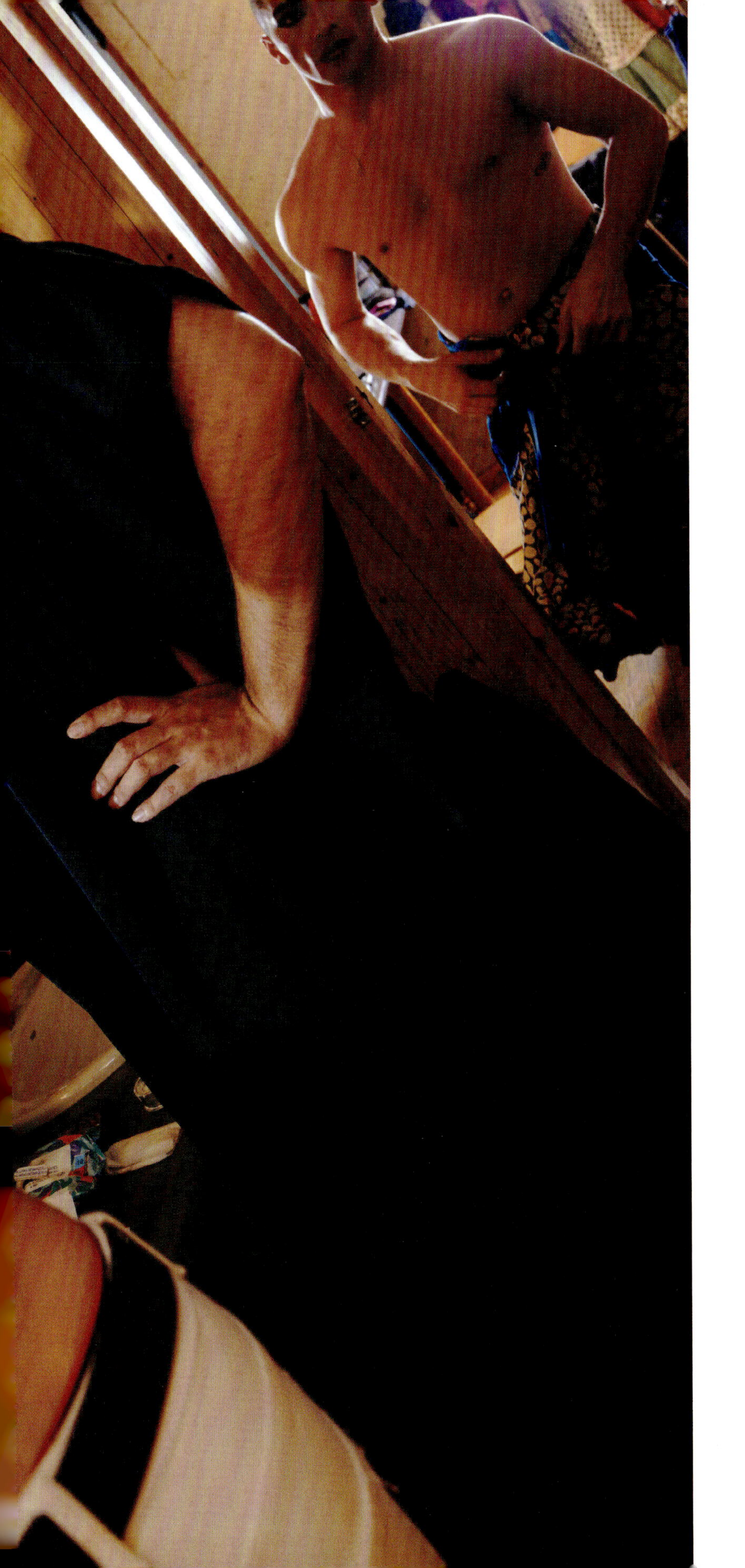

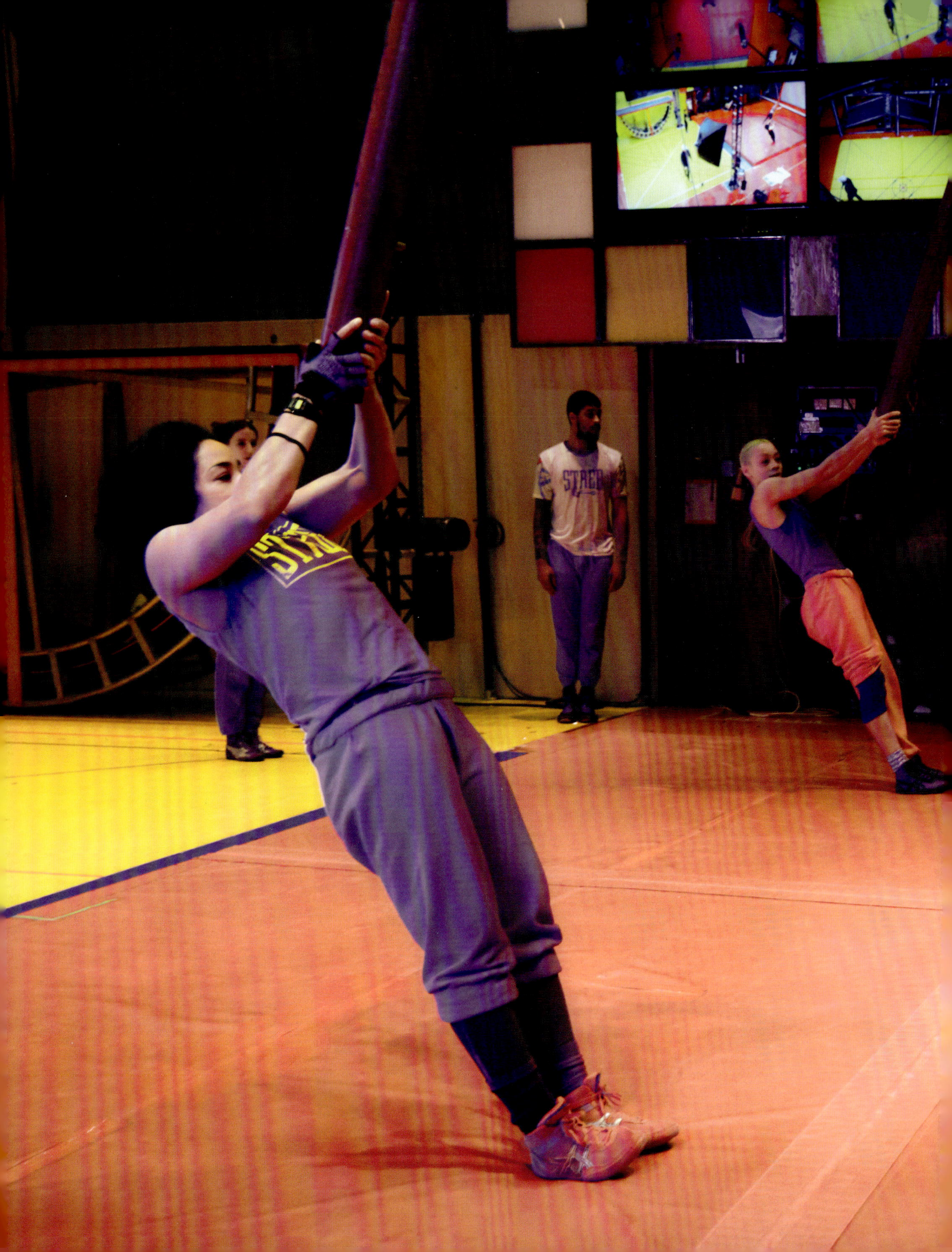

STREB EXTREME ACTION

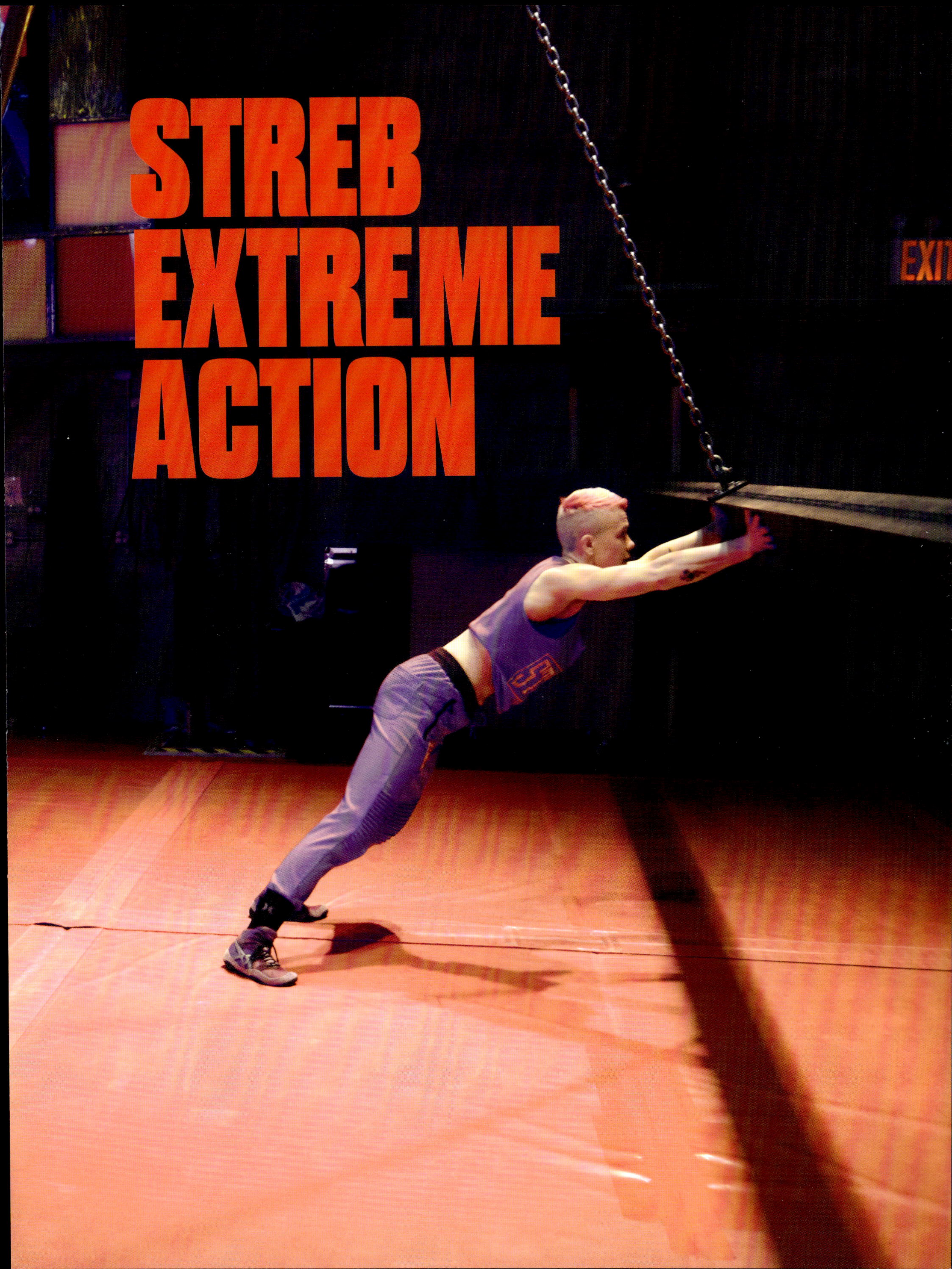

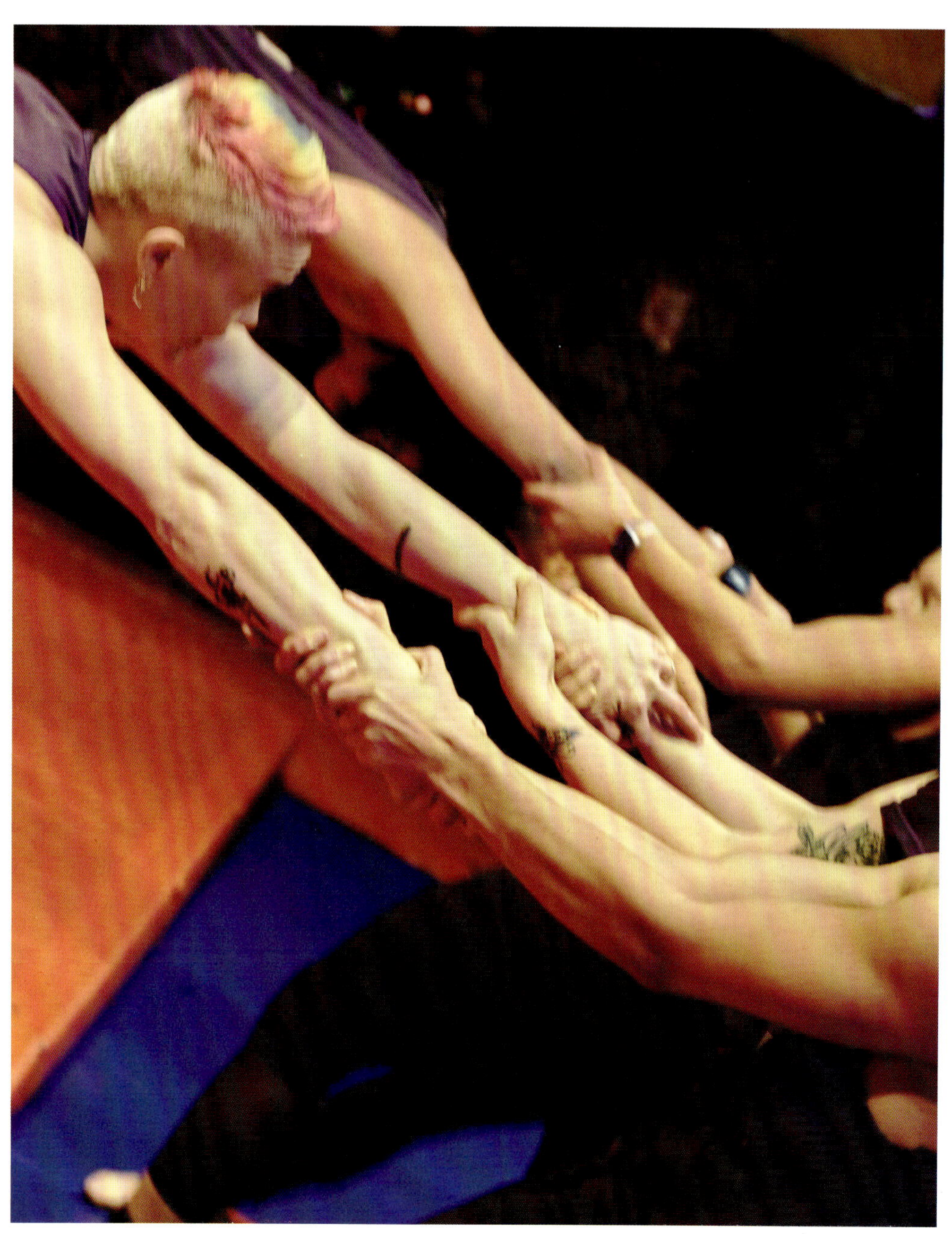

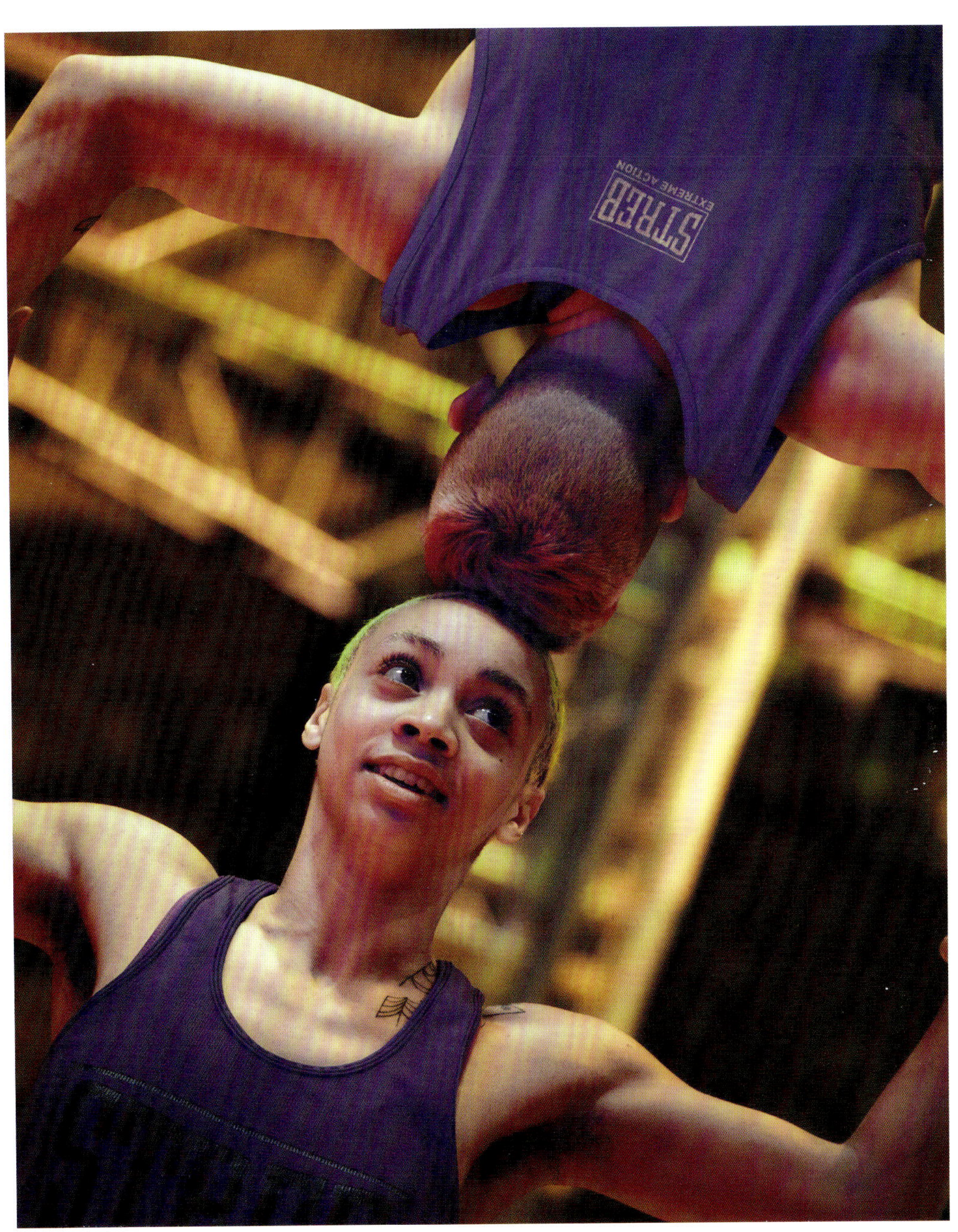
EXTREME ACTION
STREB

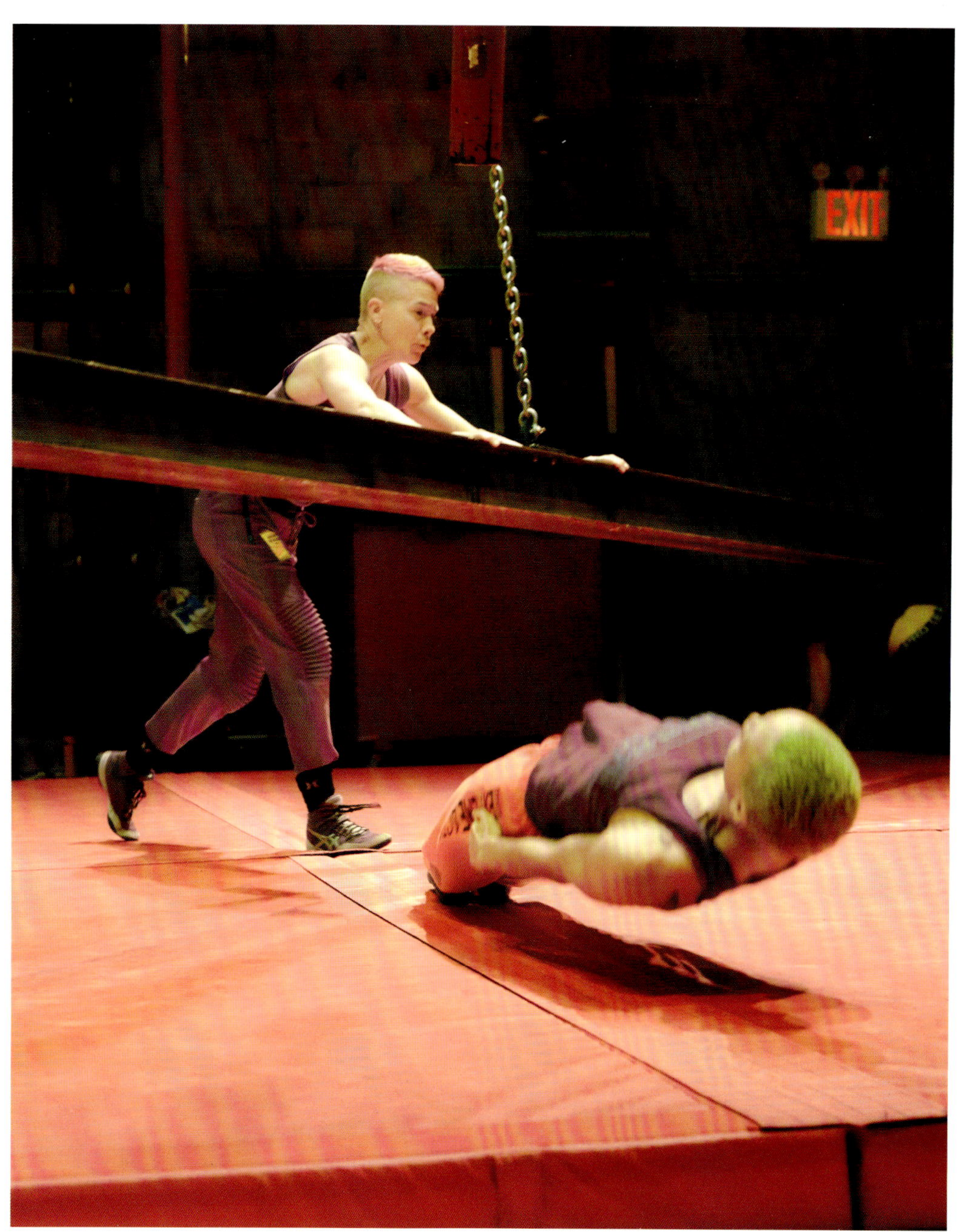
EXIT

LOOKING SLICK IN CARTOONISH RED AND BLUE JUMPSUITS, A group of performers flirts with a spinning two-ton I beam. For this piece, *Steel*, the dancers of STREB Extreme Action must fall backward and forward to dodge the metal, which, suspended from the ceiling, cuts the air like a fan's blade. Next up in the show is *Tip*, a crowd-pleaser that was first shown in 2006. Senior dancer Jackie Carlson stands within a giant, cage-like half wheel that hinges and rolls on its round side. Just as the contraption hedges dangerously toward one edge, threatening to topple over and take out a brick wall, three more performers climb aboard its flat top and shift the weight, pushing it in the opposite direction.

The performance is exhilarating and, at certain junctures, a little frightening to watch, prompting the audience, children and grown-ups alike, to gasp in awe and cover their eyes. STREB's snappy, high-flying works, which throw knives into the traditional musical and narrative qualities of dance and invent an action-based genre all their own, tend to evoke visceral reactions. To Elizabeth Streb, the mad-genius choreographer who for over three decades has been evolving this daredevil practice, an ideal Sunday afternoon involves crashing through a layer of plexiglass and diving from forty-foot scaffolding to land on a mat. *Tip*, Streb observes, is an especially confounding performance for classically trained dancers.

"It's stunning how confused you can be about where you are when you haven't gone anywhere," Streb says. "It's just memorizing distances that are circular, and it's very interesting how that confuses dancers who have studied movement probably since they were five." In many other modes of dance, she compares, a performer's "base of support is essentially the bottoms of their feet. There's no landing, there's no dealing with the forces that are just above the ground."

But of course, there has never been another choreographer like Streb. For her performers, even flight becomes possible, should one learn to do so like a human, to overcome fear and embrace the sensation of hitting the ground.

***

A few months after the show, we meet Streb at her studio, the so-called Action Lab, a former mustard factory the company has occupied since 2003. She's wearing a version of her typical uniform: a relaxed pinstripe suit with the pant legs tucked into knee-high leather motorcycle boots. Her hair is tousled into a messy, grown-out mohawk. She ascends a narrow, circular staircase up to a perch overlooking the studio and pulls up two seats at a desk littered with papers. They bear cryptic images of machines and rough outlines of choreography drawn with bright highlighters. To an outside eye, their language is impossible to decipher, a mess of symbols and scribbles.

When she says that the "tipping machine," the device Carlson almost rode into the expensive-looking row house residences next door, has in her eyes become "completely predictable," I think, Did she see what we saw? Streb yearns always to experiment, to push the danger, the surprise, and thus the excitement of her performances—or as she tells her dancers, to go "harder, faster, sooner, higher." She facilitates this through her core technique, which she calls "Pop Action," calling to mind the simplicity and approachability of the Pop Art movement. Sudden and piercing, it demands that transitions between movements be eliminated to evoke a sense of urgency and unpredictability.

The artist's technique is bolstered by an arsenal of machines that vary in shape, size, and function, which Steb designs with the help of an engineer. As we observed in *Steel*, objects are sometimes incorporated as obstacles to shape the movement. Other times, the mechanism merges with the dancer, flinging them at speeds and heights unattainable by

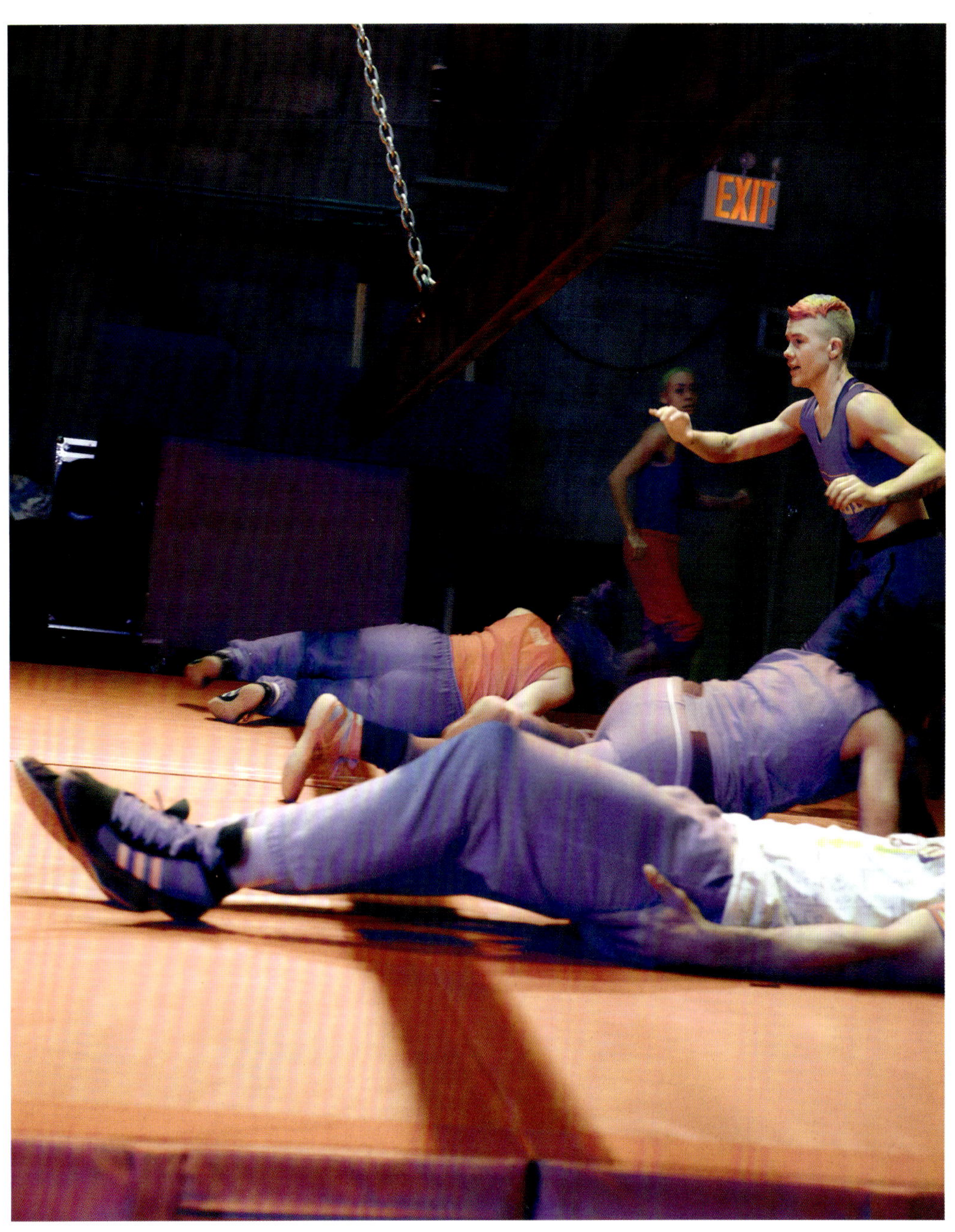
EXIT

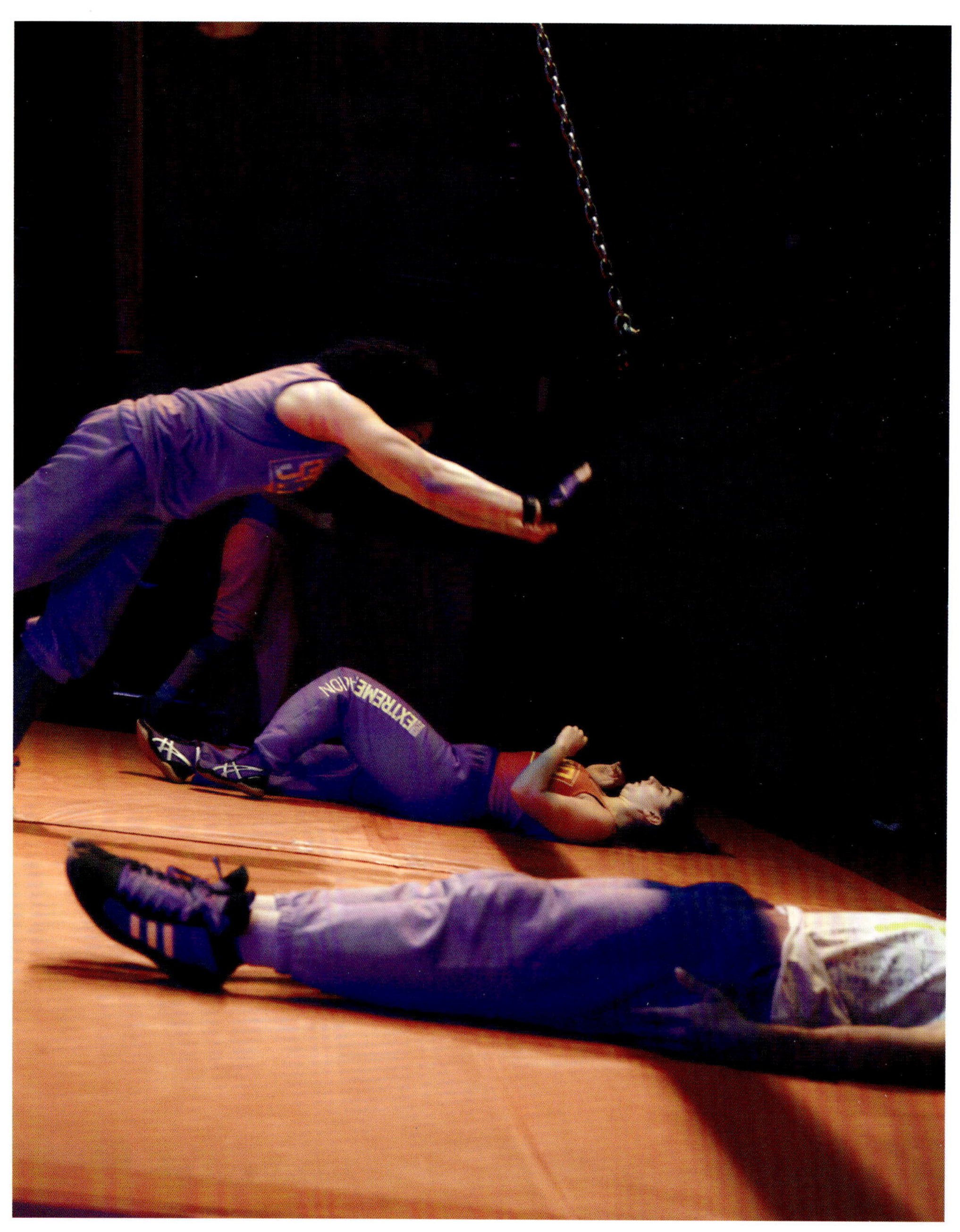
EXTREME

the body alone. "If she brings in a new piece of equipment, she'll let us have a moment of playtime with it and watch us, observe what we're doing," Carlson says. "We'll play along with each other and she'll take notes and ask questions. 'Can it be done?' We can't say it won't work. We have to show her."

It doesn't take long to realize there is something childlike about Streb. When a subject catches her fancy, her investigations run deep and intense. She graduated from the dance program at SUNY Brockport in 1972, barely earning passing grades in modern dance, but some years later, in her fifties, began attending New York University. There, she studied math, physics, and philosophy—her real passions—refusing to graduate for a decade out of a simple, earnest love for the material.

Her recent fascination with Mavericks Beach in Northern California, an anomalous place where surfers congregate to ride waves as tall as apartment buildings, led Streb to craft a new invention. The prototype, which resembles a massive roasting spit, sits at the edge of the studio. A hulking, spinning surfboard at its center invites her dancers to climb on top of it.

"I just am hooked into that, like how fast can we go in a man-made, woman-made, person-made object?" says Streb. But her pursuit involves costs and compromises. The price of production, and the tendency for the company's performances to be hard on stages, make Streb's work difficult to tour and ambitious to commission. She estimates that the first build for a machine like this would cost around $200,000. Even then, she says, "It could be a few years of failure before I actually get it right."

***

Streb has often spoken of her desire to fly and her tendency toward the extreme as innate, primal urges. She described herself as a "feral child" during her TED Talk "My Quest to Defy Gravity and Fly." Streb grew up in rural Rochester, New York, with

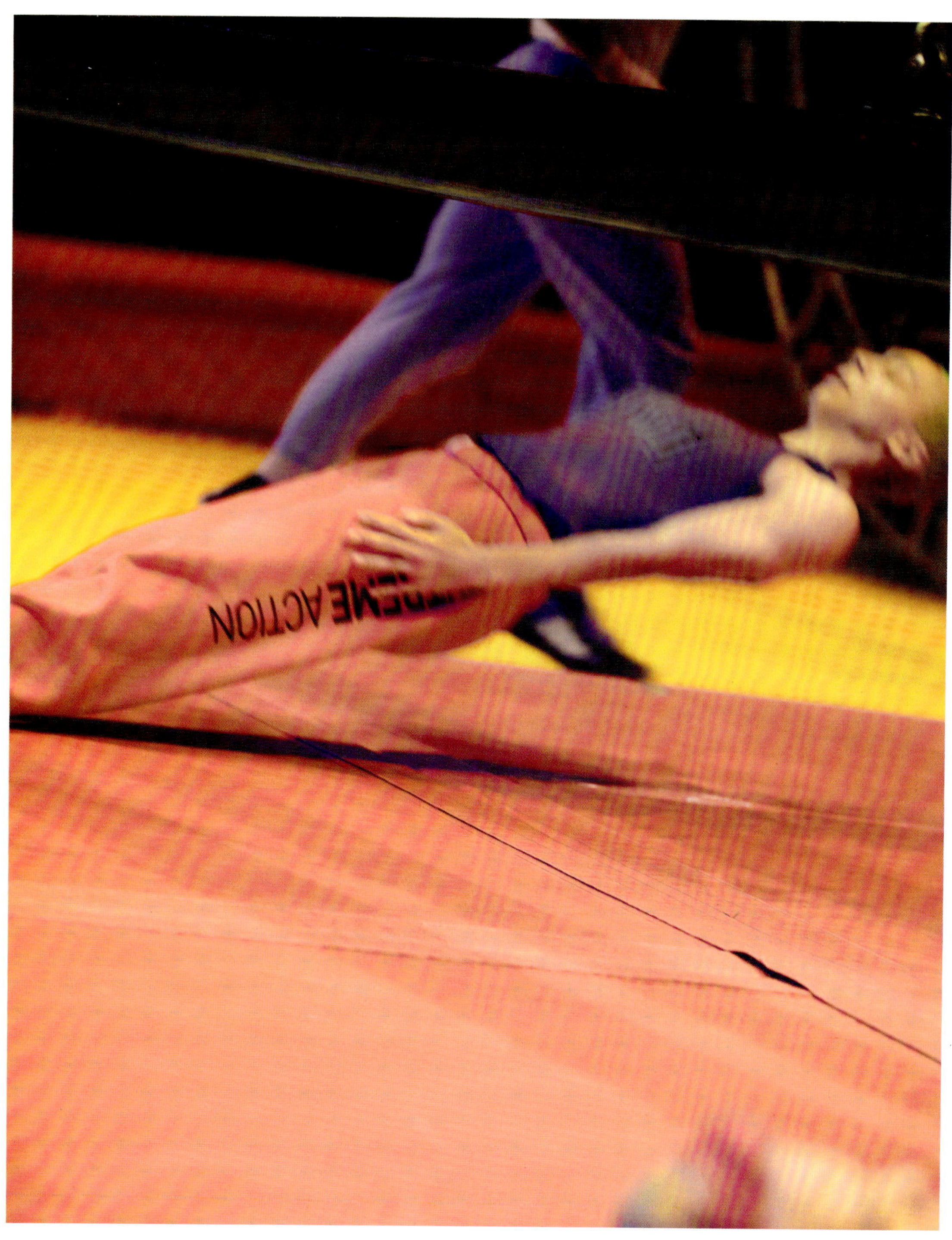

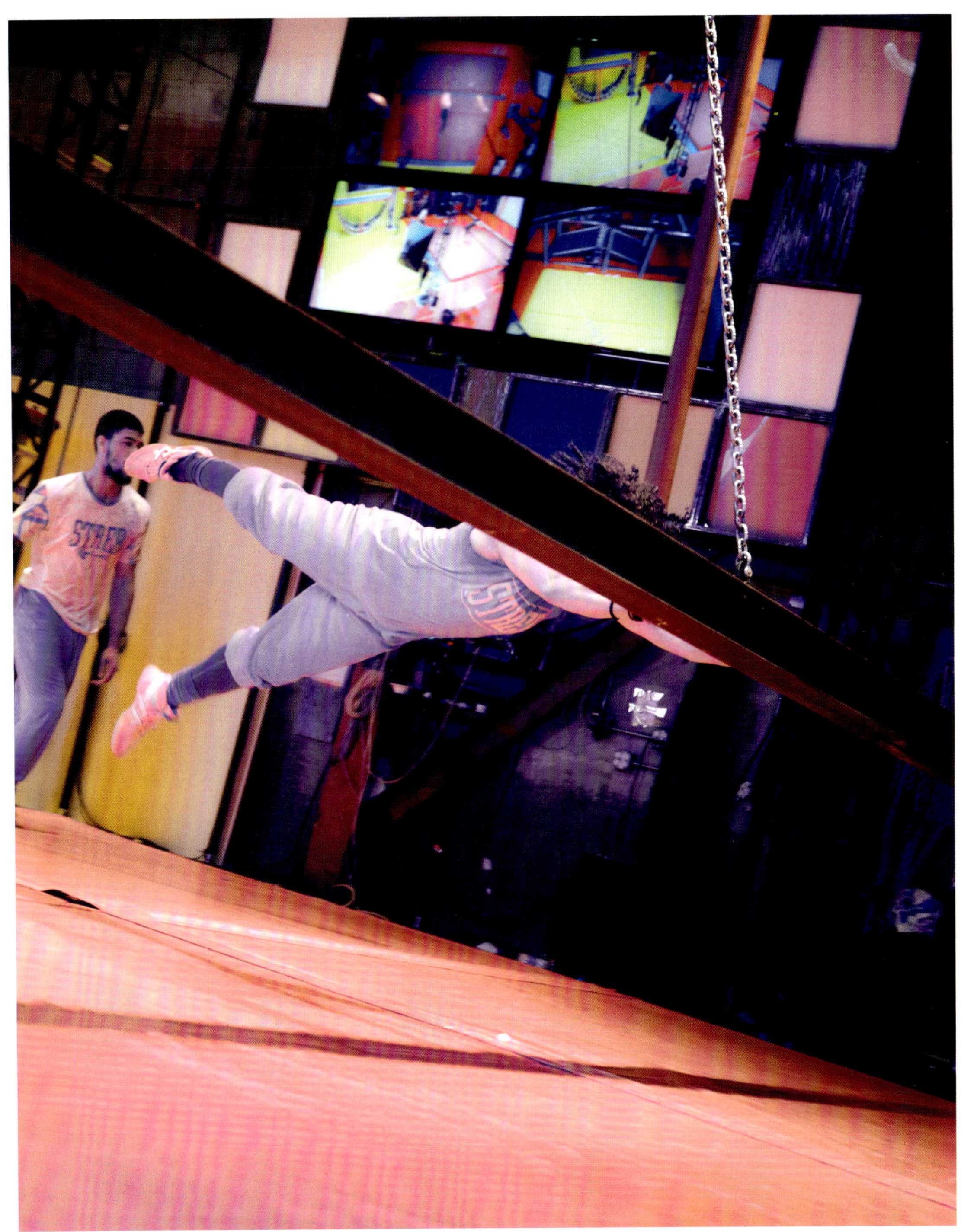

working-class adoptive parents. Her bricklayer father taught her to fish and shoot a gun. Admiring showmen like Harry Houdini and Evel Knievel, she bought her first motorcycle at fifteen years old. Her longtime partner, the journalist Laura Sanders, joked in a *New York Times* feature that it was her job to finally "domesticate" Streb; the two were married by the comedian Kate Clinton in 2019. Streb bristles at the mention. "I still can't say the word 'wife.'"

Streb developed her practice early on, in part by studying Eadweard Muybridge's photographs of animal movements. Today, her dancers resemble sparrows as they hurl themselves from a trapeze. However, because humans can't fly with wings as birds or bugs do, Streb's key to flight is learning to land, which the dancers typically do flat on their bellies.

"Part of what our job is [is] to come up with systems of tackling fear. Not running away from it but building systems where you can confront it, number one, and then also surmount it," says Cassandre Joseph, STREB's co-artistic director. Joseph joined the company in 2007 and today is the primary teacher of Streb's Pop Action technique. "Fear promotes growth," she adds.

Danger is an inherent, unavoidable part of the work, and accidents happen on occasion. Streb walks with a slight limp, having sustained years of injuries, and she gave up performing in 1998. The most severe incident occurred in 2007 when a dancer fell during a performance of *Surface*, a work that involves crashing into and climbing atop wooden boards that are propped up like pyramids. After landing hard on her back, she was rushed to a nearby hospital where she had to undergo surgery. Her career with the company ended with a metal rod implanted in her back.

But does this risk, which is so key to performing and viewing STREB's work, hint at some deeper truth? Existing in queerness itself is a perilous

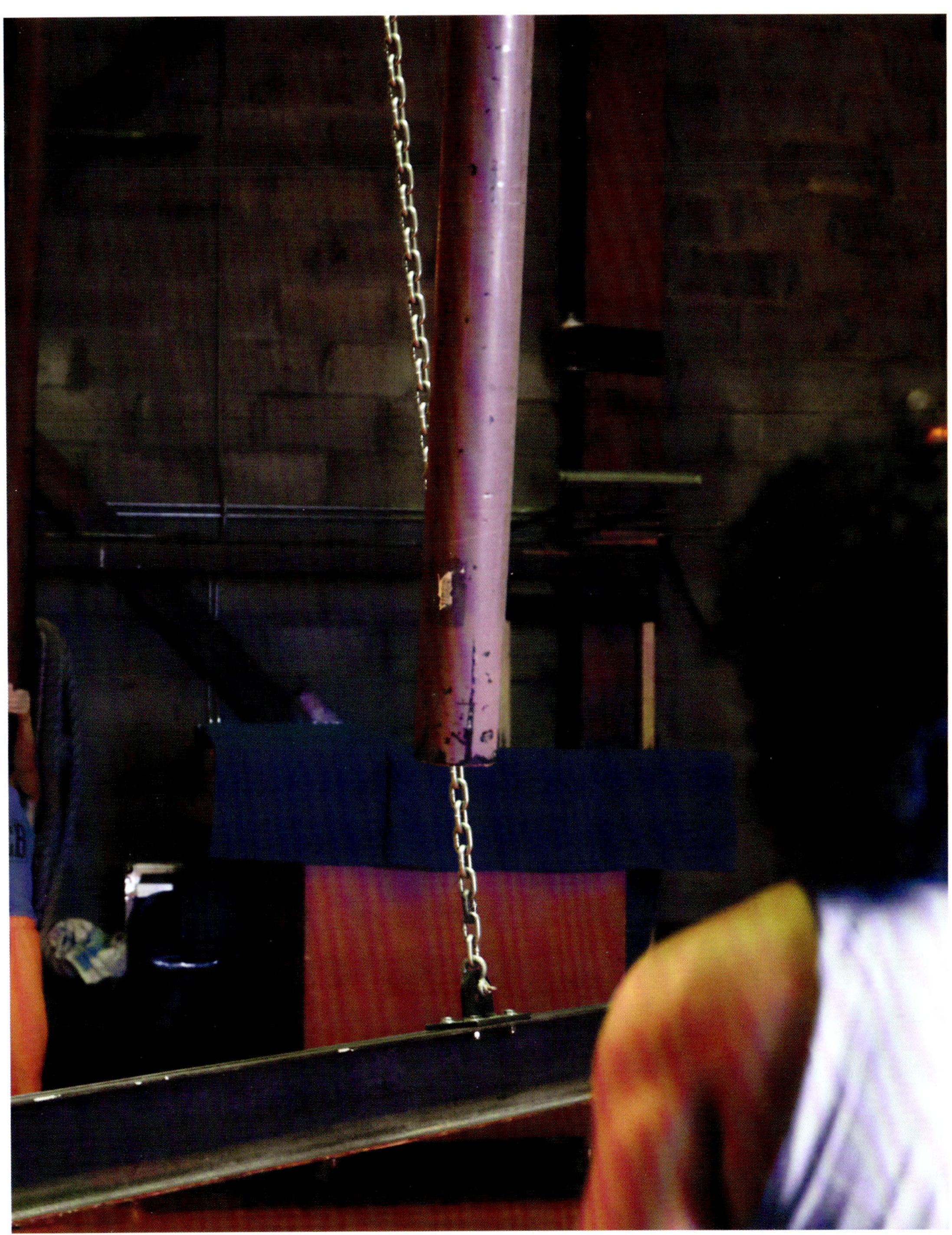

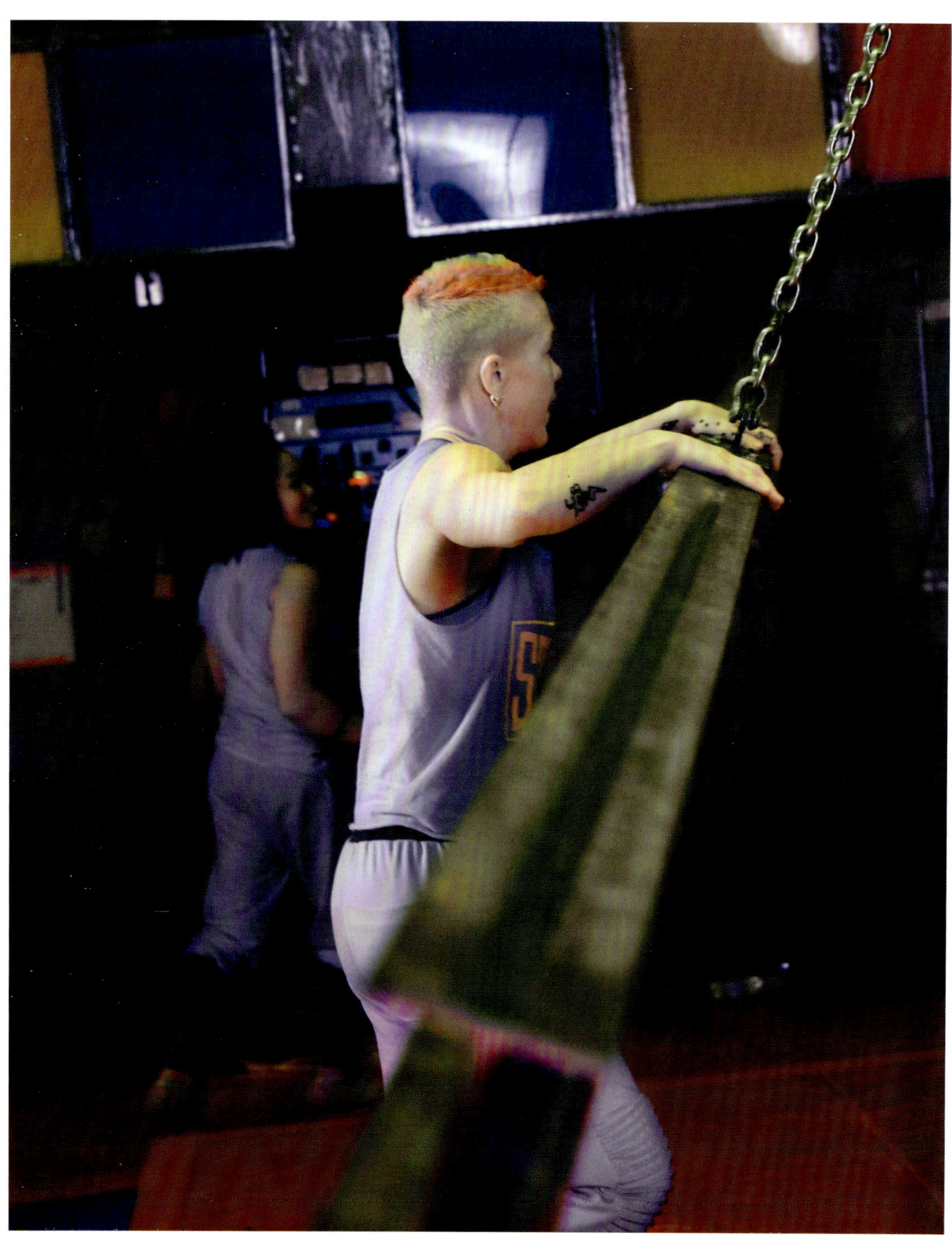

endeavor, a necessary chance we take every day to live and love in the way that we must. But sometimes, in spite of our fears, we choose flight.

"I try not to define [my work] because it's not my expertise," Streb says. There are no stories told in her work, no nods to her own biography. "I'm not trying to relegate it to meaning something besides what you see. The rhythm of the action, and how I put it together, is essentially what action at its best and most dangerous can do."

STREB's practice attracts dance outsiders and adrenaline junkies of all sorts. Carlson studied ballet, jazz, and tap from the age of six and joined the Dance Theater of Harlem in New York as a ballet dancer straight out of high school. "I didn't necessarily like being that damsel in distress that traditional ballet kind of upholds, and I didn't want the boys to help me turn," she says. "I could turn very well on my own."

Her passion for dance and a childhood dream of being a stunt double converged when she joined STREB in 2008, and today, she enjoys the wild rush that comes with testing out new arrangements. "The best part is that this work really scares me," she says. "Every day, I'm doing something that scares the shit out of me." The company, led by a gay woman and filled with LGBTQ+ people, also became a welcoming space for her to disclose her own queer identity.

"A lot of what we do is giving space to things that don't exist out there," Joseph says. "We don't want to fit the mold, and we want to give space to everyone and anyone who doesn't fit the mold and feels like they want, in some ways, to revolt." To that end, the doors to the Action Lab are always open to the public for rehearsals. STREB also offers classes for adults and children interested in confronting their fear and developing their bodies for impact. As Joseph says, "We are open to everyone and anyone who has a dream of coming in and learning how to fly."

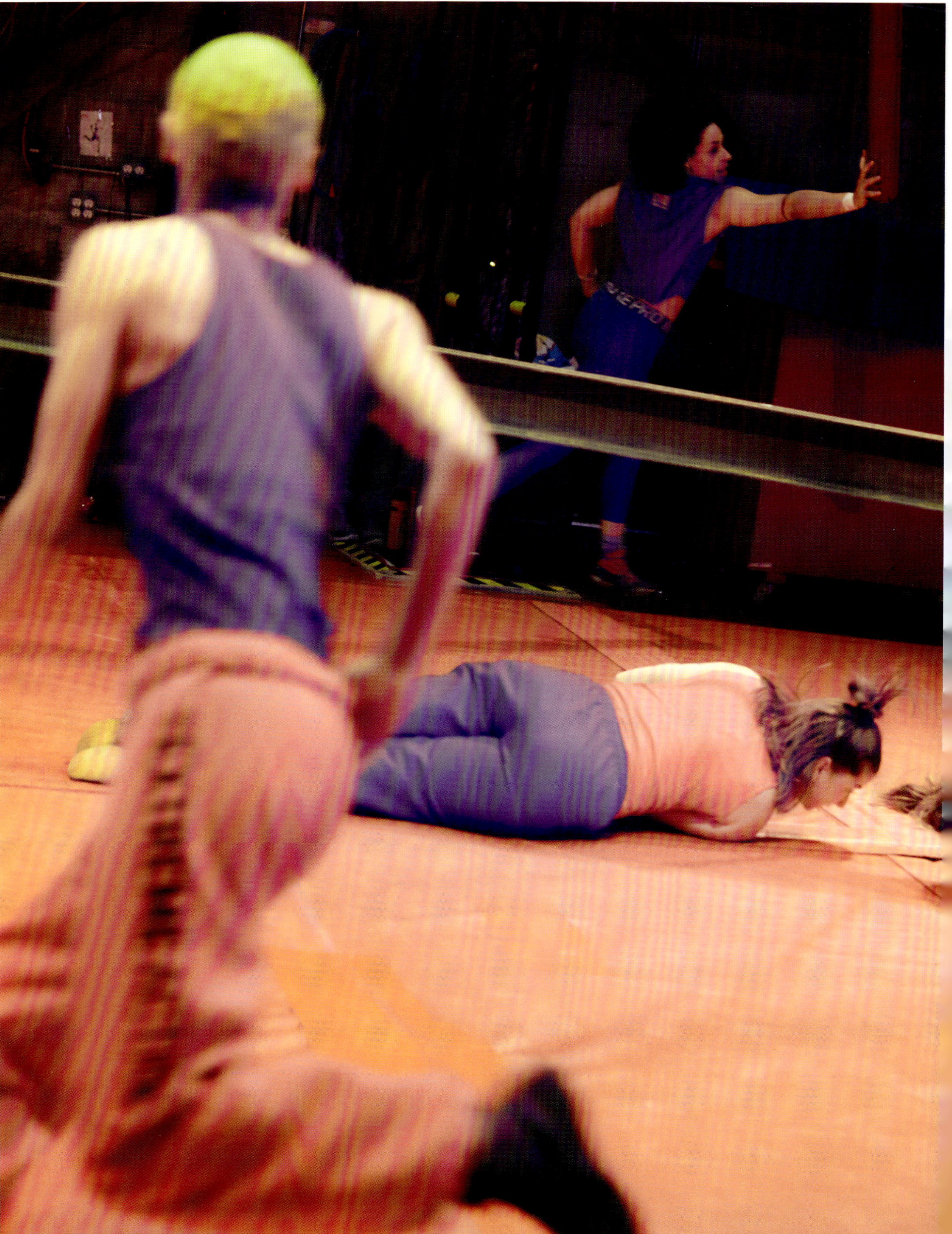

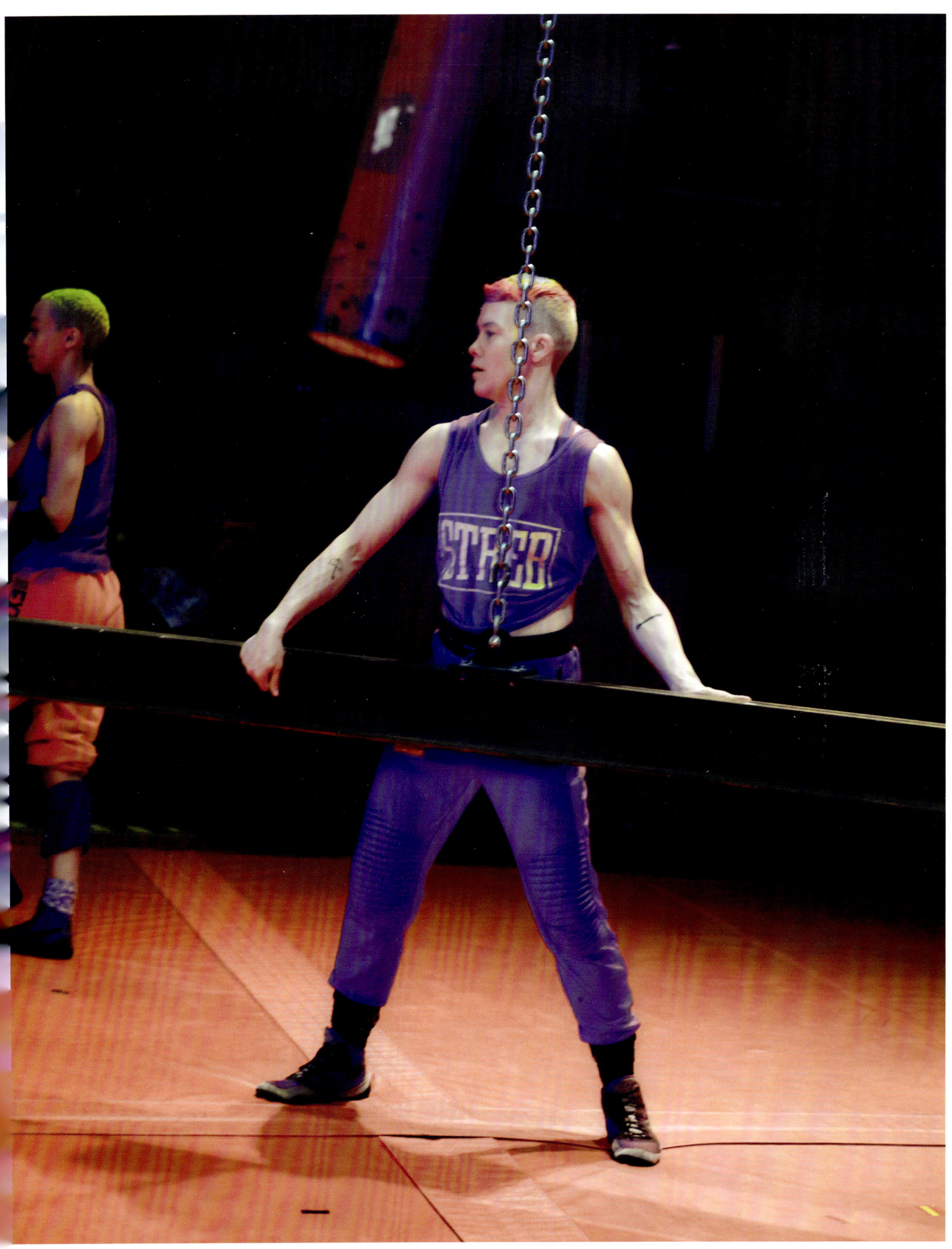

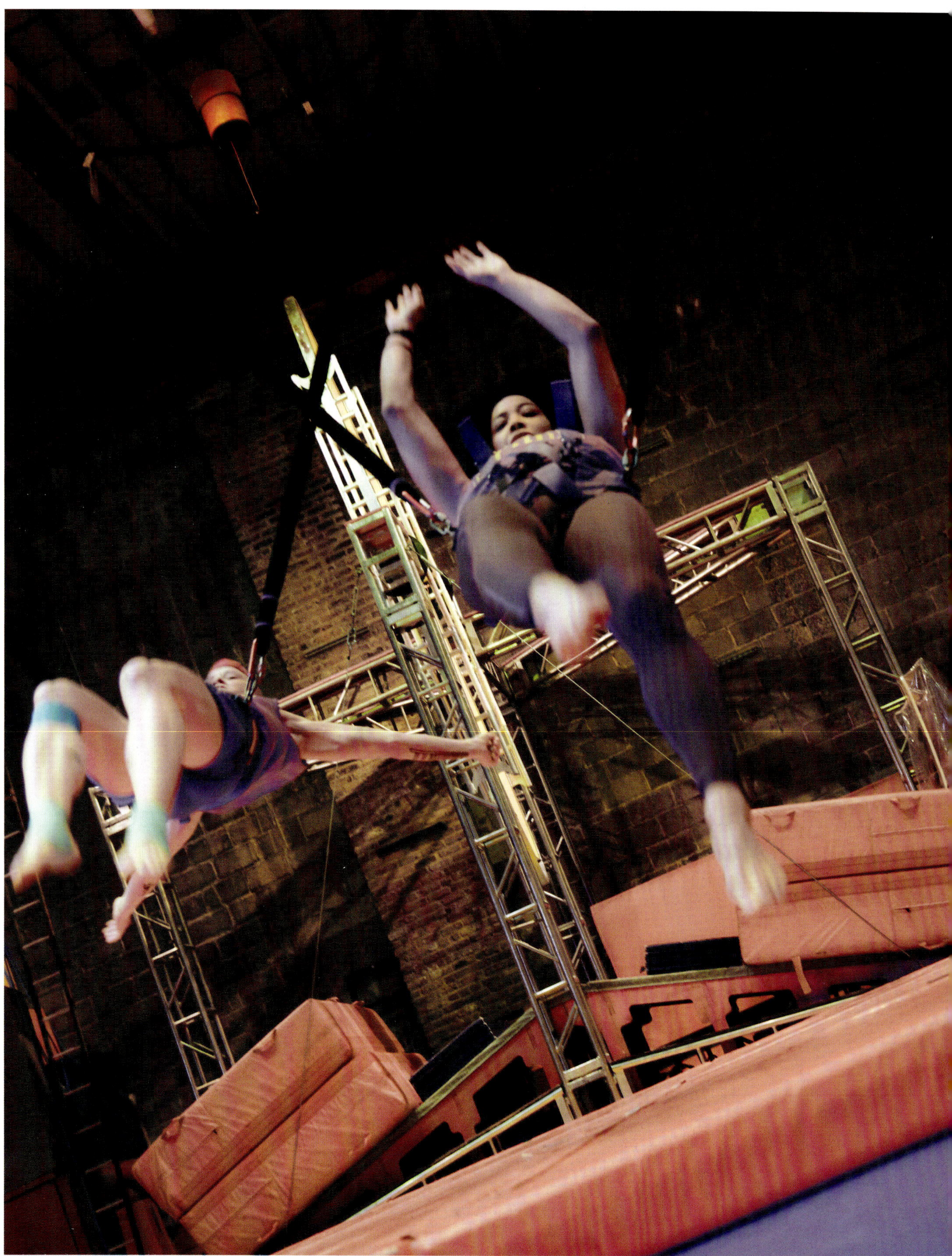

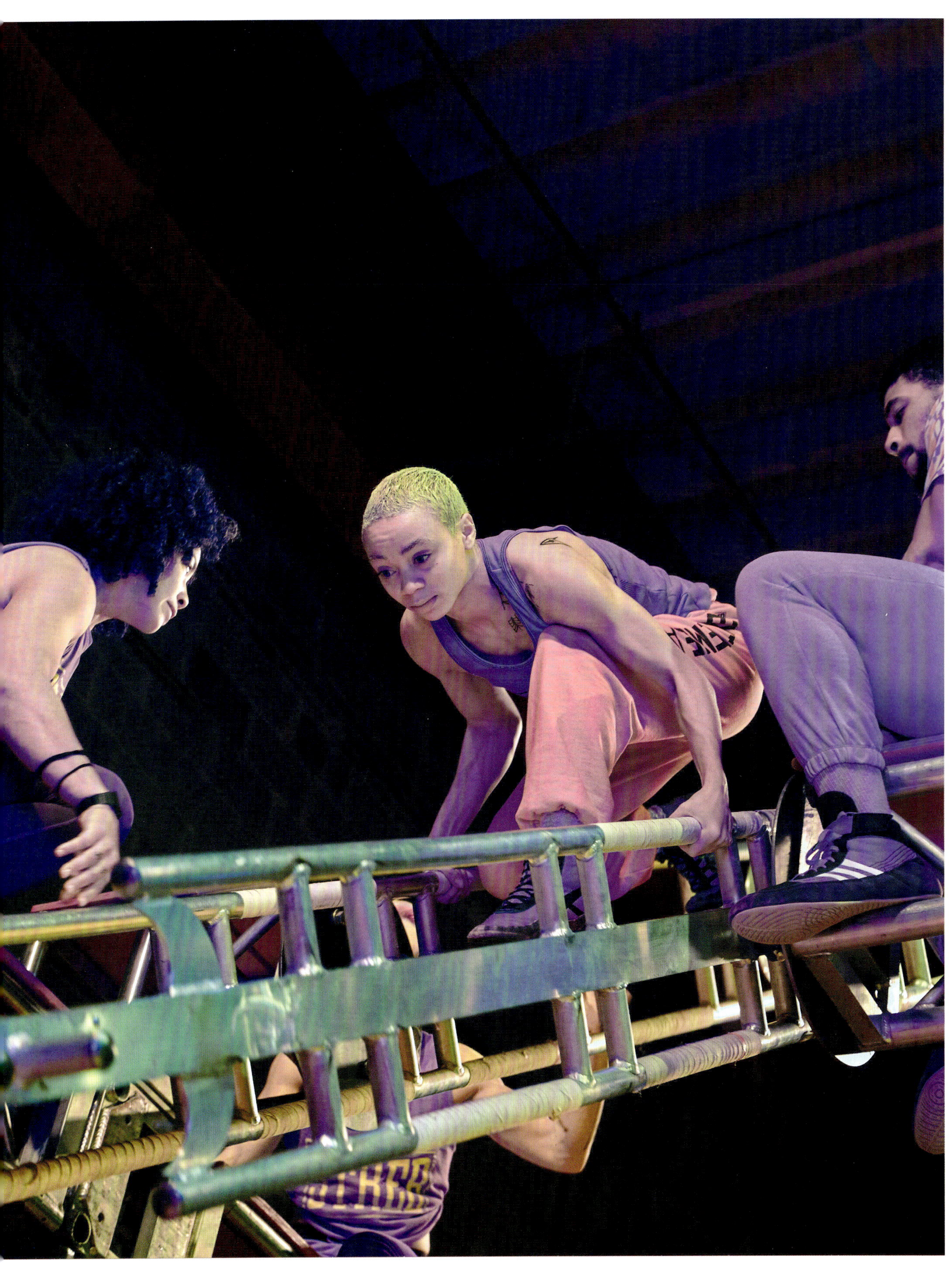

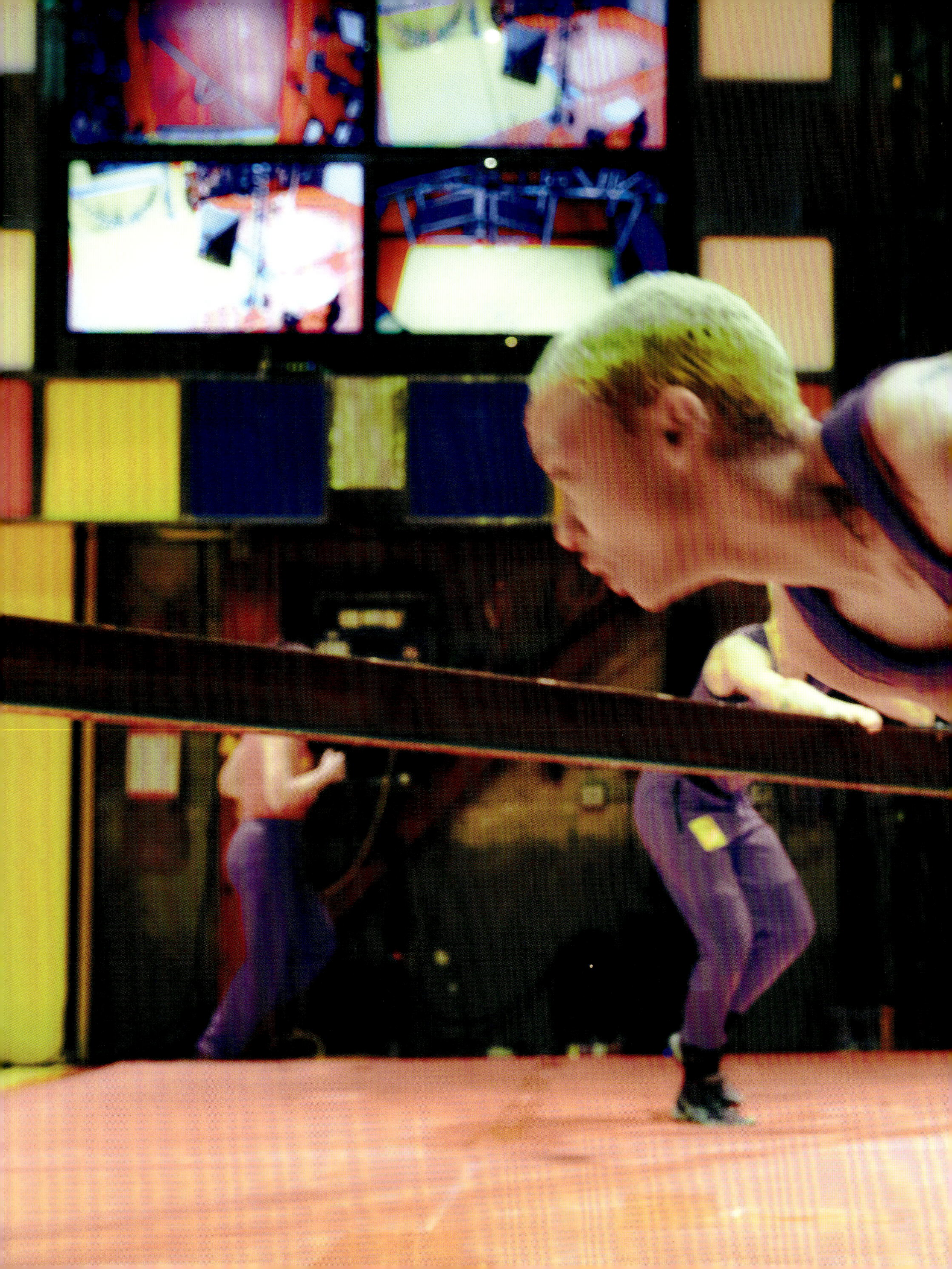

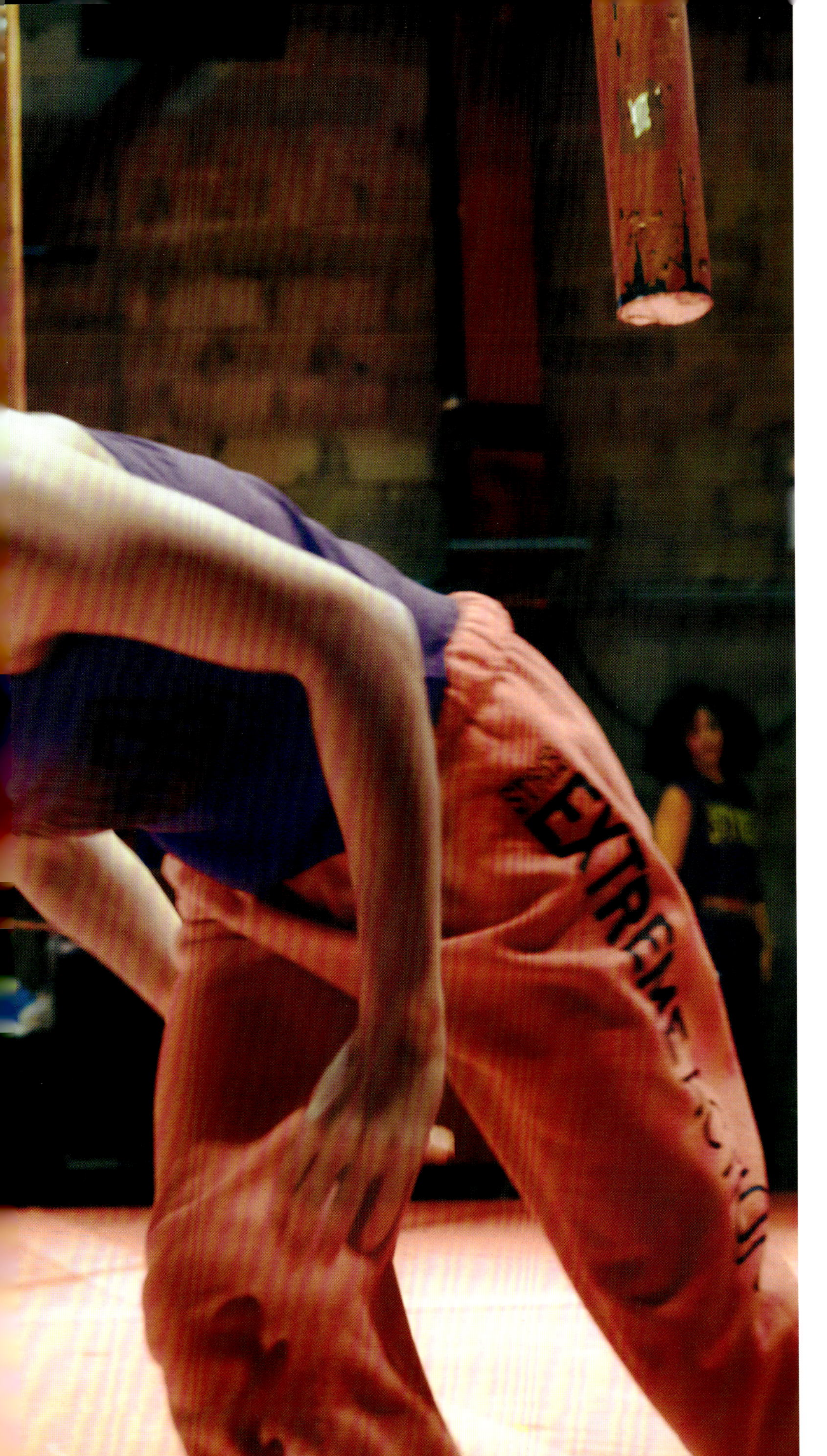
EXTREME

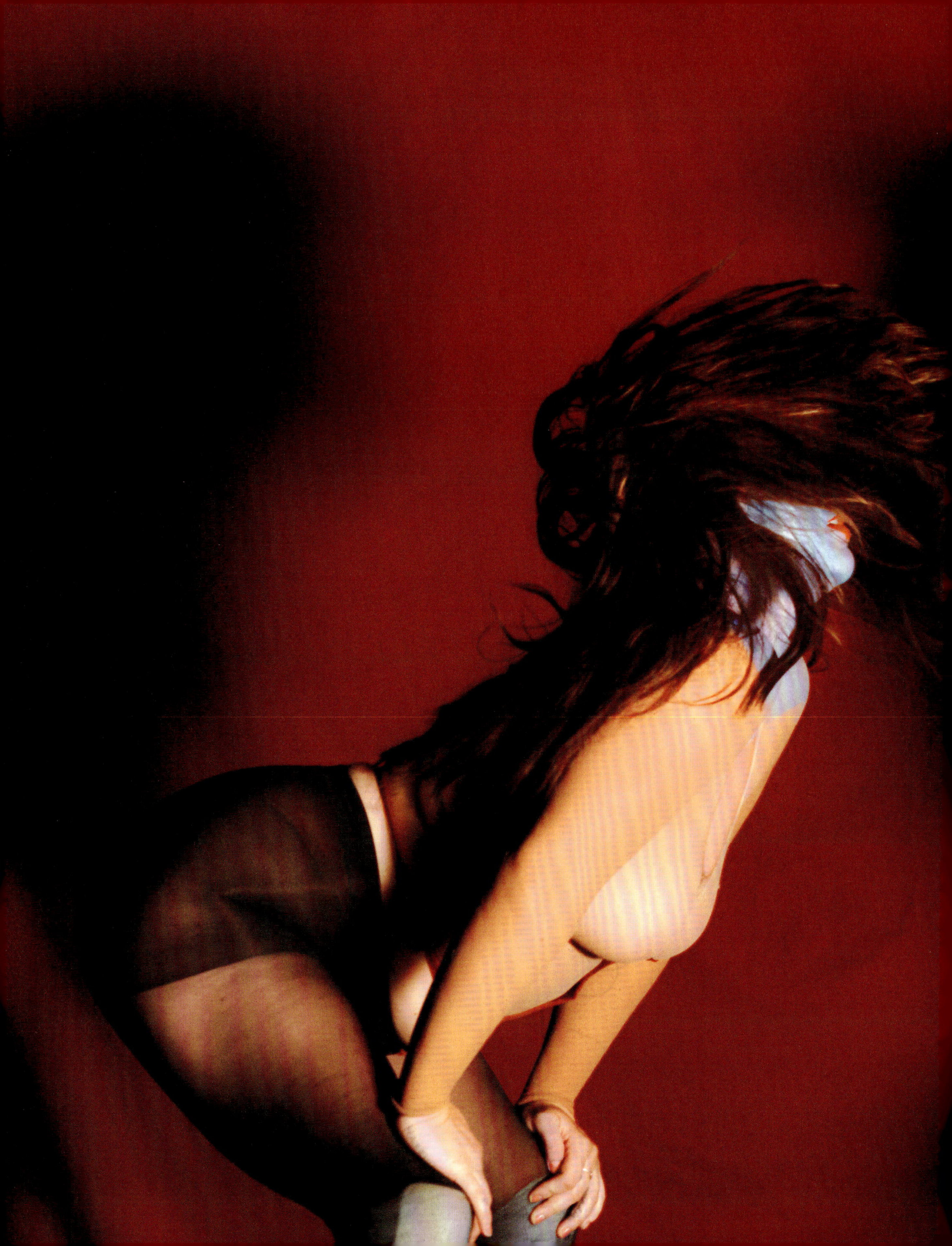

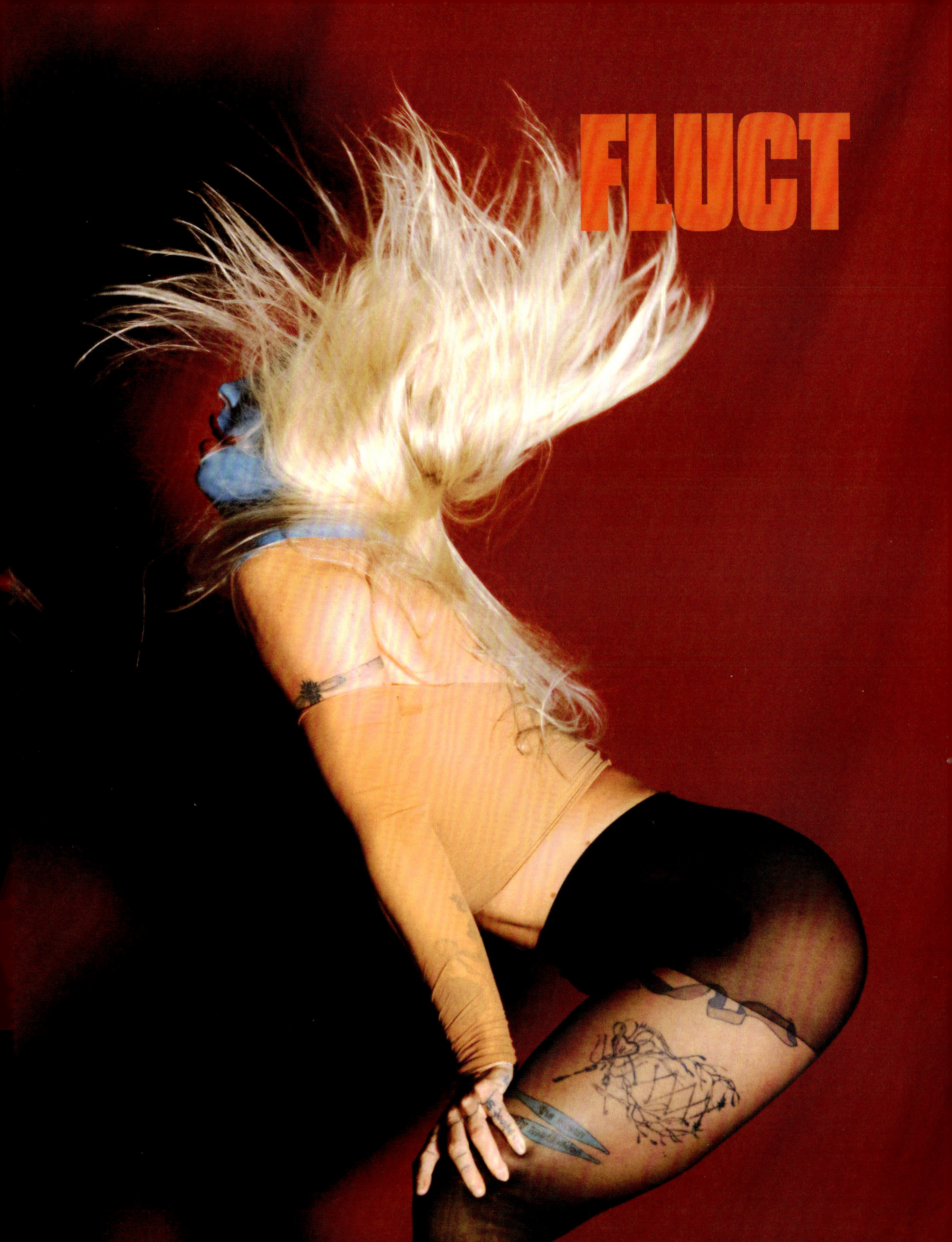
FLUCT

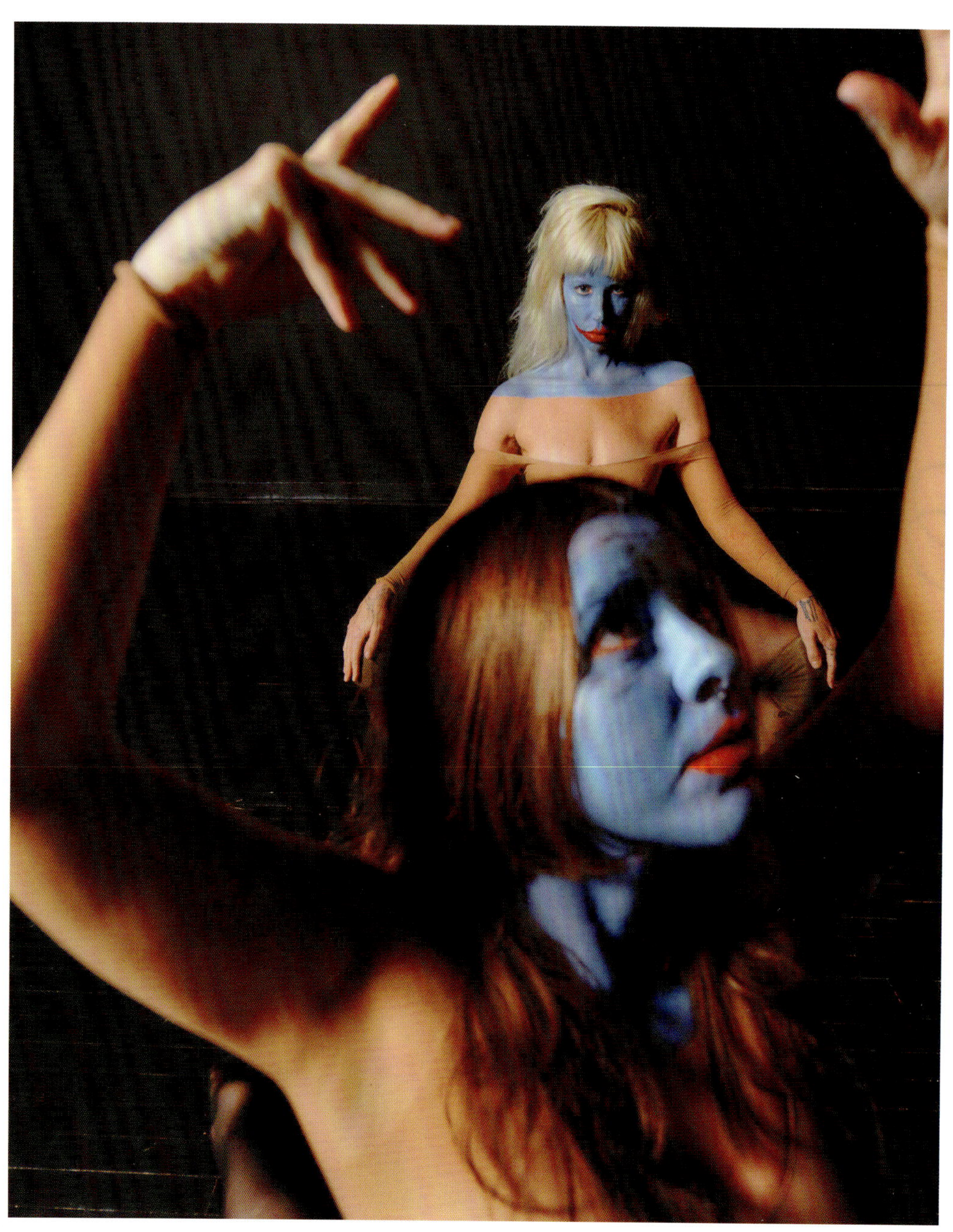

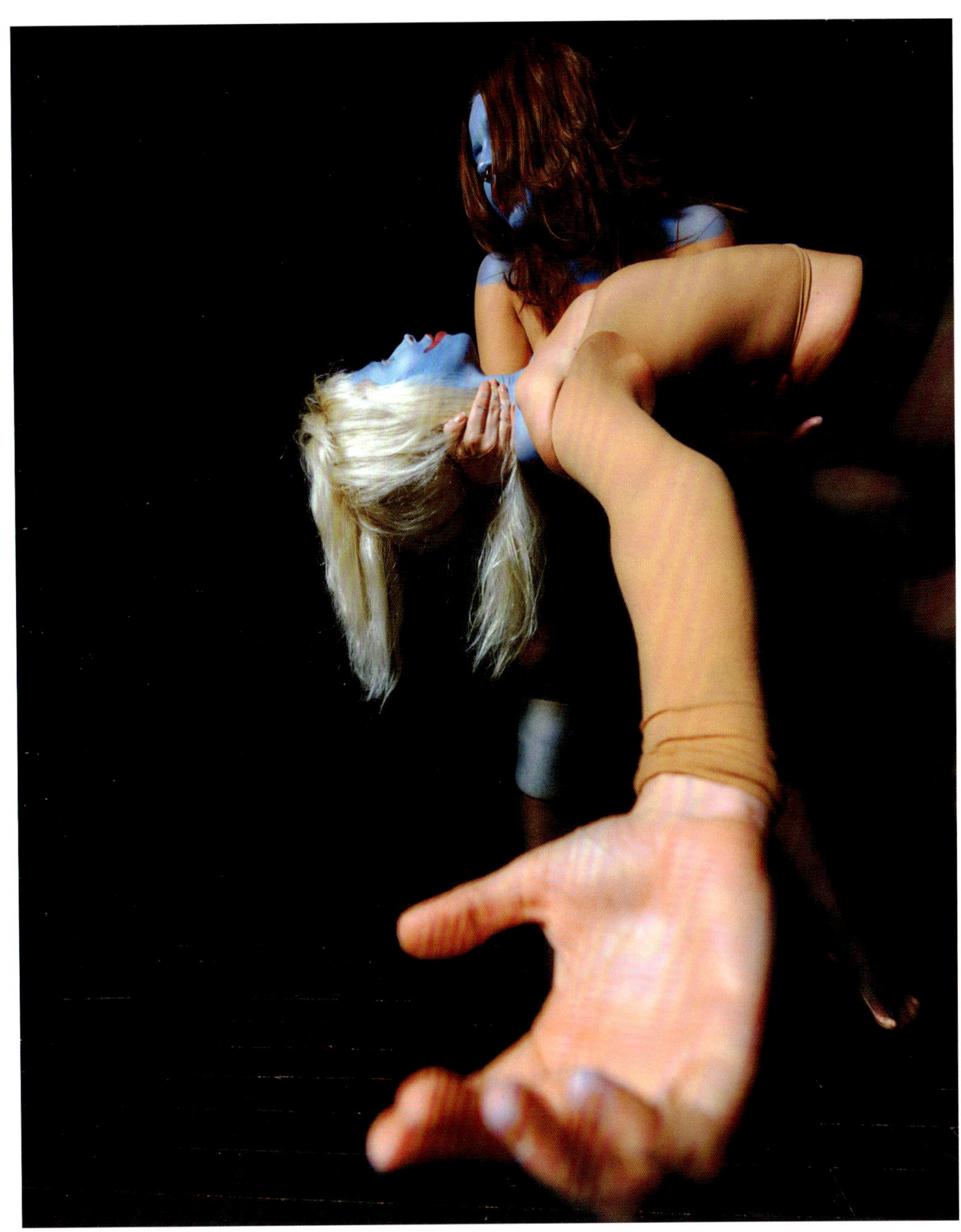

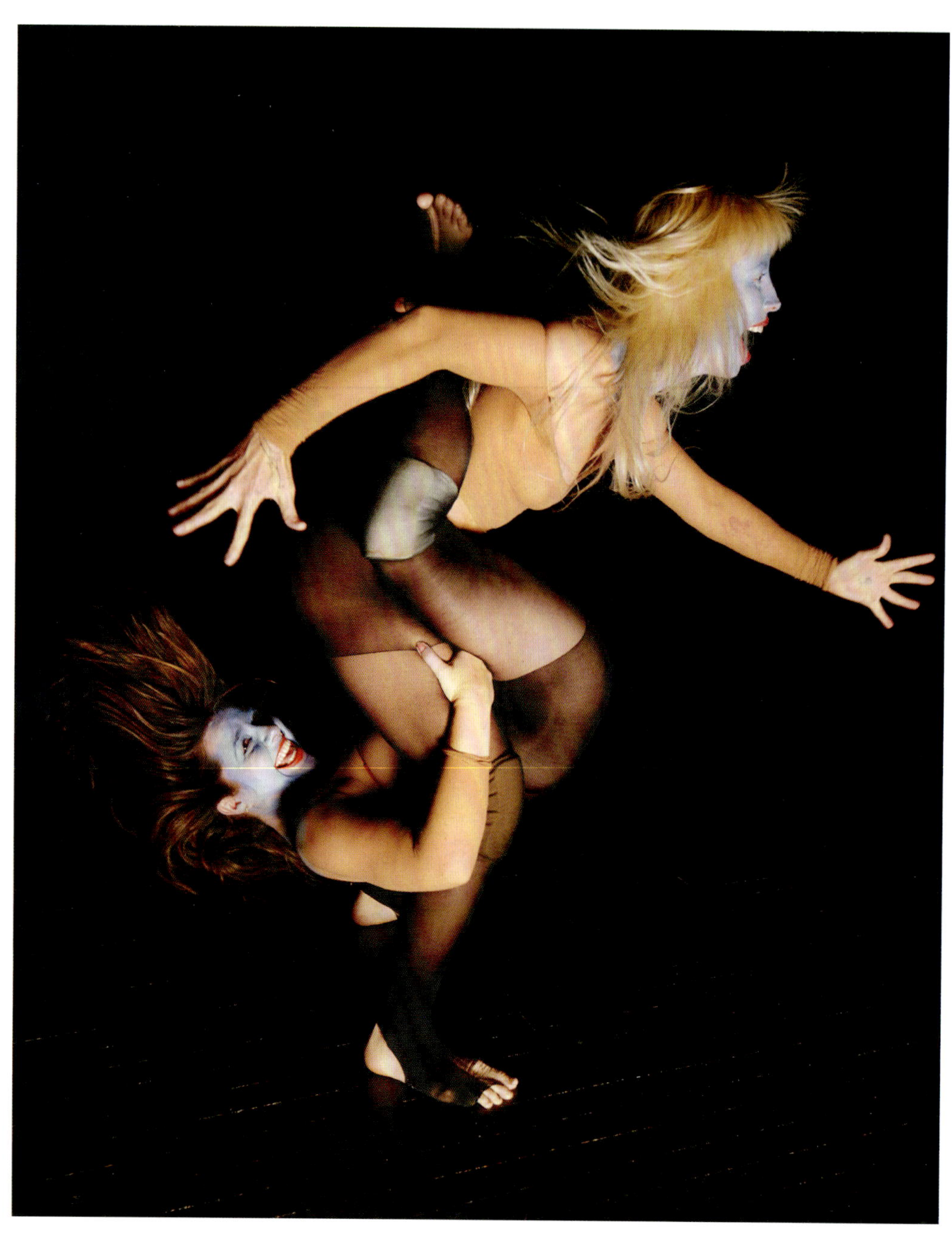

THE MUSIC OF POP PRODUCER SOPHIE HAS A VISCERAL QUALITY, even though it was entirely computer-generated and its creator opted, for many years, to remain anonymous. SOPHIE, uninterested in the limelight, hid in the darkness of a DJ booth or invited other artists to perform as proxies. It was during the promotional cycle for *Oil of Every Pearl's Un-Insides*, the first and only full album SOPHIE released before a tragic fatal accident in January 2021, that the artist finally felt ready to personify this work as a visible entity. "That was just a time when everything aligned," SOPHIE told me in 2018 for a profile published in *Out* magazine. "It's not a totally natural state of being for me to be visible. But it's something I'm learning a lot from—it can be helpful and nourishing to feel embodied."

The year before SOPHIE released *Oil of Every Pearl's Un-Insides*, the producer enlisted friends and frequent collaborators FlucT for what was billed as a live debut at the Teragram Ballroom in Los Angeles. This experimental performance duo, Monica Mirabile and Sigrid Lauren, had previously performed with SOPHIE at the New Museum in New York. During the Los Angeles show, FlucT pulled the musician into their eerie world of garish, over-the-top femininity and glitchy, culturally resonant poses. Lauren picked up and carried SOPHIE, turned upside down, atop her back. Mirabile dropped to the floor on all fours, sticking out her tongue and panting like a puppy. The performance was later immortalized with the 2018 release of the music video for "Ponyboy," the album's kinky, bass-heavy second single.

Feeling at home within one's body can be a tenuous state to grasp, especially for LGBTQ+ people who are often taught to feel at odds with their own bodies and impulses. FlucT approaches their movement practice as if it were a form of somatic therapy. Their performances offer one pathway toward embodiment through the public, often violent processing of pains held within. Watching them dance provides a momentary release from the onslaught of information and content that tell us what we need or how we must be to feel fulfilled. Lauren might hold Mirabile's leg like a rifle as a track shifts through harsh electronic fuzz. Often FlucT dances alongside live musicians or to self-edited scores played on loops, and their work was rooted in subcultural spaces before it arrived in fine art settings. These origins laid the groundwork for Mirabile's and Lauren's individual investigations as well as a blossoming of other movement makers rising from the underground.

"It's about the experience of feeling empty and then trying to fill that emptiness with what bullshit advertisements tell you will make you feel better—sex, drugs, and material," Mirabile says. "Why and what does it mean to be in a body? What does it mean to affect that body in a way that brings it out of whack? What makes you feel whole?"

The duo was exploring these and other questions well before they became a formalized partnership, back in the late aughts when they were living together in a warehouse in Baltimore with more than ten other people. Lauren had grown up in the city and recently returned after completing college on a lacrosse scholarship, and Mirabile had moved there to study interdisciplinary sculpture at Maryland Institute College of Art. They commiserated over their shared experiences. "I love my family, but they're totally dysfunctional," Mirabile says. Having studied ballet as a child before pivoting to athletics, Lauren says that "being physical always was my only safe place."

The two formed the Baltimore Experimental Dance Collective with their roommates and various other collaborators and channeled those mutual histories into visceral live works, which they showed at their home and in local clubs. "We would paint our bodies pink and wore gemstones. Half of my head was

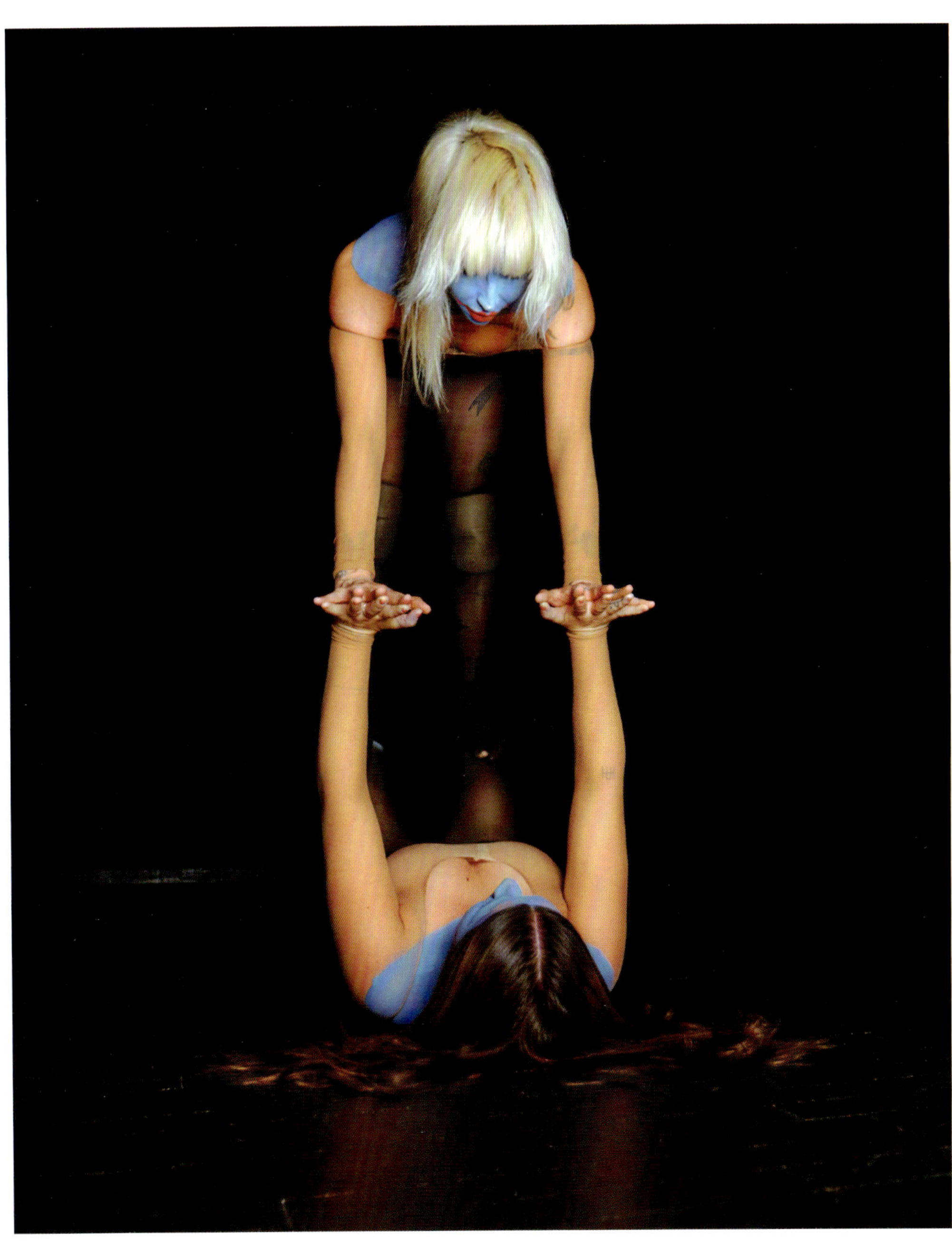

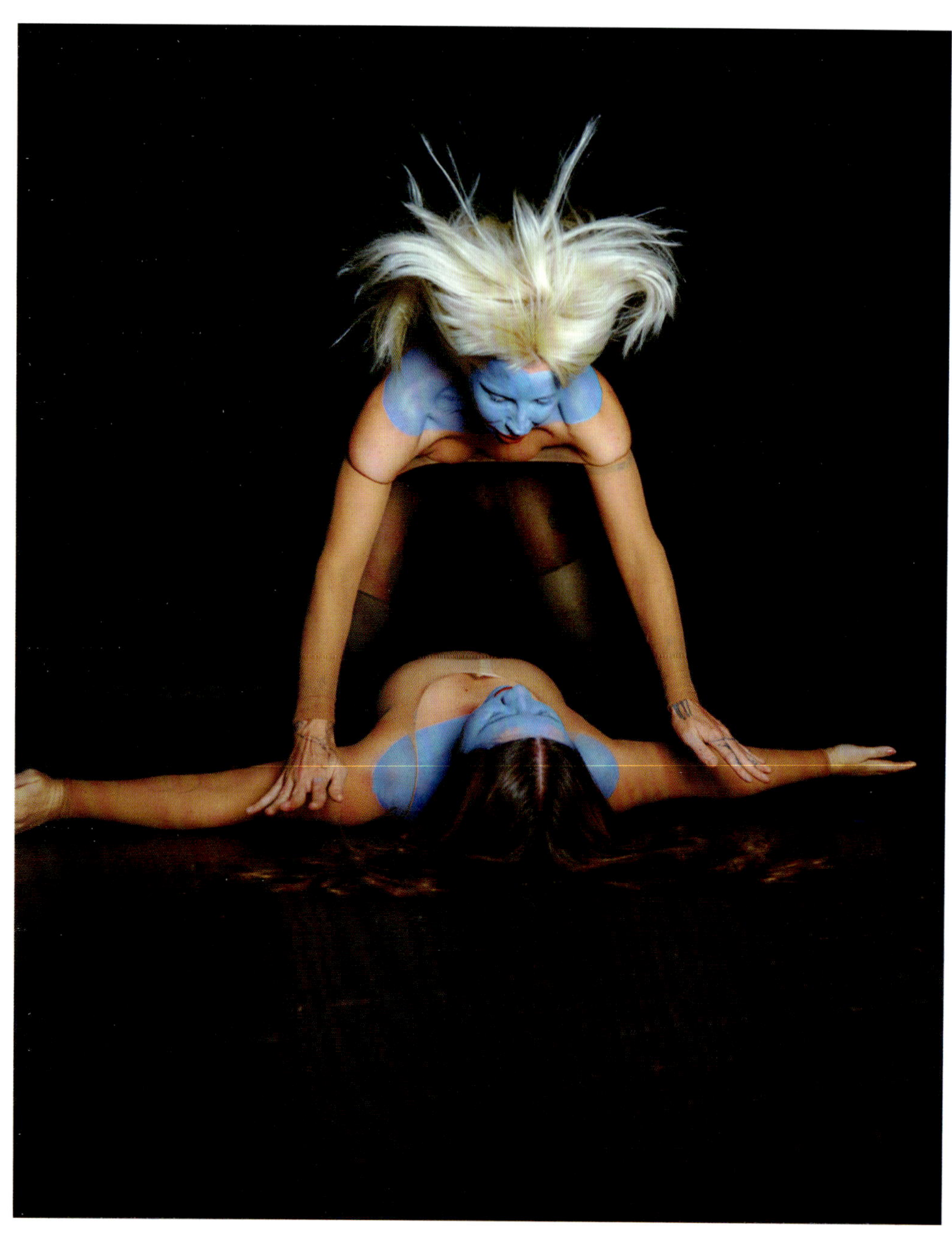

shaved and dyed with orange stripes," Mirabile recalls. "It was a little utopia in the sense of we weren't worried about who's watching. There wasn't really anyone to please."

"We were creating vocabulary from the beginning," Lauren adds. "[It was] fast, jittery, glitchy."

They coined the name FlucT in 2010 as a shorthand for the term fluctuation. "We were constantly fluctuating through these emotions that were intense—feeling really on top of it and then feeling like you have no control," Mirabile says. Soon after moving to New York in late 2012, they were staging performances in nightclubs like Bossa Nova Civic Club and the now-defunct Passion Lounge. In those spaces, their shows grew increasingly aggressive. They began forgoing a stage to dance near the audience, bombarding the viewer with all their sweat and fear. These pieces moved through a toolbox of sculptural poses that evoked recurring critiques of authority and power. FlucT's take on La Pietà, the classic image in Christian art of the Virgin Mary holding the corpse of Jesus Christ after his removal from the cross, sees Mirabile cradling Lauren. Her mouth, painted with oversize red lips, freezes in an eerily detached grin, while Lauren's arm rests on the ground. It's an image loaded with violence, care, and grief, or as Mirabile says, "It's the relationship between Sigrid and I."

In April 2014, FlucT was invited by the artist Juliana Huxtable to perform at the Queens Museum to toast the opening of the exhibition *13 Most Wanted Men: Andy Warhol and the 1964 World's Fair*. For one scene of the work they showed, *Control Top*, Lauren ripped down Mirabile's body-shaping tights to reveal a dollar bill covering her crotch. The gesture gave way to what they call the "Freak Out," when they jump, thrash wildly, or fall to the ground, "gaping, gushing, and glitching."

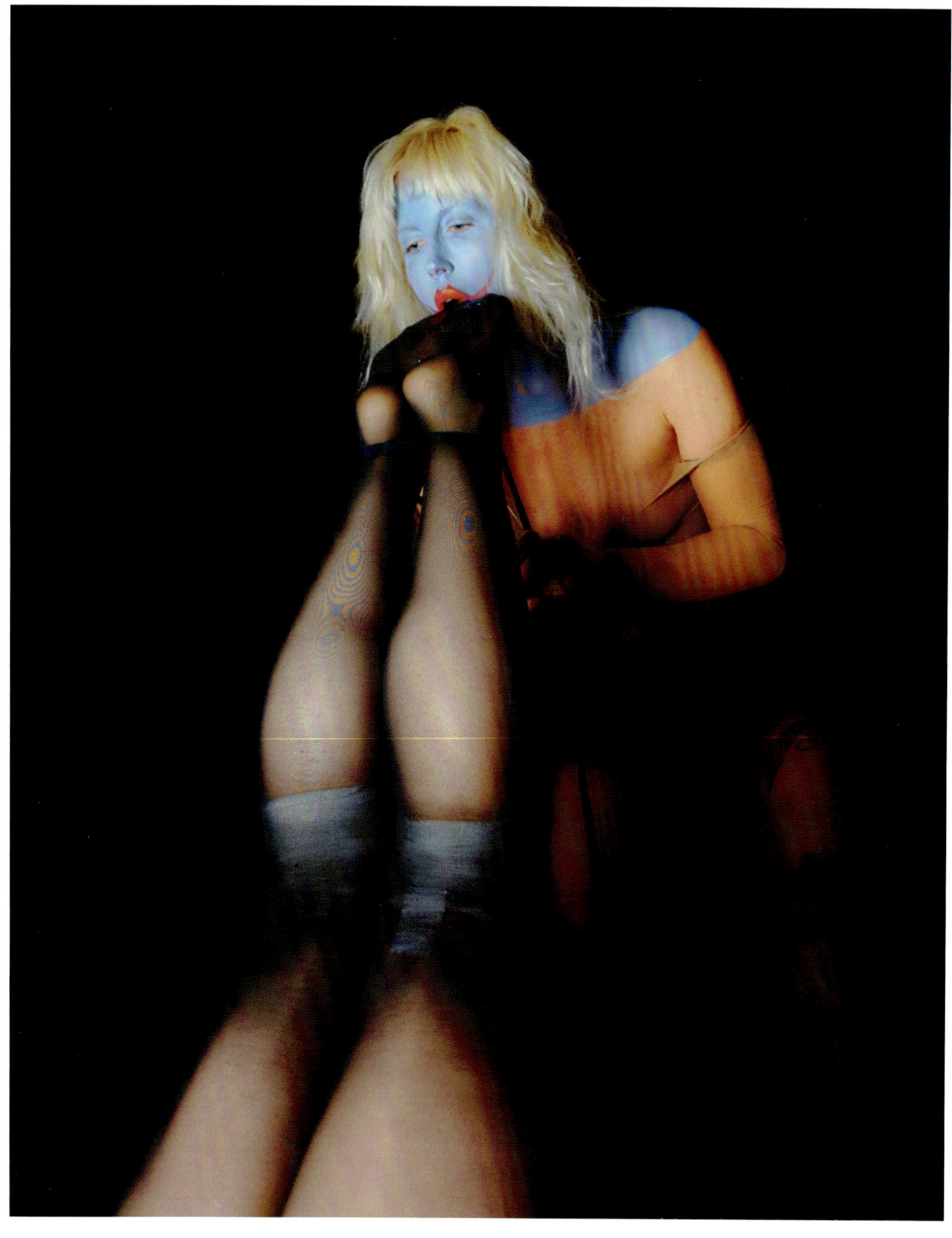

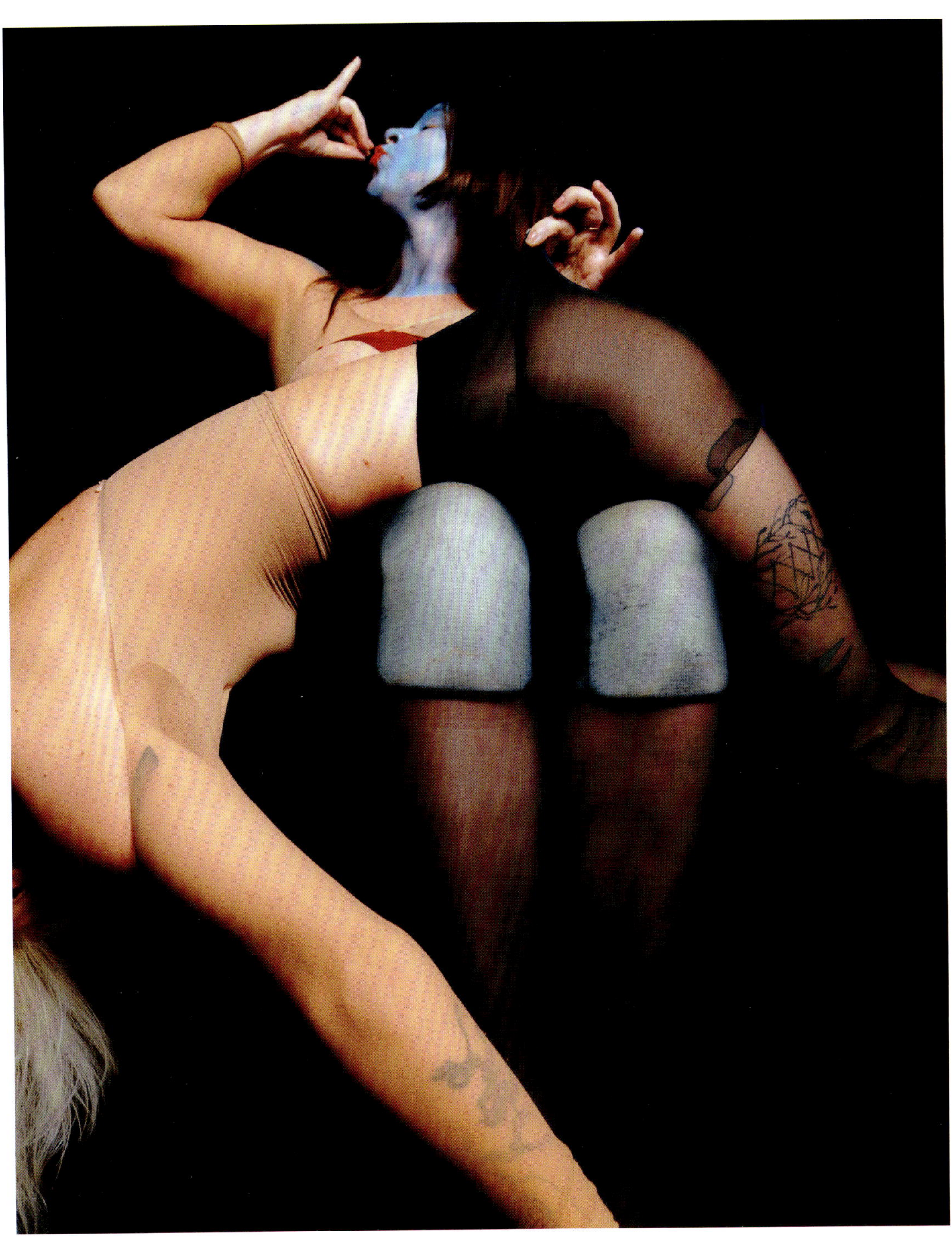

In the 2020 book *Glitch Feminism: A Manifesto*, author and curator Legacy Russell describes the glitch in contemporary art as a "vehicle of refusal, a strategy of non-performance" through which marginalized communities "create space through rupture" and forge their own identities. She asks that we consider what might typically be seen as mistakes or errors—especially regarding constructs of sexuality, race, and gender—as the things that have the potential to free us. In FlucT's performances, the glitch is a physical representation of a psychic release. "It's when I realize I'm so sick or I've been exposed to all this toxicity, and then you get out of it," Lauren says. "If you were a cartoon, your whole body would burst open and light would go everywhere."

"We were glitching because we were recognizing the dissonance that we had been experiencing our whole lives, really," Mirabile says. "So much of what we were doing was happening because of the conversations that we were having about being women in our twenties and in a society that hates women."

FlucT has performed at the Guggenheim in New York, Art Basel in Miami, and the Broad in Los Angeles, as well as in numerous galleries and nightlife environments. *Alienated Labor*, originally shown at Andrea Rosen Gallery in 2017, is in the collection of the Whitney Museum of American Art. Collaboration, with each other and other artists in their networks, has always been a key facet of FlucT's work. They continue to operate Otion Front, an accessible white-box studio tucked inside a backyard in Bushwick, which they opened in 2013. The space has helped nurture a generation of contemporary artists working across dance, music, and fashion. FlucT's collaborations with SOPHIE were developed partly in this modest workspace.

Following a friends-only November 2021 show at Performance Space New York, FlucT went on a hiatus so that

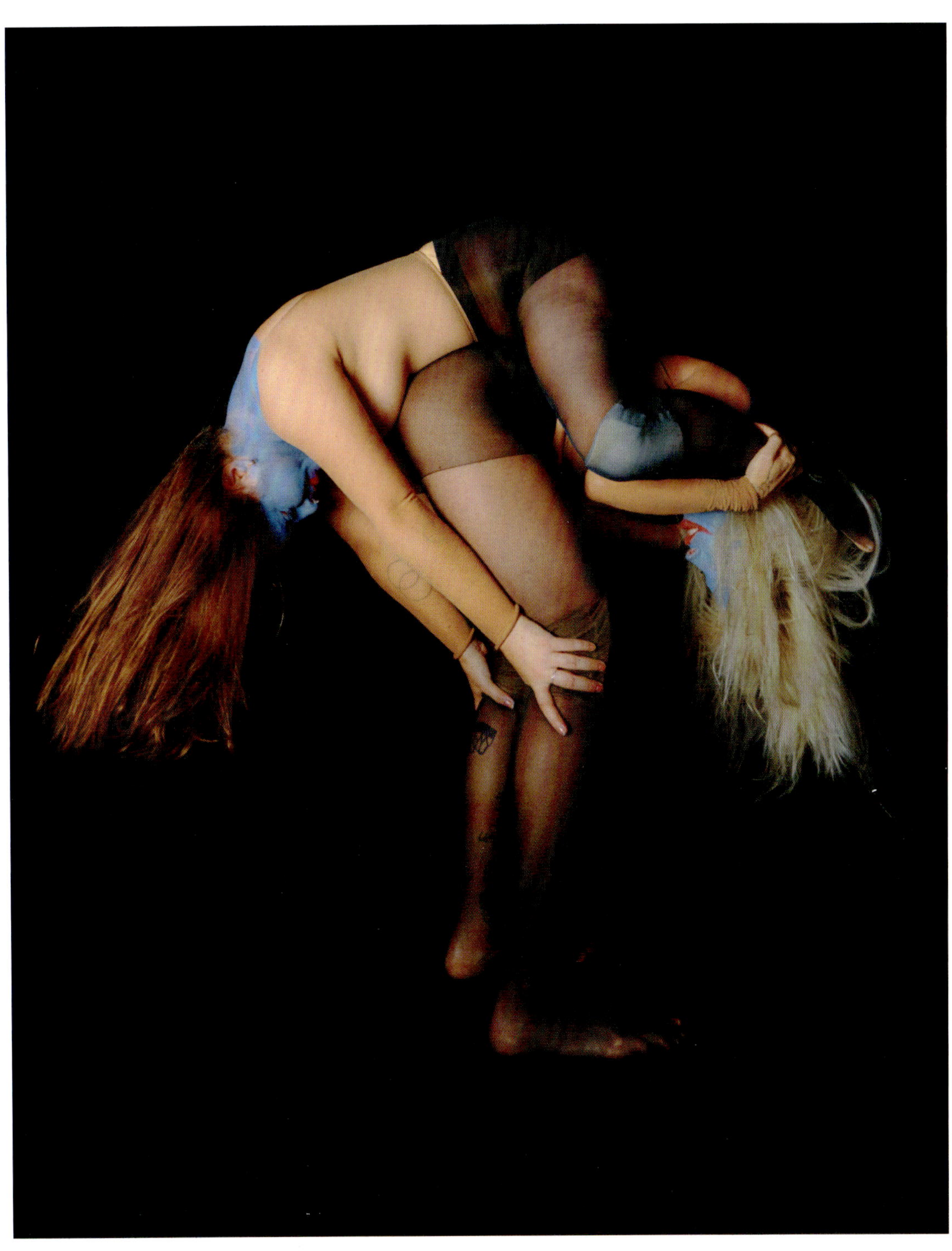

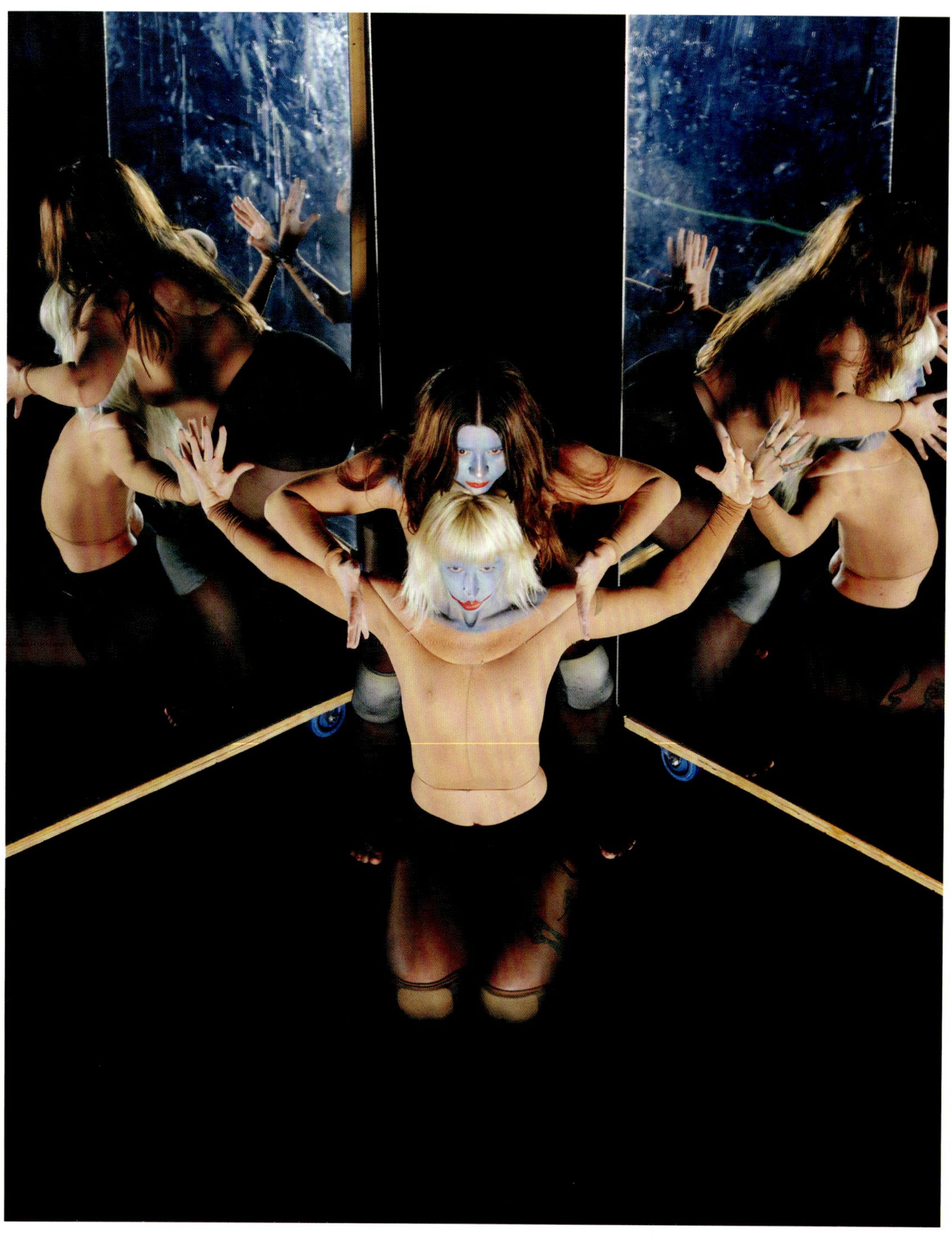

Mirabile and Lauren could pursue other projects on their own. At the time of our interview, Mirabile was curating the Open Movement series of artist-led workshops at Performance Space, where she has featured Lauren's class How to Throw a Body a Way. Lauren has used the hiatus to work as a movement director for clothing brands such as Calvin Klein, Mugler, and Peter Do. Still, the principles the two developed together continue to inform and flow into their other endeavors.

"Embodiment is a practice, something that may never be attained," Lauren says. "Just like I may never be able to do a front flip."

"We're always being and becoming at the same time," Mirabile adds. "That's what this practice is."

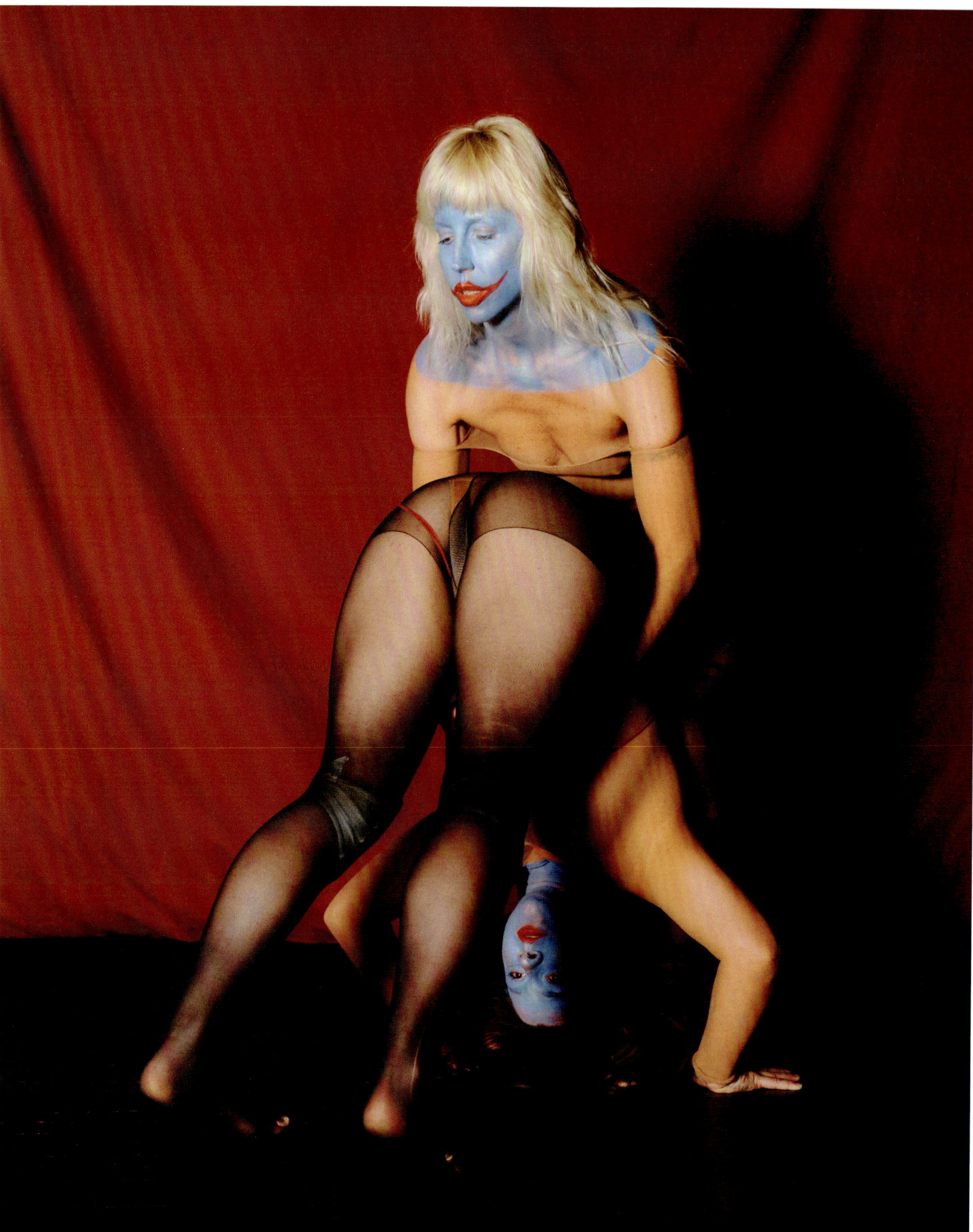

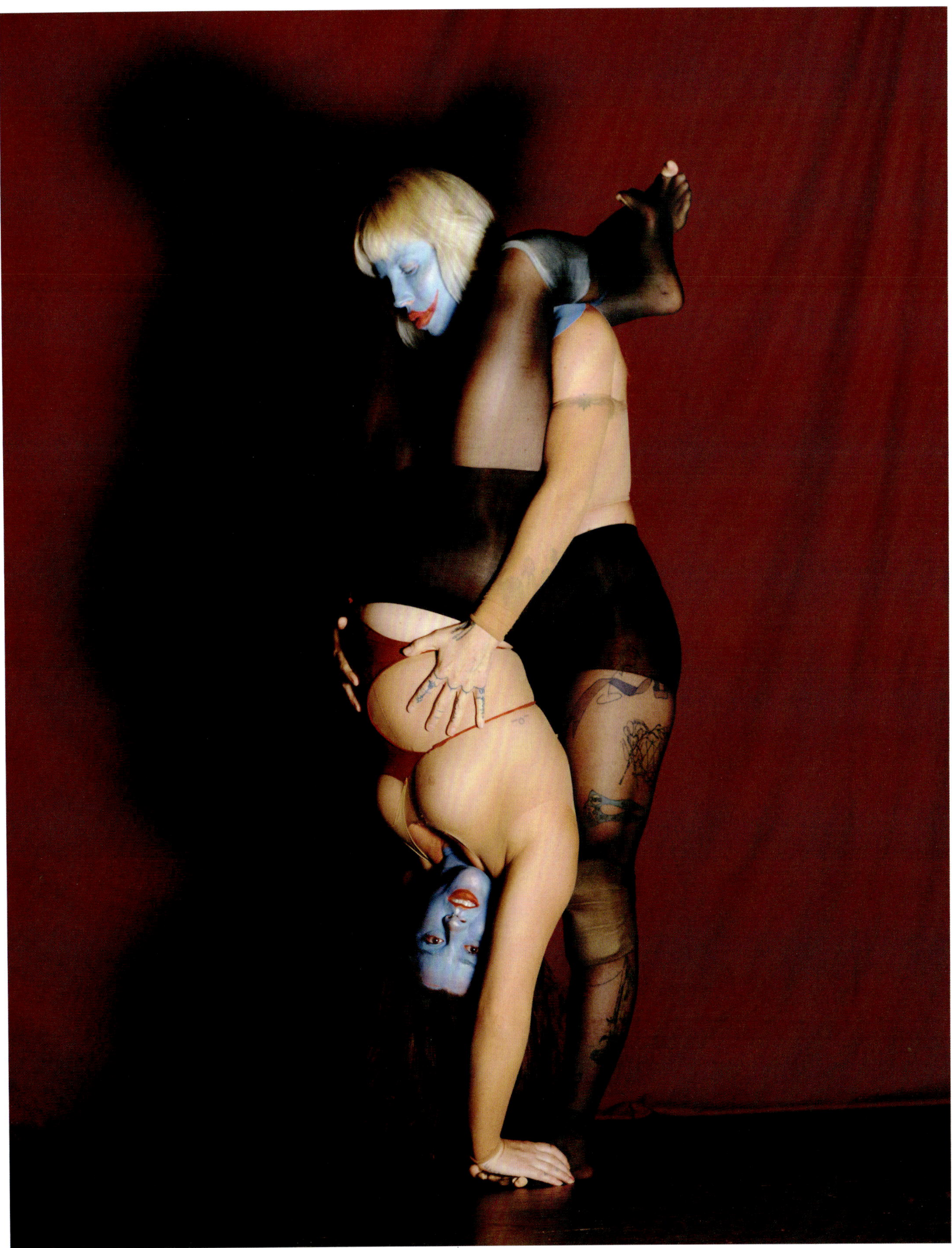

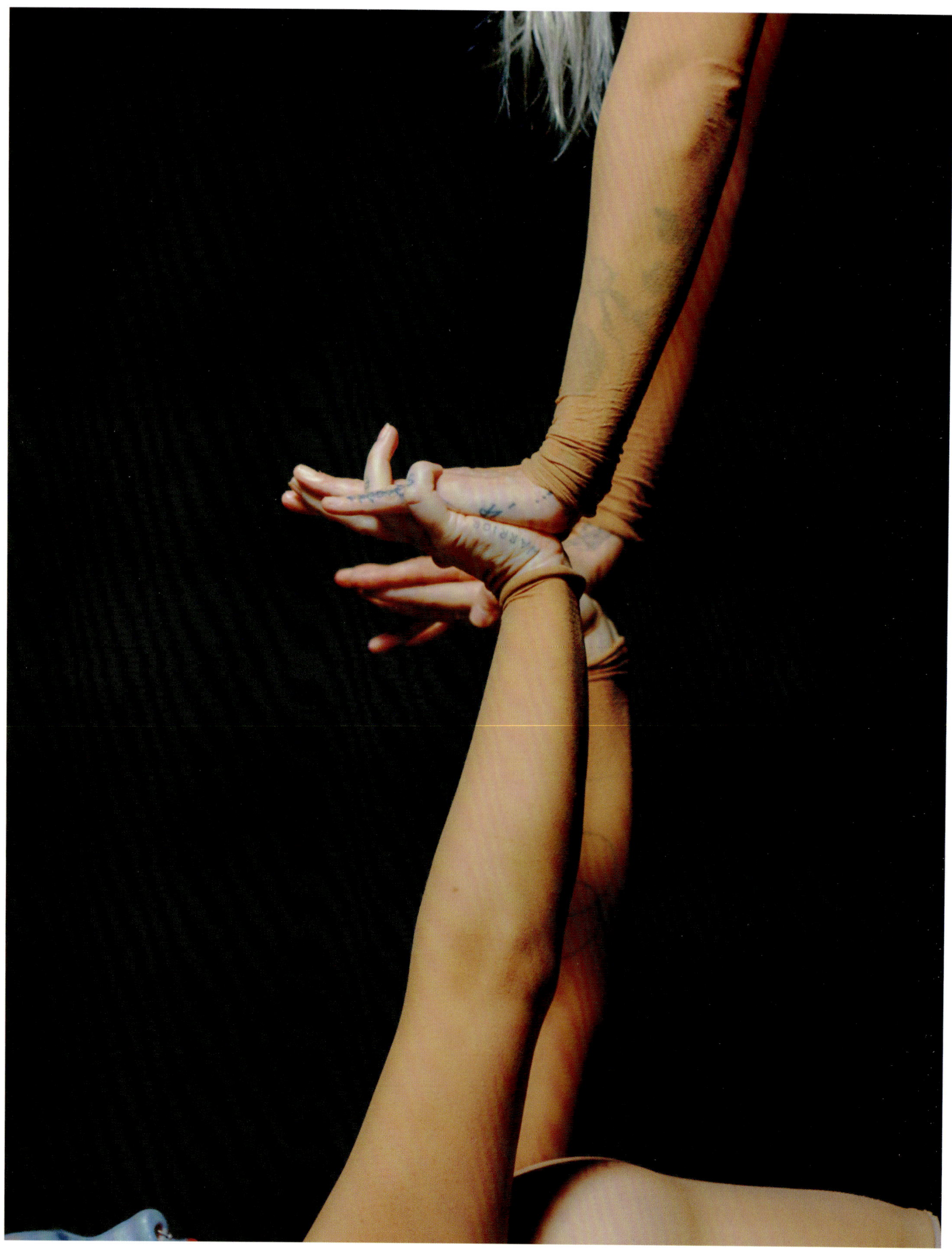

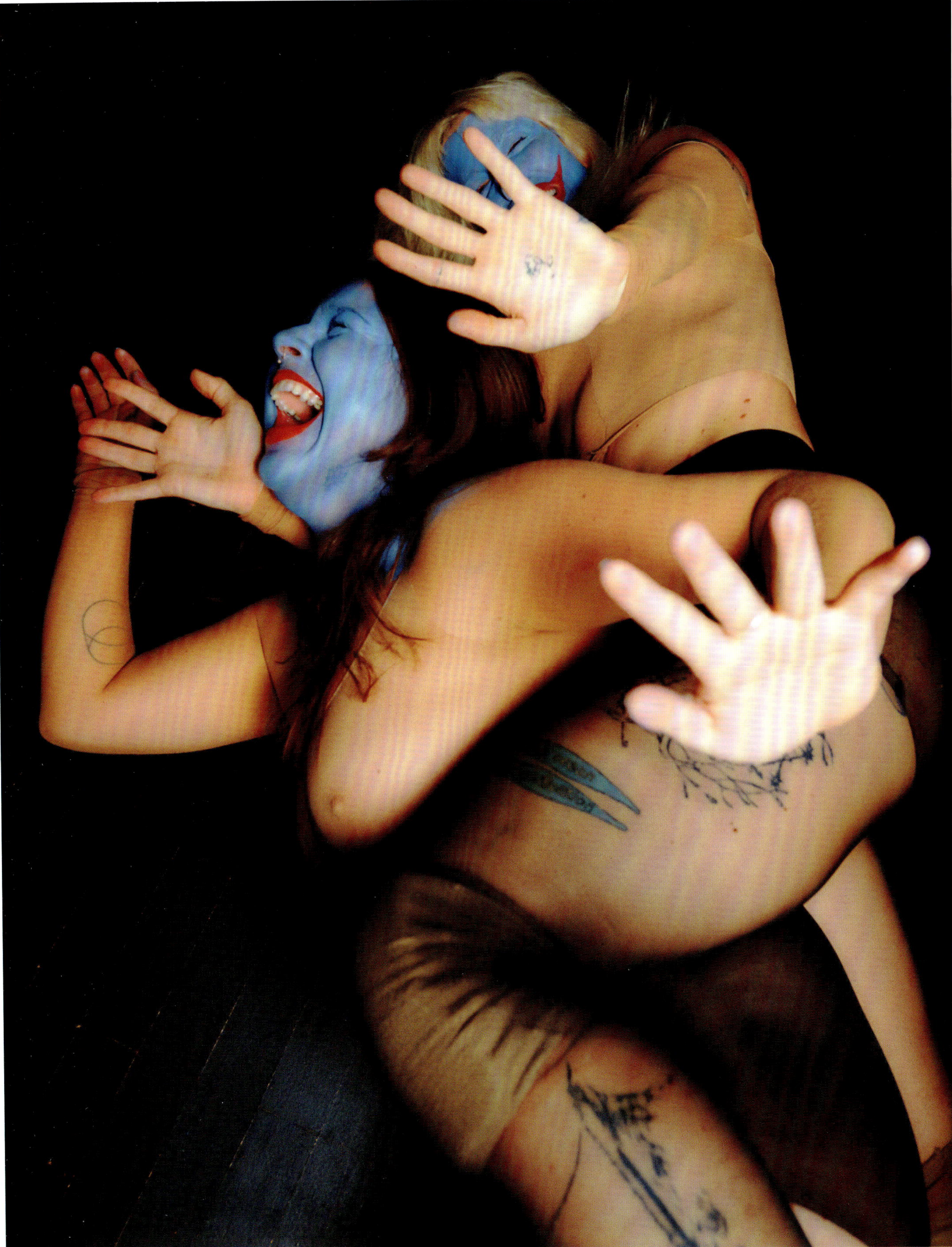

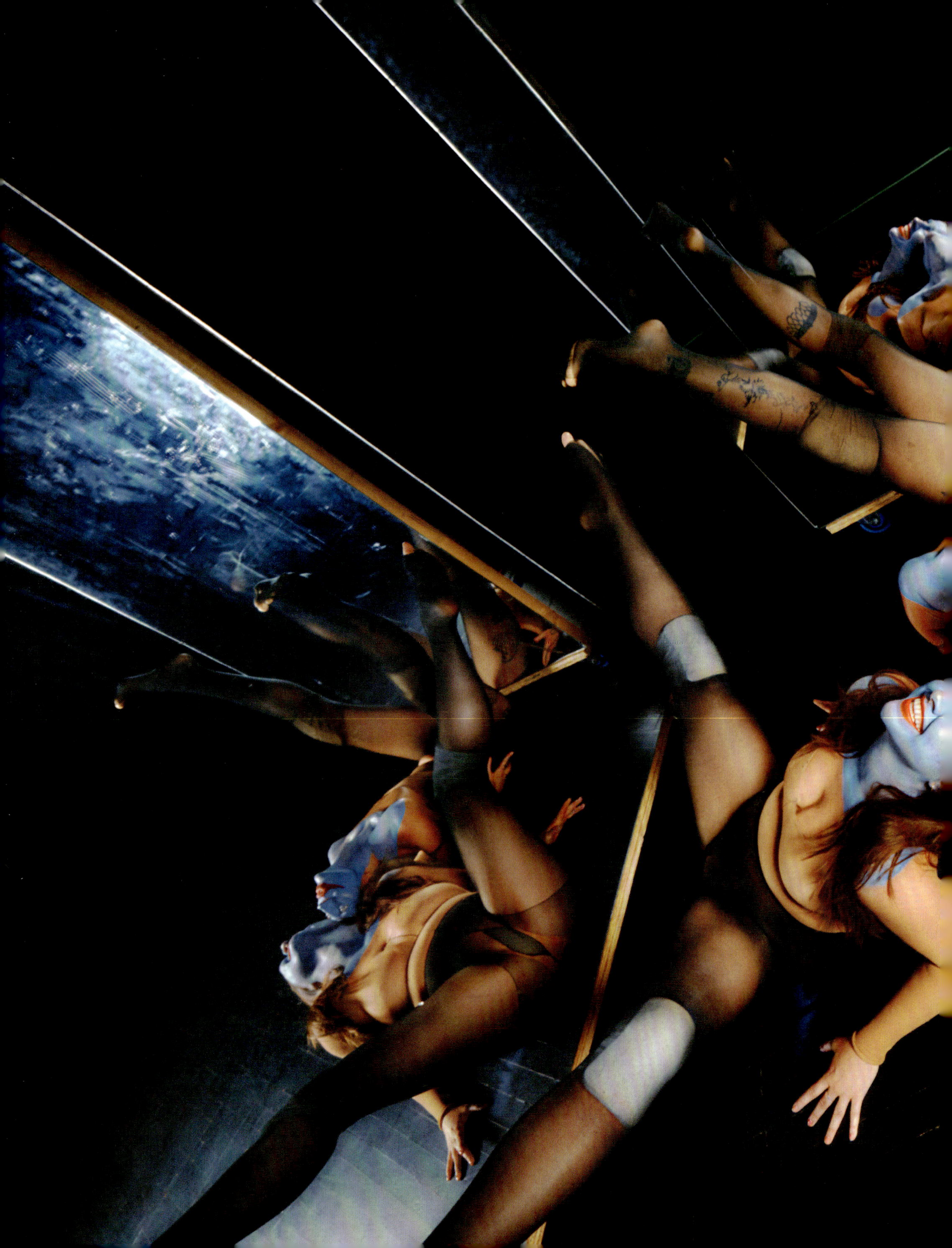

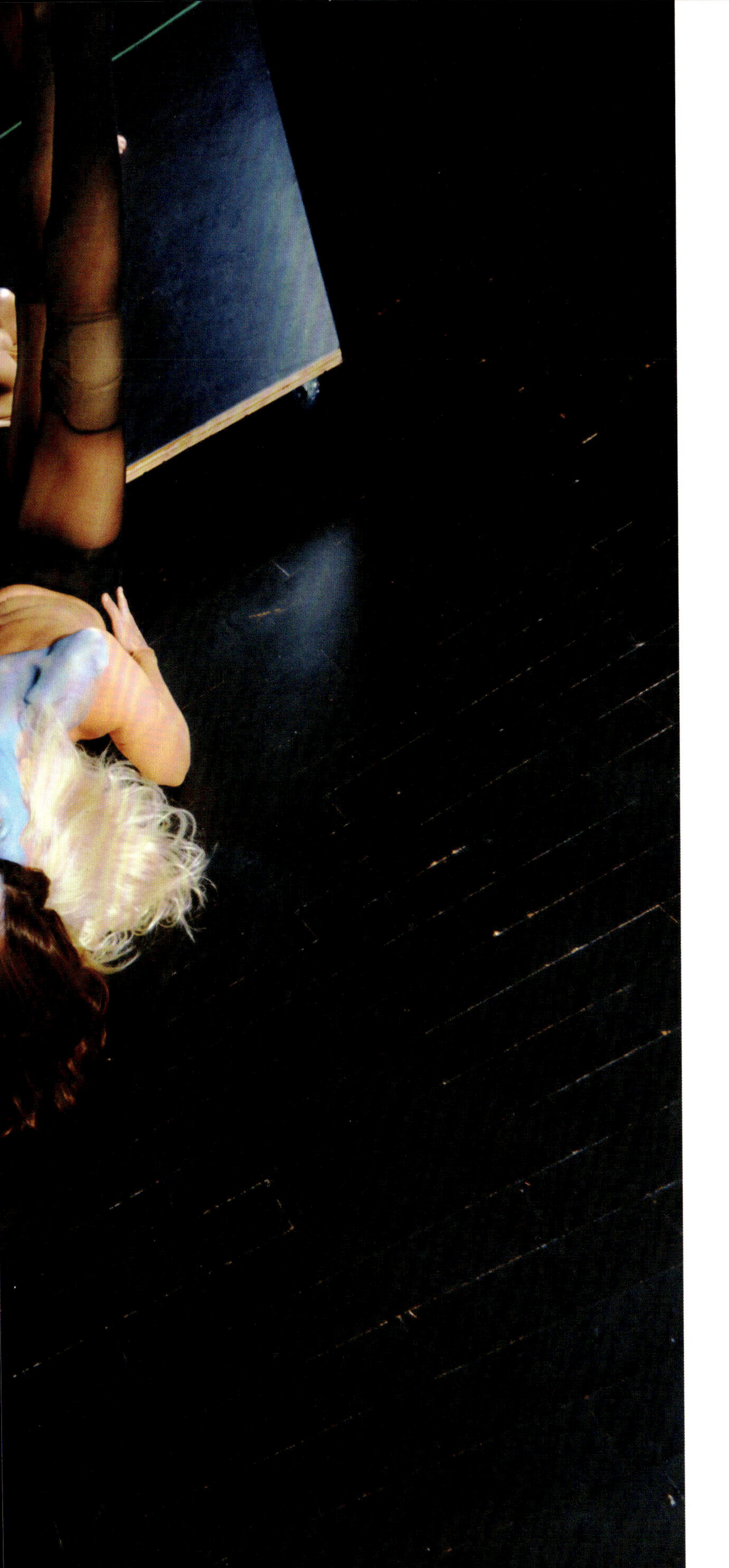

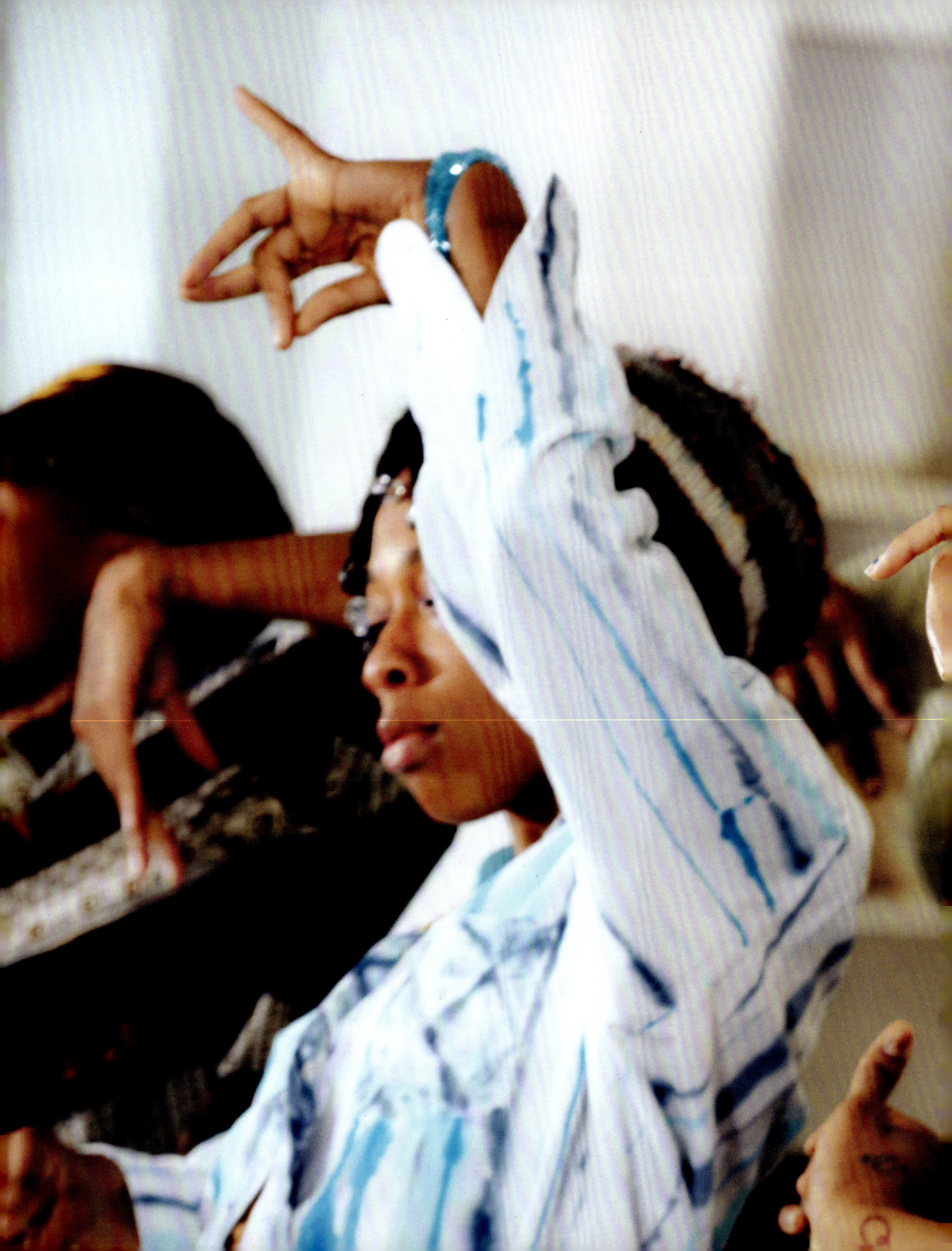

MASTERZ AT WORK DANCE FAMILY

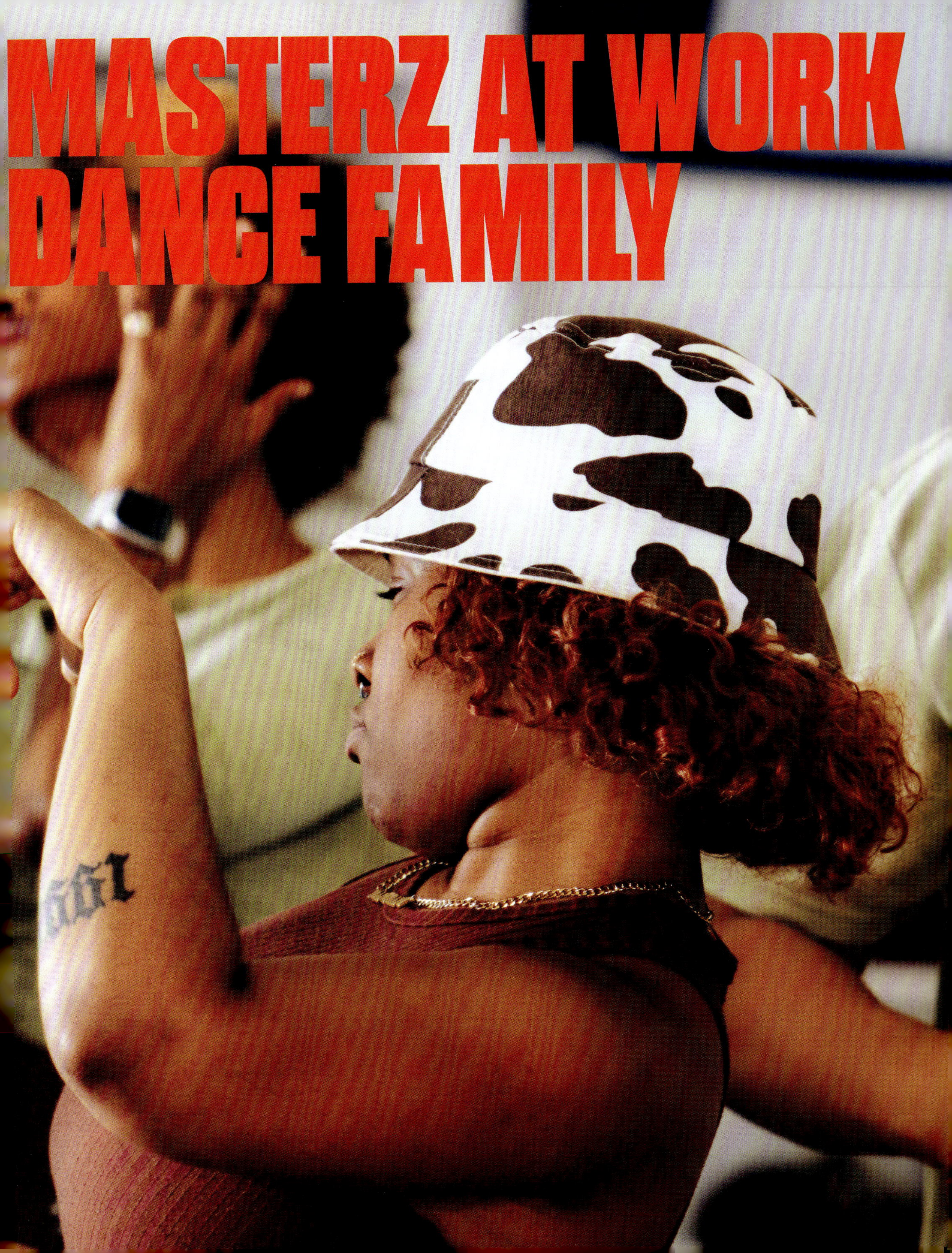

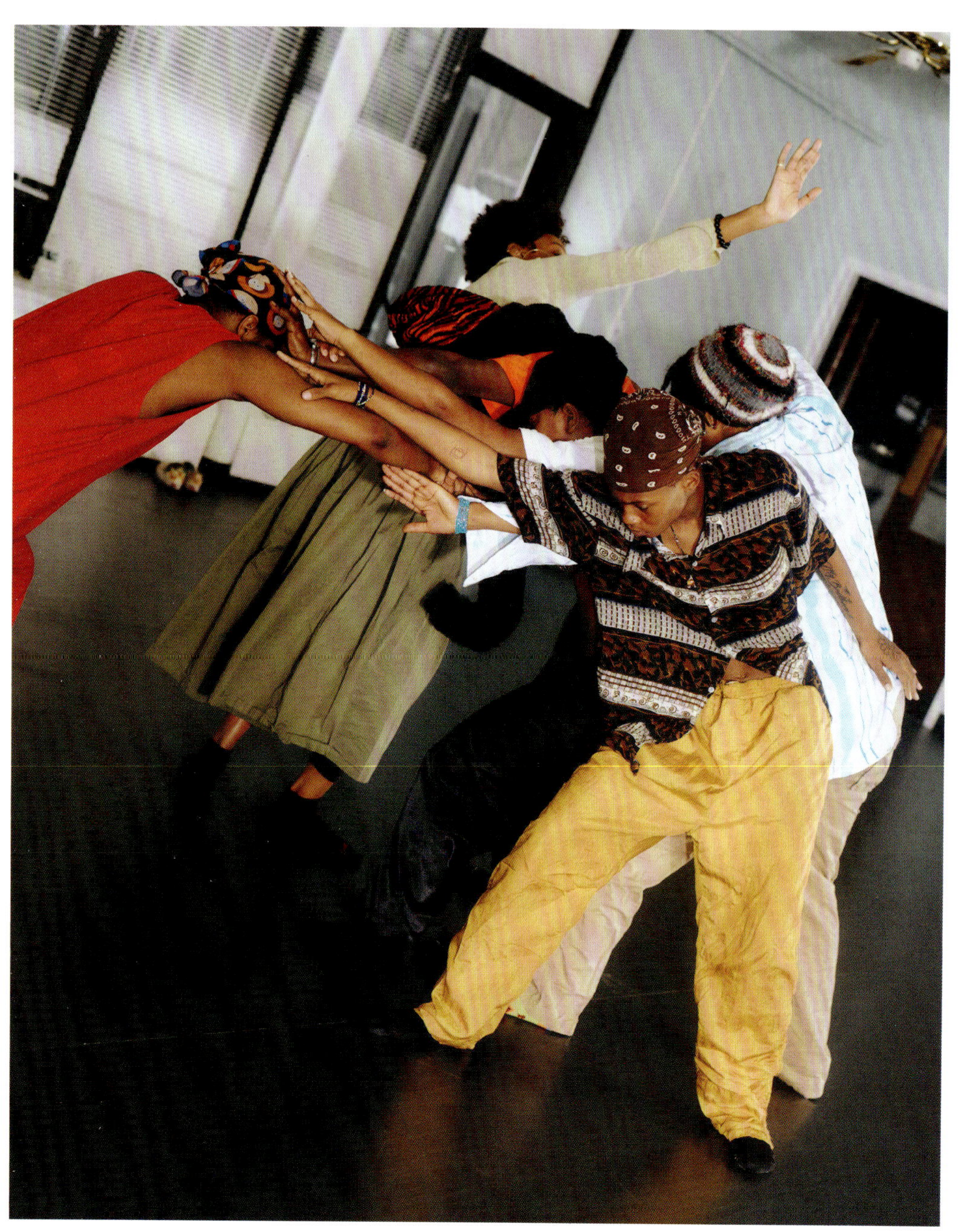

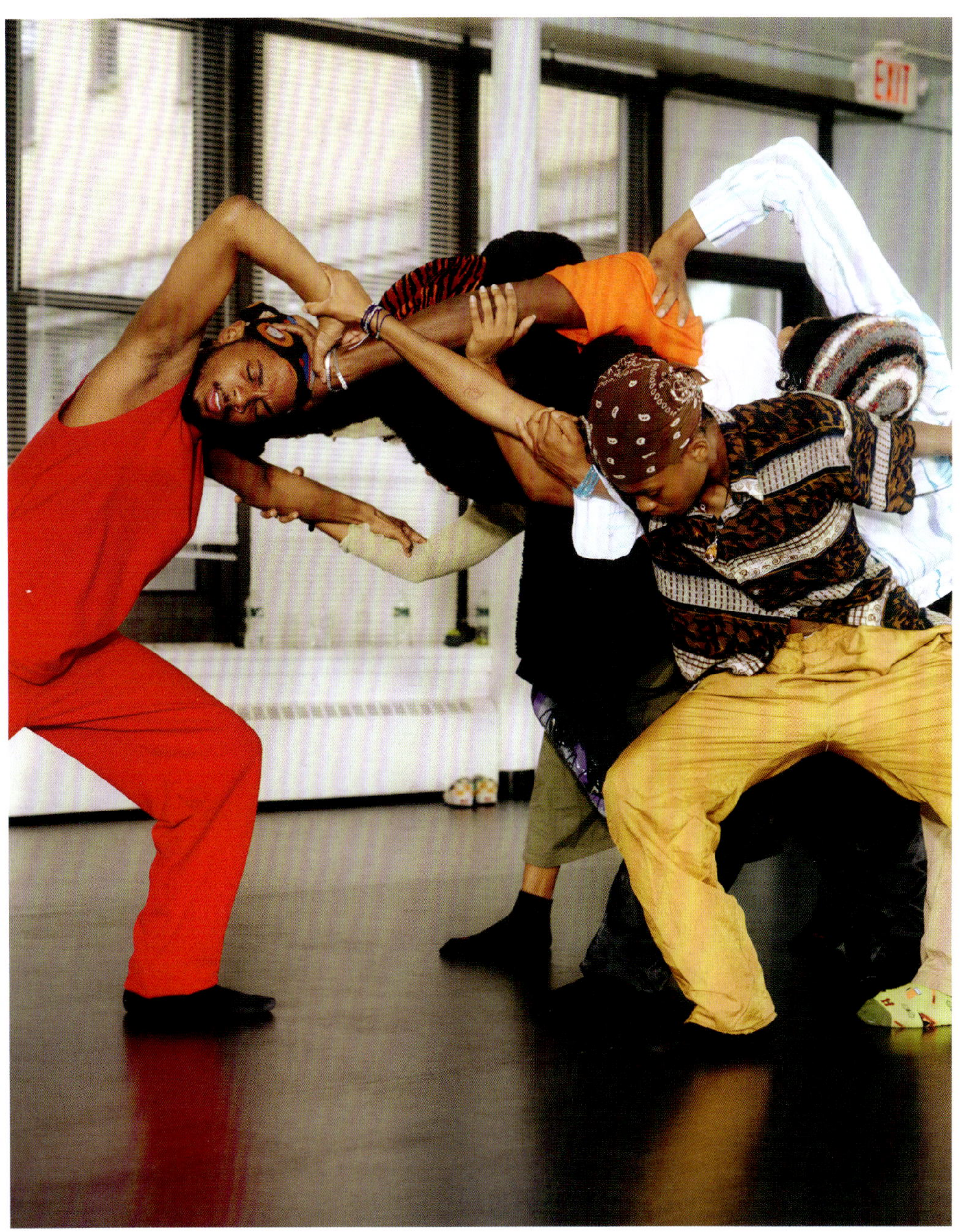
EXIT

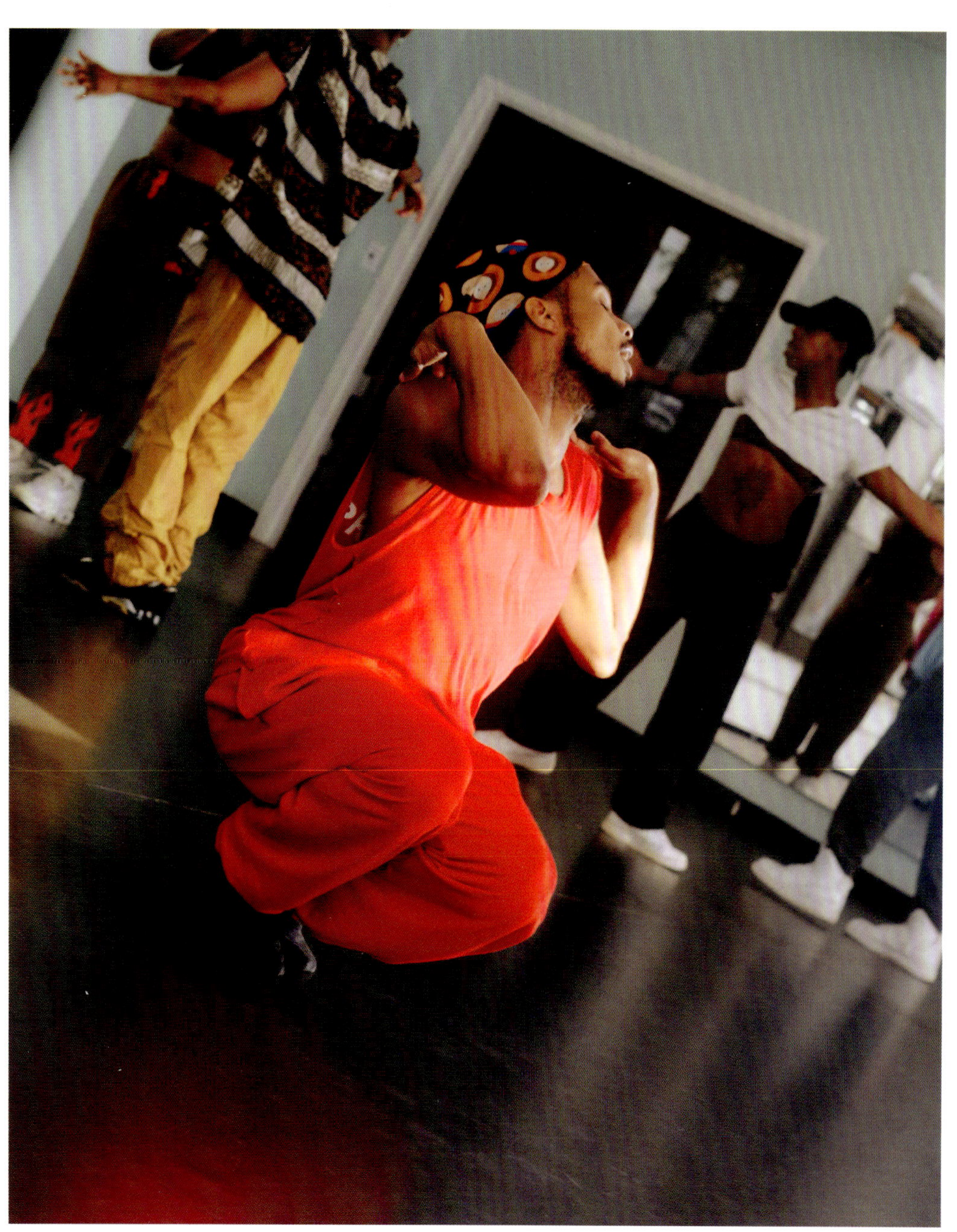

LIKE A CENTIPEDE, THE MASTERZ TOTTER INTO A LONG LINE, EACH dancer bent forward toward another's waist. "Five, six, and body-ody-ody!" shouts one member in a cow-print bucket hat, keeping time for the group. It's midafternoon on a Friday in the basement of Bethany Arts Community, a conglomeration of artist studios converted from a convent's former retreat house. The collective Masterz at Work Dance Family is rehearsing a set that will debut at the Solomon R. Guggenheim Museum, a commission by the performing arts organization Works & Process. Emotions are running hot with only three days left until showtime, but one person, watching and listening and chiming in with feedback from the edge of the room, is keeping things cool.

Courtney Washington, the company's leader and creative director, notices one performer has fallen out of sync and pulls him aside. "It's not about you; it's about *us*," she interjects, encouraging him to ramp up the strength of his stride to meet the high-energy delivery of his fellow performers. The instruction is heard. He rejoins the crew, crouching into a low duck walk and swinging his limbs into the flash-speed hand gestures of vogue. Washington, a tall figure wearing a pair of shredded denim slacks and a matching jean jacket, commands respect from the twelve dancers, all of whom she considers her children. Hers is the kind of stern but warm direction only a mother can give.

Washington has been a mother to dozens. Not in the traditional sense; she doesn't have biological or adopted children. But as a mother in the House of Balenciaga and the founder of the House of Juicy Couture—which declared victory on season three of the vogueing competition show *Legendary*—Washington has taken in and mentored countless young people. Many had been cast out by their families and, in some cases, even forced onto the streets.

She's cooked meals for them, paid their cab fare, and shown them how to compete at balls in categories like Femme Queen Realness.

Washington is a mother in the lineage of Crystal LaBeija, who, after experiencing ongoing racism in the drag pageants of 1960s New York, left the scene to found her own in Harlem, which welcomed gay and trans people, mostly Black and Latinx, and which gave rise to today's ballroom culture. Ballroom is an underground subculture in which people dance or "walk" for prizes in hyperspecific categories at elaborate events, called balls, that have their own values and social structures. The first "house" took LaBeija's name and became a model for an alternative family, built to offer support and guidance in the balls and in the world beyond them, too. Vogue, a dance that rips pose-like gestures from the glossies, has become an emblem of the community. It is, to some degree, a tactic for survival, representing much of what the balls alchemize: resilience, fantasy, and a whole lot of bite. It was with vogue that Washington got her start in this world.

"For me to be able to tell my story, I had to have that experience," she says. It was a rocky beginning—"the first time I went to the ball, I got chopped," she notes with a hearty laugh—but she quickly hit her stride in the Femme Queen Face category. Trophies and prize money, thousands of dollars of it, came later. She's since been declared a "legend," a revered title awarded to veterans of around ten years with numerous wins, second only to an "icon." Even as mainstream culture has co-opted these terms and diluted their meanings, they retain clear and specific connotations within ballroom. In Washington's world, she is a beloved elder.

By the time she walked a category at a ball for the first time, Washington had already been performing

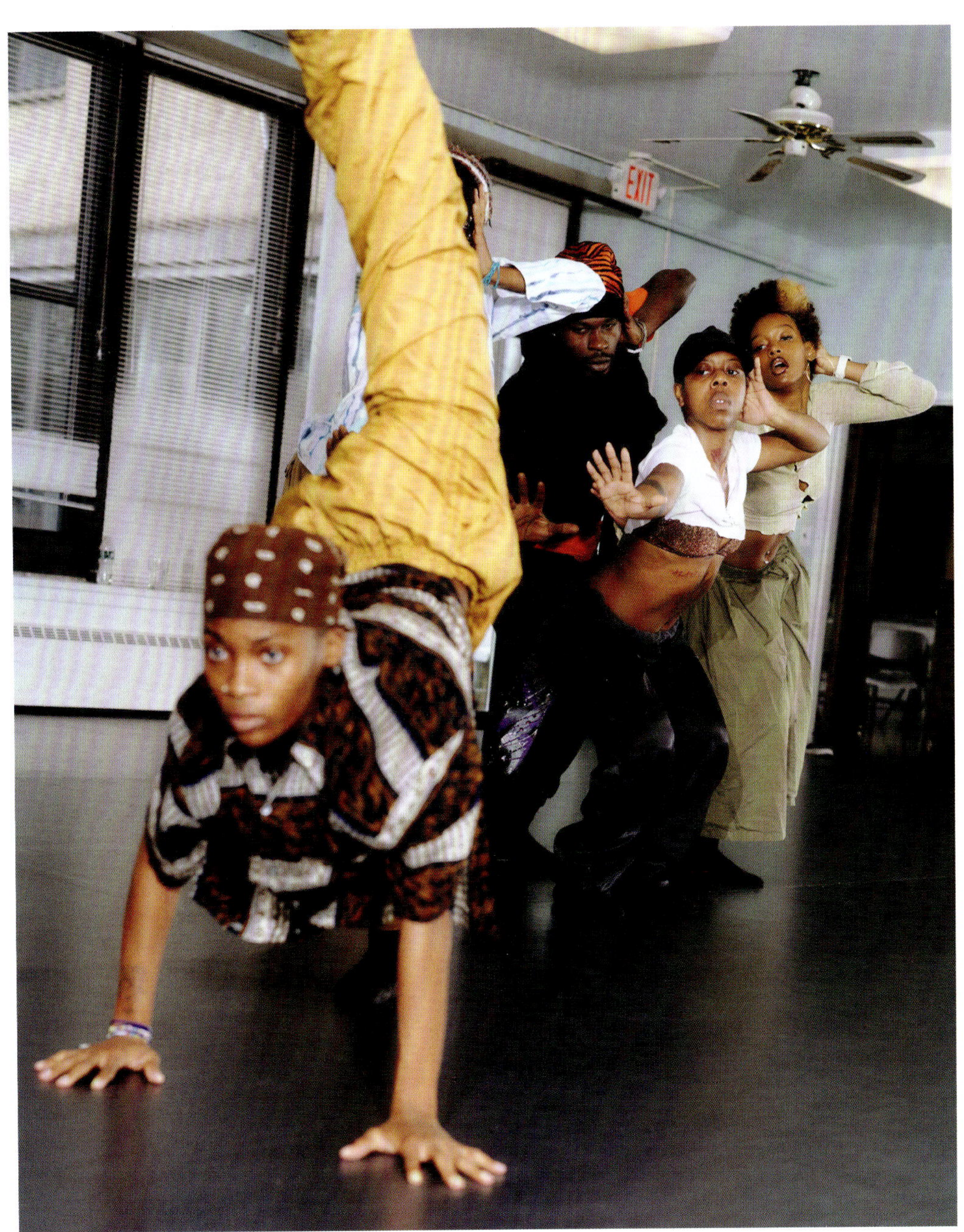
EXIT

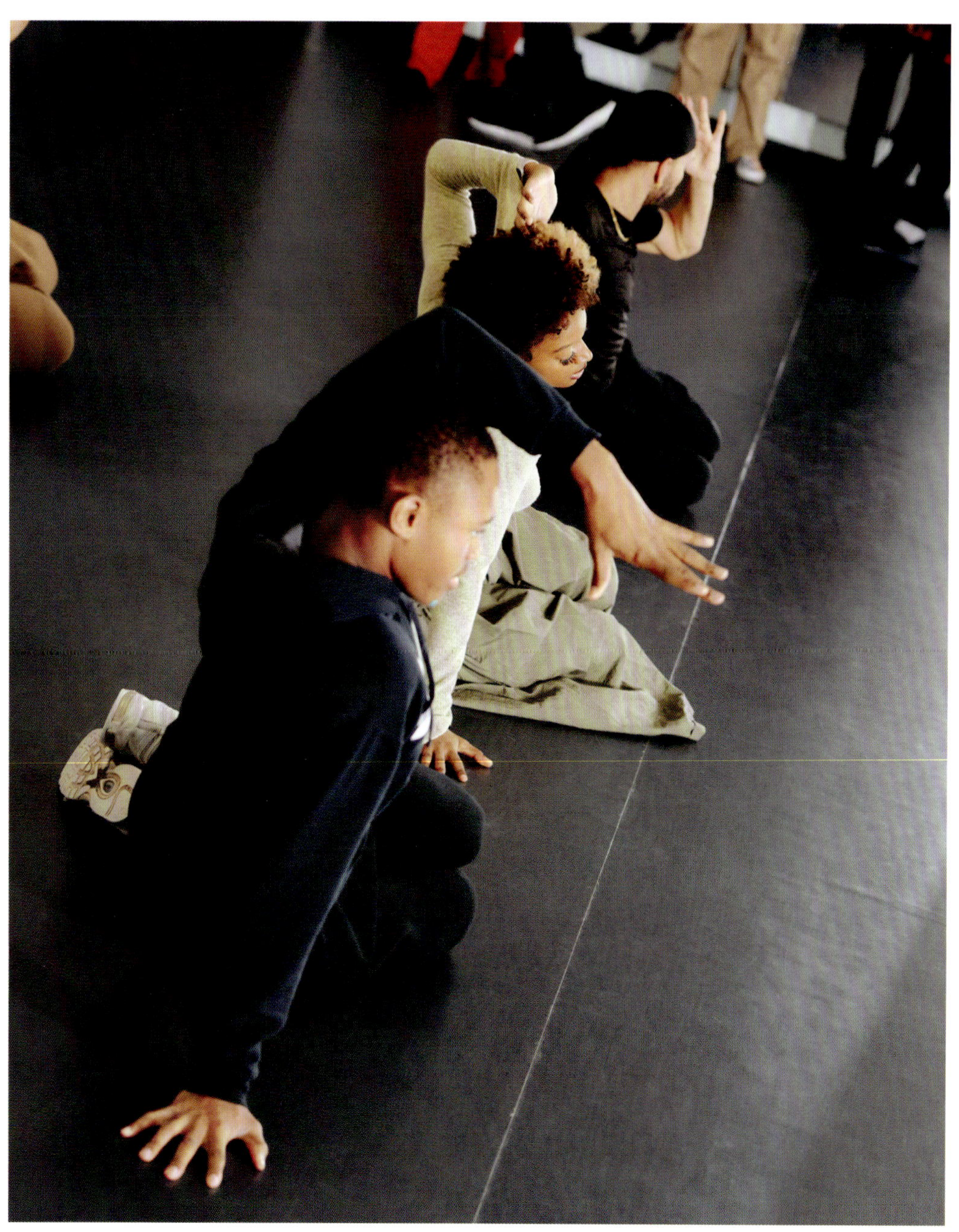

for years. Growing up within a loving family in the Bedford-Stuyvesant neighborhood of Brooklyn, she learned pan-African dance in public after-school programs. She was one of nine children, and her mother rarely had the spare funds to purchase costumes for exhibitions. But the community, seeing her natural talent and drive, would pool resources to pay her way.

She also had early ambitions as a choreographer. "I used to make dolls out of paper. I probably made one hundred of them," she recalls. "I'd write their names on the back of the paper, draw them nice outfits, and when no one was around, I would play with them." She began to craft makeshift shows using the dolls, her protean dancers, at which point the seeds of a young choreographer were planted. To this day, she says, "It's all imagination for me."

Soon, in the early aughts, Washington was making a name for herself competing in teams in New York's underground dance scene, which became her training. She developed fierce productions that she performed to hip-hop and reggae at local clubs and recreation centers. Though she appreciated the recognition that came with winning, competition was never the primary force pushing her to perform in the dance scene or later to walk the balls. It was the love of the medium and the tight bonds she formed while hanging out, fashioning looks, and simply sharing space. For that reason, she started Juicy Couture as a kiki house, a less competitive subsidiary of the ballroom scene, in 2009.

"I didn't know the power that I had in me to give," she says. "I'm seen and I'm loved, but there are people around me who are not." She adds of the balls: "There's no money that could make you feel more beautiful than that moment of showcasing your beauty to your community, and your community seeing you as just as

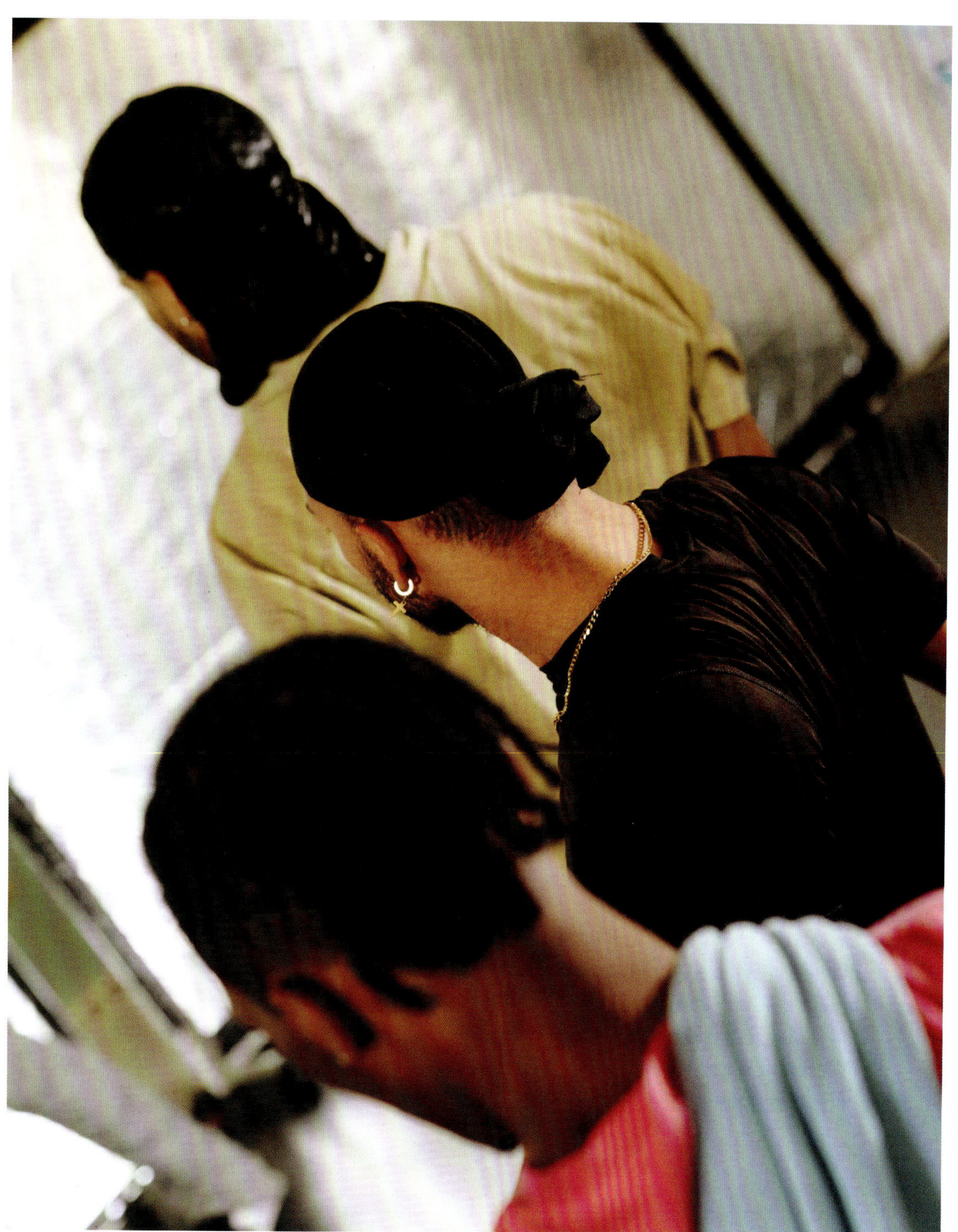

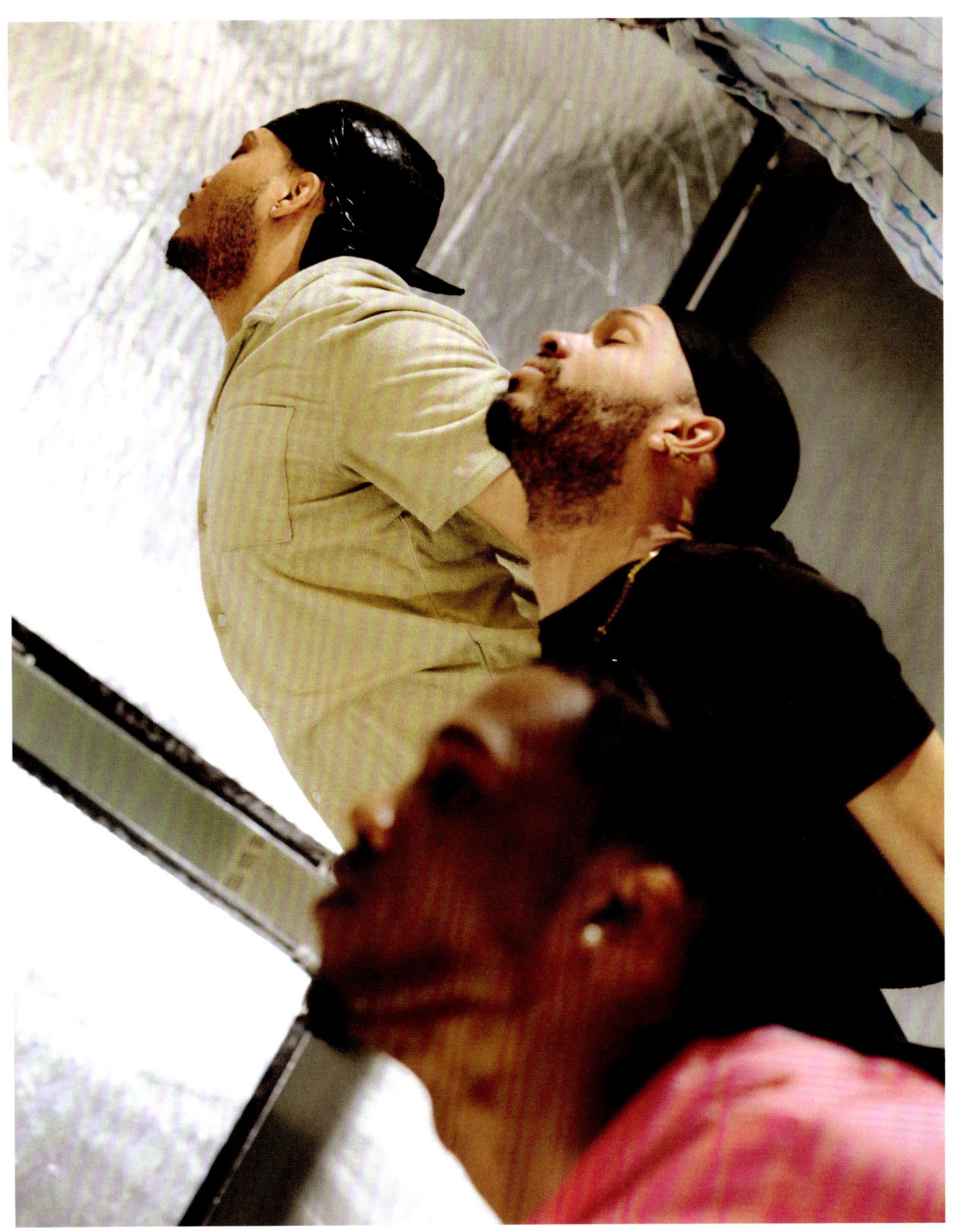

beautiful as Diana Ross or Beyoncé or Cher."

When she set out to form her own dance company, she knew how it must be structured. "I wanted to run it like it's a house," she says. "[Masterz] is a company, and it's also a family." That idea flows from Washington's tough-love leadership style down to the way choreography is developed, which is always in collaboration with her dancers. It even extends to how the group recruits new members, scouting fresh talent from showcases around the city to fill any gaps in experience or style.

One of the company's newest dancers, Armani Moore, met Washington after a performance at Choreographer's Carnival, where she had danced for the choreographer Mike da Genius, a friend of Washington's. "After the performance, [Washington] was like, 'What's your name? I'm going to give you a name. Your name's Lady Red'—because I had long red locks at the time." Washington invited Moore to attend a rehearsal at Brooklyn's Fulton Park, a public space the Masterz frequently use to practice when they are not in residence. "That was her way of saying, 'Yeah, you're with the Masterz.' It was an unspoken conversation of acceptance."

"It's not perfection she's looking for," says the dancer DeAndré Cousley, who has been with the company since 2014. "It's more about how you carry yourself in the rehearsal process, to see if you are actually going to try to get it and fight for it. It's the hunger." Trained in ballet and modern dance, Cousley was introduced to Washington after performing with the crew Organized Chaos at a showcase called Prelude New York. Now he looks forward to regular Masterz dinners at Washington's apartment, where every inch of one wall is smattered with photographs of her many children, and where Washington's eclectic music taste—everything from

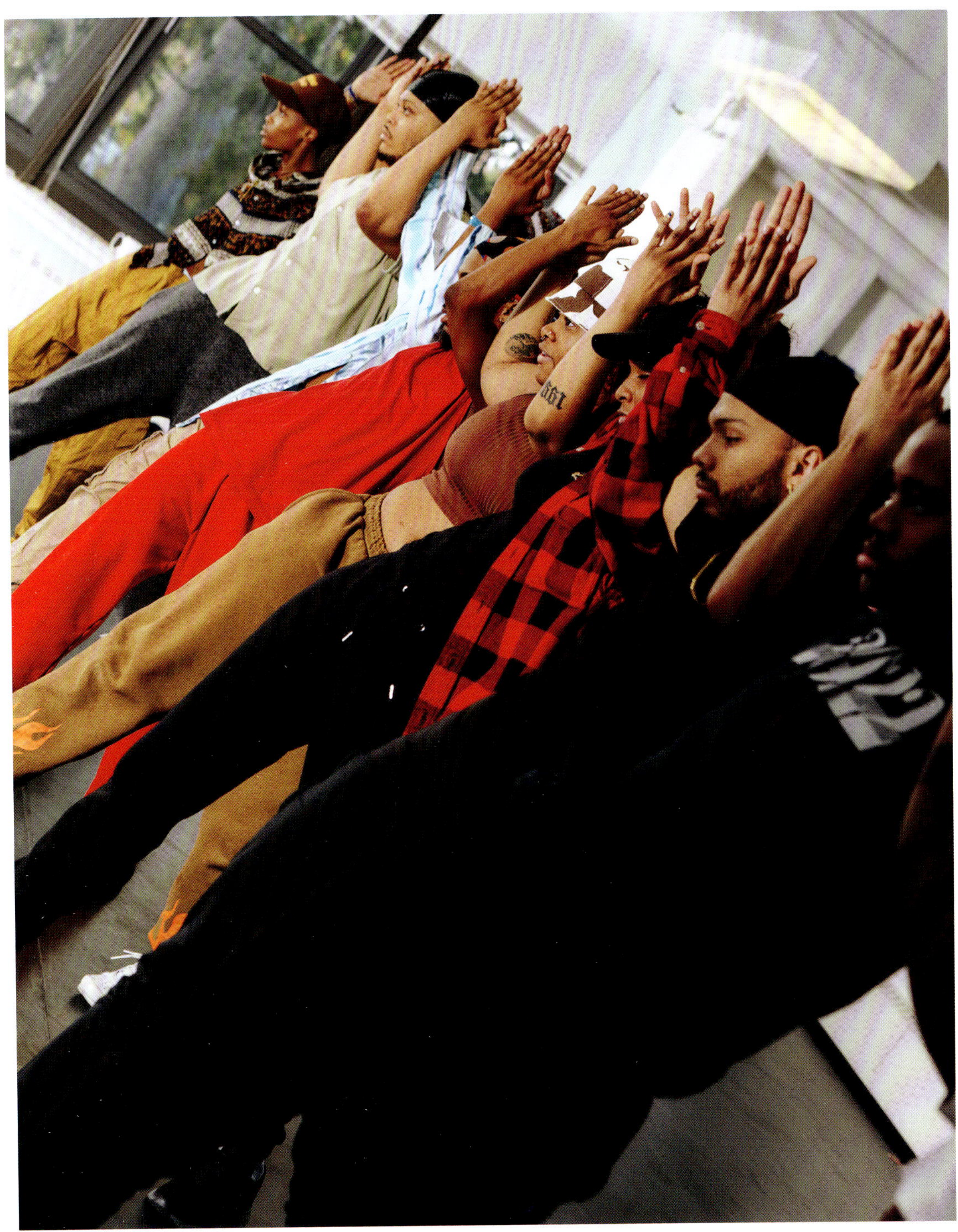

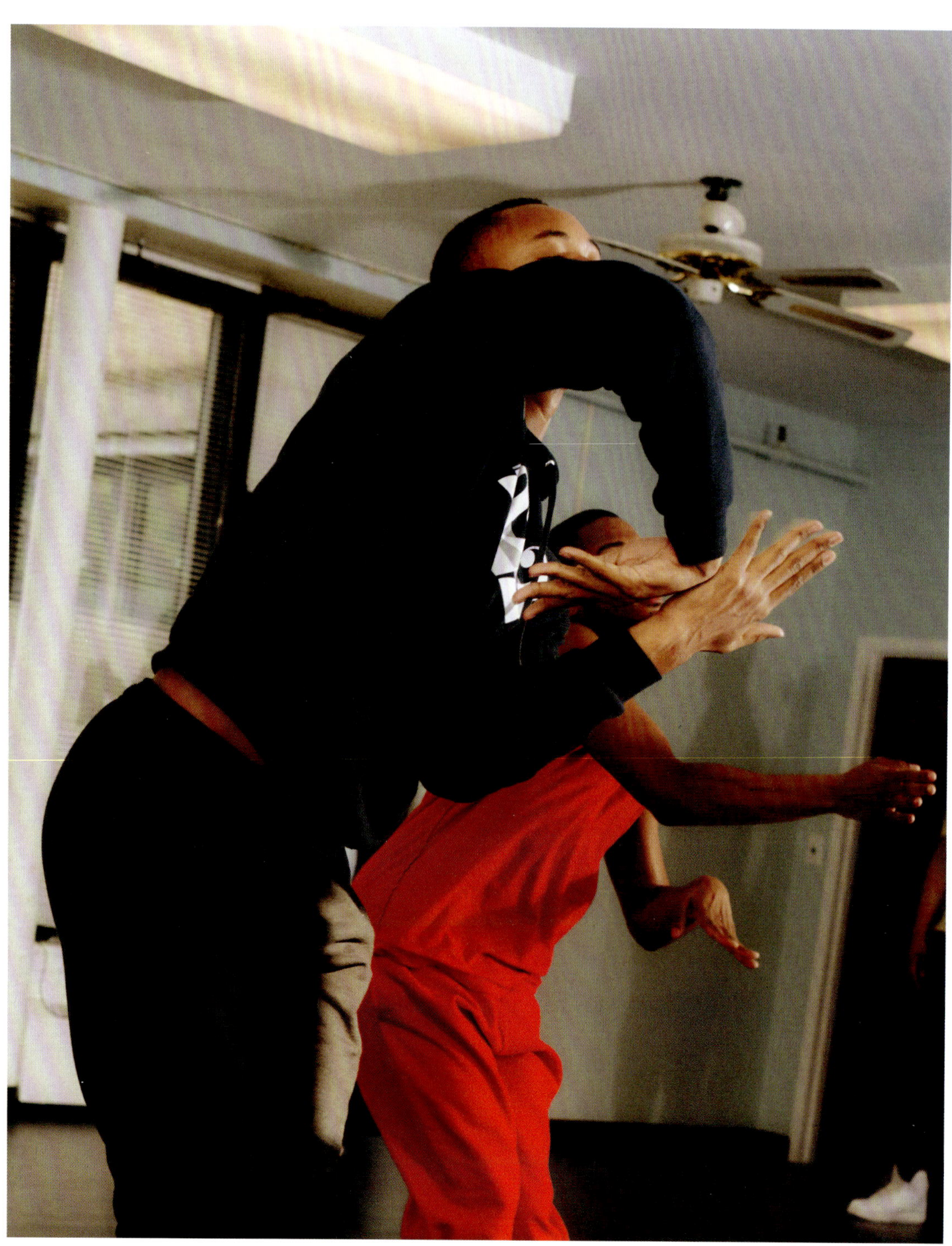

disco classics to Cakes da Killa's queer hip-hop—is on full display. "She's a jazzy girl," Cousley describes. "She definitely helped expand my musical vocabulary."

Some of those sounds can be heard on the Guggenheim's stage, where the company's hard work all comes together. The Masterz present two music videos and two live dance pieces, including their exuberant opus *ALL-INCLUSIVE*. True to its title, the performance calls upon all twelve dancers, each of whom has a solo, and vacillates among hip-hop, street jazz, and New Way vogue moves. The dancers don highlighter-colored leotards and workout gear seemingly ripped from an '80s aerobics tape, giving the number an air of nostalgia. What it represents, however—a dance company filled with young people of color, supporting the creative work of a Black trans woman within the halls of a major institution—is revolutionary.

Two weeks after the show, *Legendary* will be canceled; even as it has had a profound impact on mainstream American culture, ballroom is still underground, often referenced but rarely recognized. That fact is not lost on the audience at the Guggenheim, a mix of museum patrons and ballroom figures like Eyricka Lanvin and Omari Oricci, who in this space become one joyful family. "I'm the mother of everything I'm around," Washington says, presiding over the evening with a set of freshly painted acrylic nails and a tight white T-shirt. "I'm *your* mother."

After the show, the audience and performers spill out into the museum's rotunda, where a makeshift ball kicks off. Attendees and longtime voguers alike step up to walk in a variety of OTA, or open-to-all, categories like Runway and You Will Get Served, beneath an exhibition of paintings by Alex Katz. The museum is filled with masterpieces.

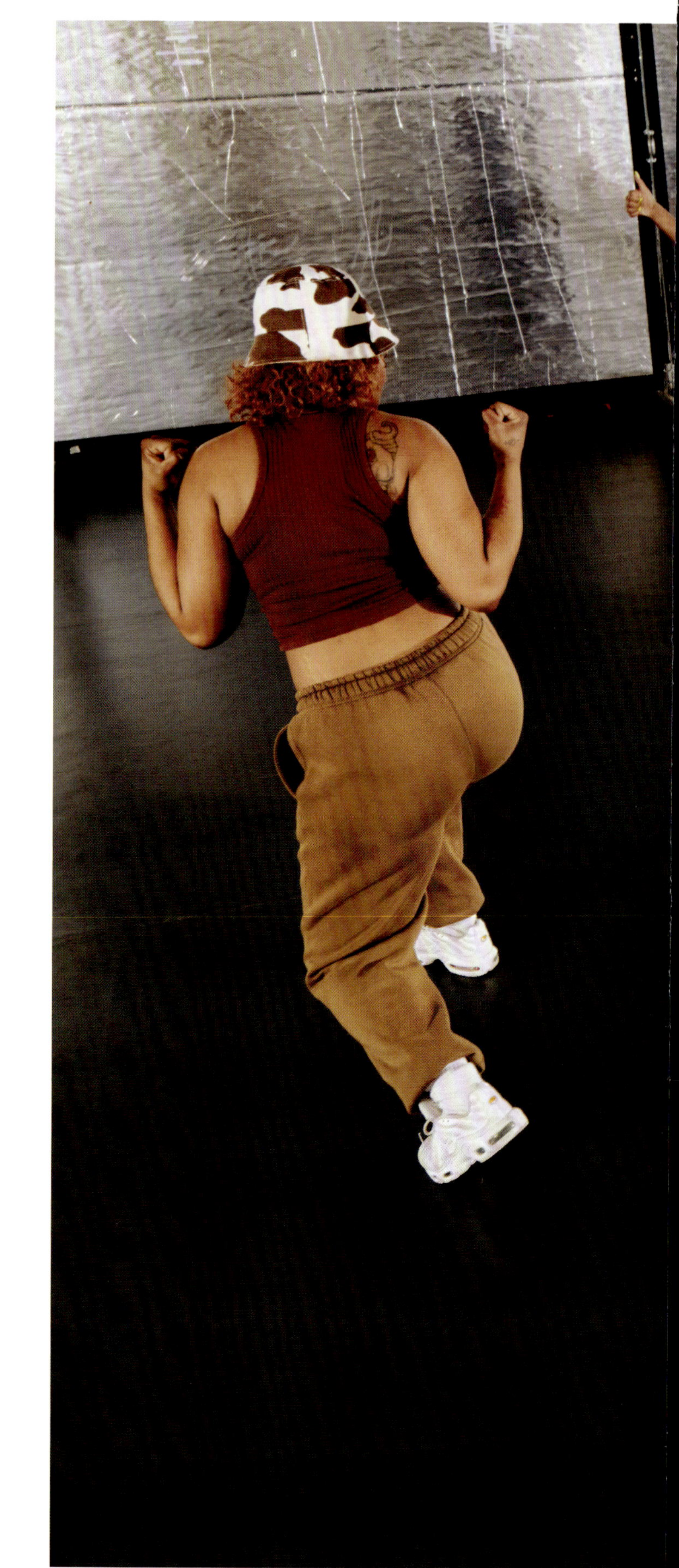

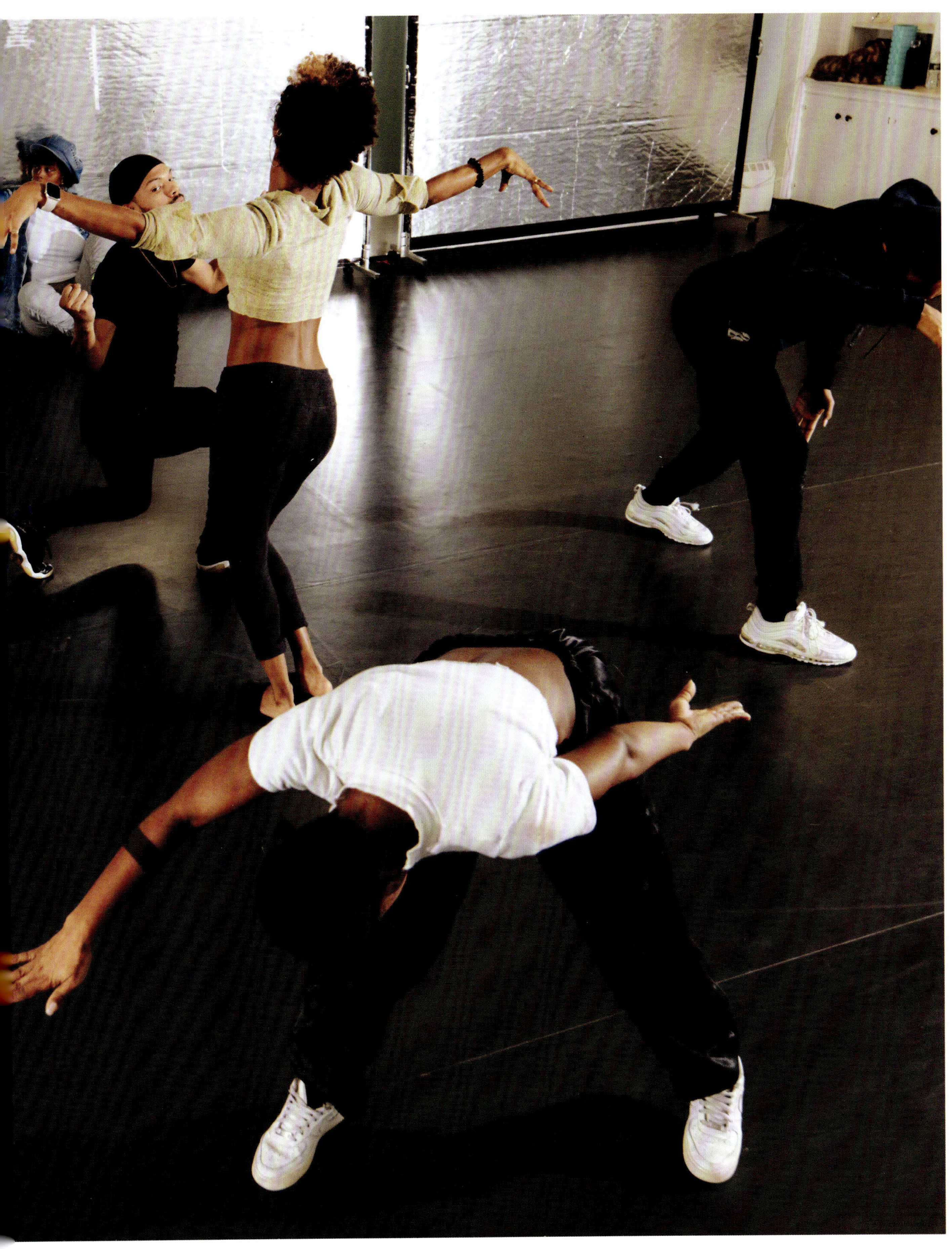

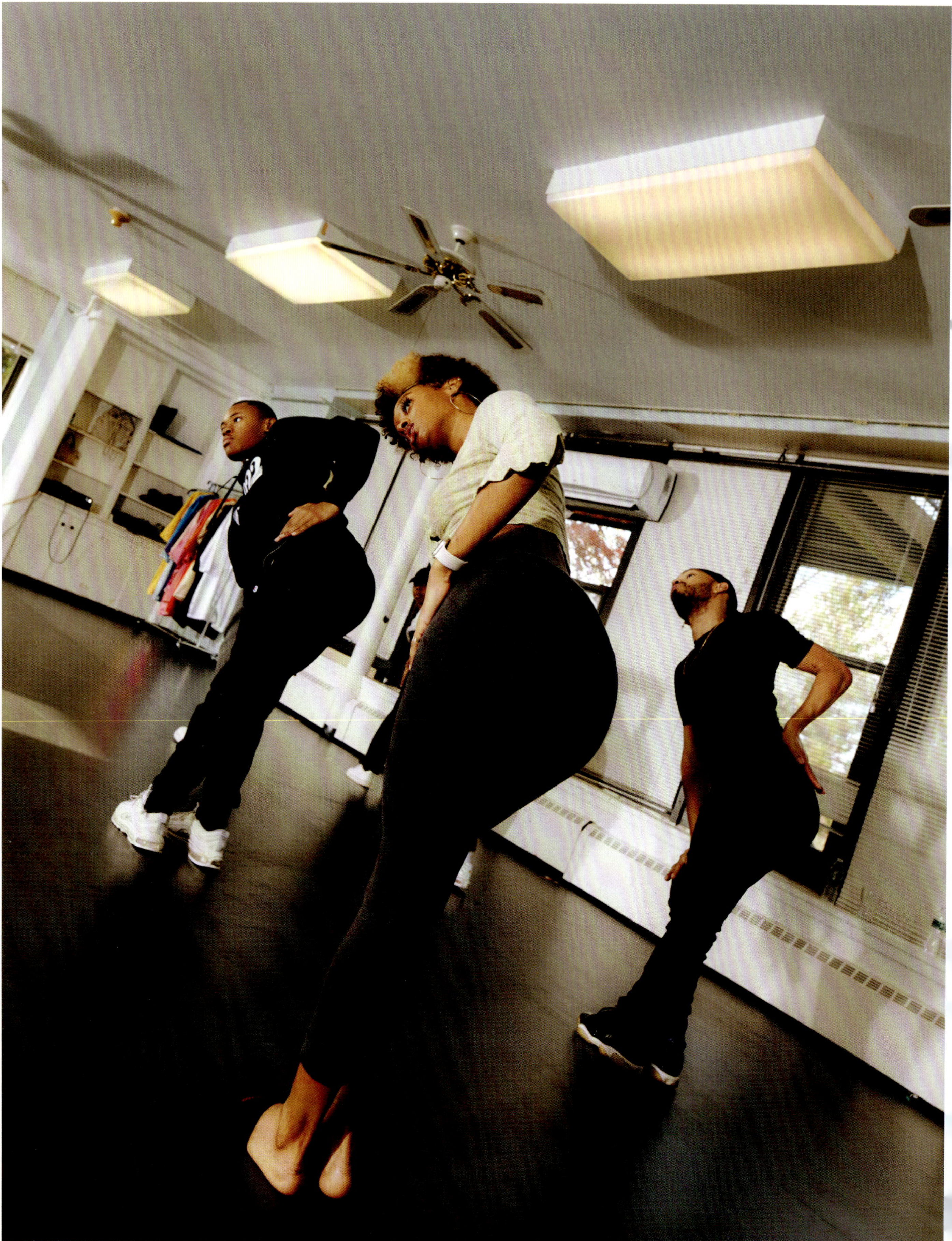

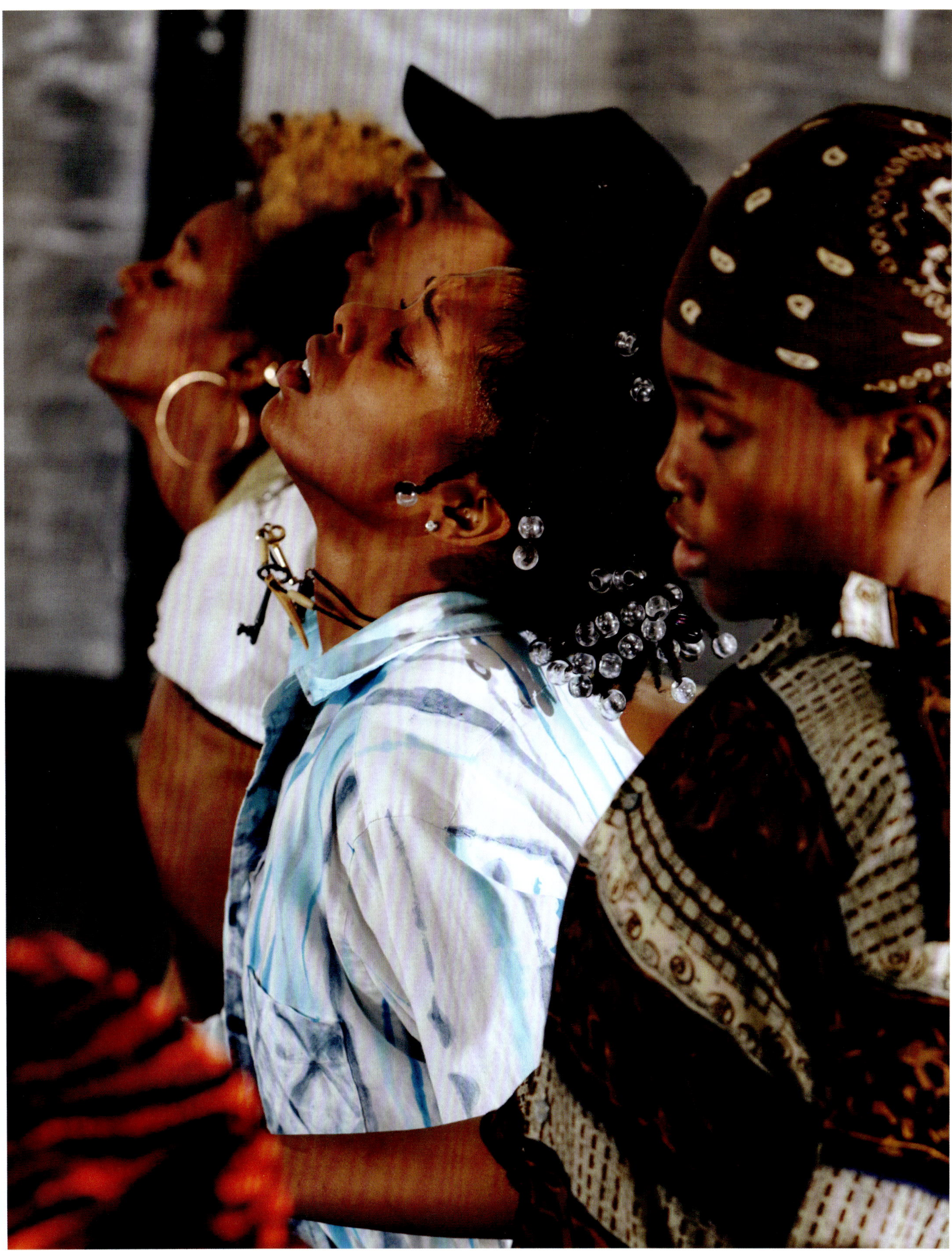

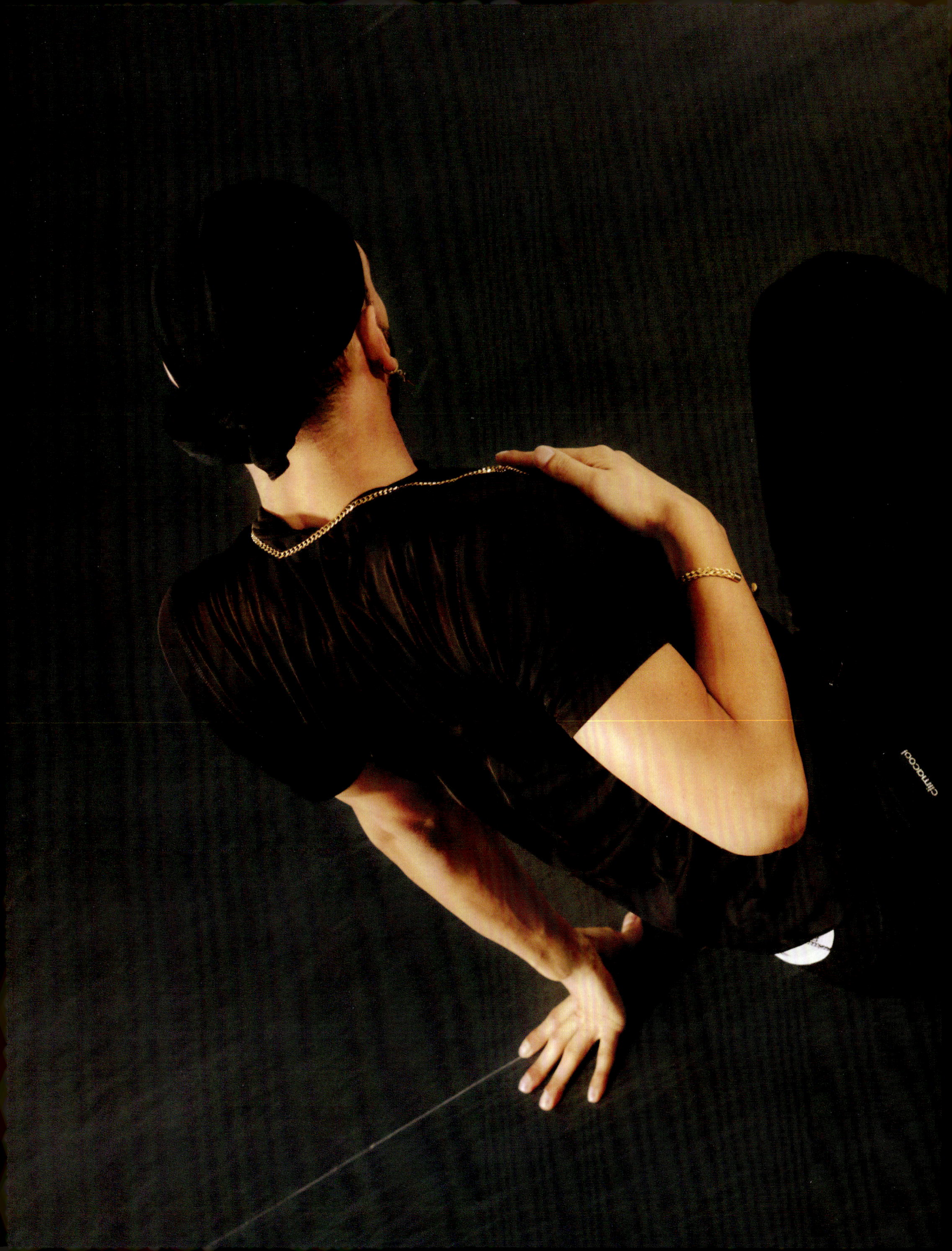
climacool

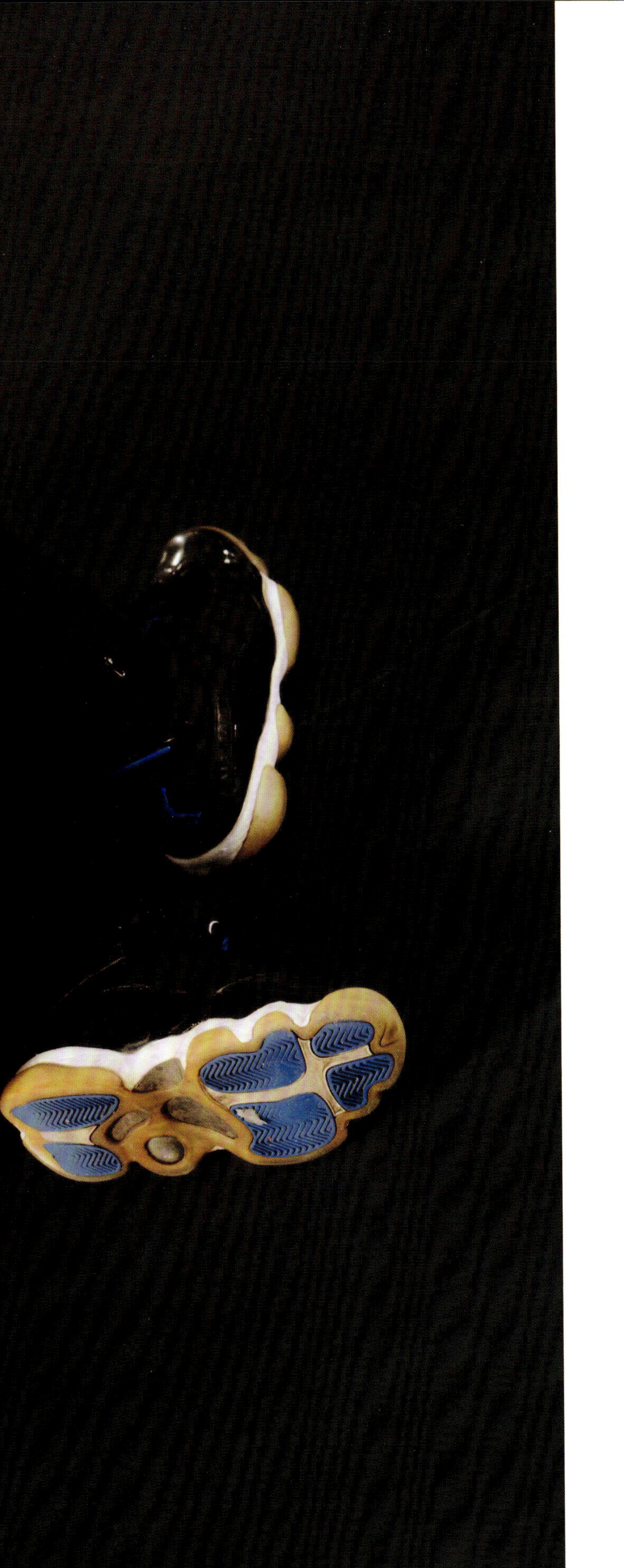

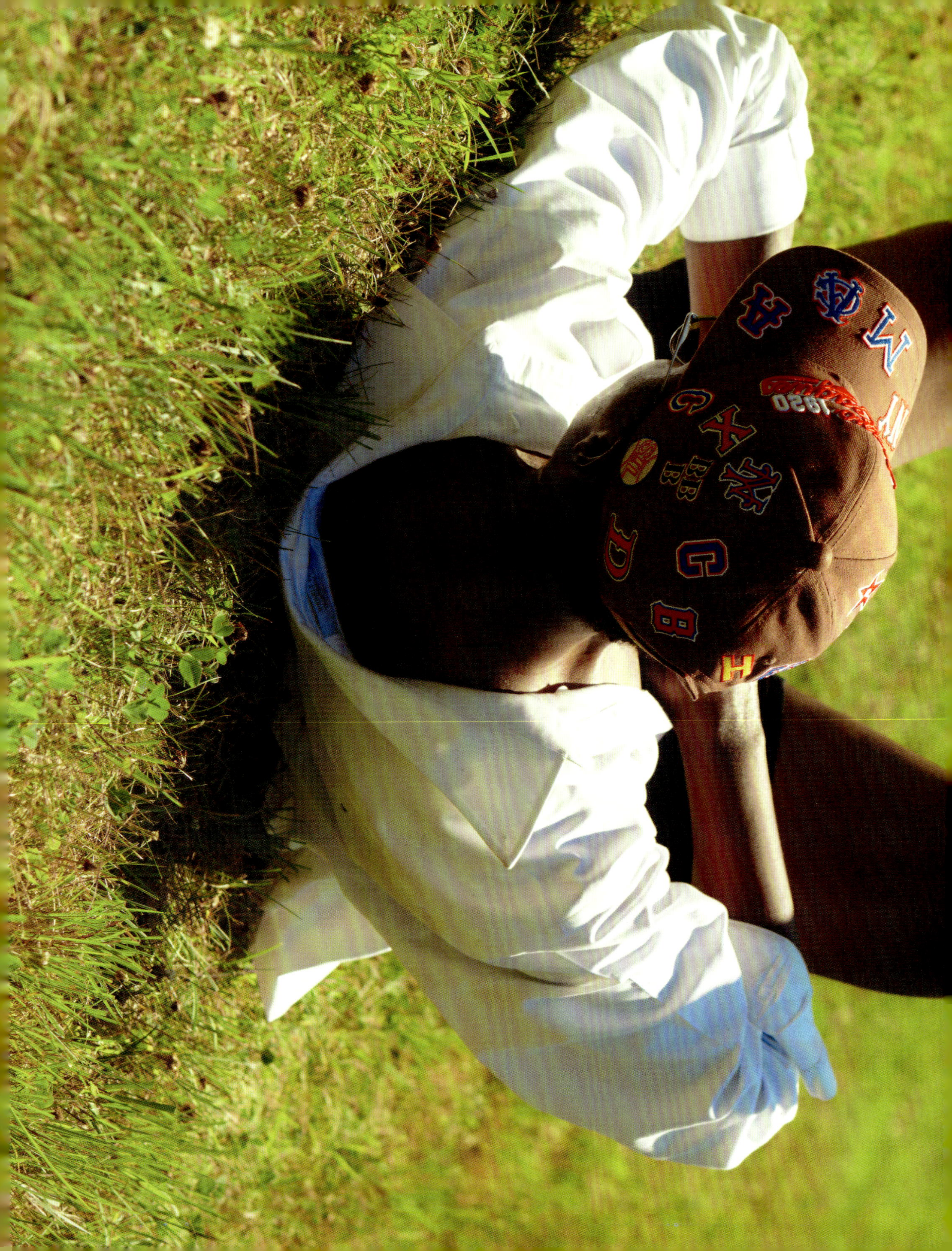

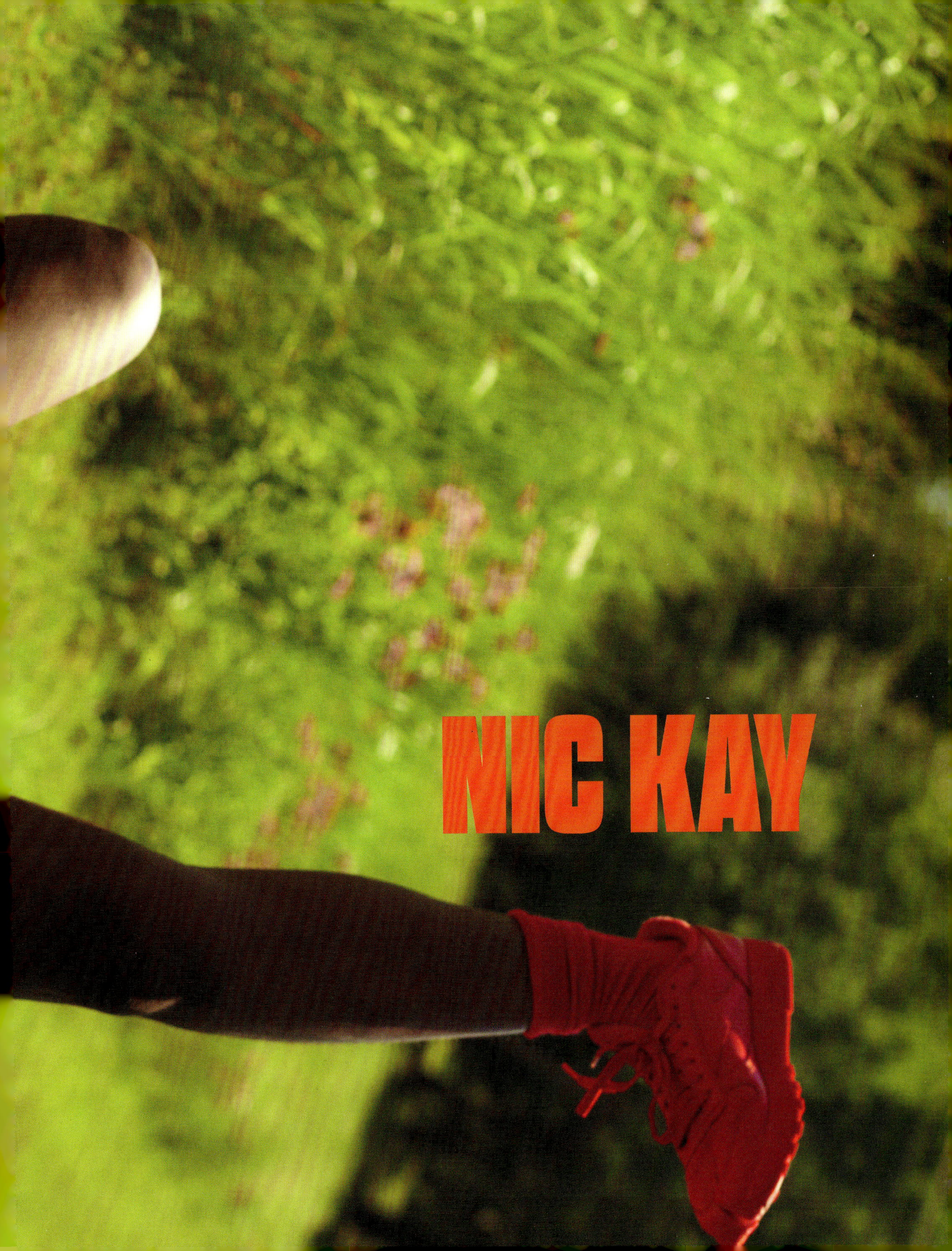

NIC KAY

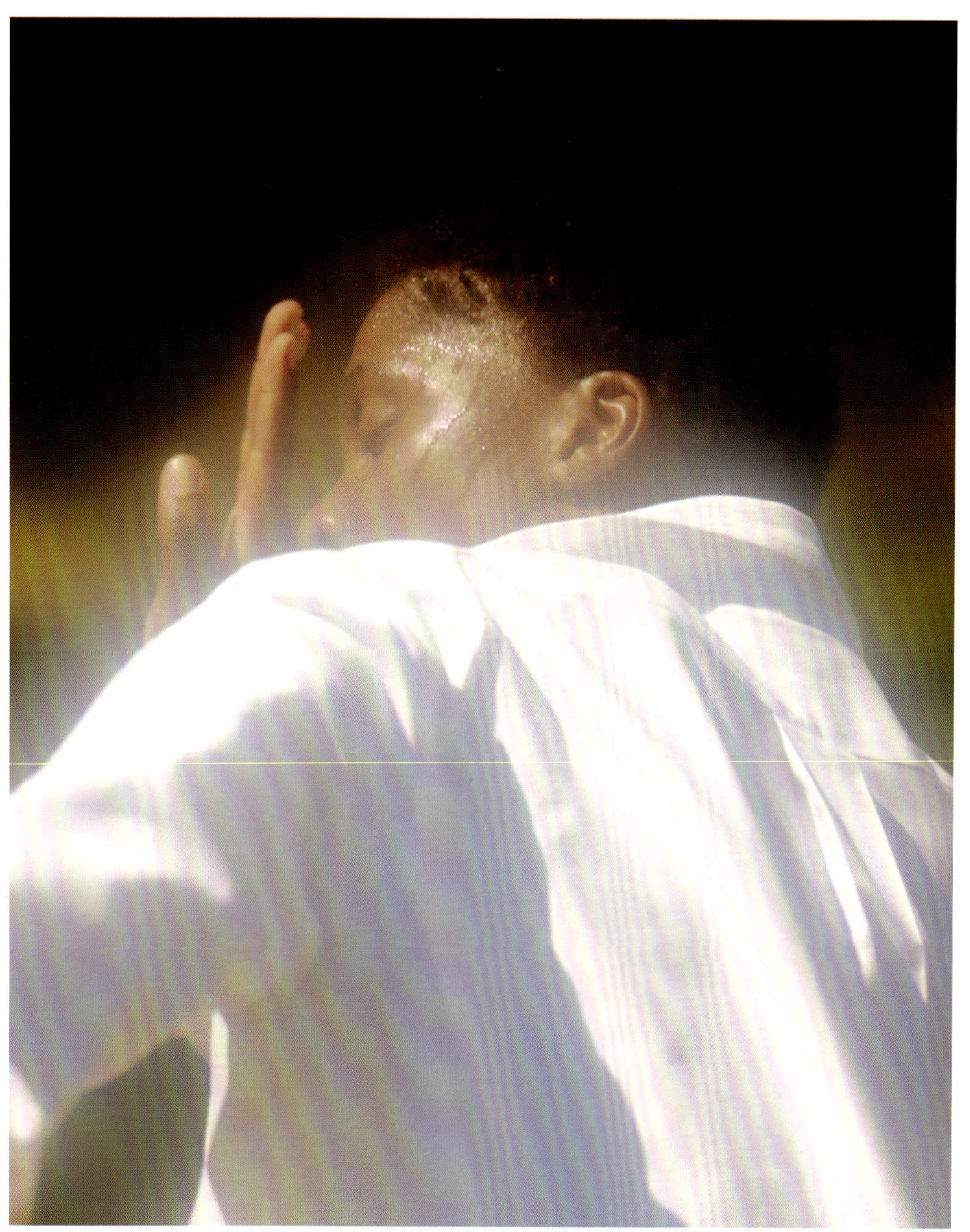

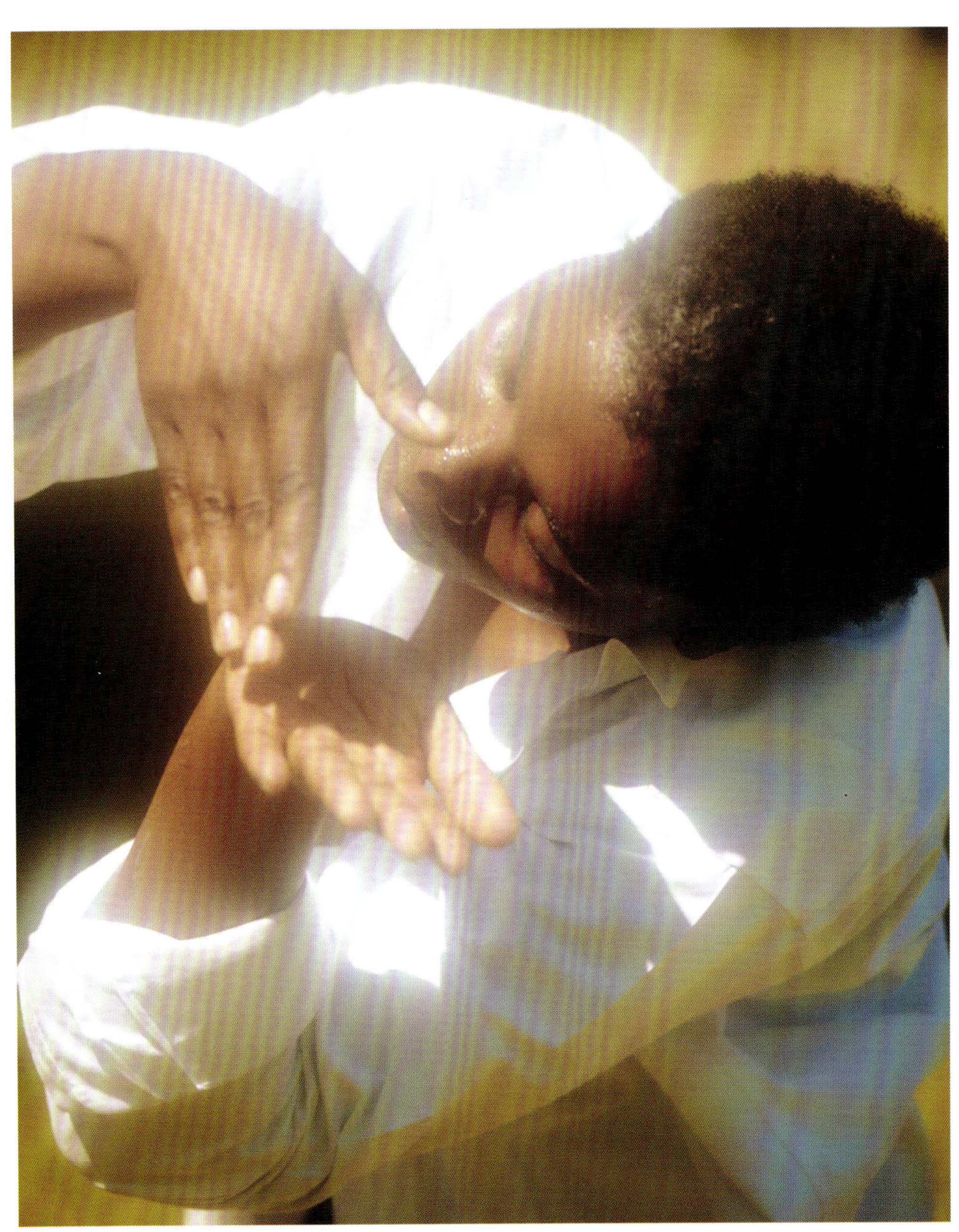

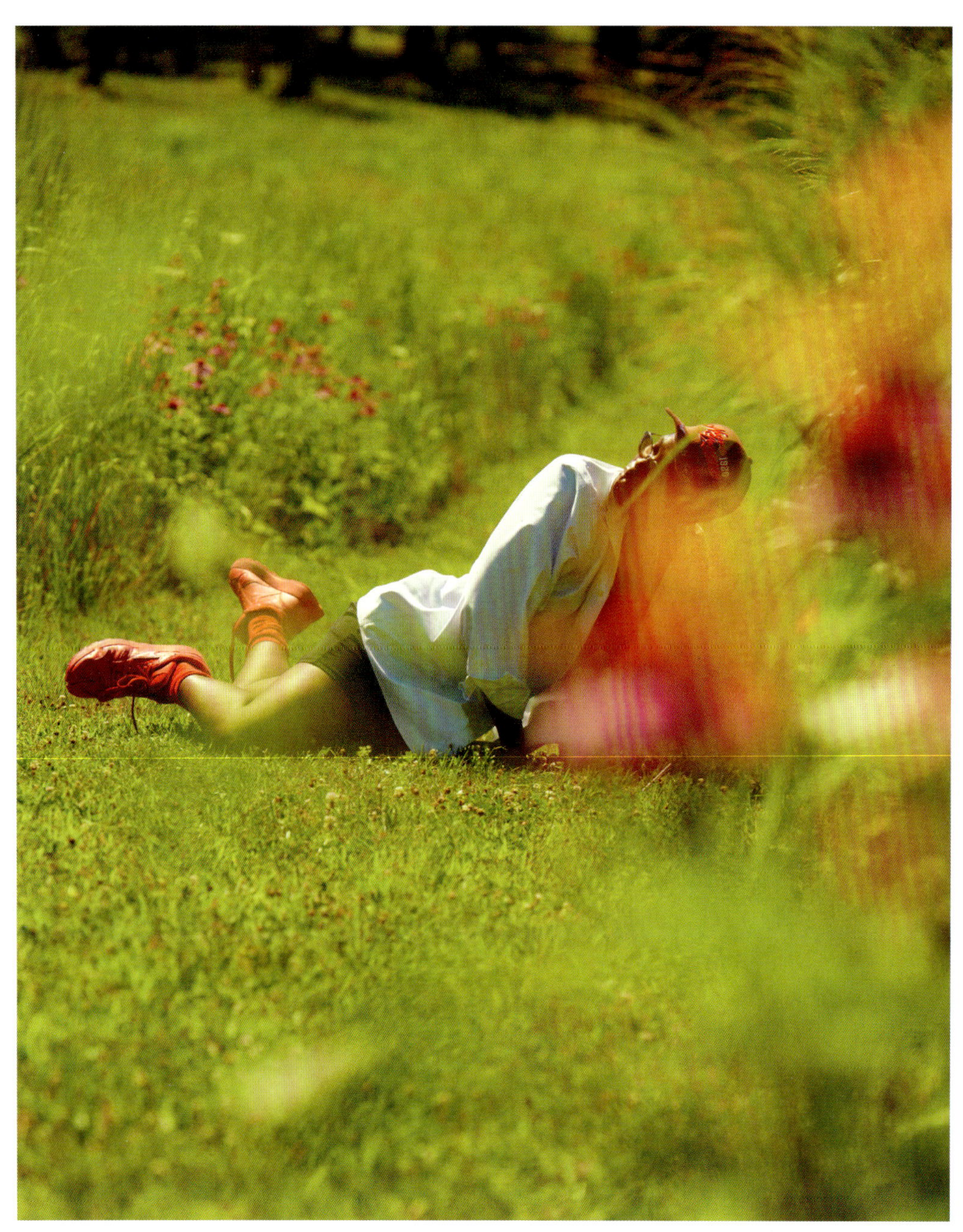

THE VIRAL DANCES CIRCULATED ON THE VIDEO-SHARING APP TIKTOK have become a deeply engrained part of popular culture, yet many of their creators—often young artists of color—haven't always been properly credited. The upbeat choreography of the Renegade, a fifteen-second segment performed to the rapper K Camp's song "Lottery (Renegade)," is typically recognized as the platform's first viral dance. The Renegade was made popular by internet sensation Charli D'Amelio before being reproduced by stars like Lizzo and Kourtney Kardashian. It took months for Jalaiah Harmon, a then fourteen-year-old dancer from suburban Atlanta, Georgia, to be recognized as the genesis of the trend.

The artist NIC Kay recognizes the power of the internet to spread such creative work and also to obscure it. Their live performances, which sometimes also yield video documentation or self-published books, incorporate elements of vogue and house music to highlight the underrecognized contributions of Black creators in culture at large, as well as the effort it takes to simply show up at a venue as a Black, gender nonconforming dancer. For their ongoing research-based project #BlackPeopleDancingOnTheInternet, which delves into the online dissemination of diasporic movement practices, they compile an archive of clips on a public Instagram account. These videos range from rhythmic dances performed to Beyoncé songs to a 3D animation by the artist Sondra Perry. "I'm fascinated with Black youth who are creating prolific moments," they explain. "The ways in which their talent and beings are co-opted are in alignment with Black historic performance practices in the United States but also around the world."

The Renegade became central to a work NIC staged while completing their MFA thesis at Bard College, an art university located in Red Hook, New York. As students arrived in a classroom, they sat down in chairs that had been arranged in a series of circles facing the center of the room. A clip was played from "Lottery (Renegade)," emphasizing the repetition of the word *wait*, while the circular arrangement suggested that a dancer would emerge to occupy the empty space and entertain the group. No one did. In the void NIC created, the absence of the performer was keenly felt.

NIC grew up in the South Bronx, a borough where Mexican, Dominican, West African, and various other communities converge. Their earliest memories are set to the overlapping sounds of reggae and '90s hip-hop. They separated from their religious parents early on, graduating in 2011 from the Professional Performing Arts high school in Hell's Kitchen while bouncing between shelters and friends' apartments. In place of that relationship, they found another family in the kiki scene, a less competitive subsidiary of the ballroom community centered on LGBTQ+ youth. Having never studied dance formally, they came to movement from a place of desire—a longing to be something or to be part of something. They learned by mimicking the high-speed gestures of the voguers who made the downtown piers their playground.

"It was the first time I found a way of moving that lit me up," they say. "In vogueing, I found a power in the type of femininity that I wanted to be in the world."

NIC moved to Chicago in 2012, initially to pursue a career acting in theater, which they felt had become oversaturated and inaccessible in New York. By then, they had already taken jobs performing in others' creations. In the Italian artist Vanessa Beecroft's *VB64,* NIC's naked body was painted plaster white as they either laid still or moved about a gallery in varying degrees of slowness, depending on the hour, to muddy the divide between art and life. Relocating to a new city,

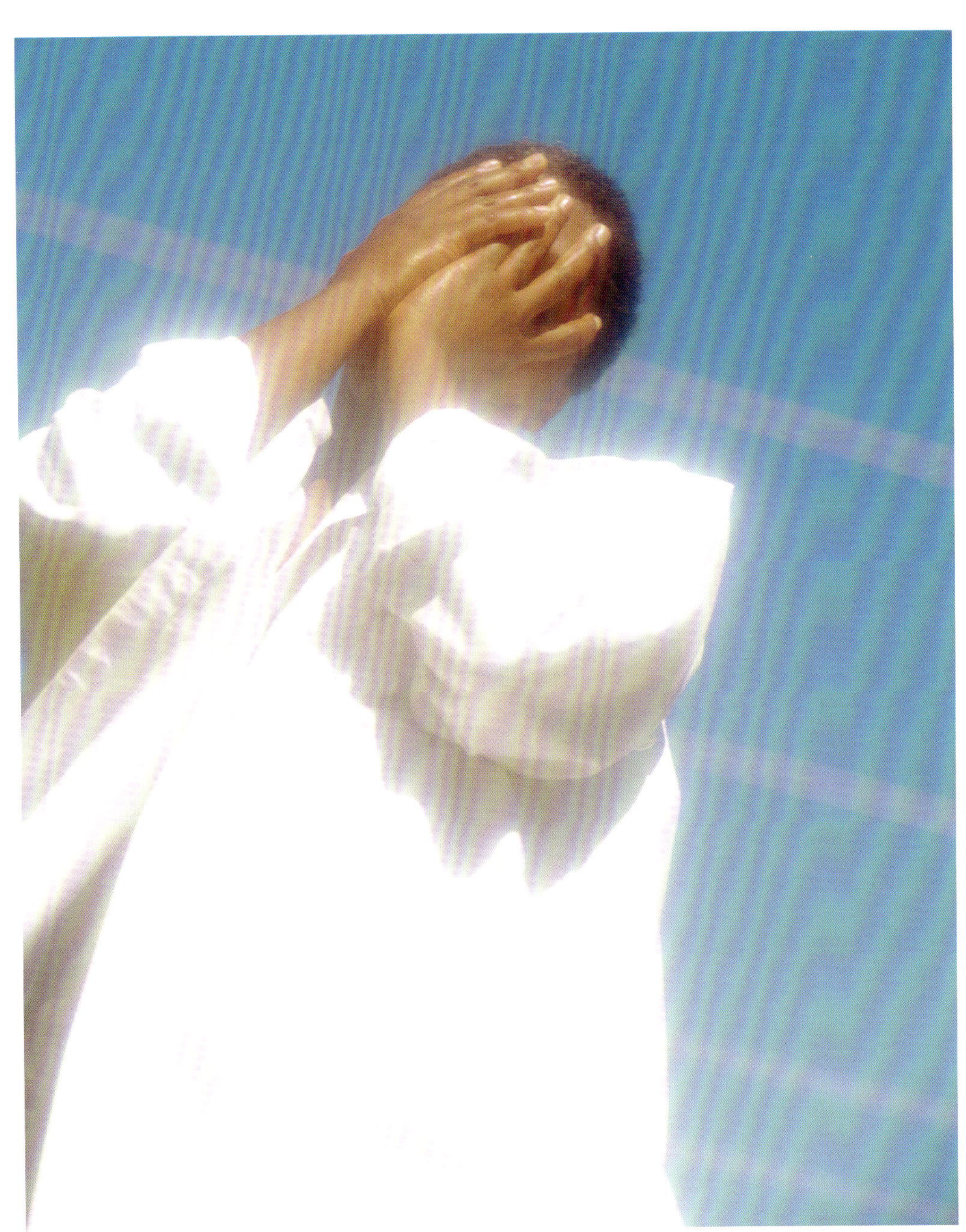

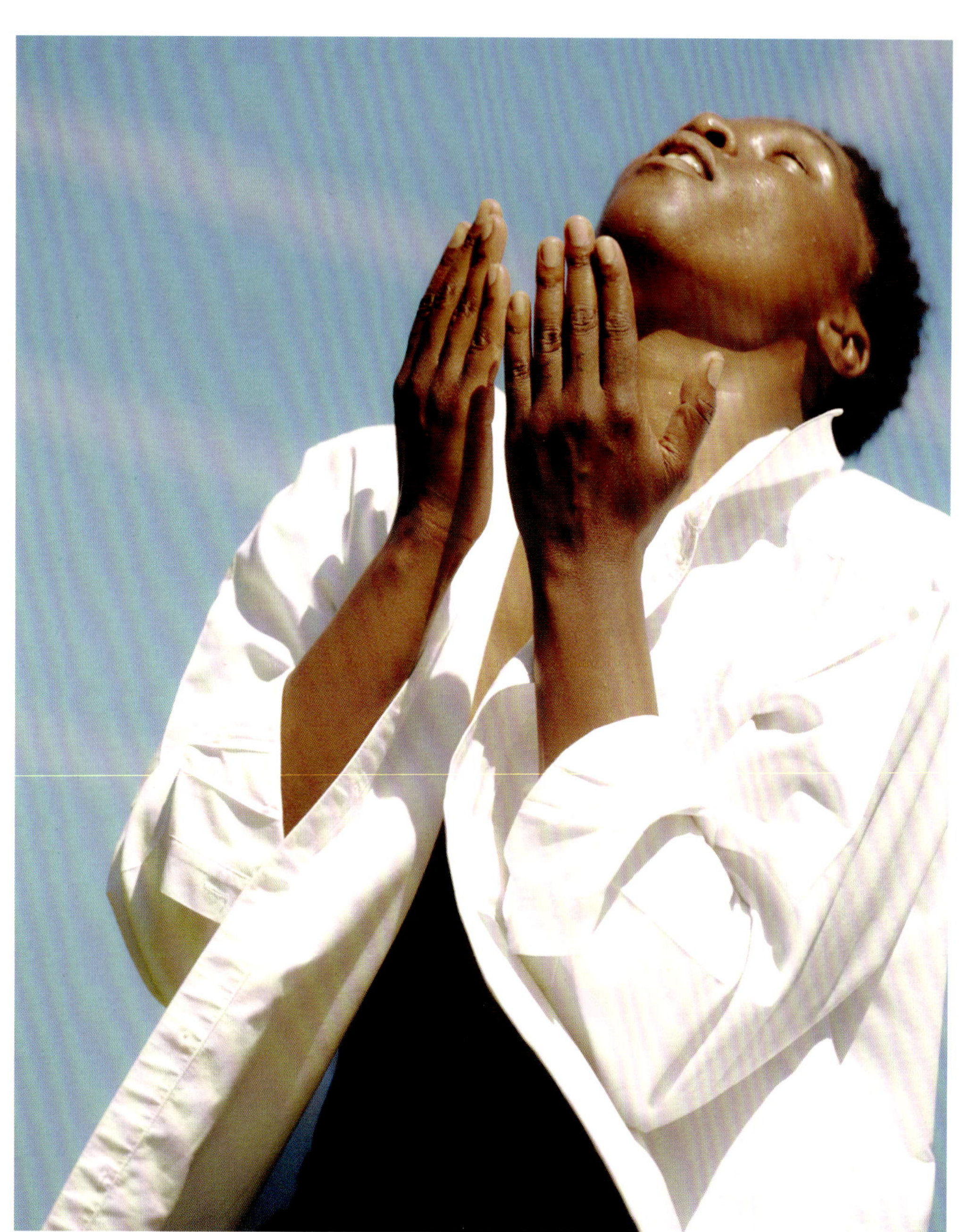

however, allowed them to develop a movement vernacular of their own. They began staging performances at nightclubs with the roving party Chances Dances, and in that space, onstage and within crowds of other gyrating bodies, everything they had learned up to that point—"vogueing and the different types of Black improvisational dance styles I learned as a kid"—converged.

Around this time, NIC would record themself dancing on their laptop's Photo Booth app to measure their progress, checking the lines they created with their form in the absence of a studio mirror. This started as a necessity, when they lacked access to a proper rehearsal space, but it has since become a key facet of their process. In one case, they documented a portion of a freestyle and uploaded it to YouTube with the title "us for this is."

NIC rehearsed using video as a tool while preparing for a 2022 showcase at the BOFFO performance festival, which takes place each summer in the Pines region of Fire Island. One afternoon, they ventured into the sprawling garden behind the house where they lived while completing their MFA program. They stationed their computer atop a green bucket at the edge of an open trail, flanked on either side by tall grass and pink daisies in bloom. As they began to dance, they covered their face with their palms and tossed their white button-up atop their head, whipping it behind them as though it were a bundle of long, elegant hair. In this freestyle, as in many of their performances, hand gestures factor heavily into NIC's intuitive choreography. They point their fingers, using their arm's motion as the guide for the rest of the body.

"It's important for me to know why I'm making the thing to begin with," they explain. "If I'm not trying to have the best arabesque, what dance or studio practice helps me tap into what my thing is? A lot of it

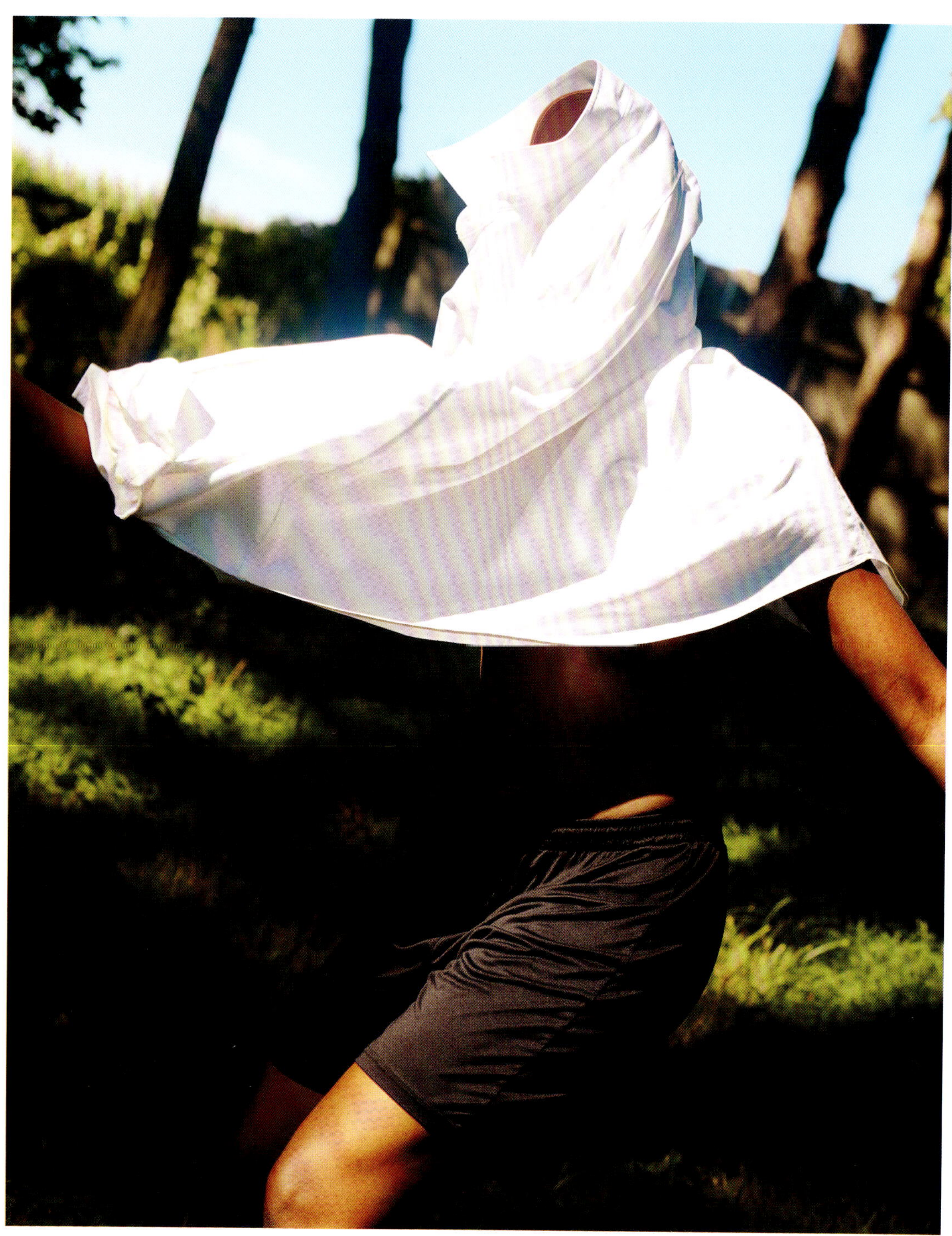

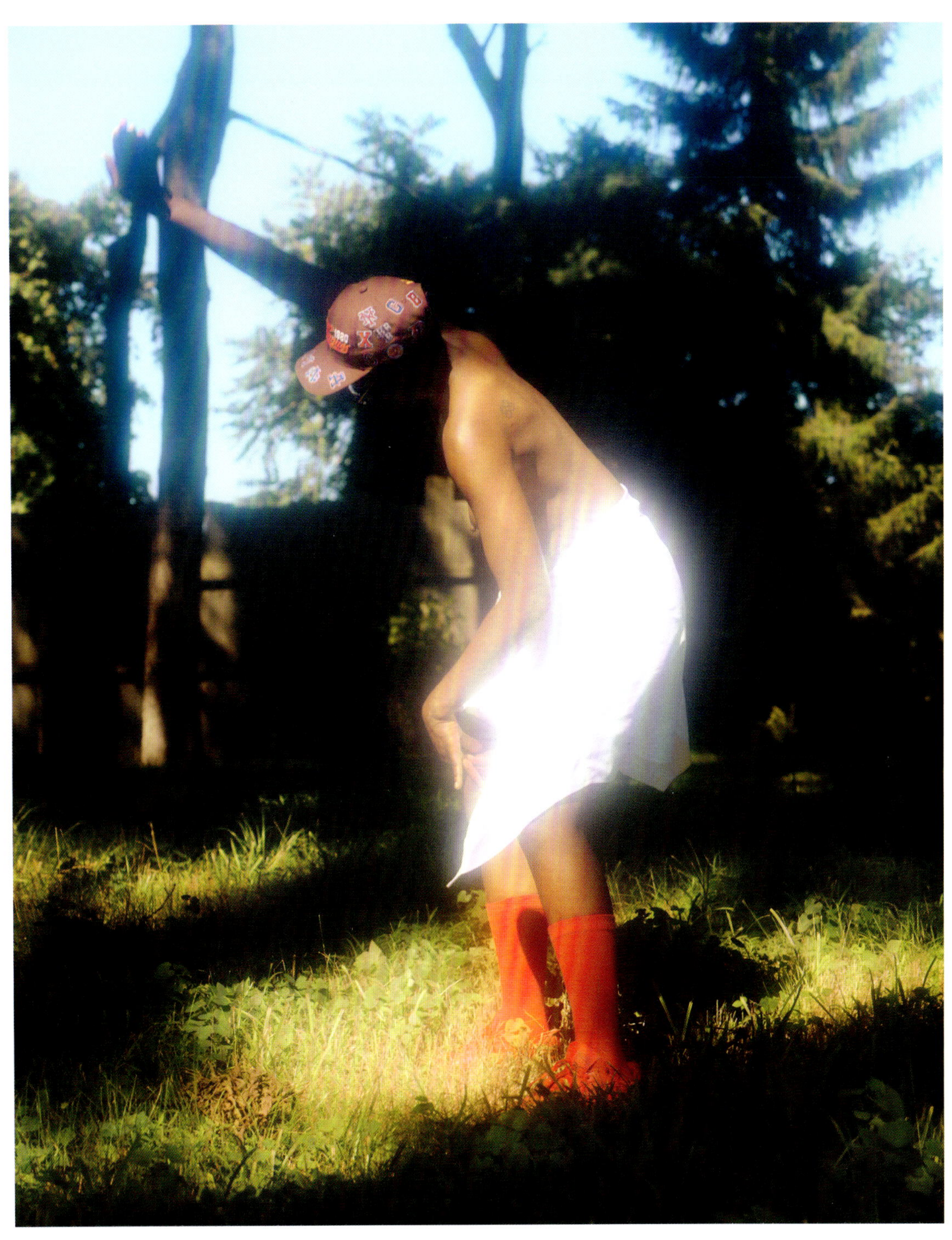

is understanding my desire, trying to work through memories."

The August debut of NIC's BOFFO performance, titled *Today's Gonna Be a Good Day, Respectfully*, was met with a mixture of confusion and delight. Emerging from a nearby beach house, the artist stepped onto the glowing stretch of sand that served as a stage. They were wearing a mascot head resembling a fuzzy brown bear, with bulging black eyes and round ears. For about ten minutes, they arched their palms and pointed their fingers, flicked their limp wrists, bounced atop their knees, and dropped to the ground, while electronic music beat into their headphones, invisible and silent to the onlookers. Drops of sweat pooled at their collarbone under the pummeling weight of the bear head and the scorching heat of the afternoon sun.

The performance continued like this throughout the day in brief intervals, a necessary precaution to avoid overheating. This segmentation compounded the absurd effect of the costuming, as the bear's disappearance and reappearance went mostly unexplained to the audience who had gathered there. But for NIC, the image of the bear was instantly recognizable. The costume was a reference to the mascots that entertain in Times Square or at children's birthday parties. NIC pulled the idea not from an unearthed memory but from the countless videos they have discovered on TikTok, which they continue to study daily as if it were a map to some exquisite treasure. They selected their costume knowing their audience—mostly gay men of a certain tax bracket—would have their own sordid associations with the animal.

"Instagram and TikTok are not really critical spaces, and I think that NIC makes both those sites critical through their performance," says the artist Richard Kennedy, who was a curator for that year's BOFFO and

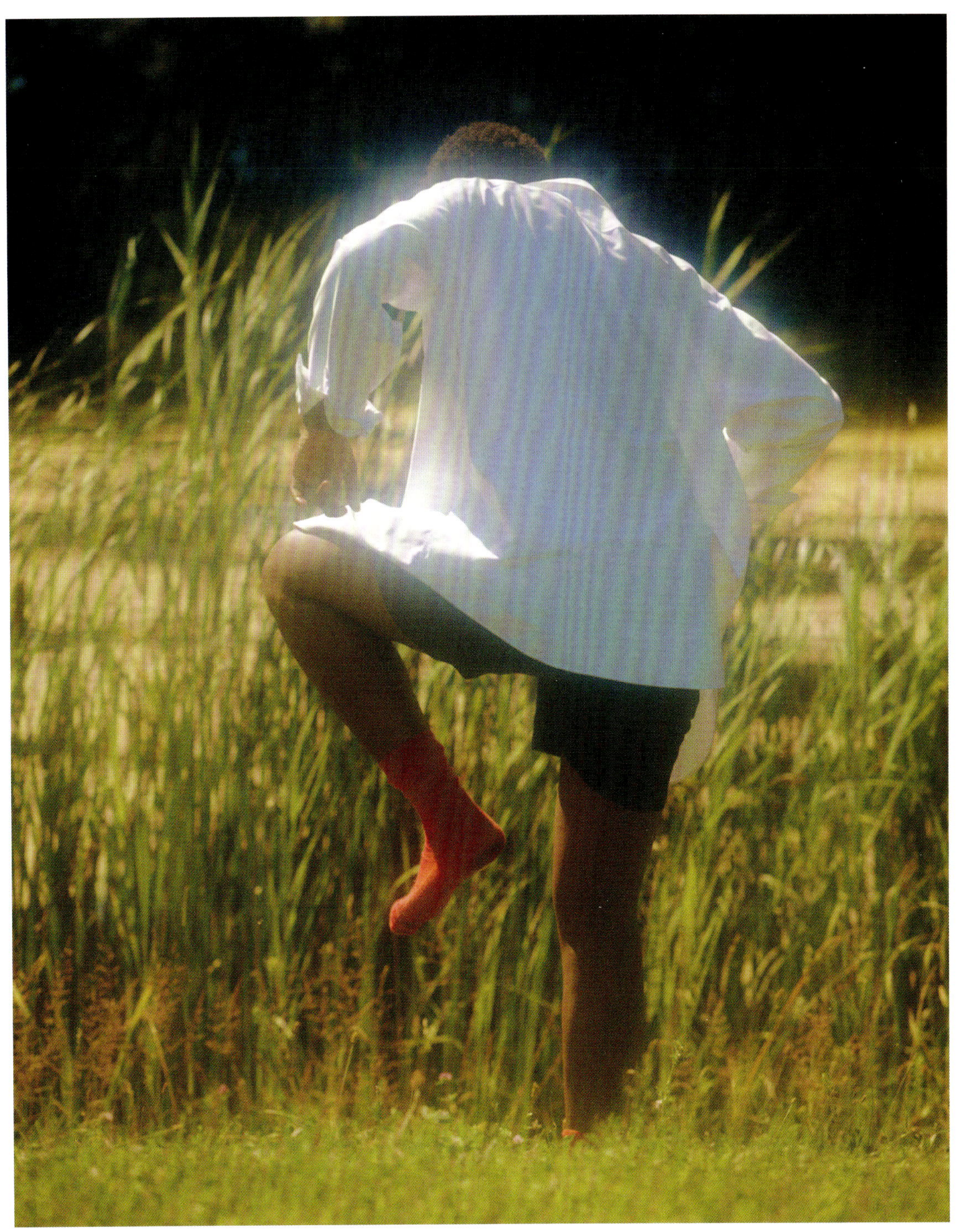

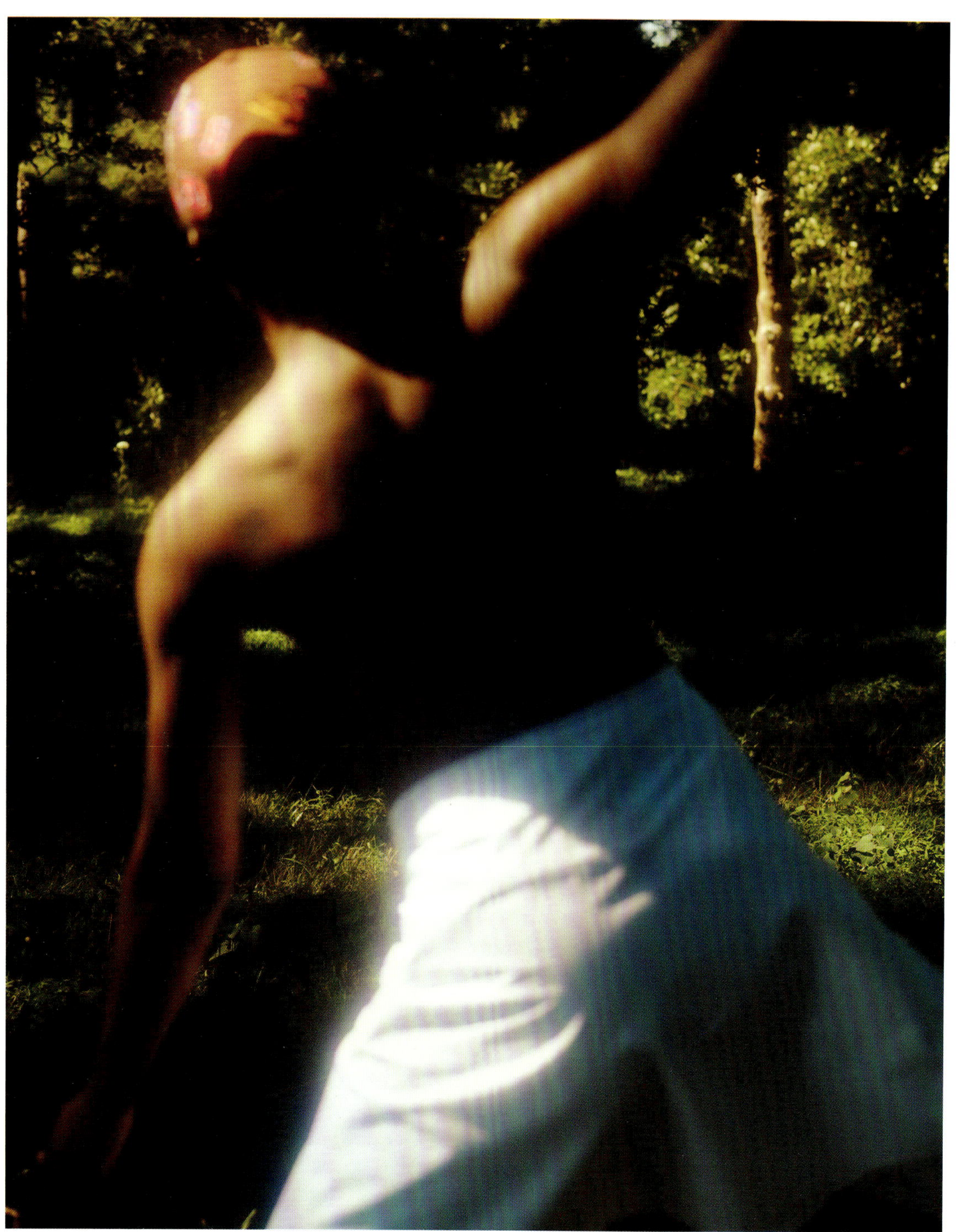

invited NIC to perform. "There's a level of humor that goes hand in hand with NIC's intellectual rigor." While other artists have incorporated transformative costuming into similarly durational performances—in the film *Starting Over*, Nayland Blake tap-dances inside a 146-pound bean-filled bunny suit until collapsing from exhaustion—NIC was interested in the ensemble's ability to hide the body, perhaps obscuring one's identity altogether and thus refuting spectacle.

They explained: "That was really the excitement about it: the disappearance of what is identifiably a Black performer, Black queer performer, Black gay performer, and seeing what happens with that abstracting. So, are Black people dancing on the internet when you see those mascots dancing to particular types of music?"

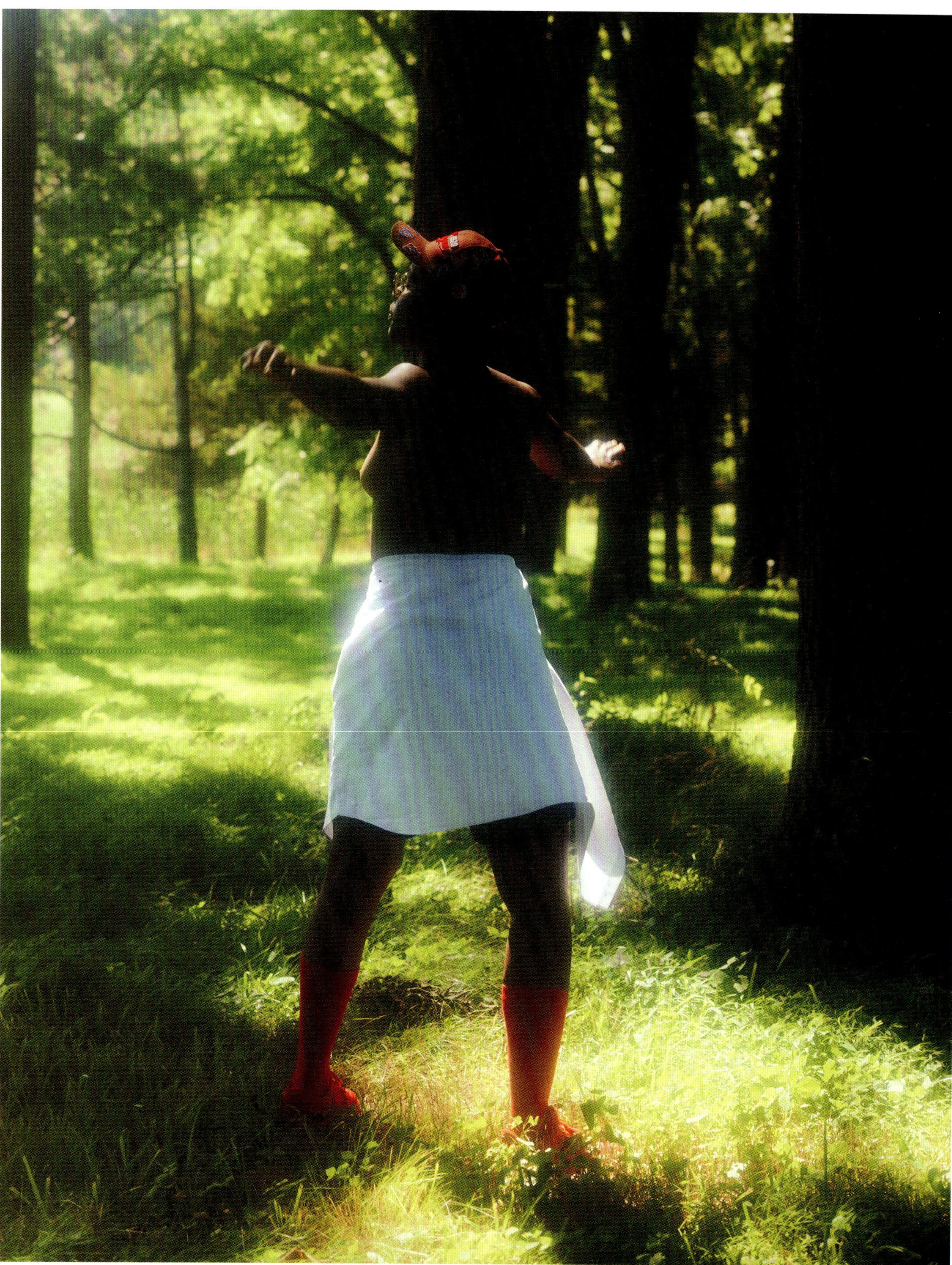

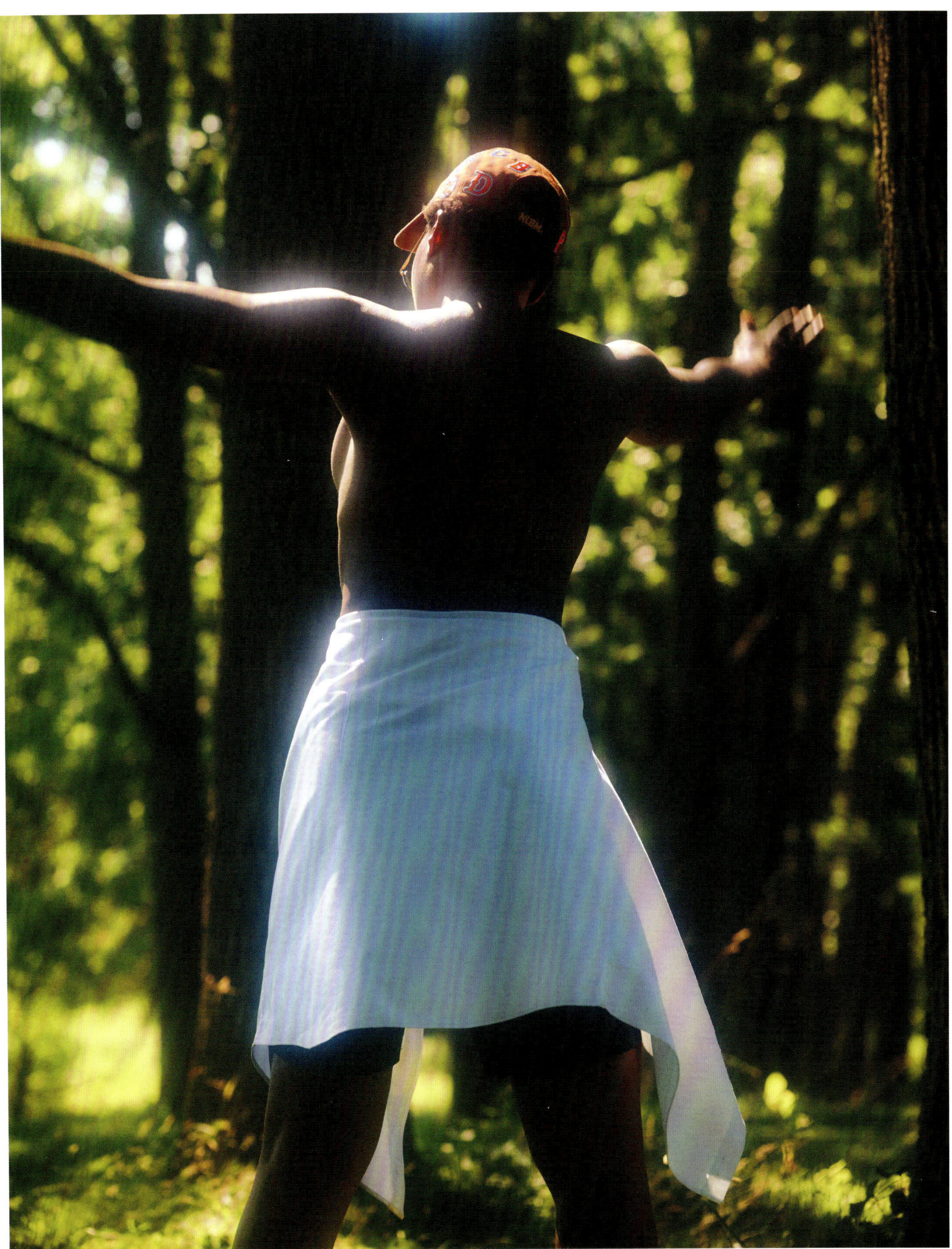

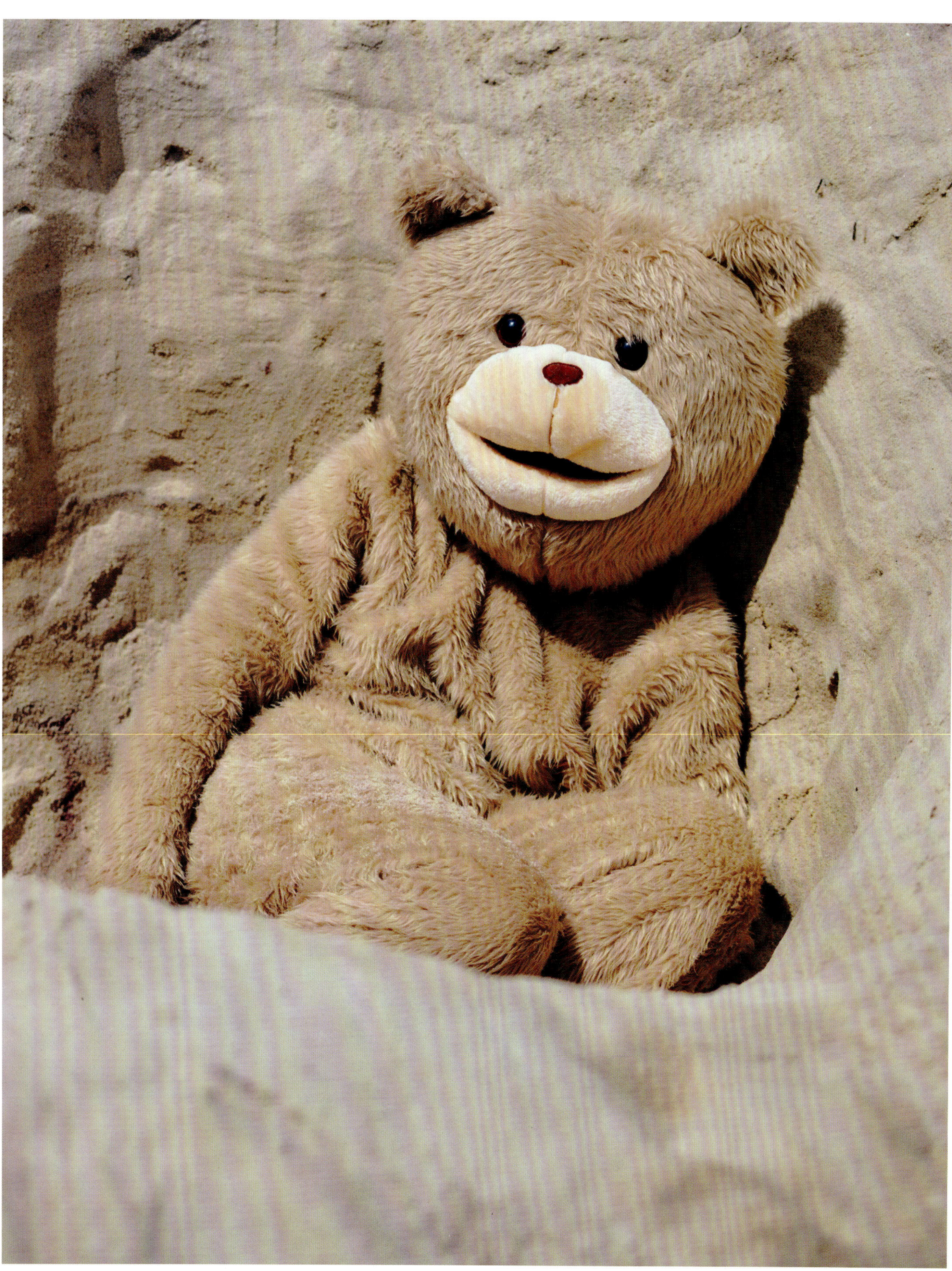

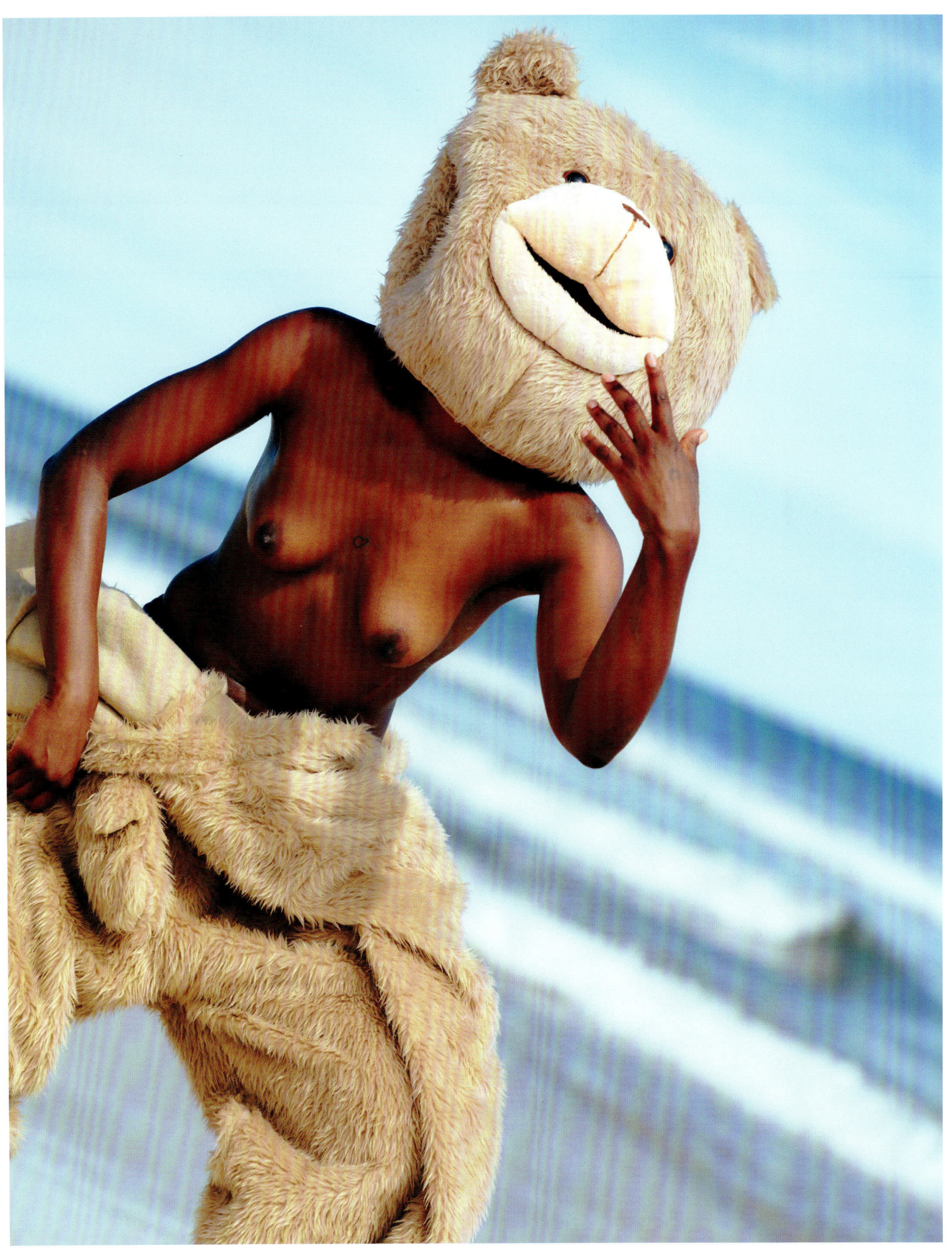

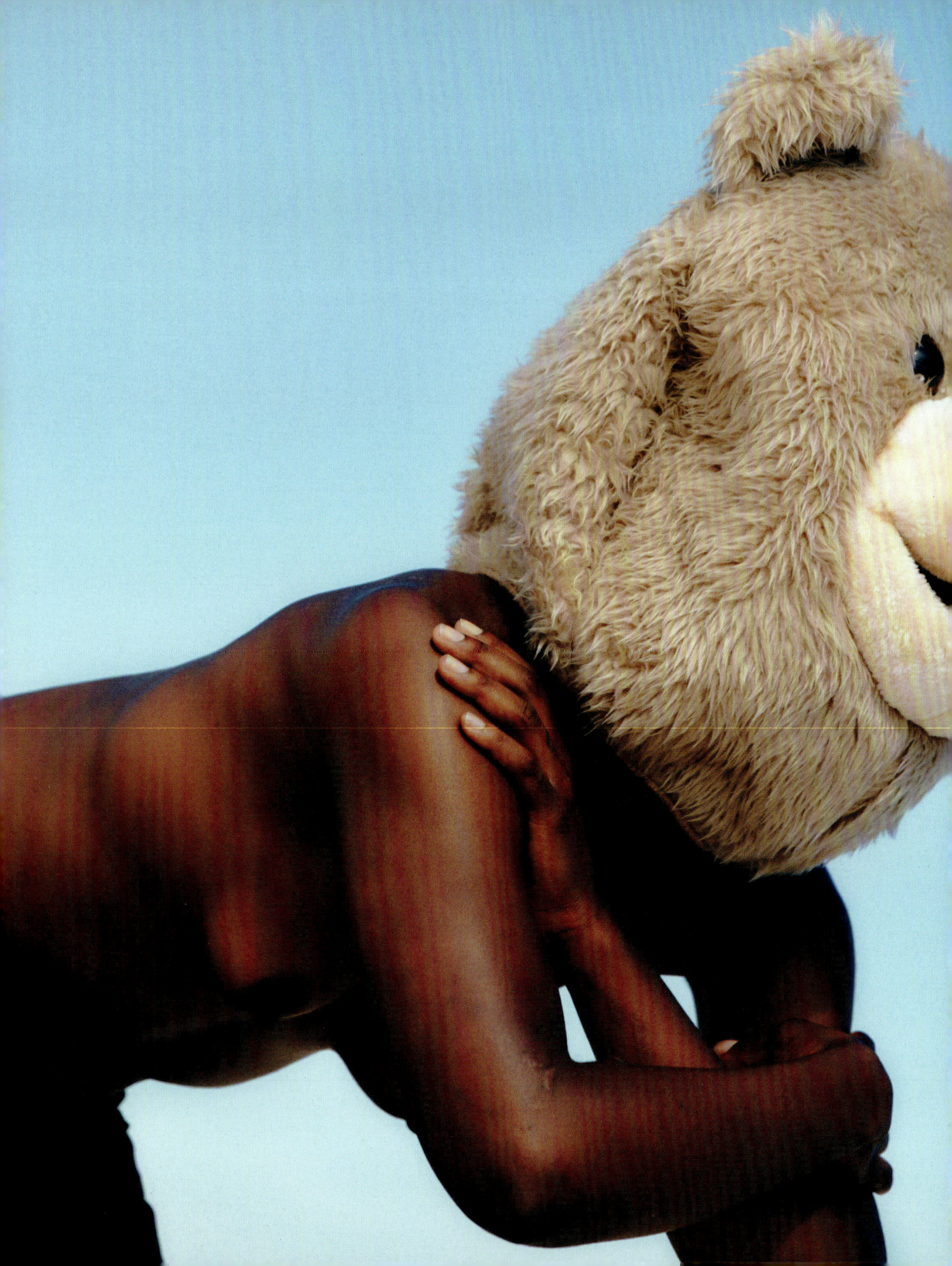

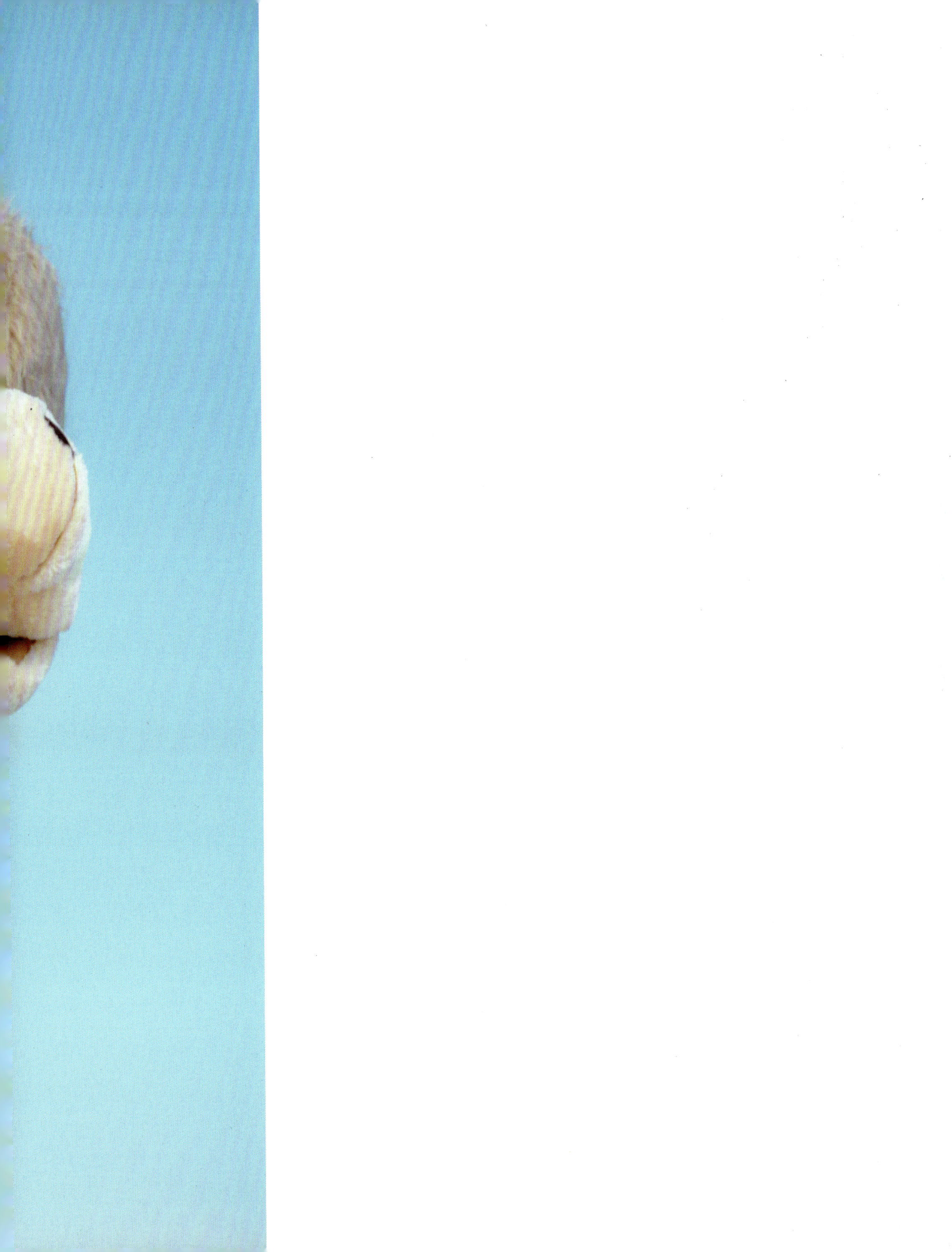

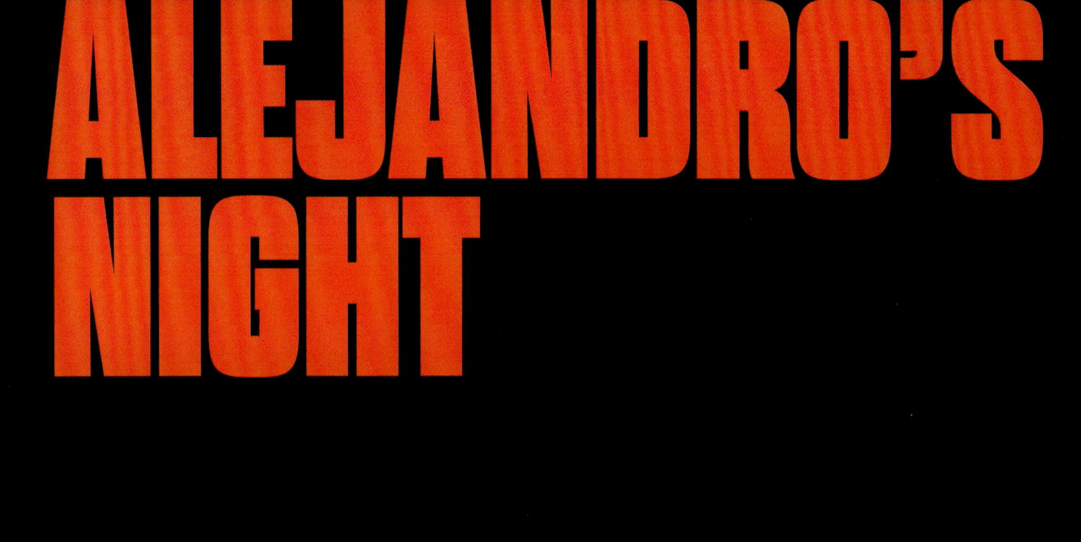
ALEJANDRO'S
NIGHT

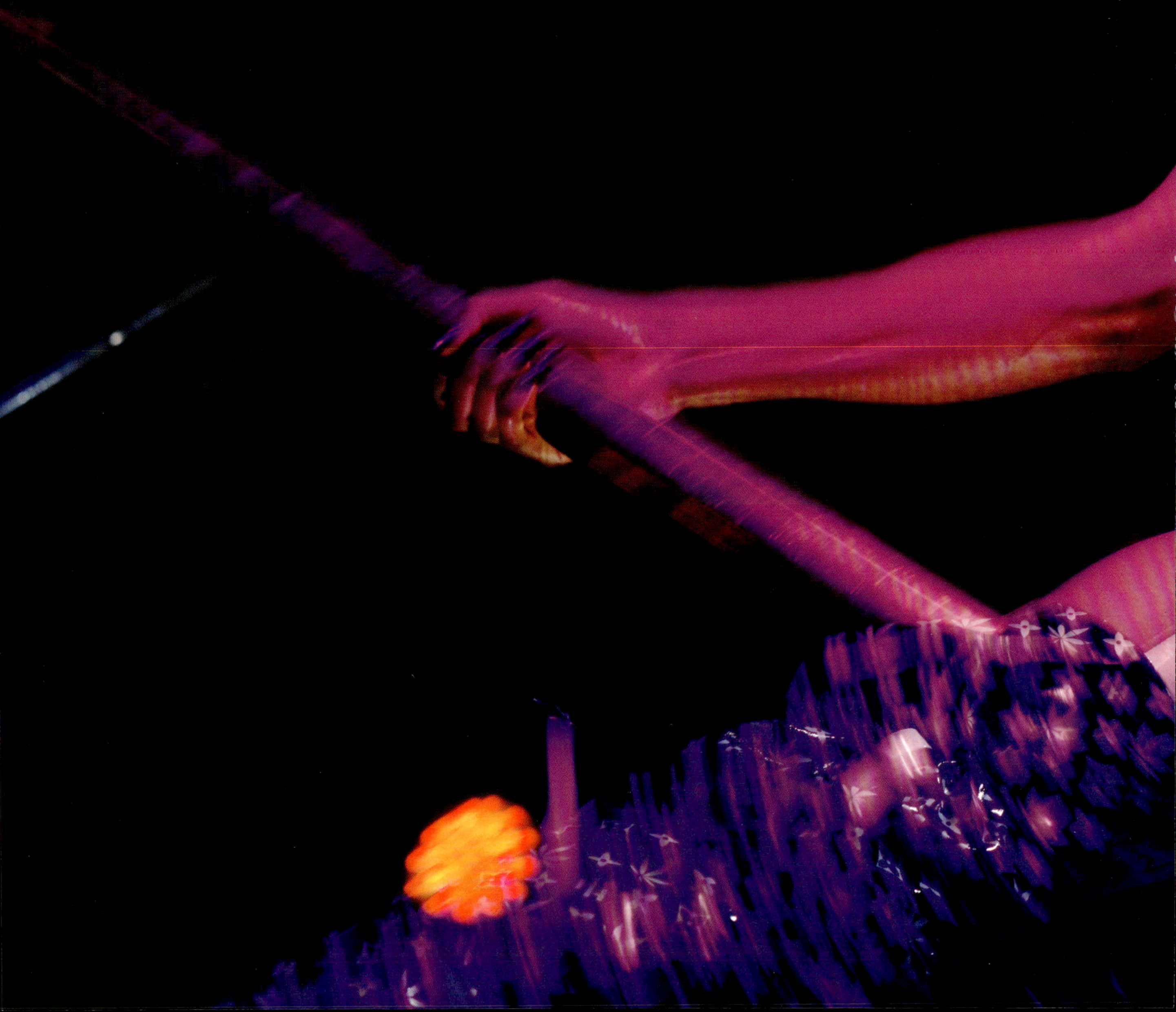

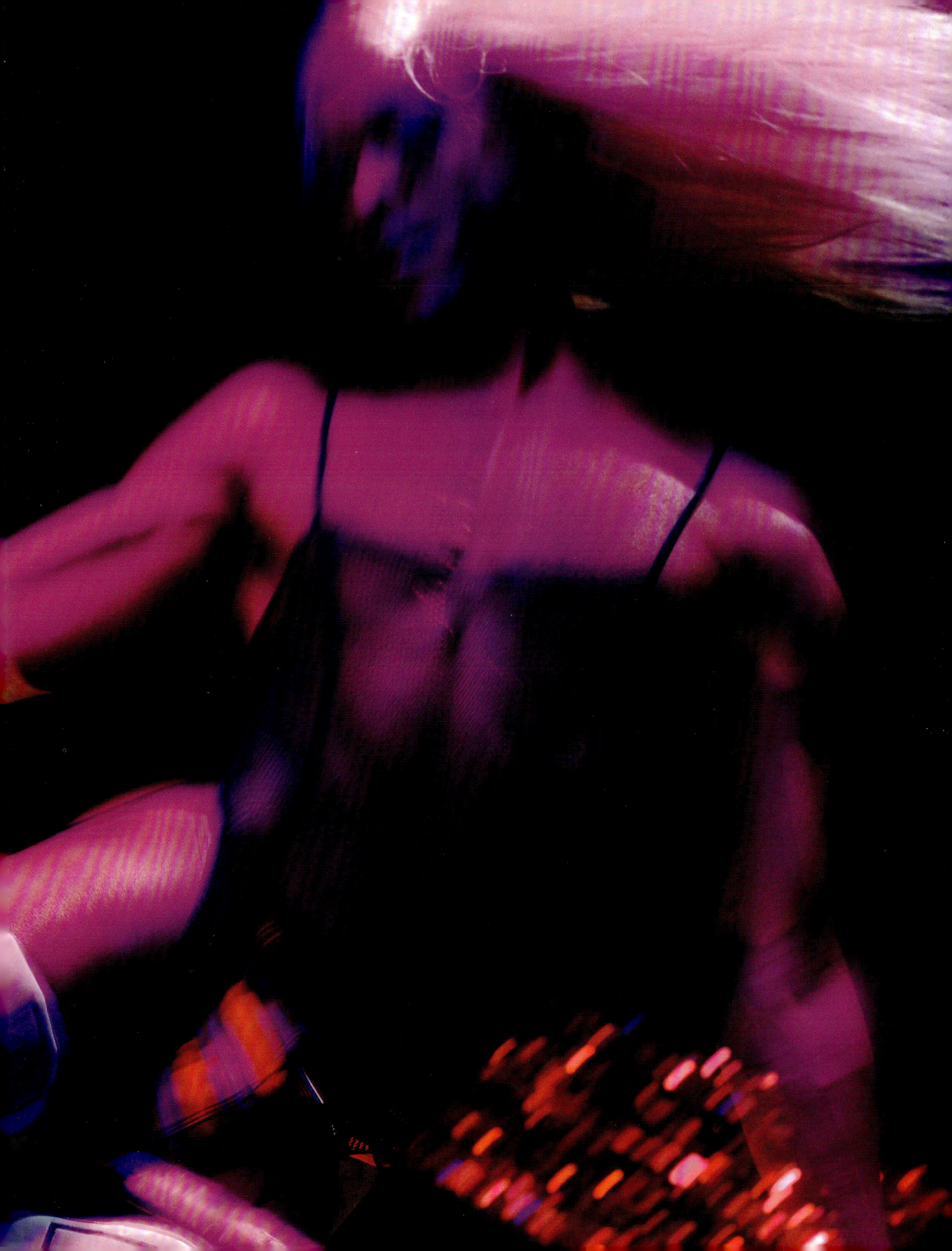

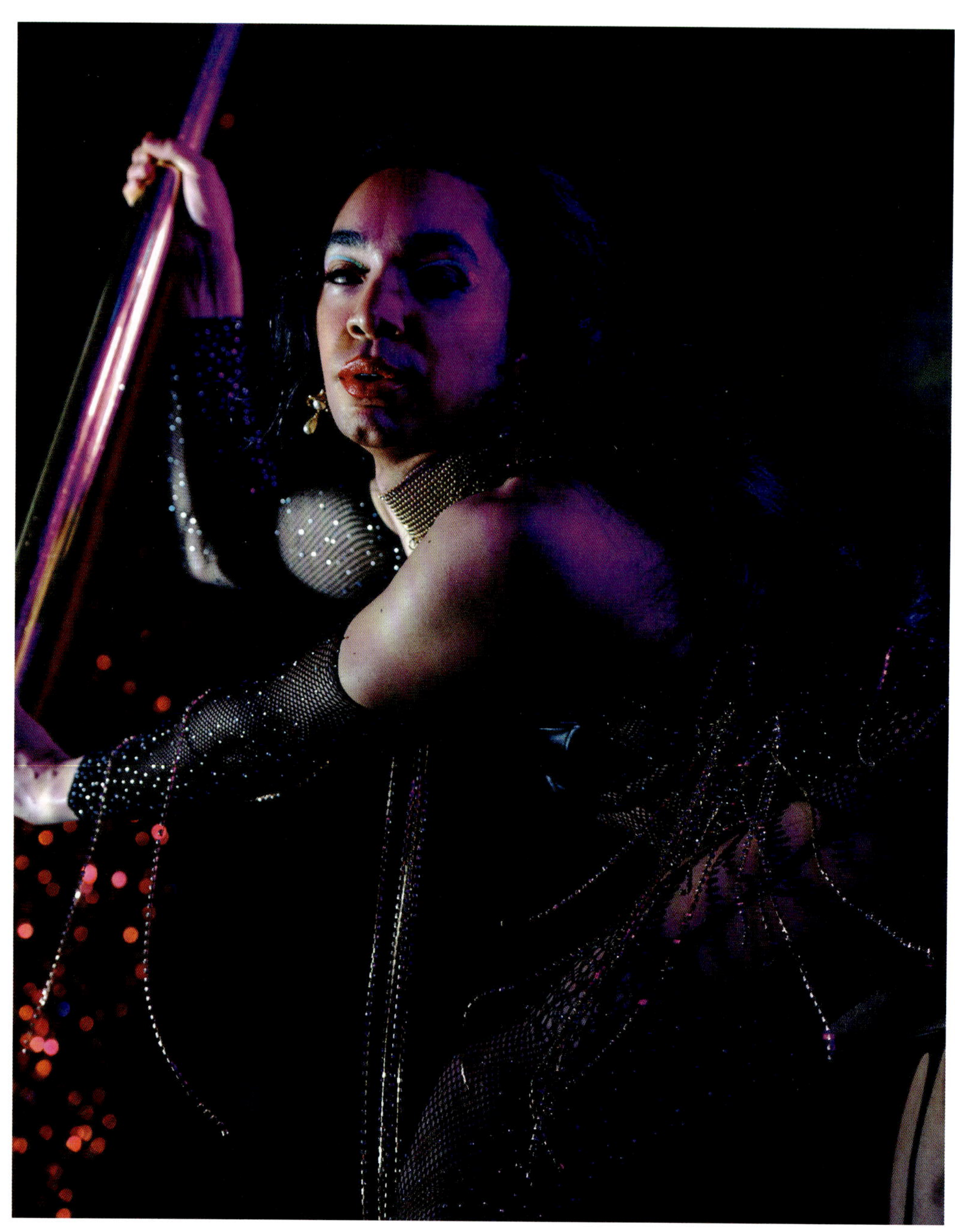

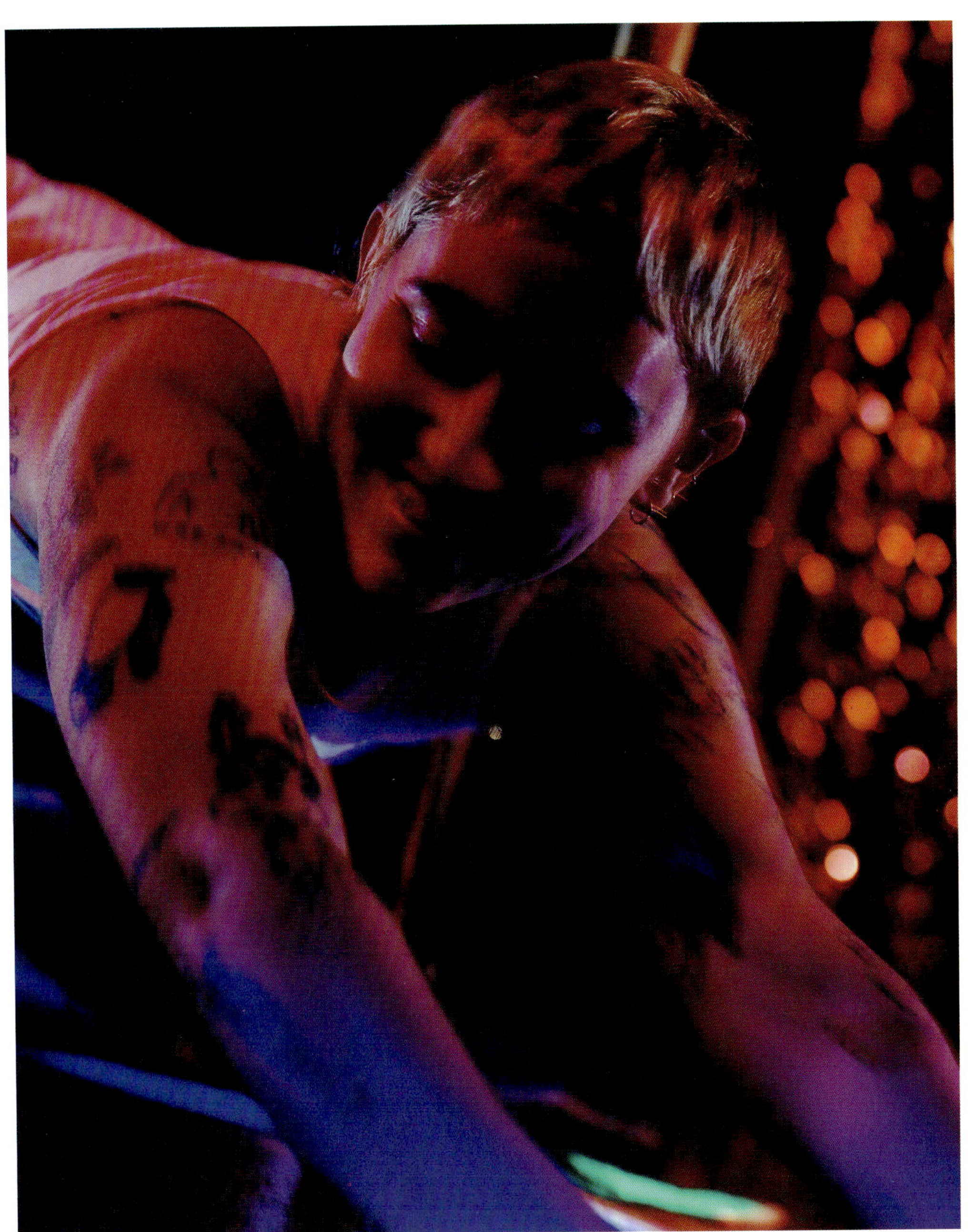

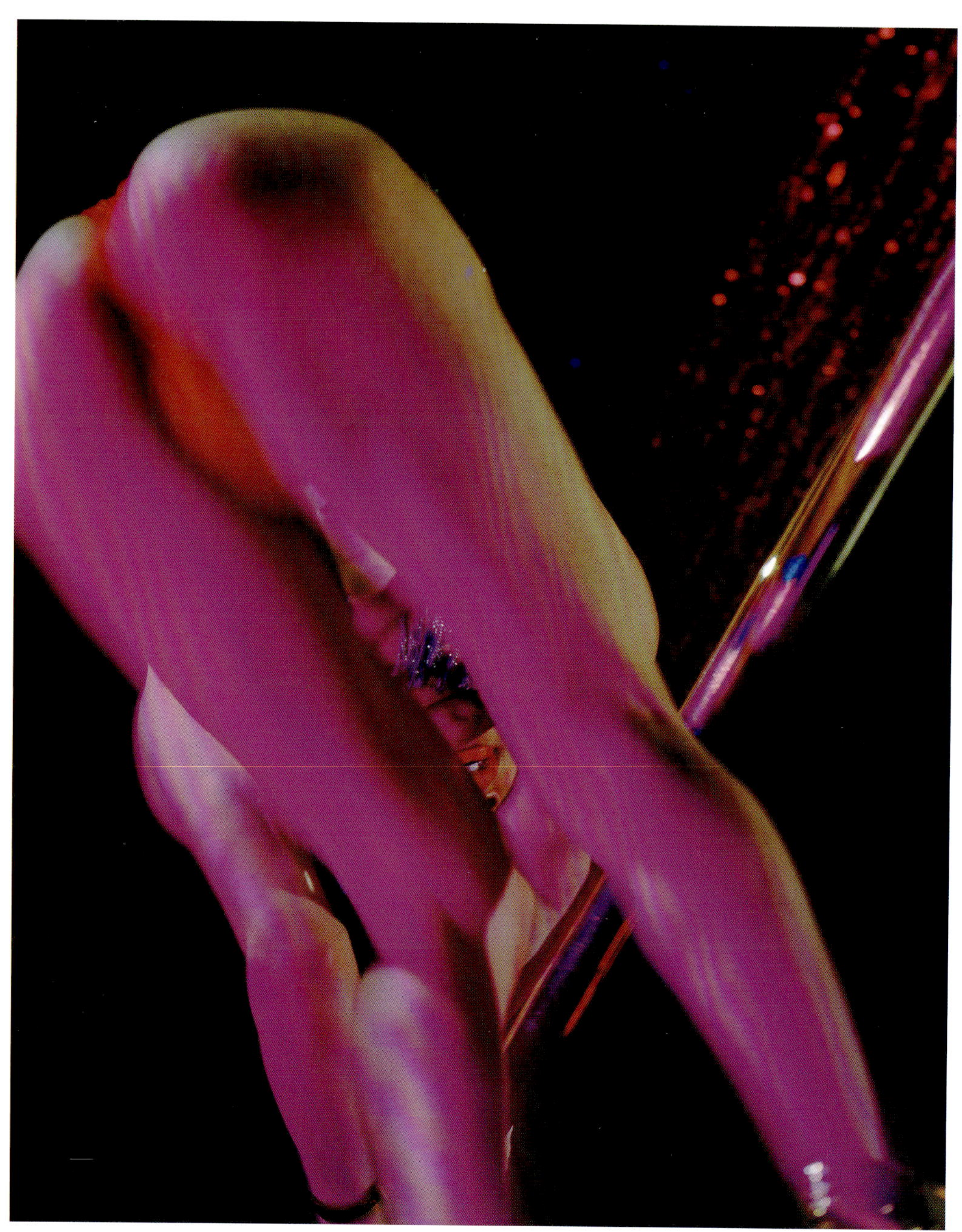

A DANCER, SCANTILY CLAD BUT FOR A SHROUD OF FAUX FUR– lined chiffon, edges toward a pole. It's a Wednesday night at the downtown Los Angeles bar Precinct. He falls to his back with a mischievous smirk, maintaining eye contact with an audience member seated beside the platform. The murmurs of Enya's "Only Time" hum in the background; usually a meditation on the healing that comes with the passing of days, in this context the song, soft and slow as a lullaby, sounds like a promise of some sensuous future tryst.

This dancer, Ken Dahl, has been honing his craft since he was twenty-two. He was born in Monroe, Washington, a rain-soaked town sleeping in the shadow of the Cascade mountains, but he moved to Seattle in 2017 and landed a job at a club then known as Little Darlings. It was a dimly lit joint housed within an austere building in the city's Belltown neighborhood, a short walk from Dahl's apartment at the time. Though he has since taken classes to strengthen his technique, he had no formal pole dancing training when he was starting out, instead picking up everything he could while on the job.

"I learned from watching my associates, other strippers. I'd be like, 'I want to do that' and would try until I succeeded," he recalls. "The stripper mom would have me come in right when the club opened and teach me a trick. But even then, I didn't know the names of the tricks. I didn't even know if I was doing proper form, but that was what I had." He quickly took to the movement, appreciating the intimate moments it facilitated between the performer and their audience—"that sleepy, daydreamy, sexy feeling where it gets to be more erotic than sexualized."

As he later considered a gender-affirming surgery that would alter his chest, he faced a difficult decision. The procedure would bring his body into better alignment with his identity, yet he knew it could also threaten the livelihood he earned in traditional club environments, which catered to the assumed desires of straight, cisgender men. Dahl ultimately decided to move forward with the operation in 2017, putting his dancing on pause and pivoting to drag performance. Still, his passion for striptease never subsided, and at the recommendation of Selena the Stripper and The Goddess Cori—cohosts of Heaux in the Kneaux, a podcast about sex work—he discovered Alejandro's Night, a gender-expansive strip party. There, in December 2021, he was back on the pole for the first time in four years.

Held monthly in Precinct's back room, past the main bar where fried chicken sandwiches are served up hot, Alejandro's feels like a delicious secret whispered between friends. This performance-driven strip night takes its name from a Lady Gaga song. With an all-inclusive vision, it puts transmasculine performers of color in the spotlight. From behind a pair of glittering red curtains, dancers of all body types and in varying stages of undress advance toward a floor-to-ceiling pole, the nexus for a series of gravity-defying flips and spins. As clothing comes off, each reveal is met with increasingly elated screams from the crowd. Flurries of green bills, falling like snow, blanket the stage.

Alejandro's is one of a growing number of events popping up around the country that aim to fill a gap in nightlife: spaces for pole dancing to be safely performed and enjoyed by queer and trans people. Elsewhere in Los Angeles, there's Fantasy Suite, which recurs at a Hollywood bar called the North End and celebrates bigger bodies in addition to LGBTQ+ performers. Alejandro's originated in November 2020 and grew out of a sister event called Jolene that created a platform primarily for transfeminine performers.

"Some of the dancers we have are really strong," says Alejandro's event producer Face, who also performs as

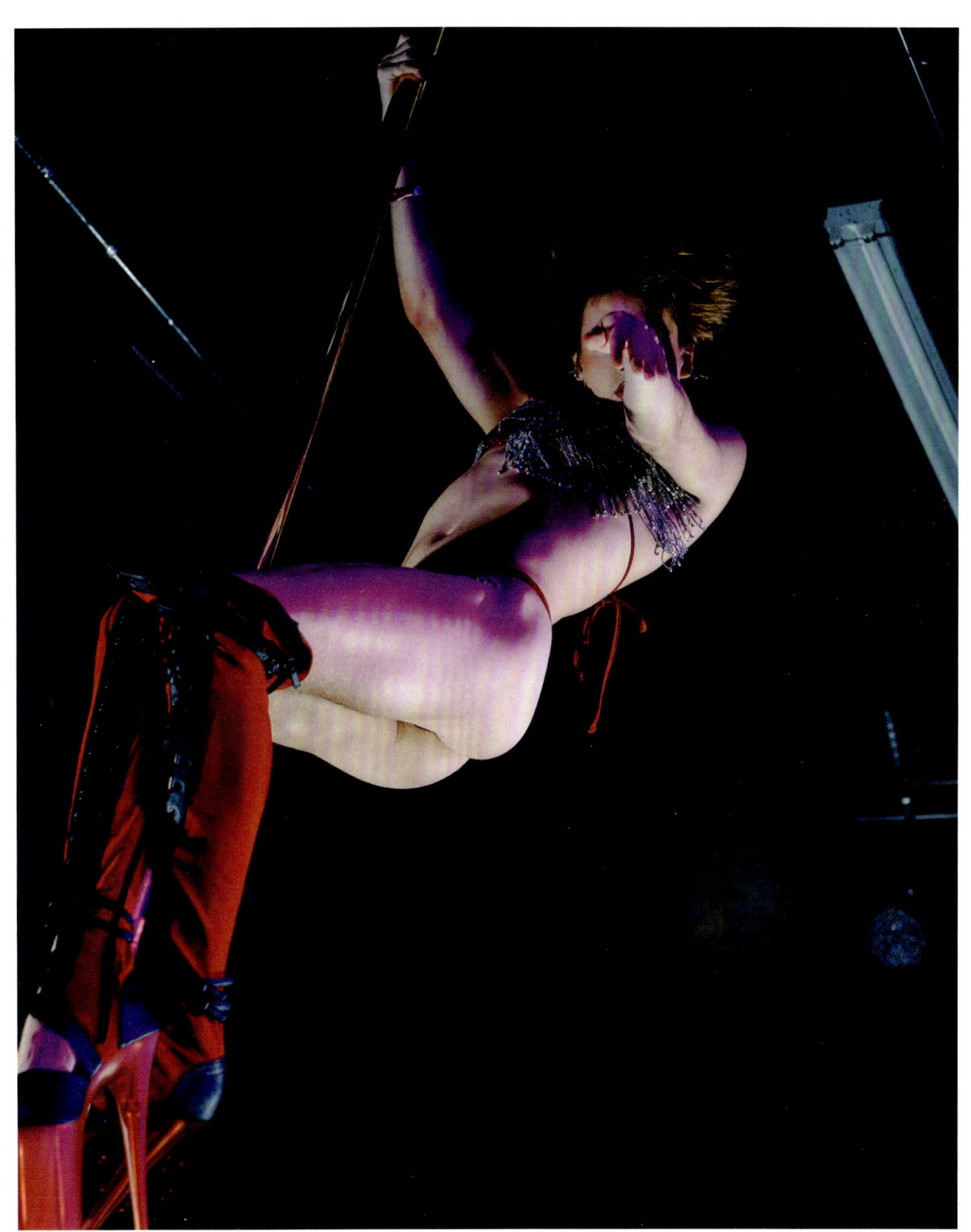

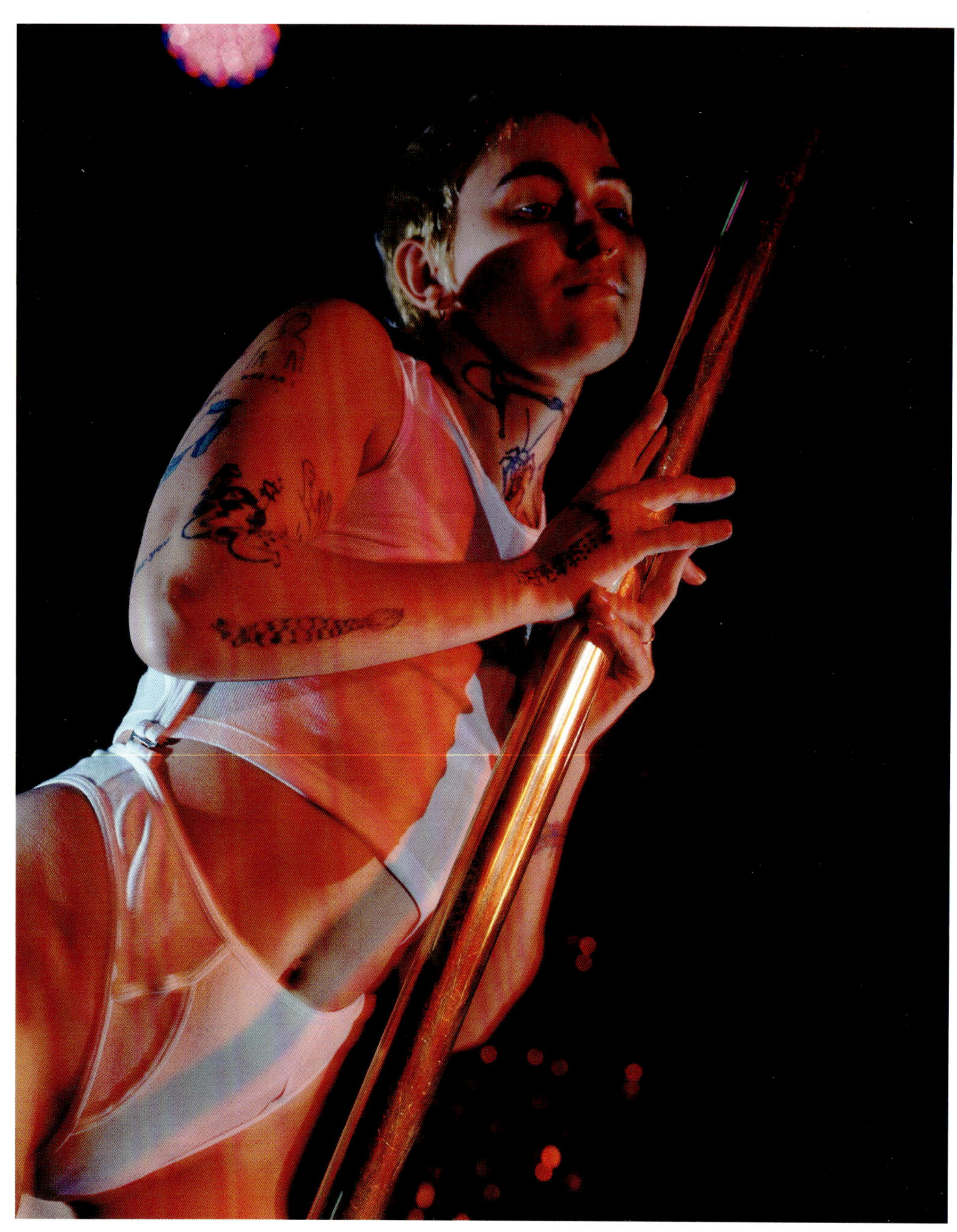

the Diamond Prince. "They really do this as a living and practice their craft. Some people are just here to perform, and they have regular day jobs. No matter who those people are, when you get onstage, there's nothing but love."

Born and raised in nearby Long Beach, Face began dancing in traditional clubs when he was eighteen. At first, it was a way for him to make money during a time when he needed it, but he soon became an in-demand performer touring through cities in Texas, Georgia, and Nevada. He enjoyed the hustle this involved and cherished the friends he met along the way. Yet he, like Dahl, held an underlying fear that, once he began his transition, there would be no place for him in the industry.

He performed at Alejandro's for the first time in December 2020 and took over production in spring 2021. Now he casts every show, coordinates with the bar, oversees the social media promotion, and, as the evening's lovingly named "stripper dad," tends to the needs of the performers—often with a drink in hand. Backstage prior to the show, in a narrow dressing room lined with mirrors and event posters, he gathers the dancers for a group huddle, an important pre-show ritual he adopted from his time playing high school basketball and wrestling.

"Some of them are quiet; they're doing their makeup and they're [keeping] to themselves," he says. "I challenge them. I question them. I'm like, 'Are you guys ready to make some money?!' And I make them scream, shout. I get them excited."

One night in January 2022, the party's lineup was composed entirely of trans performers for the first time. Face tasks himself with opening Alejandro's. His warm, cheery candor offstage tightens into a steely stare. He takes the stage with a series of heavy stomps, his boots leaving behind loud thuds. He lunges onto

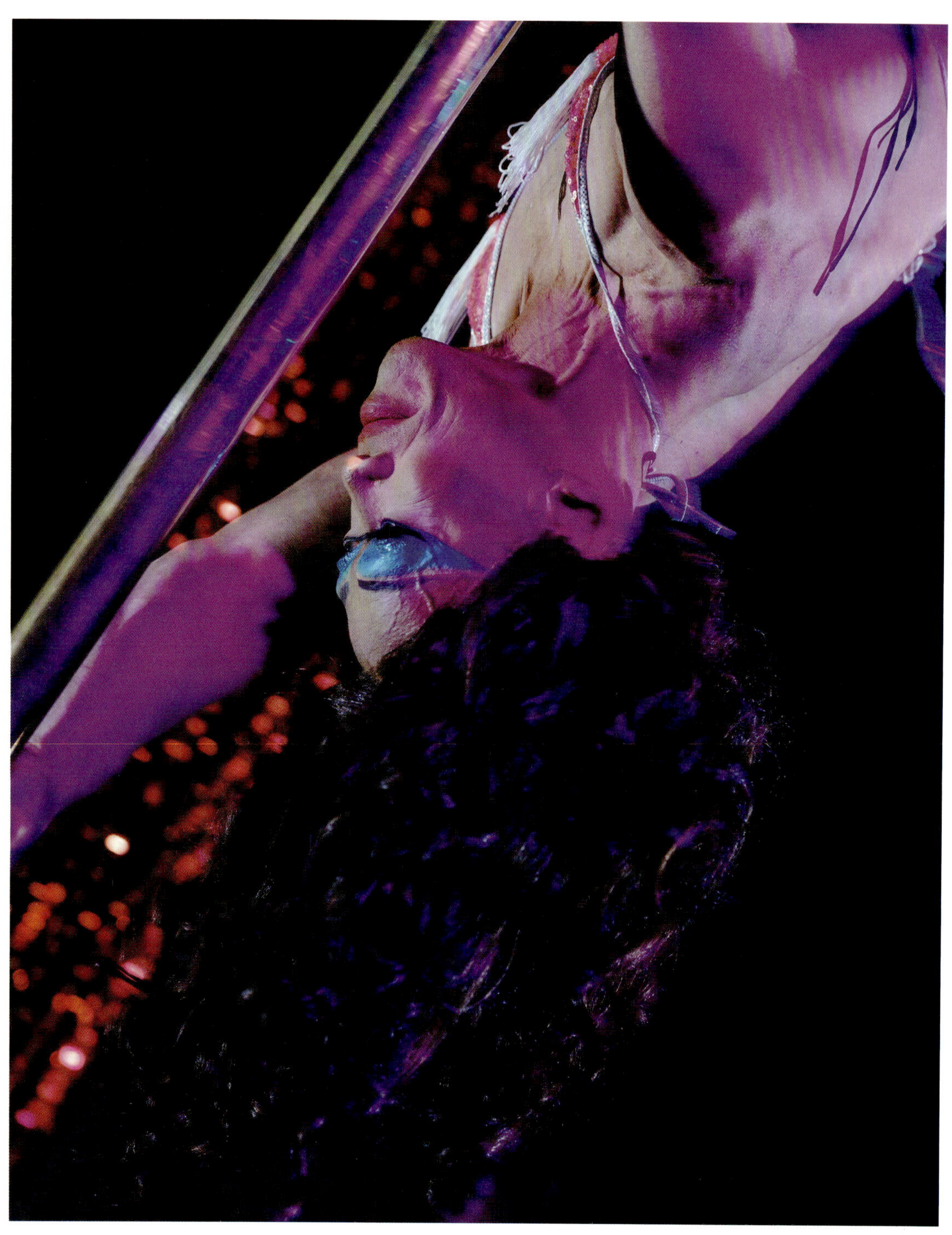

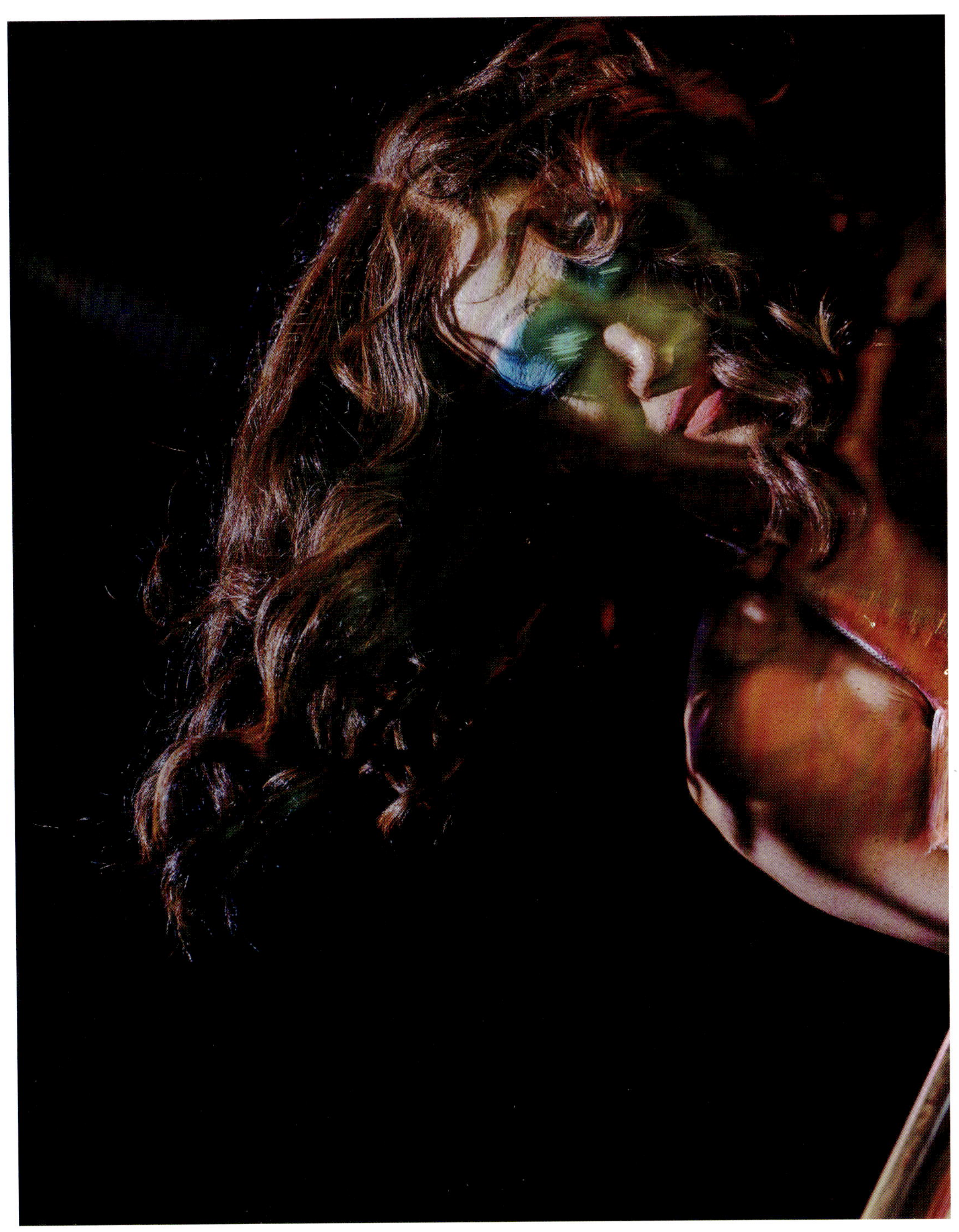

the pole, around which he hooks his leg, spins, and inverts, before returning to the ground to close out the number. Facing the audience, he thrusts his pelvis. Although once dancing felt like portraying a character, Face says, here he can perform squarely as himself.

Every dancer is asked to perform three numbers throughout the evening, and each is wildly different from the last. A fan describes Becky Peach, a dancer sporting a waterfall of pin-straight blond hair, as the "Beyoncé" of the show. Her star power is undeniable as she floats midair in a Superman pose, holding herself upright by clutching the pole between her thigh-high boots, which are dotted with images of marijuana leaves in the style of Louis Vuitton's monogram print. Kayan, a dancer and instructor who arrived at pole by way of fitness classes, sits on the ground with their legs splayed, then smacks their sky-high heels together with a tremendous thwack. Their rhinestone bra clings to muscular shoulders. Pole dancing, though often made to appear delicate in form, requires a tremendous amount of physical strength.

Growing up in Los Angeles's Chinatown neighborhood, Kayan says they often felt insecure "about the way I look, about the way I dress, about the way how people viewed me." Three years of dancing transformed their insecurities into strengths, and they found that they began to feel comfortable wearing less and less clothing the more they performed. "It's like peeling layers off me," they explain. "The thing about pole is it empowers you. It makes you feel so secure with everything you're doing. Everything else doesn't matter."

Pole dancing has deep roots that, in some traditions, date back to twelfth-century acrobatics. In the United States, it largely evolved out of suggestive belly dances performed in Great Depression–era traveling shows.

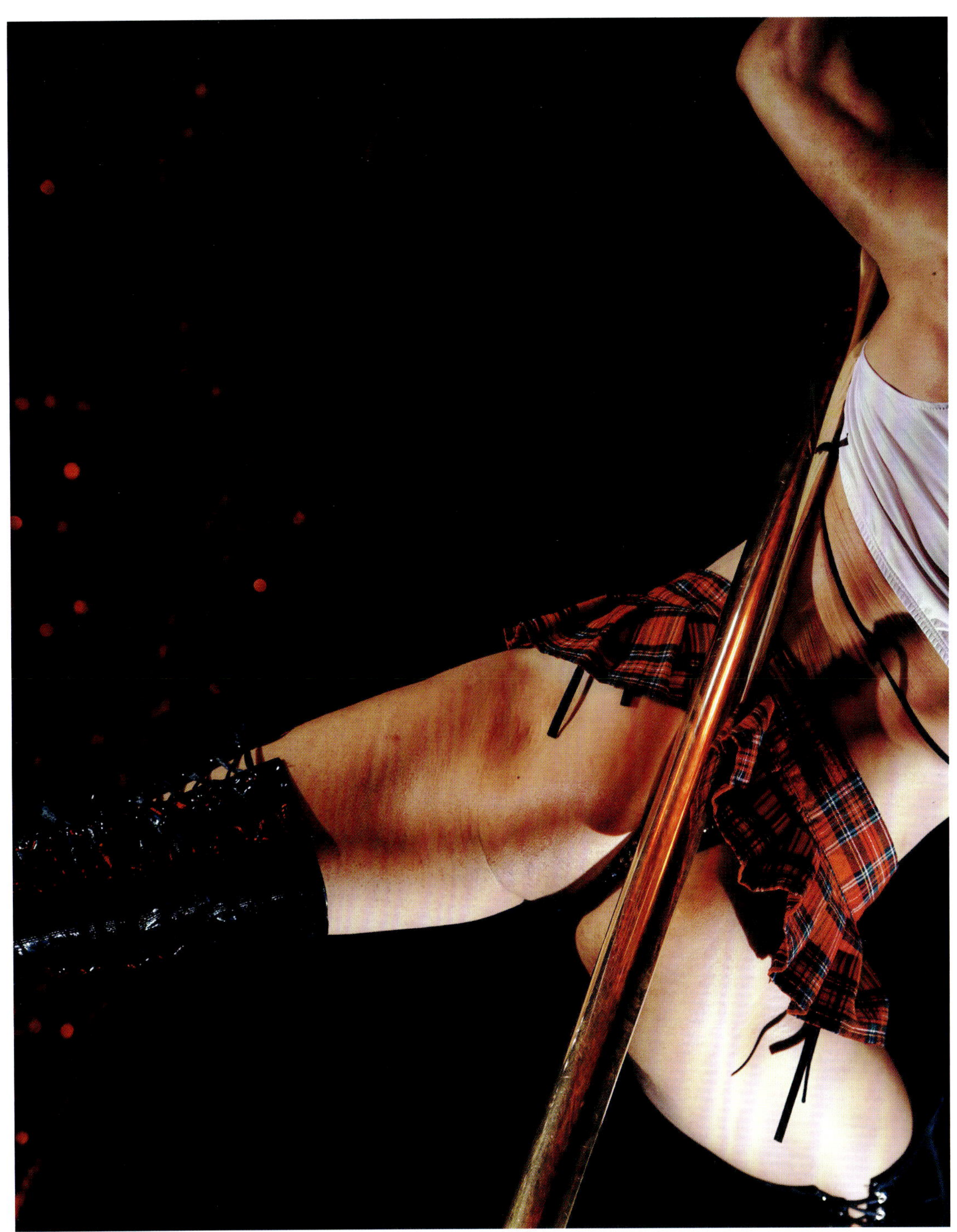

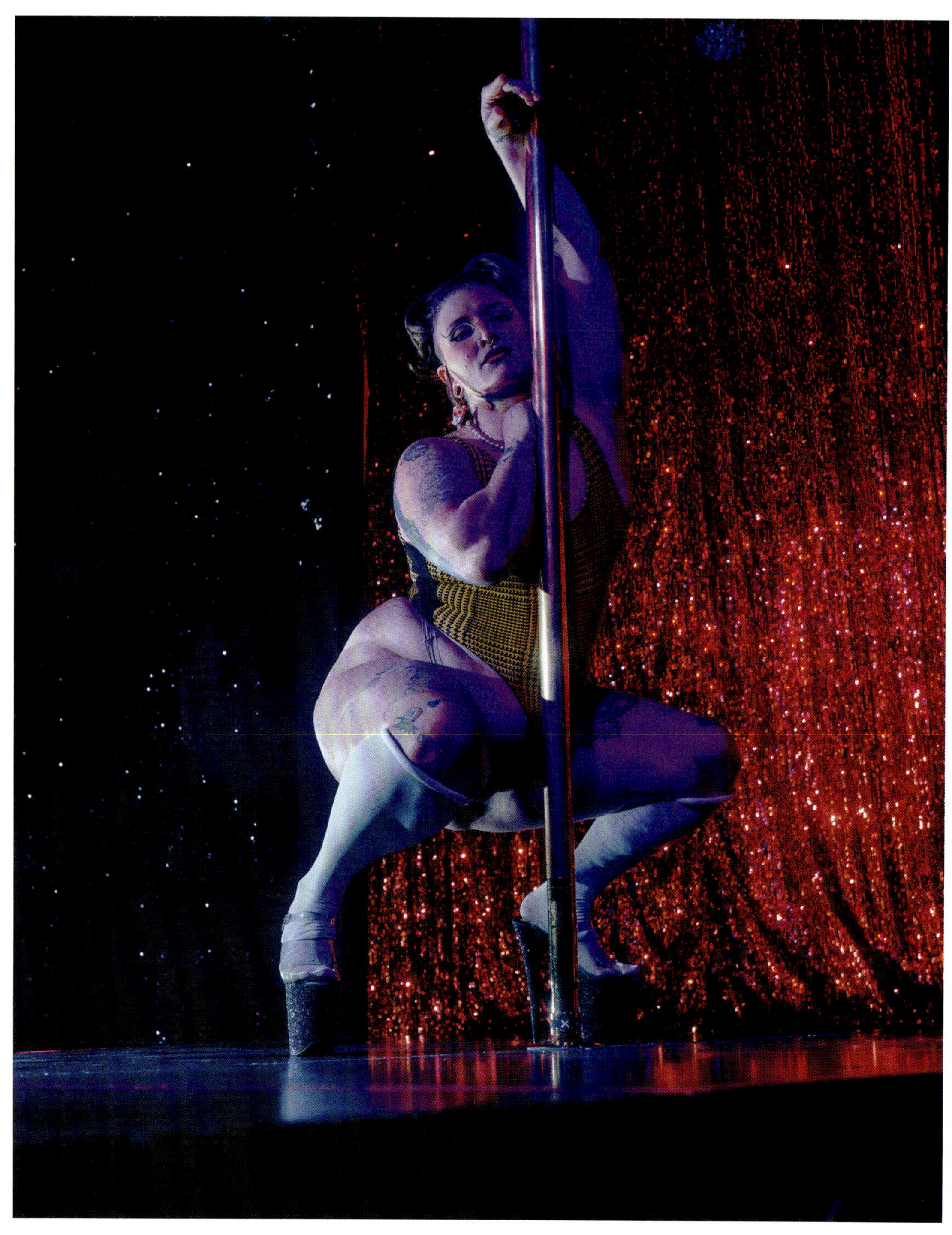

The performances went brick and mortar in the 1950s when strip clubs began popping up around the country, and by the 1970s, nearly all strip clubs included poles in their acts. Pole dancing exists today as a competitive sport and as a fitness trend, yet it is still circulated widely in strip clubs, where the gaze punctures everything, dictating how dancers should look and how they must interact with patrons. Alejandro's, and queer- and trans-centered events like it, offer an alternative, where dancers are celebrated as they are—and compensated for it too.

One dancer says he has already accrued over $300 in tips after only his second performance. Part of the fun is in the exchange—of money, yes; of power, probably; but also of glances, of intimate moments and secrets shared. A stagehand, wearing little but a pair of shrunken leather shorts, arrives to scoop the cash into a bucket. It's time for the next dance.

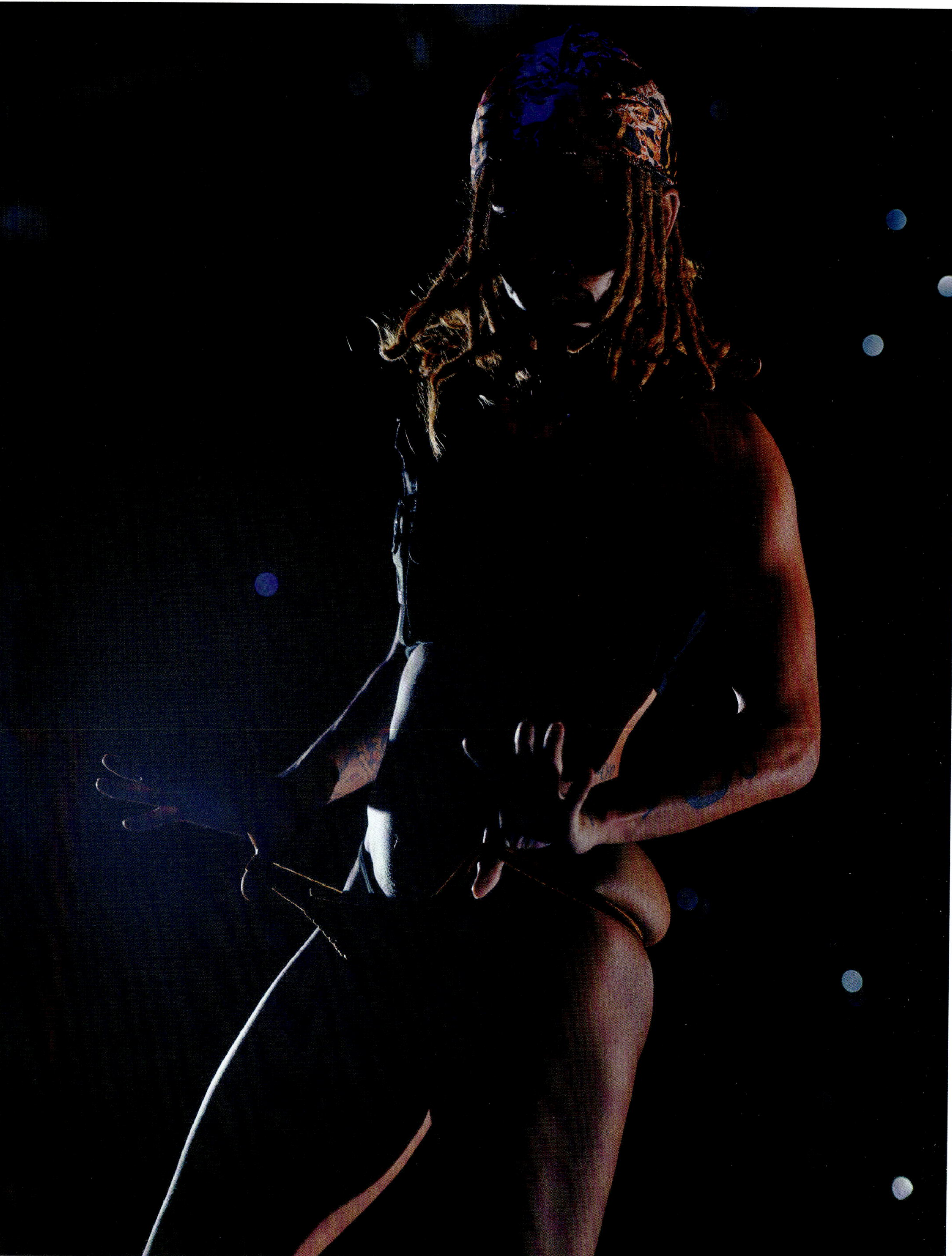

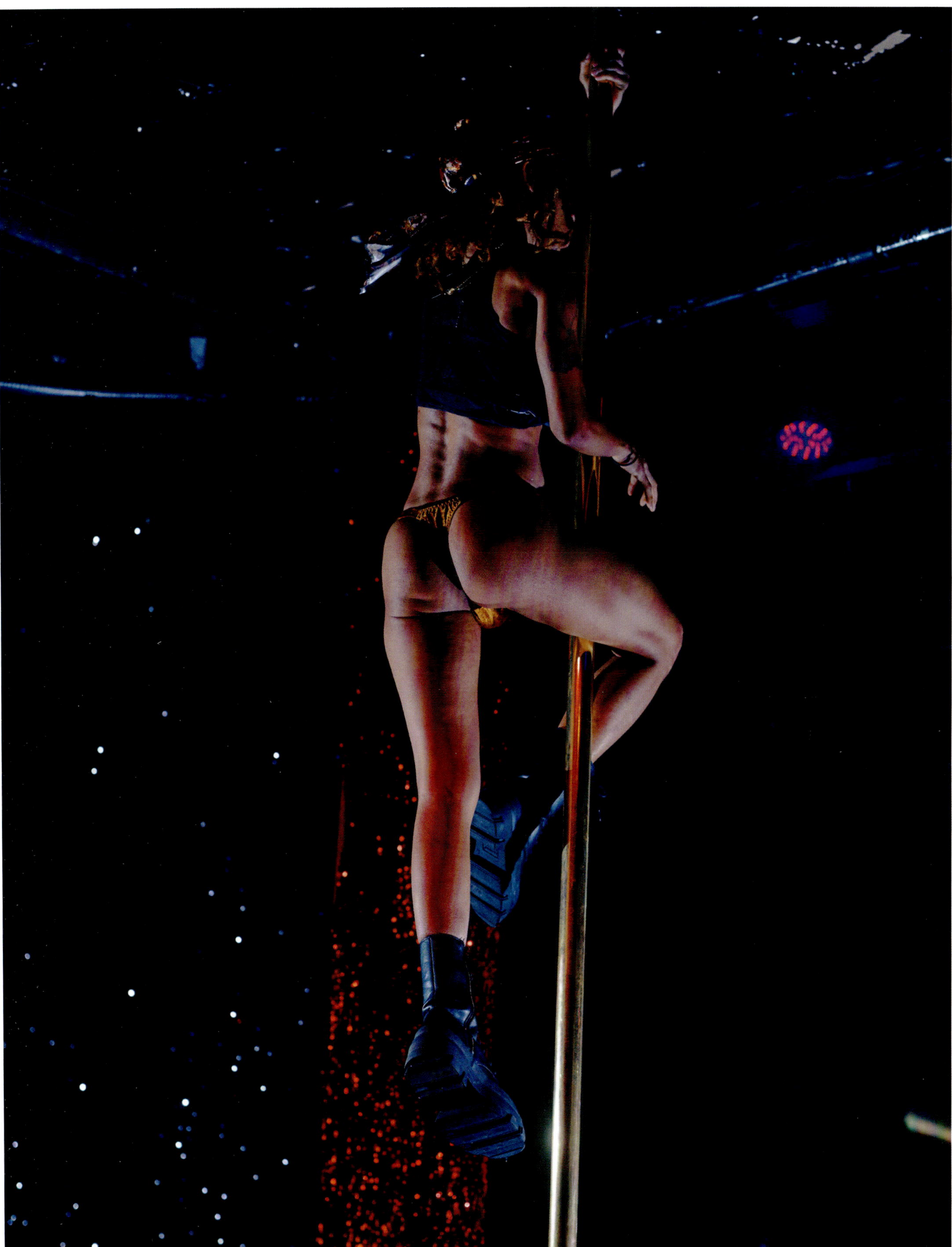

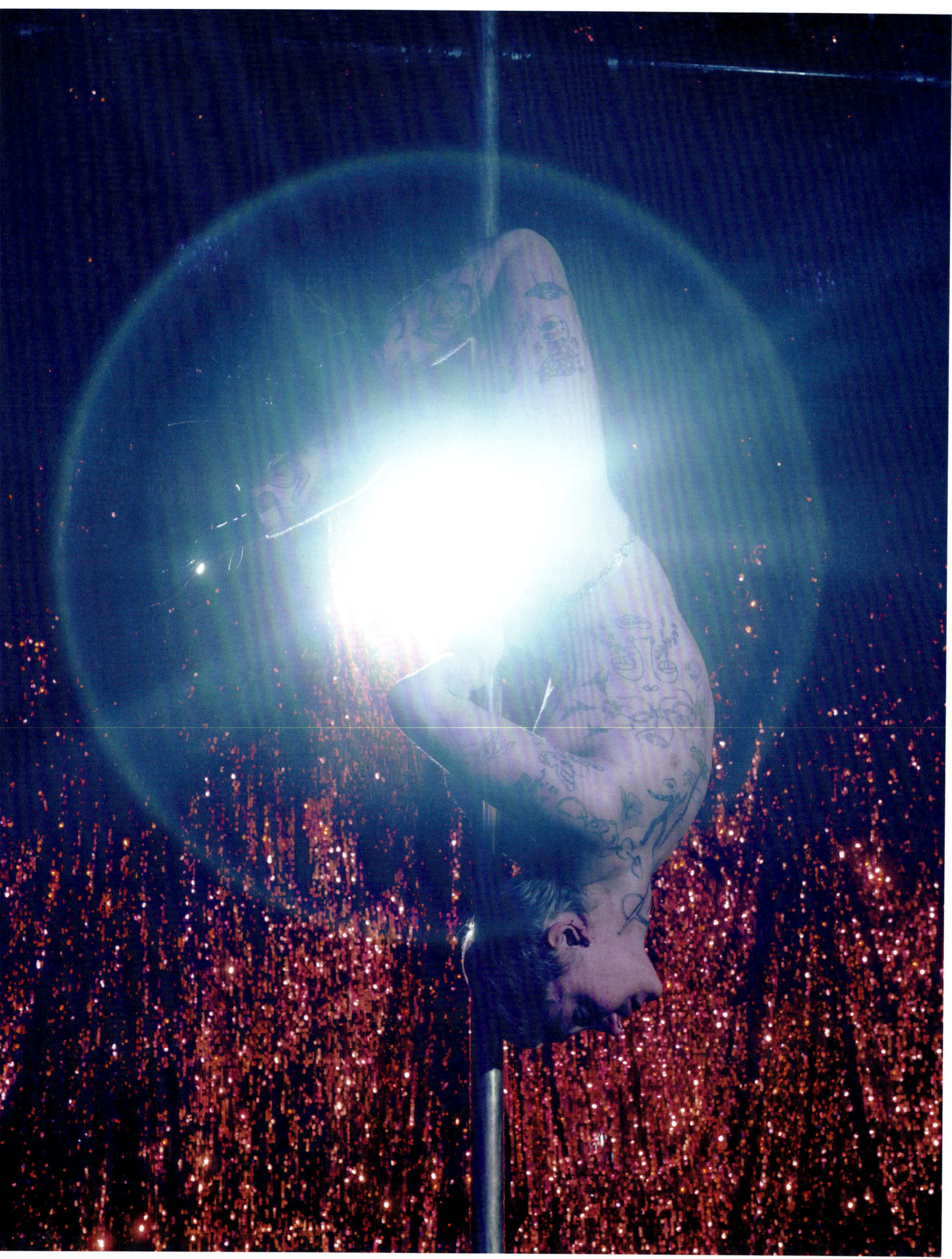

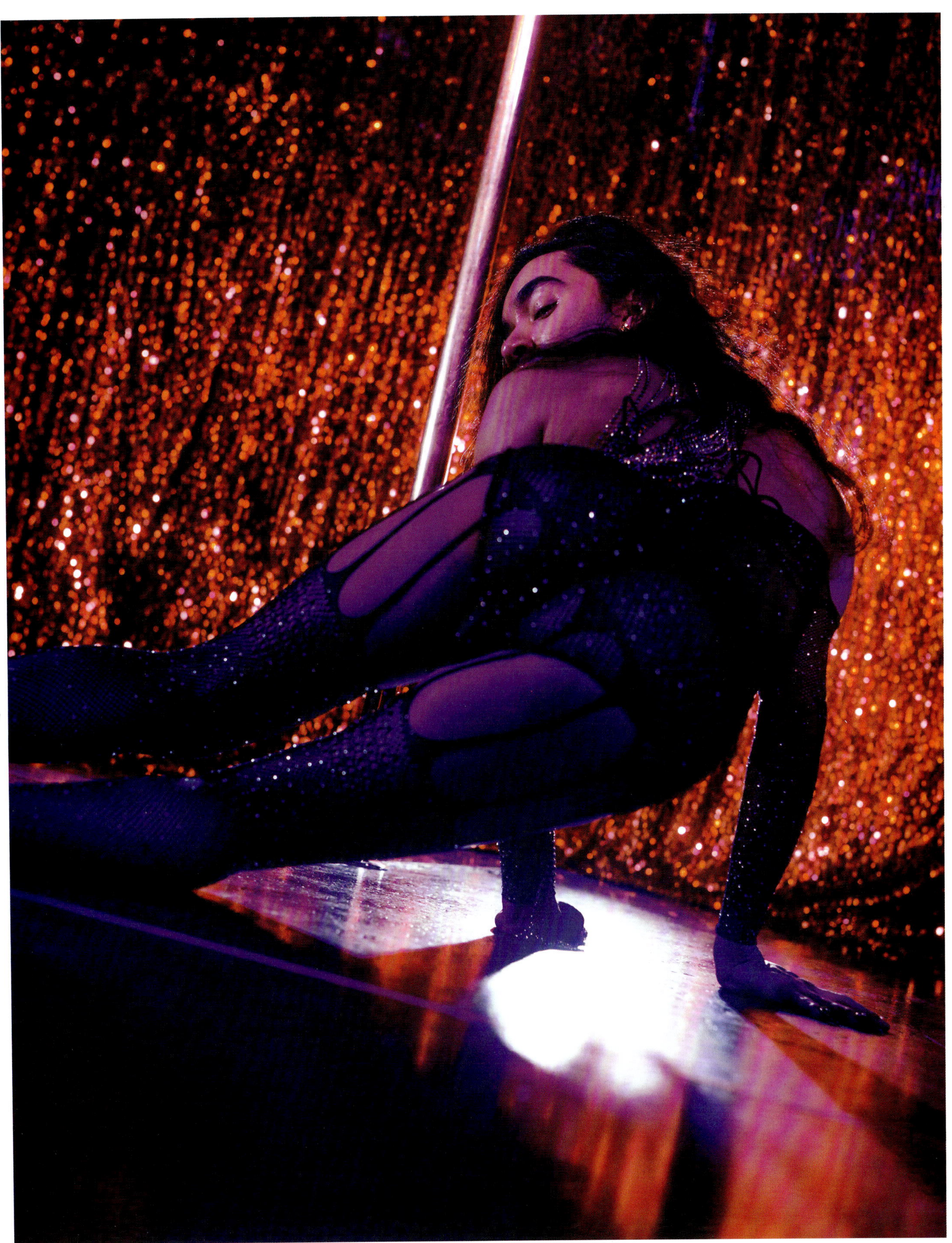

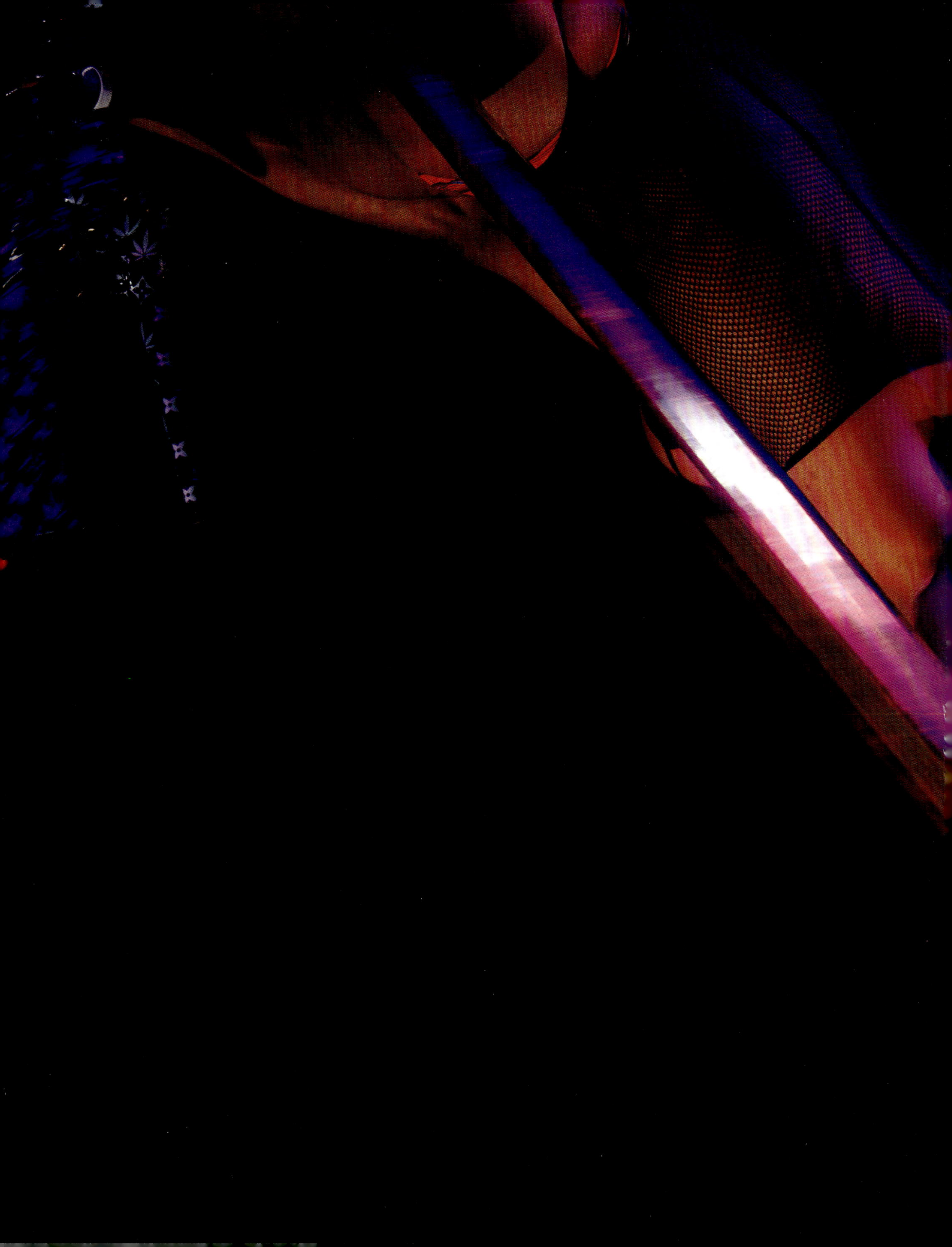

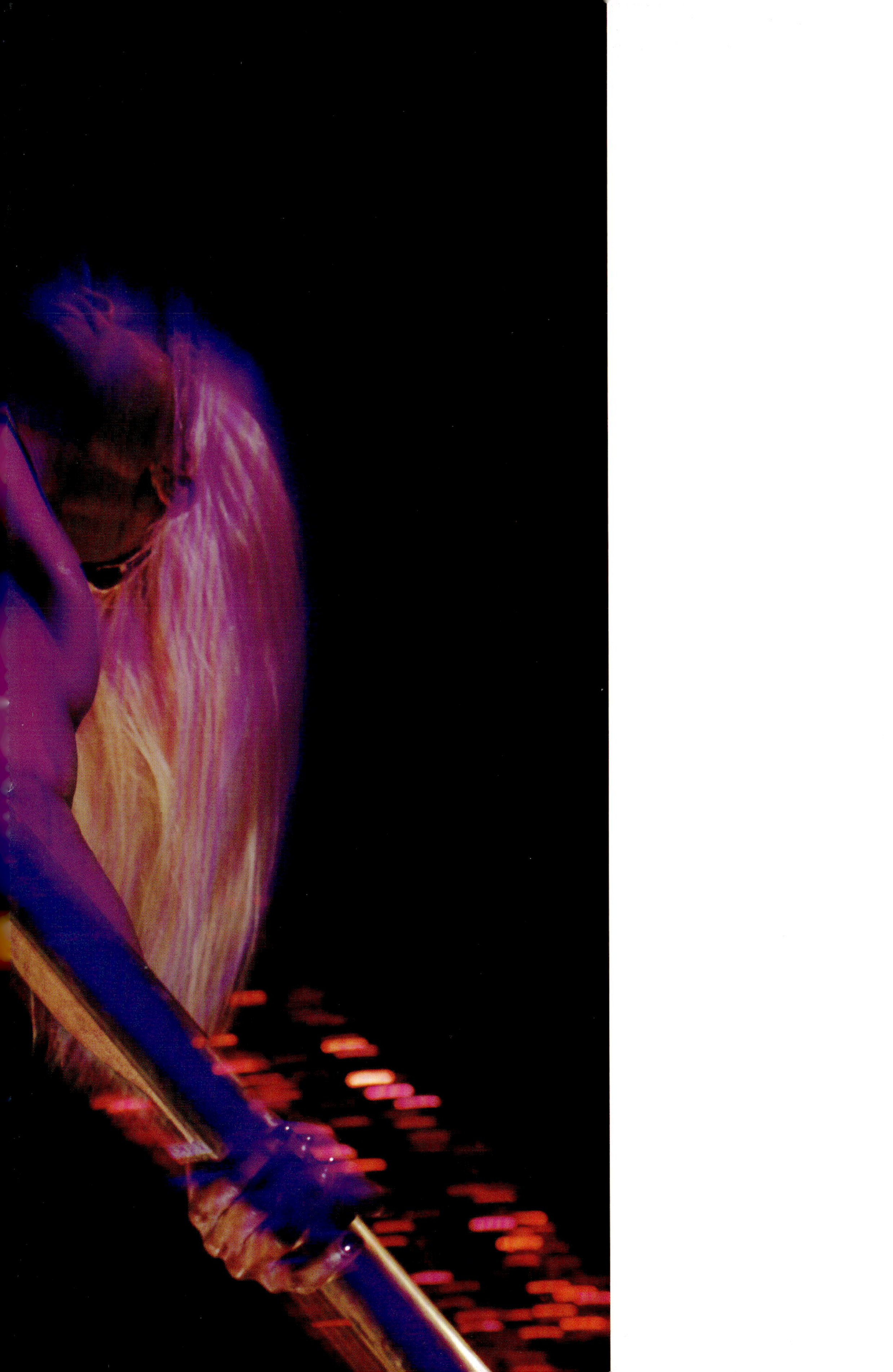

ACKNOWLEDGMENTS

Thank you to everyone who, at any point throughout this process, read, looked, connected, supported, translated, assisted, or critiqued.

Adriane Anderson. Ashley Malloy. Christopher Alexander. Christopher Rudolph. David Oramas. Duke Dang. Emily Keegan. Eve Lyons. Fran Tirado. George Schramm. Gerardo Ismael Madera. Inés Garcia. Jessie Wender. Justin J. Wee. Kay Thebez. Ken Castaneda. Kenta Murakami. Mars Hobrecker. Michelle Tabnick. Mimi d'Autremont. Loganne Bond. Lyudmila Zotova. Patrick Hosken. Samuel Viklund. Stephen Nthusi Reber. Vanessa Golembewski. Virginia Lowman.

Thank you to the wonderful team at Chronicle Books, especially our editor, Mirabelle Korn, and our agent, Ayla Zuraw-Friedland, at Frances Goldin Literary Agency.

And thank you, most of all, to the featured artists for trusting us in sharing your stories.

BIBLIOGRAPHY

Croft, Clare, editor. *Queer Dance: Meanings and Makings*. New York: Oxford University Press, 2017.

Garafola, Lynn. "The Travesty Dancer in Nineteenth-Century Ballet." *Dance Research Journal* 17, no. 2 (1985): 35–40.

George, Cassidy. "Queer Butoh: Finding Belonging in the Dance of Darkness." *New York Times*. Updated June 21, 2020. https://www.nytimes.com/2020/06/21/arts/dance/queer-butoh-virus.html.

Holguín, Sandie. "The Complicated History of Flamenco in Spain." *Smithsonian Magazine*. Updated October 24, 2019. https://www.smithsonianmag.com/travel/complicated-history-flamenco-spain-180973398/

Lorenz, Taylor. "The Original Renegade." *New York Times*. Updated August 28, 2021. https://www.nytimes.com/2020/02/13/style/the-original-renegade.html.

Phillips, Tom. "IMPRESSIONS: Queer Butoh 2022, Vangeline Theater/New York Butoh Institute in Collaboration with the Brick." *The Dance Enthusiast*. Updated July 6, 2022. https://www.dance-enthusiast.com/features/impressions-reviews/view/Queer-Butoh-Vangeline-Theater-New-York-Butoh-Institutie-The-Brick.

Russell, Legacy. *Glitch Feminism: A Manifesto*. New York: Verso, 2020.

Scelfo, Julie. "A High-Level Collaboration on a SoHo Loft." *New York Times*. Updated December 14, 2011. https://www.nytimes.com/2011/12/15/garden/elizabeth-streb-and-laura-flanders-at-home-with.html.

Wakin, Daniel J. "A Troupe Known for Daredevil Choreography Copes with a Casualty." *New York Times*. Updated June 2, 2007. https://www.nytimes.com/2007/06/02/arts/dance/02stre.html.

Watlington, Emily. "Our Work Is Working." *Art in America* (October 2022): 36–43.

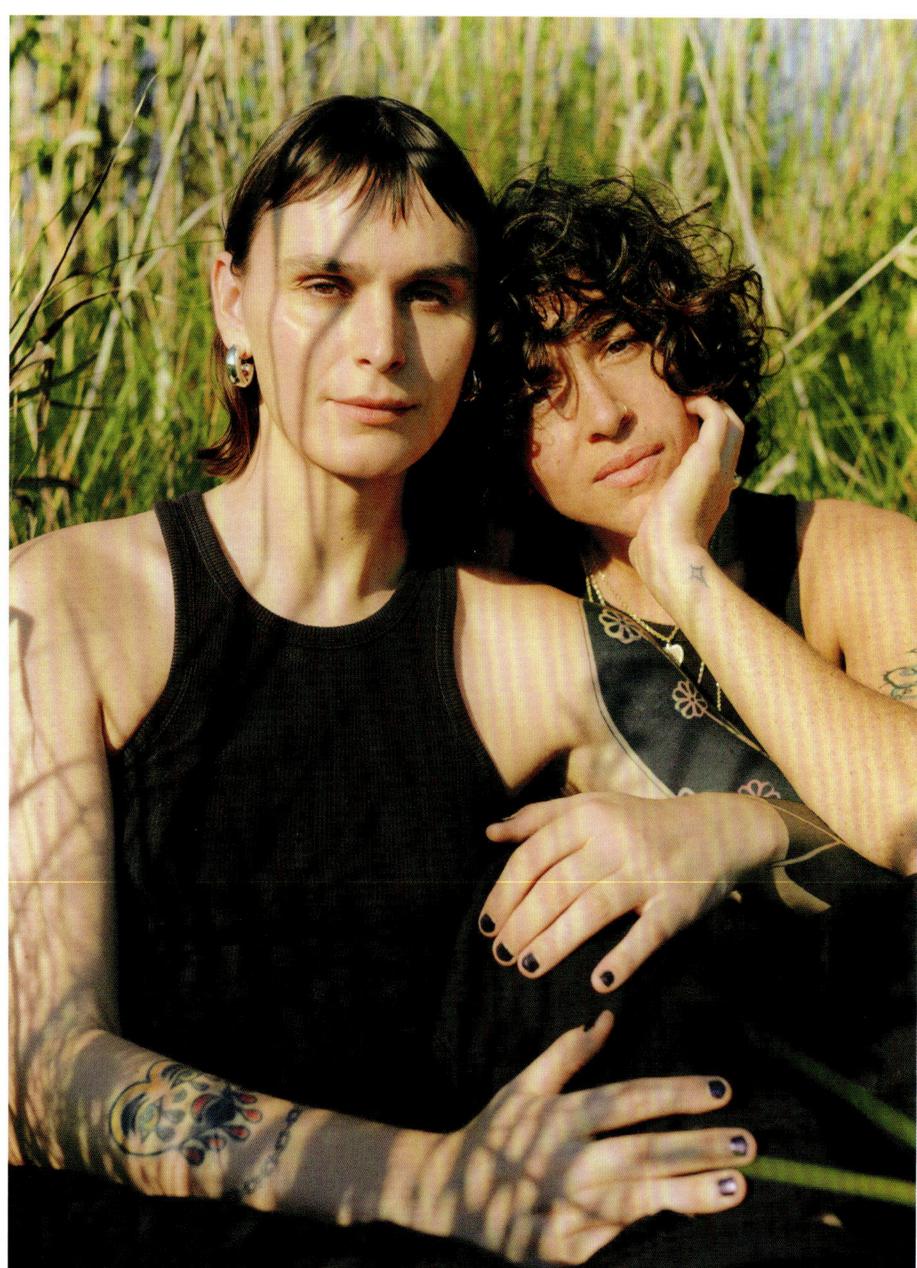

PHOTO BY HEATHER STEN

Coco Romack is a writer and editor who has contributed to the *New York Times, Architectural Digest*, and *Artforum*, among other publications. Originally from Seattle, Coco now lives in Brooklyn.

Yael Malka is a Bronx-born, Brooklyn-based photographer and artist. She has exhibited at the Leslie-Lohman Museum of Art, and her photographs have been published in the *New York Times*, the *New Yorker*, and *Vogue*.